René Descartes

Philosophical Essays and Correspondence

Edited, with Introduction, by
ROGER ARIEW

Hackett Publishing Company, Inc.
Indianapolis/Cambridge

For SAA, DAA, and DBA

06 05 04 03 02 01 00   1 2 3 4 5 6 7 8 9

For further information, please address

Hackett Publishing Company, Inc.
P.O. Box 44937
Indianapolis, IN 46244-0937

www.hackettpublishing.com

Cover design by Listenberger Design & Associates.

Interior design by Meera Dash.

Library of Congress Cataloging-in-Publication Data

Descartes, René, 1596–1650.
  [Selections. English 2000]
  Philosophical essays and correspondence / Descartes ; edited by Roger Ariew.
    p. cm.
  Includes bibliographical references and index.
  ISBN 0-87220-503-7 (cloth)—ISBN 0-87220-502-9 (paper)
    1. Philosophy. 2. Descartes, René, 1596–1650—Correspondence. I. Ariew, Roger. II.
Title.

B1837.A75 2000
194—dc21   99-049303

The paper used in this publication meets the minimum requirements of American National
Standard for Information Services—Permanence of Paper for Printed Library Materials,
ANSI Z39.48-1984

Contents

Introduction

Descartes: Life and Times

René Descartes was born in Touraine on March 31, 1596, at La Haye (now known as Descartes), the son of Joachim Descartes (councilor to the parliament of Brittany) and Jeanne Brochard.[1] His mother died the next year on May 13, as a result of the birth of another son who lived only three days; his father remarried around 1600. René spent his childhood at the home of his maternal grandmother, Jeanne Sain, together with his older siblings, Pierre and Jeanne. Pierre left in 1604 to study at the Jesuit college just established at La Flèche, in Anjou, and René later followed him there, probably in 1607, at Easter. The younger Descartes spent eight or nine years at La Flèche, until about 1615. Jesuit education at the time consisted of five years of French and Latin grammar, with a year of rhetoric from Greek and Roman authors, culminating in the last three years with the philosophy curriculum and some mathematics: logic and ethics; natural philosophy and mathematics;[2] and metaphysics. In general, these studies followed the pattern of the textbooks written by Jesuits of the University of Coimbra (the Conimbricences) or Collegio Romano (Franciscus Toletus, for example). That is, they involved lectures and commentaries on the works of Aristotle, which were generally interpreted according to a Thomism that had itself weathered three centuries of commentary and criticism.[3] After La Flèche, the younger Descartes studied law, like his father, his older brother, and his younger half-brother. He received an M.A. in canon and civil law from the University of Poitiers in November 1616.[4]

---

1. For more details about René Descartes's life and times, see Stephen Gaukroger, *Descartes. An Intellectual Biography* (Oxford: Clarendon, Press, 1995), and Geneviève Rodis-Lewis, *Descartes, His Life and Thought* (Ithaca: Cornell University Press, 1998).

2. The course in mathematics would have followed the textbooks written by the Collegio Romano Jesuit Christopher Clavius. Descartes is reported to have said in 1646 that he had no other instruction in algebra than his reading of Clavius more than thirty years before—that is, before 1616, when he was a student at La Flèche (*Oeuvres de Descartes*, eds. Charles Adam and Paul Tannery, vol. IV, pp. 730–1). Adam and Tannery's edition, just cited, is the standard edition of Descartes's works; references to it are abbreviated as AT volume, page—in this case: AT IV, 730–1. The numbers in the margins of this volume are also to this edition. This enables the reader to cross-reference the original text and other translations.

3. For more information on 17th-century scholastic philosphy and its relation to Descartes's, see Roger Ariew, *Descartes and the Last Scholastics* (Ithaca: Cornell University Press, 1999). Samples of various philosophical essays, including portions of relevant 17th-century scholastic texts forming the background to Descartes's philosophy, may be consulted in *Descartes' Meditations: Background Source Materials,* Cambridge Philosophical Texts in Context, eds. and trans. Roger Ariew, John Cottingham, and Tom Sorell (Cambridge: Cambridge University Press, 1998).

4. The dedication from Descartes's law theses was discovered at the city library of Poitier in 1986.

At the age of twenty-one, having gained a measure of independence from his father, Descartes enlisted at Breda, in the Netherlands, as a gentleman soldier in the army of Maurice of Nassau, Prince of Orange, a Protestant ally of France during the war between the Netherlands and Spain. However, the period of Descartes's enlistment was characterized by a truce in that war, and Descartes did not participate in any military action; on the other hand, army life provided him with the opportunity to travel. At Breda, on November 10, 1618, he had a chance encounter with Isaac Beeckman, who translated for him into Latin a mathematical problem posted in Dutch. A warm friendship ensued, Descartes demonstrating his mathematical abilities to Beeckman and Beeckman teaching him the application of mathematics to problems of physics: "You alone have roused me from my state of indifference and reawakened the learning that had almost disappeared by then from my memory," Descartes later told Beeckman.[5] On New Year's Eve, Descartes offered Beeckman as a gift his first work, a mathematical treatise on musical theory called *Compendium musicae*. He also began writing his thoughts down in a notebook.[6] However, Beeckman returned to his home in Middelburg, and, in search of military action in March 1619, Descartes set off to Germany at the start of the Thirty Years' War to enlist in the Catholic army of Maximilian of Bavaria. Again, he seems not to have found any military action, but in his travels he witnessed the coronation of Emperor Ferdinand II at Frankfurt and met the mathematician Joannes Faulhaber at Ulm. He spent the winter in the Catholic principality of Neuberg, on the shores of the Danube, in a "stove-heated room," as he described it.[7] "Full of enthusiasm," he perceived "the foundations of a wonderful science."[8] He recorded that, on the night of November 10, 1619, he had three strange dreams that set him on the right course of life.[9] At the time he was working on various mathematical projects—for example, the *Mathematical Treasury* of Polybius the Cosmopolitan (a pseudonym he considered adopting) on universal mathematics—and had begun the *Rules for the Direction of the Mind,* a treatise on method, which he left unfinished around 1628. He noted in his notebook that in 1620 he "began to understand the foundations of a wonderful discovery,"[10] probably having to do with the solution of third- and fourth-degree equations by means of a circle and a parabola.

Having definitively abandoned his military career, Descartes returned to Paris sometime in 1621. There he reacquainted himself with Marin Mersenne, an older student from La Flèche. Mersenne had joined the Minim order and established a circle of mathematicians, technicians, and physicists who met in his cell at the

---

5. AT X, 162.

6. See *Preliminaries* and *Observations*.

7. AT VI, 11.

8. AT X, 189.

9. For the content of the three dreams, see Gaukroger, chap. 4, and Rodis-Lewis, chap. 3.

10. AT X, 216.

Minims' convent near the Place Royale.[11] Descartes worked with two members of that circle, the mathematician Claude Mydorge and the technician Jean Ferrier, on optics and the construction of lenses. He also took the opportunity to sell the inheritance left to him from his mother's estate, thereby providing himself with a modest income through most of his life, but also losing the title "Seigneur du Perron," which he had adopted in his monogram, RSP.

Other financial matters required Descartes to take a lengthy trip through Italy. While he was away, Parisian intellectuals were discussing the trial of the libertine poet Théophile de Viau and the condemnation of fourteen anti-Aristotelian theses posted by the alchemists and atomists Etienne de Clave, Jean Bitaud, and Antoine Villon. De Viau died shortly after being released from jail, and de Clave, Bitaud, and Villon were prevented from defending their theses and exiled from Paris. On his return to Paris in April 1625, Descartes continued his association with the Mersenne circle, which included exchanges with the chemist and engineer Etienne de Villebressieur and the mathematician-astrologer Jean-Baptiste Morin. He also frequented literary and theological circles and became friends with the essayist Guez de Balzac, the religious apologist Jean de Silhon, and the Oratorian theologian Guillaume Gibieuf, among others. Together with Mersenne, these turned into some of Descartes's principal correspondents. At the time Descartes was making progress on his method for avoiding sophisms (described in *Rules for the Direction of the Mind*), so that he seemed ready to "mount the stage of the world." He recounted a meeting at the residence of the papal ambassador in which a M. de Chandoux, an alchemist, talked about his own new philosophy. Descartes wrote that he used the occasion to correct Chandoux: "I made the whole company acknowledge what the art of reasoning well can do for the mind of those who are only barely clever and how my principles are better established, more true, and more natural than any of the others received up to now by the learned world."[12] The large and distinguished audience included Cardinal Pierre de Bérulle, founder of the Oratorians, a militant Catholic order. According to Descartes, Bérulle granted him a private audience and encouraged him to develop his philosophy as an antidote to atheism. But Paris was not allowing Descartes enough uninterrupted time to work on his various projects, and even the French countryside did not provide sufficient peace and quiet; Descartes left for the Netherlands near the end of 1628, and, although he moved frequently, he stayed in that country for most of the next twenty years (until his disastrous trip to Sweden in 1649), returning for the first time to Paris for a short visit in 1644. He described the charms of Amsterdam to Balzac, contrasting it with Paris and the French countryside:

> However accomplished a country home may be . . . the very solitude you hope for is never altogether perfect. . . . It can happen that you will have a quantity of little

---

11. For more on Mersenne, see Peter Dear, *Mersenne and the Learning of the Schools* (Ithaca: Cornell University Press, 1988). A selection from Mersenne's works, in English translation, is available in Ariew, Cottingham, and Sorell, pp. 136–75.

12. AT I, 213.

neighbors who will bother you at times, and whose visits will be even more bother-
some than those you get in Paris. Instead, in this large city where I live, everyone
but me is engaged in a trade, and as a result is so attentive to his own profit that I
could live my whole life without ever being noticed by anyone. I walk each day
amid the bustle of the crowd with as much freedom and tranquility as you could
obtain in your country walks, and I pay no more attention to the people I meet than
I would to the trees in your woods. . . .[13]

Descartes became reacquainted with Beeckman in the Netherlands, but the two
had outgrown their relationship; they had a nasty exchange of letters in 1630 and
a superficial reconciliation in 1634, a few years before Beeckman's death in
1637. Descartes made new friends and developed a following in Dutch intellectual circles; among his associates were the mathematician Jacob Golius, the
physicians Henricus Reneri and Henricus Regius,[14] the logician Adriaan
Heereboord, and the statesman and poet Constantijn Huygens (father of the poly-
math Christiaan Huygens). While in the Netherlands Descartes took the opportunity to enroll as a student at the Universities of Frankener (in 1629) and Leyden
(in 1630). As soon as he arrived, he began a small treatise in metaphysics, now
lost; as he said, "The first nine months I was in this country I worked at nothing
else." He revealed, in one of the famous letters he wrote to Mersenne on the creation of the eternal truths, that he thought he "found out how one can demonstrate the truths of metaphysics in a way that is more evident than the
demonstrations of Geometry"; he claimed that he tried to begin his studies in this
way and that he "would never have known how to discover the foundations of
physics, if [he] had not sought them by that path"—a path consisting in attempting to know God and the self.[15] However, by summer 1629, Descartes became
intrigued with the reported phenomenon of parhelia, or multiple suns, and began
working on meteorology, optics, and physics. The essays *Meteors* and *Dioptrics*
date from this period, as do the beginnings of *The World* with its lengthy chapter
on man (the single manuscript was published posthumously separately as *The
World or Treatise on Light* and *Treatise on Man*). In the fall of 1633, Descartes
was preparing *The World* for publication when he heard that Galileo had been
condemned by the Catholic Church the previous June for defending the motion
of the earth. Descartes stopped the publication of his treatise, which contained
the proposition deemed heretical, because, as he said, all the things he explained
in his treatise "were so completely dependent on one another, that the knowledge
that one of them is false is sufficient for the recognition that all the arguments
[he] made use of are worthless." And Descartes added that he "would not for
anything in the world maintain [these propositions] against the authority of the

13. AT I, 203.
14. Reneri was the first to teach Cartesian philosophy; he did so at the University of
Utrecht as early as 1635, even before Descartes's first formal publication. Regius became
the follower of Descartes from whom Descartes eventually had to distance himself; see
the end of the Preface to the *Principles* and *Notes Against a Program*.
15. AT I, 144.

church."[16] Instead, he prepared drafts of the *Dioptrics* and *Meteors,* scientific treatises on less controversial topics, and began to work on a preface linking them together, something he once called "the history of my mind,"[17] that became the *Discourse on Method.* At the start of 1636 he added the *Geometry,* as another of the essays appended to the *Discourse* to demonstrate the soundness of his method. The printing of Descartes's first publication was completed in June 1637. Issued anonymously at Leyden, the work was entitled *Discourse on the Method for Conducting One's Reason Well and for Seeking the Truth in the Sciences, with Dioptrics, Meteors, and Geometry, Which Are Essays of This Method.*

It should be noted that Descartes conceived a daughter, Francine, from a union with a servant named Hélène Jans. Francine was born in July 1635 and baptized in August as the daughter of "René, son of Joachim." In August 1637 Descartes arranged to have Francine join him as "his niece" and employed her mother as a servant. In 1640, Descartes planned a trip to France with Francine, so as to leave her and her education in the charge of a relative. However, Francine caught scarlet fever and died in September of that year. Descartes learned the next month of the death of his father. It was reported that, because of the publication of the *Discourse,* Descartes's father said he was disappointed to have a son who was ridiculous enough to have himself bound up in calf-leather.[18] Descartes's sister, Jeanne, also died shortly thereafter. Consoling a friend after the death of his brother, Descartes told him that he shared his pain and explained that he was not one of those who thought that tears and sadness were not appropriate for men: "Not long ago I suffered the loss of two people who were very close to me, and I found out that those who wanted to prevent me from being sad only made things worse, whereas I was consoled by the kindness of those whom I saw to be touched by my grief."[19] It is true that Descartes did not specify which two of the three recent deaths made him sad, but it could be conjectured that he was thinking of his daughter and sister.[20]

Although Descartes published the *Discourse on Method* anonymously, he also insisted, as part of the publishing contract, on receiving many author's copies; these he sent to people far and wide: close friends, the nobility, various intellectuals, Jesuits, and others. For example, Descartes indicated in a letter that, of the three copies of the *Discourse* enclosed, one was for the recipient of the letter, another for Cardinal Richelieu, and the third for the king himself.[21] He even sent the volume to one of his old teachers amd described it as a fruit belonging to the

16. AT I, 285.
17. AT I, 570.
18. Charles Adam, *Vie de Descartes* (Paris: Cerf, 1910), pp. 433–4.
19. AT III, 278–9.
20. Most commentators assert without argument that Descartes had in mind his father and daughter; some assert, also without argument, and perhaps maliciously, that Descartes was referring to his father and sister.
21. AT I, 387.

recipient, since its first seeds were sown in his mind by him.[22] When Descartes published the *Meditations,* he also published a series of *Objections* and *Replies* to the work. He had hoped to do the same thing with the *Discourse.* In Part Six of the *Discourse,* Descartes announced: "I shall be very happy if [my writings] are examined, and, in order to have more of an opportunity to do this, I am imploring all who have any objections to make against them to take the trouble to send them to my publisher and, on being advised about them by him, I shall try at the same time to append my reply to the objections; and by this means, seeing both of them together, readers will judge the truth all the more easily."[23] However, his request for objections (and his sending out copies) did not succeed as well as he wished. He wrote to Huygens: "As for my book, I do not know what opinion the worldly people will have of it; as for the people of the schools, I understand that they are keeping quiet, and that, displeased with not finding anything in it to grasp in order to exercise their arguments, they are content in saying that, if what is contained in it were true, all their philosophy would have to be false."[24] Ultimately, Descartes received a number of responses to the *Discourse;* among them were a critique by Libertius Fromondus, an anti-atomist, and several sets of objections by Plempius, a student of Fromondus, and Jean-Baptiste Morin.[25] Descartes also reported the more hopeful response from someone at his old school: "I have just received a letter from one of the Jesuits at La Flèche, in which I find as much approbation as I would desire from anyone. Thus far he does not find difficulty with anything I wanted to explain, but only with what I did not want to write; as a result, he takes the occasion to request my physics and my metaphysics with great insistence."[26] So, to satisfy this and other such demands, Descartes produced his metaphysics. In 1640, he expanded Part Four of the *Discourse* into *Meditations on First Philosophy* (published in 1641).

Descartes first sent the manuscript of the *Meditations* to some Dutch friends, who transmitted it to Johan de Kater (or Caterus), a Dutch Catholic theologian.[27] He then appended Caterus's objections and his replies to the manuscript and had Mersenne circulate the whole package to various intellectuals. Mersenne col-

---

22. AT I, 383.

23. AT VI, 75.

24. AT II, 48.

25. Descartes was asked by Mersenne whether foreigners formulated better objections than the French. Descartes replied that he did not count any of the objections received as French other than Morin's. He referred to a dispute with Pierre Petit, which he dismissed, saying that he did not take Petit seriously but simply mocked him in return—for more on the exchange between Descartes and Petit, see Jean-Luc Marion, "The Place of the *Objections* in the Development of Cartesian Metaphysics," in *Descartes and His Contemporaries,* eds. Roger Ariew and Marjorie Grene, pp. 7–20. Descartes then listed the foreign objectors: Fromondus from Louvain, Plempius, an anonymous Jesuit from Louvain, and someone from the Hague (AT II, 191–2).

26. AT II, 50.

27. For more on Caterus, see Theo Verbeek, "The First Objections," and Jean-Robert Armogathe, "Caterus'Objections to God," in Ariew and Grene, pp. 21–33 and 34–43.

lected sets of objections from Thomas Hobbes, Antoine Arnauld, and Pierre Gassendi and put together two other sets of the objections of various philosophers and theologians. Separately, Descartes became embroiled in a controversy with the Jesuit mathematician Pierre Bourdin. Bourdin sent a seventh set of objections, and Descartes published it with the second edition of the *Meditations* (in 1642).[28] The *Objections* and *Replies* enable one to see genuine philosophical debate conducted on the spot. This is true for the confrontation between Descartes and Caterus's scholasticism. It is especially true for Descartes's battle with Hobbesian materialism. Hobbes accepted none of Descartes's arguments and the debate became increasingly heated.[29] Arguably, the best set of objections was the one written by Arnauld, at the time a theology doctoral candidate at the University of Paris. In the critical but sympathetic exchange one can see Arnauld's keen analytical mind working. In his criticism of Descartes's notion of material falsity, in his comments on God as positive cause of himself, and in his questioning whether the *Meditations* are circular, Arnauld makes significant contributions to the discussion.[30]

In 1644, Descartes further revised his philosophy into textbook form and disseminated it with his physics as *Principles of Philosophy*.[31] Interestingly, Descartes wrote the bulk of Part I of the *Principles* at the same time as he was writing his replies to the various objections to the *Meditations*. On December 31, 1640, he said in a letter to Mersenne: "I have resolved to use this year for writing my philosophy in such an order that it can easily be taught. And the first part, which I am now working on, contains almost the same things as the *Meditations* that you have, except that it is in an entirely different style, and that what is said

---

28. As an appendix to the second edition of the *Meditations,* Descartes also published a long letter to Bourdin's superior, Father Dinet, complaining about Bourdin's objections.

29. Thomas Hobbes (1588–1679) spent most of his life as tutor, secretary, and financial manager in the service of the earls of Devonshire and Newcastle. His extensive travels in Europe brought him into contact with many of the leading thinkers of the time, including Galileo, whom he visited in 1636, and Mersenne, to whose circle he belonged while in Paris in 1635, and then again when in exile in Paris from 1640 to 1651. The work for which he is best known, in which he defends his materialist philosophy, is *Leviathan, or the Matter, Forme, and Power of a Commonwealth Ecclesiasticall and Civill* (1651). For more on Hobbes, see Tom Sorell, ed., *Cambridge Companion to Hobbes* (Cambridge: Cambridge University Press, 1996).

30. Antoine Arnauld was born in Paris in 1612. He was admitted to the Paris Faculty of Theology in 1643 and expelled in 1656. Throughout his life Arnauld engaged in public controversies on philosophical and theological topics. He became the leading spokesman in France for the Jansenist movement and one of the more outspoken defenders of Cartesian philosophy. Arnauld's philosophical work included the *Port-Royal Logic* (1662), written with Pierre Nicole, and *Of True and False Ideas* (1683)—both broadly Cartesian projects. For more on Arnauld, see Steven Nadler, *Arnauld and the Cartesian Philosophy of Ideas* (Princeton: Princeton University Press, 1989).

31. Descartes dedicated the *Principles* to Princess Elisabeth of Bohemia, one of his more important correspondents from their first meeting in 1643 until his death.

at length in the one is more abridged in the other, and vice versa."[32] One of Descartes's more colorful ways of describing the *Principles* was to say that it would make his *World* speak Latin,[33] that is, with it he would be able to teach his physics to an educated 17th-century international audience. In keeping with this intent, the *Principles* was often published with the Latin translation of the *Discourse on Method, Dioptrics,* and *Meteors* (*Specimina philosophiae seu dissertatio de methodo, dioptrice et meteora,* 1644). Together these treatises were responsible for Descartes's considerable international scientific reputation.[34]

Descartes became embroiled in several controversies during the period after the publication of the *Meditations.* In 1643 the academic senate of the University of Utrecht, following the recommendation of its rector Gysbertus Voetius, prohibited the teaching of the new philosophy. Here is a portion of the Utrecht edict, as quoted by Descartes himself:

> The professors reject this new philosophy for three reasons. First, it is contrary to the ancient philosophy that universities throughout the world have taught thus far with the greatest success, and it undermines its foundations. Second, it turns away the young from this sound and ancient philosophy and prevents them from reaching the heights of erudition; once they have begun to rely on this so-called philosophy, they are unable to understand the technical terms used in the books of traditional authors and in the lectures and debates of their professors. And, finally, various false and absurd opinions either follow from the new philosophy or can be imprudently deduced from it by the young, opinions that are in conflict with other disciplines and faculties and, above all, with orthodox theology.[35]

The reasons for the prohibition clearly ran the gamut from pragmatic to pedagogical to doctrinal concerns. Voetius's ire was primarily directed against the teaching of Regius, a professor at the University of Utrecht and Descartes's disciple. Descartes and Regius counterattacked with a polemical letter against Voetius in 1643, but the city council of Utrecht regarded the letter as defamatory and issued a warrant against Descartes. Descartes sought the protection of the French ambassador against the warrant, and the affair abated somewhat. In 1645 the University of Utrecht reaffirmed its prohibition against the works of

---

32. AT III, 276.

33. In a letter to Huygens, talking about his new project that will become the *Principles,* Descartes said: "Perhaps these scholastic wars will cause my *World* to be brought into the world. I believe it would be out already, were it not that I would want first to teach it to speak Latin. I would call it *Summa Philosophiae,* so that it would be more easily introduced into the conversation of the people of the schools, ministers as well as Jesuits, who are now persecuting it and trying to smother it before its birth." (AT III, 523)

34. For more on Descartes as a physicist, see Daniel Garber, *Descartes' Metaphysical Physics* (Chicago: University of Chicago Press, 1992).

35. AT VII, 592. Descartes defends himself in AT VII, 596–8.

Descartes. Similar troubles arose at the University of Leyden in 1647, which resulted in a prohibition against the teaching of Descartes's works in 1648.[36]

In the same period Descartes oversaw the French translation of the *Meditations* and *Principles* (both published in 1647). He also made a few trips to France (in 1644, 1647, and 1648), the first since his departure to the Netherlands in 1628. During the first two trips he resided with Claude Picot, a member of Mersenne's circle and the translator of the *Principles* into French. Descartes was able to review some of Picot's translation as early as 1644, and, in 1646–1647, he made significant corrections to it, including the addition of replies to some objections. Thus, the French translation of the *Principles* ought to be seen as a separate revised edition of the work. Descartes also added to it a large new preface in the guise of a letter to the translator. The trips to France allowed Descartes to be reconciled with such critics as Bourdin and Gassendi. They also provided the occasion for him to meet Claude Clerselier, the future translator of the *Objections* and *Replies* and executor of his literary estate, and Hector-Pierre Chanut, Clerselier's brother-in-law and future French ambassador to Sweden and to the Netherlands.

With Chanut as an intermediary, Descartes began a correspondence with Queen Christina of Sweden. Queen Christina invited Descartes to spend the summer of 1649 at Stockholm, but Descartes delayed the visit. He even refused to board the ship the queen sent for him that spring. Finally, Descartes departed for Sweden in the fall, after a personal visit from Chanut. At Queen Christina's bidding in December 1649, Descartes began discussing philosophy with her at her palace, during the early hours of the morning, around five o'clock. Descartes did not last the winter, catching pneumonia at the beginning of February and dying about a week later.

Descartes was buried in Stockholm; his body was transferred to Paris in 1667 and reburied at the Abbey of Sainte Geneviève. His skull was separately sent to Paris and displayed in the Musée de l'Homme (where it still resides, though no longer on display). Descartes was reburied once more around 1817 in a chapel of the church of Saint Germain-des-Prés, where he still rests. In 1793, the Revolution passed an edict transferring his remains to the newly erected Pantheon, but the edict was never carried through.

Descartes's literary estate was also transferred to France by Chanut. Clerselier received the manuscripts and proceeded to produce various posthumous publications: the *Rules, The World,* a three-volume set of *Correspondence,* and several collections of Descartes's works. He also became an advocate of Cartesian philosophy. Cartesianism gained a following during the second half of the 17th century,[37] but that also produced a severe backlash. Here is an account of how

---

36. For more about the intellectual context leading to these events, see Theo Verbeek, *Descartes and the Dutch: Early Reactions to Cartesian Philosophy 1637–1650* (Carbondale, IL: Southern Illinois University Press, 1992).

37. For more on the first Cartesians, see Richard A. Watson, *The Breakdown of Cartesian Metaphysics* (Indianapolis: Hackett Publishing Company, 1998).

Descartes's followers were perceived by François Babin, a theologian and administrator of the College of Angers. Babin was clearly horrified by the attitudes of the new philosophers:

> Young people are no longer taught anything other than to rid themselves of their childhood prejudices and to doubt all things—including whether they themselves exist in the world. They are taught that the soul is a substance whose essence is always to think something; that children think from the time they are in their mothers' bellies, and that when they grow up they have less need of teachers who would teach them what they have never known than of coaches who would have them recall in their minds the ancient ideas of all things, which were created with them. It is no longer fashionable to believe that fire is hot, that marble is hard, that animate bodies sense pain. These truths are too ancient for those who love novelty. Some of them assert that animals are only machines and puppets without motion, without life, and without sensation; that there are no substantial forms other than rational soul; and by completely contrary principles . . . others teach that the souls of animals are immortal, spiritual, and created directly by God, as are those of men.

For Babin, something had gone terribly wrong. Cartesian philosophy was causing contempt for traditional learning, to the point of causing disrespect for religion and government. Babin continued his account, moving from pedagogical and epistemic to metaphysical and theological issues, and ultimately to political ones:

> The Cartesians assert that accidents are not really distinct from substance; that it would be well to guard oneself from attributing some knowledge or certainty to the testimony of our senses. . . . They make the essence of all bodies consist in local extension, without worrying that Christ's body does not better accommodate their principles and our mysteries; they teach that something does not stop being true in philosophy even though faith and the Catholic religion teach us the contrary—as if the Christian and the philosopher could have been two distinct things. Their boldness is so criminal that it attacks God's power, enclosing him within the limits and the sphere of things he has made, as if creating from nothing would have exhausted his omnipotence. Their doctrine is yet more harmful to sovereigns and monarchs, and tends toward the reversal of the political and civil state.[38]

Although Descartes made some converts to his new philosophy, he did not succeed in getting his work adopted in the curriculum of the schools. Here and there one can find Cartesian principles taught, by, for example, some ill-fated Oratorian professors at Angers in the 1670s and Edmond Pourchot at the University of Paris in the 1690s. One can also find Cartesian propositions included in disputations, but the discussions are mostly negative. For most of the 17th century, the official response to Descartes's philosophy was unfavorable. At various times, Descartes had waged fierce battles with his opponents. As we have said, he fought with the Jesuits in the 1640s and had problems and was officially

---

38. François Babin, *Journal ou relation fidele de tout ce qui s'est passé dans l'université d'Angers au sujet de la philosophie de Des Cartes en l'execution des ordres du Roy pendant les années 1675, 1676, 1677, et 1678* (Angers 1679), p. 2.

condemned by Protestants at Utrecht circa 1644, and Leyden, 1647. After Descartes's death he was condemned by Catholics at Louvain (1662); these condemnations culminated with Descartes's works being put on the *Index of Prohibited Books* by the censors of Rome in 1663. The fighting intensified with numerous attacks in print. The Cartesians counterattacked with satires and learned essays. The anti-Cartesians also responded with their own satires. Ultimately, the dispute spilled into the official political arena, the domains of the king, of the universities, and of the teaching orders: the king issued an edict against the new philosophy in 1671; various faculties of the University of Paris condemned Cartesianism in the period 1671–1691; there were skirmishes at Angers and Caen during 1675–1678; the Jesuits, in a pact with the Oratorians, prohibited the teaching of Cartesianism in 1678 and formally condemned it in 1706. Cartesianism finally won the war in the 1720s, when it became widely taught in universities, including the University of Paris, but that victory was short lived because of the ascendancy of Newtonianism. The view of Descartes in the 18th century was that he had succumbed to the spirit of system.

But even Descartes's opponents could not prevent themselves from showing their admiration in the midst of their criticism. For example, the Jesuit René Rapin wrote of Descartes that he "is one of the most extraordinary geniuses of these times. . . . In truth, he teaches one to doubt too much, and that is not a good model for minds who are naturally credulous; however, in the end, he is more original than the others."[39] Perhaps Descartes's legacy can be best encapsulated by a comment from the often critical G. W. Leibniz: "[W]hen I think of everything Descartes has said that is beautiful and original, I am more astonished with what he has accomplished than with what he has failed to accomplish."[40]

Principle of Selection for the Volume

René Descartes: Philosophical Essays and Correspondence is a reader in the philosophy of René Descartes in English translation for an American audience. It provides Descartes's most important texts in their entirety, that is, both the 1637 *Discourse on Method* and the 1641 *Meditations*. It also includes substantive selections from other main Cartesian texts: *Rules* (1618?–1628?); *The World* (1632); *Objections* and *Replies* (1641); *Principles* (1644; 1647); *Notes Against a Program* (1647); *Passions of the Soul* (1649); and *Search After Truth* (1641?–1649?). Moreover, the volume surrounds these texts with a selection of the most significant of the philosopher's correspondence, in order to allow the reader to understand his thought more fully and to situate it within the framework of his contemporaries'concerns. The intent of the volume is simply to provide a representation of the totality of Descartes's philosophical accomplishments

---

39. René Rapin, *Réflexions sur la philosophie,* in *Oeuvres* (Paris 1725), p. 366.
40. *Leibniz: Philosophical Essays,* eds. and trans. Roger Ariew and Daniel Garber (Indianapolis: Hackett Publishing Company, 1989), p. 2.

(taken broadly to include natural philosophy) and their relations to one another. Arguably, Descartes's masterpiece is the *Meditations,* but to understand that work, one has to appreciate it in contrast with its previous reflection in the *Discourse,* its restatement in the *Principles,* and the debates it provoked in the *Objections* and *Replies* and in the correspondence.

It is evident that Descartes himself viewed the *Meditations* as a continuation of the *Discourse.* The opening line of the *Meditations* even refers the reader back to the time of the *Discourse,* and, as the *Discourse* makes plain, the argument of the *Meditations* is intended to be integrated into a larger framework as the foundation of the new sciences. As Descartes said to his closest correspondent Mersenne, "I will tell you, between us, that these six meditations contain all the foundations of my physics. But it will not do to say this, if you please; for those who favor Aristotle would perhaps find it more difficult to approve of them. And I hope that those who read them will accustom themselves insensibly to my principles, and will recognize the truth before noticing that they destroy those of Aristotle."[41]

Thus the *Meditations* attempts a complete intellectual revolution: the replacement of Aristotelian philosophy with a new philosophy in order to replace Aristotelian science with a new science. For a 17th-century Aristotelian, a body is matter informed by substantial and accidental forms, and change is explained by the gain or loss of such forms: in mutation by theacquisition of a substantial form, and in what Aristotelians would call true motion (that is, augmentation and diminution, alteration, or local motion) by the successive acquisition of places or of qualitative or quantitative forms. The mechanist program consisted in doing away with qualitative forms and reducing all changes to something mathematically quantifiable: matter in motion. As Descartes said in *The World,* not only the four qualities called heat, cold, moistness, and dryness, "but also all others, and even all the forms of all inanimate bodies, can be explained without needing to assume anything in their matter other than the motion, size, shape, and arrangement of its parts."[42] Accordingly, Descartes does not need substantial forms and does not explain mutation as change of form, whether substantial or accidental. He finds no forms other than the ones he has described quantitatively. For Descartes, the only motion is local motion; hence he states: "The philosophers also suppose many motions they think can be accomplished without any body changing place. . . . As for me, I do not know of any motion other than the one which is easier to conceive of than the geometers' lines, the motion that makes bodies pass from one place to another."[43]

However, considering the *Meditations* as part of Descartes's larger program of the reform of science should not prevent one from regarding it as a philosophical treatise standing by itself (and vice versa). It has often been thought that there

41. AT III, 297–8.
42. AT XI, 26.
43. AT XI, 40–1.

is a conflict between considering a philosopher's works developmentally and regarding them, as it were, internally, or as independent units.[44] But this does not need to be the case. Martial Gueroult, a major Cartesian commentator, did in fact consider the *Meditations* internally, as Descartes's great achievement against which Descartes's other writings might be measured; but he did not think that his approach was inconsistent with developmental or more properly historical approaches.

It might be instructive to see how Gueroult thought about his own work. According to him, "Historians have two techniques at their disposal for [discovering the enigma proposed to them by the work of the great geniuses]: textual criticism itself and analysis of structures." He adds: "For Descartes'philosophy, textual criticism (problems of sources, variations, evolutions, etc.) has been amply practiced: the remarkable work of Gilson, Gouhier, Laporte, and others are known by all. On the other hand, the analysis of structures has been little attempted."[45] Gueroult in consequence proposed for himself the work of discovering the structures of the *Meditations,* what he called the laying bare of the architectonic elements. And he found support for this endeavor in Descartes's writings.[46] Hence Gueroult, using "textual criticism," discovered that "analysis of structures" was needed in this case at this time. He concluded, "It seems that once the requirements of historical critique are satisfied, the better method is truly the analysis of the structure of the work."[47] Thus Gueroult's historiography is intended to be subordinate to developmental approaches. According to his own view, there is no genuine conflict between developmental approaches and his laying bare of the architectonics of the *Meditations.* Naturally, one can always disagree with any of Gueroult's analyses or results. And if it could be shown that he was guilty of an anachronism—that he read earlier developments in Descartes's philosophy in terms of later ones—presumably he would have accepted the finding as a legitimate external criticism.

It would be unfortunate if Gueroult's representation of Descartes's *Meditations* was simply inconsistent with considering the *Meditations* as a step in Descartes's development. Gueroult, like Descartes, thought of the *Meditations* as a single block of certainty in which everything is so arranged that nothing can

---

44. For example, Gaukroger asserts: "Commentators on Descartes in the twentieth century, especially (but by no means exclusively) in Anglophone philosophy, have not taken much notice of Descartes' intellectual development, assuming that the *Discours de la méthode* (1638) [sic], the *Meditationes* (1641), and the *Passions de l'âme* (1649) somehow capture and sum up the whole of his thought" (p. 11). According to Gaukroger, commentators who assume that such works are completely self-contained use an approach diametrically opposed to his; he adds, "implausible as I believe it is, such a line of interpretation is still commonly favoured among Descartes commentators" (p. 460).

45. Martial Gueroult, *Descartes' Philosophy Interpreted According to the Order of Reasons,* trans. Roger Ariew, vol. I, p. xviii. Etienne Gilson, Henri Gouhier, and Jean Laporte are major French Descartes interpreters and Gueroult's contemporaries.

46. For example, AT VIIIb, 41; AT VII, 9–10; and AT III, 266–7.

47. Gueroult, p. xix.

be taken away without the whole thing dissolving. According to Gueroult, the unification of the Cartesian movement within the *Meditations* is accomplished in that its perspectives are complementary: to the hypothesis of the evil genius, which plays a role of segregation, elimination, and purification in the first three Meditations, corresponds the dogma of divine veracity, which is a heuristic principle, an organ of reintegration, and a rule of discipline in the last three Meditations. Gueroult consequently thought of the *Meditations* as a diptych, a work of art in two panels. He saw the first three Meditations as the first panel, ruled by the darkness of the principle of universal deception, with a battle being fought against it by the truth of the existence of the self—a mere point of light— a narrow but piercing exception to the principle of doubt, culminating with the defeat of the principle and the victory of the exception. The second panel is then ruled by the blinding light of God's absolute veracity—that is, the principle of universal truth—and fought against by the existence of error, a narrow point of darkness and seeming exception to that principle, puncturing the light of universal veracity in the same way that the existence of the self punctured the darkness of universal deception. However, here the battle culminates with the victory of the principle, the triumph of light over darkness.

A Bibliographical Note on Descartes's Main Works

Descartes's principal publications were as follows:

Rules for the Direction of the Mind: *Regulae ad Directionem Ingenii*, in *Opuscula posthuma, physica et mathematica* (Amsterdam: P. & J. Blaeu, 1701). Unfinished manuscript; sections of this work are referred to as Rule 1, Rule 2, etc. There is a new edition: *Regulae ad directionem ingenii. Texte critique établi par Giovanni Crapulli avec la version hollandaise du XVIIeme siècle* ('s-Gravenhage: Martinus Nijhoff, 1966).

The World: *Le Monde de Mr. Descartes ou Le Traité de la Lumiere*, & des autres principaux objets des Sens. Avec un Discours du Mouvement Local & un autre des Fièvres, composez selon les principes du même auteur (Paris: Jacques Le Gras, 1664). There is a new, well-annotated edition treating the *Treatise on Man* as its eighteenth chapter: *Le Monde, L'Homme*, eds. Annie Bitbol-Hespériès and Jean-Pierre Verdet (Paris: Éditions du Seuil, 1996).

Treatise on Man: *L'Homme* de René Descartes, & un *Traité de la Formation du Foetus* du mesme Autheur. Avec les Remarques de Louys de la Forge, Docteur en Medecine, demeurant à la Fleche, sur le Traité de l'Homme de René Descartes, & sur les Figures par luy inventées (Paris: T. Girard, 1664). See *The World*.

Discourse on Method: *Discours de la Methode* Pour bien conduire sa raison, & chercher la verité dans les sciences. Plus *La Dioptrique*. *Les Meteores*. et *La*

Geometrie. Qui sont des essais de cete Methode (Leyden: Ian Maire, 1637); the three attached treatises are known as *Dioptrics, Meteors,* and *Geometry,* and collectively as *Essays.* There are six parts to the *Discourse* (i.e., *Discourse,* Part 1, or Discourse 1). A reproduction of this edition is available (Lecce: Conte Editore, 1987).

Meditations*: Renati Des-Cartes Meditationes de Prima Philosophia,* in qua Dei existentia et Animae immortalitatis demonstratur (Paris: Michel Soly, 1641). *Renati Des-Cartes Meditationes de Prima Philosophia,* In quibus Dei existentia, et animae humanae a corpore distinctio, demonstratur. His adjunctae sunt variae objectiones doctorum vivorum in istas de Deo et anima demonstrationes; cum Responsionibus Authoris. Secunda editio septimis objectionibus antehac non visis aucta (Amsterdam: L. Elzivier, 1642). Printed at the head of both editions of the *Meditations* were the *Letter to the Deans and Doctors of the Sorbonne—Sapientissimis Clarissimique Viris Sacrae Facultatis Theologiae Parisiensis Decano et doctoribus, Renatus Des-Cartes S. D.—* together with three preliminary pieces, *Preface to the Reader,* Table of Contents, and *Synopsis* of the *Meditations*: *Praefatio ad Lectorem, Index,* and *Synopsis sex Sequentium Meditationum.* The *Meditations* was divided into six Meditations; thus Meditation One (or First Meditation), Meditation Two, etc. Published with the *Meditations* were *Primae Objectiones*; *Responsio Authoris* ad Primas Objectiones; *Objectiones Secundae*; *Responsio* ad Secundas Objectiones; *Objectiones Tertiae cum Responsionibus Authoris*; *Objectiones Quartae* ad Virum Clarissimum Epistola; *Responsio* ad Quartas Objectiones; *Objectiones Quintae* Eximo viro Renato Cartesio P. Gassendus S.; *Responsio Authoris* ad Quintas Objectiones; *Objectiones Sextae*; *Responsio* ad Sextas Objectiones; and in the second edition, *Objectiones Septimae* cum Notis Authoris sive Dissertatio de Prima Philosophia and *Admodum Reverendo Patri Patri Dinet* Sociatatis Jesu Praeposito Provinciali per Francia Renatus Des Cartes S. D.—these are known as *Objections I, Replies I, Objections II, Replies II,* etc., and *Letter to Dinet.* A reproduction of the 1642 edition is available (Lecce: Conte Editore, 1994).

Principles of Philosophy*:* Renati Des-Cartes *Principia Philosophiae* (Amsterdam: L. Elzivier, 1644). The work was divided into four parts, each containing numerous articles (art.). The edition was prefaced by a dedicatory letter to Princess Elisabeth—*Serenissimae Principi Elisabethae,* Frederici Bohemiae Regis, Comitis Palatini et Electoris Sacri Romani Imperii, Fillae Natu Maximae. The 1647 French translation was also accompanied by a *Preface*: *Lettre de l'Autheur* à celuy qui a traduit le livre, laquelle peut icy servir de Preface. A reproduction of the 1644 edition is available (Lecce: Conte Editore, 1994).

Passions of the Soul*: Les Passions de L'Ame.* Par René Des Cartes (Paris: H. Le Gras, 1649). A reproduction of the 1650 edition is available (Lecce: Conte Editore, 1996).

Selected Bibliography of Primary and Secondary Sources

Primary Sources

Adam, Charles, and Paul Tannery, eds. *Oeuvres de Descartes,* 2d. ed. Paris: Vrin, 1964–1974. This is the main edition of the works of Descartes.

Ariew, Roger, John Cottingham, and Tom Sorell, eds. and trans. *Descartes' Meditations: Background Source Materials*, Cambridge Philosophical Texts in Context. Cambridge: Cambridge University Press, 1998. A selection of works by Descartes's contemporaries translated into English.

Descartes, René. *Treatise of Man.* Ed. and trans. Thomas Steele Hall. Cambridge, MA: Harvard University Press, 1972.

Descartes, René. *The World/Le Monde.* Trans. Michael S. Mahoney. New York: Abaris, 1979.

Descartes, René. *Principles of Philosophy.* Trans. V. R. Miller and R. P. Miller. Dordrecht: Reidel, 1983.

Descartes, René. *The Philosophical Writing of Descartes*, Vols. 1 and 2. Trans. John Cottingham, Robert Stoothoff, and Dugald Murdoch. Vol. 3, Trans. John Cottingham, Robert Stoothoff, Dougald Murdoch, and Anthony Kenny. Cambridge: Cambridge University Press, 1985–1991. This is the largest collection of the works of Descartes in English translation.

Descartes, René. *Passions of the Soul.* Trans. Stephen H. Voss. Indianapolis: Hackett Publishing Company, 1989.

Descartes, René. *The World and Other Writings.* Ed. and trans. Stephen Gaukroger. Cambridge: Cambridge University Press, 1998.

Secondary Sources

Ariew, Roger. *Descartes and the Last Scholastics.* Ithaca: Cornell University Press, 1999.

Ariew, Roger, and Marjorie Grene, eds. *Descartes and His Contemporaries.* Chicago: University of Chicago Press, 1995.

Chappell, Vere, and Willis Doney, eds. *Twenty-Five Years of Descartes Scholarship, 1960–1984: A Bibliography.* New York: Garland, 1987. A continuation of G. Sebba's bibliography.

Cottingham, John, ed. *The Cambridge Companion to Descartes.* Cambridge: Cambridge University Press, 1992.

Curley, Edwin M. *Descartes Against the Skeptics.* Cambridge, MA: Harvard University Press, 1978.

Frankfurt, Harry G. *Demons, Dreamers, and Madmen: The Defense of Reason in Descartes's Meditations.* Indianapolis: Bobbs-Merrill, 1970.

Garber, Daniel. *Descartes' Metaphysical Physics*. Chicago: University of Chicago Press, 1992.

Gaukroger, Stephen. *Descartes. An Intellectual Biography*. Oxford: Clarendon Press, 1995.

Grene, Marjorie. *Descartes*. Indianapolis: Hackett Publishing Company, 1998.

Gueroult, Martial. *Descartes' Philosophy Interpreted According to the Order of Reasons*, 2 vols. Trans. Roger Ariew. Minneapolis: University of Minnesota Press, 1984–1985.

Marion, Jean-Luc. *On Descartes' Metaphysical Prism*. Chicago: University of Chicago Press, 1999.

Marshall, John. *Descartes' Moral Theory*. Ithaca: Cornell University Press, 1998.

Rodis-Lewis, Geneviève. *Descartes, His Life and Thought*. Ithaca: Cornell University Press, 1998.

Sebba, Gregor. *Bibliographia Cartesiana, A Critical Guide to the Descartes Literature, 1880–1960*. The Hague: M. Nijhoff, 1964.

Shea, William R. *The Magic of Numbers and Motion: The Scientific Career of René Descartes*. Canton, MA: Science History Publications, 1991.

Verbeek, Theo. *Descartes and the Dutch: Early Reactions to Cartesian Philosophy 1637–1650*. Carbondale, IL: Southern Illinois University Press, 1992.

Watson, Richard A. *The Breakdown of Cartesian Metaphysics*. Indianapolis: Hackett Publishing Company, 1998.

Wilson, Margaret. *Descartes*. London: Routledge and Kegan Paul, 1978.

Acknowledgments

Discourse on Method, Meditations, and *Objections* and *Replies* were translated by Donald Cress: *René Descartes, Discourse on Method* (3rd ed., Indianapolis: Hackett Publishing Company, 1998) and *René Descartes, Meditations on First Philosophy* (3rd ed., Indianapolis: Hackett Publishing Company, 1993). The selections from the *Principles, Notes Against a Program, Passions of the Soul,* and *Search After Truth* were translated by Elizabeth S. Haldane and G. R. T. Ross: *The Philosophical Works of Descartes* (Cambridge: Cambridge University Press, 1911). These were revised substantially by Marjorie Grene and Roger Ariew. All the other selections and the correspondence were translated by Marjorie Grene and Roger Ariew.

I wish to thank Donald Cress, Daniel Garber, and Marjorie Grene for their numerous helpful suggestions with respect to this project.

Brief Chronology of Descartes's Life and Works

1596	born in Touraine at La Haye on March 31
1607–15	studies at the Jesuit college of La Flèche in Anjou
1616	receives M.A. in law from the University of Poitiers in November
1618	enlists in the Netherlands in the army of Prince Maurice of Nassau; has a chance encounter with Isaac Beeckman; composes first work, on musical theory
1619	travels in Germany; has three strange dreams, November 10, that set him on the right course of life; works on *Rules for the Direction of the Mind,* which he leaves unfinished in 1628
1620	notes that he "began to understand the foundations of a wonderful discovery"
1621	returns to Paris but also takes an extended trip to Italy in the next few years
1624	trial of the libertine poet Théophile de Viau and condemnation of anti-Aristotelian theses posted by the alchemists and atomists Etienne de Clave, Jean Bitaud, and Antoine Villon
1628	leaves for the Netherlands
1629	begins a small treatise in metaphysics (now lost); begins working on the essays *Meteors* and *Dioptrics* and the treatise *The World* (with its lengthy chapter on man)
1633	Galileo condemned for defending the motion of the earth; stops the publication of *The World*
1635	birth of his daughter, Francine, in July, baptized August 7 (dies September 1640)
1637	publishes *Discourse on Method* with *Dioptrics, Meteors,* and *Geometry*
1641	publishes *Meditations on First Philosophy* with *Objections*—sets by Caterus, Thomas Hobbes, Antoine Arnauld, Pierre Gassendi, and two sets collected by Marin Mersenne—and his *Replies*
1642	publishes the second edition of the Meditations with a new set of *Objections* by the Jesuit Pierre Bourdin and his *Replies,* plus the *Letter to Father Dinet*
1643	the University of Utrecht prohibits the teaching of the new philosophy (reaffirmed in 1645); starts a correspondence with Princess Elisabeth of Bohemia
1644	briefly returns to France for the first time; publishes *Principles of Philosophy*
1647	publishes French translations of the *Meditations* and *Principles,* plus *Notes Against a Program*
1648	the University of Leyden prohibits the teaching of his works
1649	leaves for Sweden in the fall; publishes *Passions of the Soul*
1650	dies at Stockholm on February 11

I

EARLY WORKS AND CORRESPONDENCE (TO 1637)

Preliminaries and *Observations* (1619)

Actors, called upon the stage, put on a mask so that we cannot see the blush on   *X, 213*
their faces. So, as I am about to mount the stage of the world where I have been
a spectator so far, I advance masked.

   In my youth, when I was shown ingenious discoveries, I used to ask myself   *214*
whether I could not invent them by myself even without reading the author. In
this way, I gradually came to notice that I was using determinate rules. [. . .]

   Most books, as soon as you have read a few of their lines and looked at some
of their diagrams, are completely understood. The rest is there only to fill the
pages.

   The *Mathematical Treasure* of Polybius the Cosmopolitan[1] gives the true way
of solving all the difficulties of mathematical science; it demonstrates that the
human mind cannot achieve anything more with respect to these difficulties. The
work is aimed at people who promise to show new miracles in all the sciences,
so that it can shake them out of their laziness and reject their boldness. It also
intends to lighten the tortuous labor of the many who struggle night and day with
some of the Gordian knots of that science, and who uselessly consume their intellectual resources. The work is offered for a second time to the learned of the
world, and particularly to the most celebrated Rosicrucian Brothers in Germany.[2]

   The sciences are now masked. If the masks were taken off, they would appear   *215*
in all their beauty. Anyone who would see the linkage of the sciences, would not
find them any more difficult to retain in the mind than a series of numbers.

   All minds have prescribed limits that cannot be surpassed. Those who cannot
make use of principles in discovery, because of some defect of mind, can still
recognize the true value of the sciences; and this will suffice for them to arrive
at correct judgments of the value of things.

* * *

   I call the diseases of the soul vices. They are less easy to diagnose than the dis-   *215*
eases of the body; for we have often experienced the true health of the body, but
never that of the soul. [. . .]

Selections on pp. 1–45 translated by Marjorie Grene and Roger Ariew.

1. A pseudonym Descartes was contemplating using for himself.

2. The Brothers of the Rosy-Cross was a secret society established in Germany and devoted
to the reformation of all knowledge. Descartes's dedication of his work to them might be
ironic; indeed, the whole paragraph seems to be a parody of Rosicrucian manifestos.

1

216   In the year 1620, I began to understand the foundations of a wonderful discovery. I had a dream in November 1619, containing Ode Seven of Ausonius, beginning "Quod vitae sectabor iter?" [What course of life shall I follow?]

X, 359   *Rules for the Direction of the Mind* (1618?–1628?)

1. The end of all studies should be to direct the mind toward the enunciation of solid and true judgments on all things presented to it.

It is the custom of people, whenever they notice any similarity between two things, to attribute to both of them, even in those respects in which they differ, whatever they have found to be true of either one. So they make a false comparison between the sciences, which all consist in the cognition of the mind, and the arts, which demand a certain belief and disposition of the body. They see that one person cannot learn all the arts at the same time, but that a person who practices

360   only one art more easily emerges an excellent artist. For the same hands cannot so easily be applied both to tilling the fields and to strumming on the lyre, or to several different occupations of this kind, as to only one of them. Hence they have held the same opinion of the sciences, and, distinguishing them from one another by the diversity of their objects, they thought it proper to pursue each one of them singly to the neglect of all the others. But in this they are plainly mistaken. Since all the sciences are nothing but human intelligence, which always remains one and the same, however different the subjects to which it is applied, and which receives no more alteration from those subjects than does the light of the sun from the variety of things it illumines, there is no need to impose any boundaries upon the mind; nor, indeed, does the knowledge of one truth, like the practice of a single art, keep us from the discovery of another, but rather assists us. Indeed, it amazes me how most people study with the greatest diligence the customs of humans, the properties of plants, the motions of the stars, the transformations of metals, and the objects of other such disciplines, while at the same time almost no one thinks about good sense, or about universal intelligence, although as a matter of fact all other things are to be valued, not for themselves, but because they contribute something to universal intelligence. Thus it is not without reason that we set down this first rule, since nothing takes us farther afield from the right road for seeking truth than the direction of our studies to particular ends rather than to this one general one. Nor am I speaking of perverse and reprehensible ends, like vain glory or the love of filthy lucre; it is clear that

361   pretended arguments and sophistries suited to vulgar minds open a much easier road to them than the solid knowledge of truth could do. But I am thinking even of decent and laudable ends, since we are often more subtly deceived by these— as, for example, if we pursue sciences useful either for the comforts of life, or for that pleasure which is found in the contemplation of truth, and which is almost the only happiness in this life that is pure and untroubled by pain. For these legitimate fruits of the sciences we can certainly expect to attain; but, if we think about these things in the midst of our studies, they often make us omit much that is necessary to the knowledge of other things—whether because such material appears at first sight of little use, or of little interest. It must be recognized, however, that all the sciences are so related to one another that it is much easier to learn them all at one time than to separate one from the others. If therefore anyone wishes seriously to investigate the truth of things, he should not choose any single science; for they are all interconnected and reciprocally dependent. He should rather think only of increasing the natural light of reason, not in order to resolve this or that problem of the School, but in order that in every particular situation of his life his intellect may show his will what choice to make. Soon he will be amazed to find that he has made much greater progress than those who study particular things, and that he has attained not only what others desire, but also higher things which they could not expect to reach.

2. We should concern ourselves only with those objects of which our *362*
minds appear to be adequate in gaining their certain and indubitable
knowledge.

All science is certain and evident knowledge. He who doubts of many things is not more learned than he who has never thought about them. Indeed, the former seems even more ignorant than the latter, if he has conceived a false opinion of any of them. So it is better not to study at all than to occupy oneself with objects so difficult that, in our inability to distinguish true from false, we are forced to admit doubtful things for certain; for in these matters there is not so much hope of increasing our learning as there is danger of diminishing it. And so through this proposition we reject all knowledge that is only probable, and we declare that only those things ought to be believed which are perfectly known and of which there can be no doubt. Scholars may perhaps have convinced themselves that there is little knowledge of this kind, because they have neglected to reflect on it as being too easy and open to anyone at all—a vice common to the human race. But I warn them that such knowledge is much more plentiful than they think and sufficient to demonstrate with certainty innumerable propositions on which they have been able until now to argue only with probability. And because they have thought it unworthy of a scholar to admit ignorance of any- *363* thing, they have been accustomed to adorn their false arguments so well that they come to persuade themselves, and so they have ended up trumpeting them as true.

Indeed if we observe this rule well there will be very few things we may suitably undertake to learn. For there is scarcely one question in the sciences on which clever people have not often disagreed. But each time the judgments of two people diverge on a single point, it is certain that at least one of them is wrong and not even one of them, it seems, has scientific knowledge. For if the argument of the one was certain and evident, he would be able to expound it to the other in such a way as finally to convince his intellect also. Therefore we see that in all such probable opinions we cannot acquire perfect science, for we may not without temerity hope for more than others have achieved. Consequently, if our reckoning is correct, there remain of all the sciences already discovered only arithmetic and geometry to which the observation of this rule reduces us.

Nevertheless we do not therefore condemn that manner of philosophizing so suitable for jousting that others have already invented, that is, the scholastics' weapons of probable syllogisms. They do indeed train the minds of children and stimulate them by a certain emulation. It is much better to mold them with opin-
364 ions of this kind, uncertain though they seem when disputed among the erudite, than to leave them free to themselves. For perhaps without a guide they might cast themselves into some abyss; but while they follow in their masters' footsteps, they may indeed deviate somewhat from the truth, yet they will certainly take a road that is more secure at least in this sense, that it has already been tried by those who are more prudent; and we ourselves rejoice that we were once trained in the schools in this way. But since we are now freed of that obligation that bound us to the words of our masters, and since as adults we withdraw our hand from under the rod, if we wish seriously to set ourselves rules with the help of which we may ascend to the height of human knowledge, we must surely admit among the first the one that warns us not to abuse our leisure, as do many who neglect everything simple and are occupied only with arduous matters. They certainly make the subtlest conjectures on such subjects and devise very probable arguments. But after many labors they finally notice too late that they have only increased their doubts, without having learned any science.

But now, since we just said that of all the disciplines known by others, only arithmetic and geometry are free from every taint of falsity and uncertainty, we should examine more carefully the reason why this is so. And for this purpose we
365 must observe that we can arrive at knowledge of things by two paths, namely by experience or by deduction. We must observe, further, that while experiences of things are often deceptive, deduction or a pure inference of one thing from another, though it may be passed over if it is not noticed, can never be erroneously executed by an intellect even minimally rational. And I find of little use for this purpose those bonds by which the dialecticians seek to rule human reason, although I do not deny that they are most suitable for other uses. For all the error to which people are subject (people, I say, not beasts), results, never from faulty inference, but only from the fact that experiments insufficiently understood are admitted or that judgments are asserted rashly and without basis.

From this the explanation is evident why arithmetic and geometry are much more certain than other disciplines. The reason is that they alone are concerned with an object so pure and simple that they suppose absolutely nothing which experience has rendered uncertain, but they consist entirely in consequences rationally deduced. They are therefore the easiest and clearest of all the sciences, and have the kind of object we require, since in them it appears that human nature scarcely ever errs, except through inattention. Nevertheless, we ought not to wonder if many apply their minds more readily to other arts or to philosophy. For this happens because everyone feels free to guess with more confidence in
366 an obscure than in an evident subject matter, and because it is much easier to make conjectures on any random question than to arrive at truth itself in a single one, however simple.

From all this one must conclude, not, indeed, that one must learn nothing but arithmetic and geometry, but only that those who seek the right road of truth should not occupy themselves with any object concerning which they cannot possess a certainty equal to that of the demonstrations of arithmetic and geometry.

3. Concerning the objects presented to us we should investigate, not what others have thought nor what we ourselves conjecture, but what we can intuit clearly and evidently or deduce with certainty, since scientific knowledge is acquired by no other means.

The books of the ancients should be read, since it is a tremendous advantage for us to be able to use the labors of so many persons: as much to learn what has been correctly discovered in the past as to be counseled what more remains to be thought out in all the disciplines. On the other hand, there is great danger that perhaps some traces of the errors acquired by too attentive a reading of those authors may remain with us, however unwilling we may be and however much we guard against them. For writers are in fact so inclined that whenever, through thoughtless credulity, they have slipped into a judgment on some controversial subject, they always try by the subtlest arguments to draw us along in the same direction. Whenever, on the contrary, they have happily discovered something certain and evident, they never display it except in a wrapping of various detours,   *367* either because they fear that the dignity of their discovery might be diminished by the simplicity of the argument, or else because they begrudge us the obvious truth.

Yet even if they were all guileless and open, and never imposed upon us any doubtful opinions as true, but expounded every subject in good faith, we should still be perpetually uncertain which of them ought to be believed, since scarcely anything has been pronounced by someone whose contrary has not been asserted by another. And it would not help to count votes, so that we might follow the opinion held by the greater number of authorities. For when it is a case of a difficult question, it is more likely that the truth should have been discovered by few than by many. But even if all of them agreed, their doctrine would still be inadequate. For instance, we shall not turn out to be mathematicians, even though we keep in mind all the demonstrations of others, unless we are equipped intellectually for the solution of any kind of problem. Nor shall we turn out to be philosophers if we have read all the arguments of Plato and Aristotle but are unable to form a solid judgment on a given question. In fact we seem in this fashion to have learned not sciences but histories.

Further, we should be warned never at any time to admit any conjectures whatsoever as an admixture to our judgments on the truth of things. This counsel is of no small importance. For the chief reason why nothing is found in the vulgar philosophy so evident and certain as to be incapable of controversial treatment is this: scholars, not content with knowing what is clear and certain, first hazarded   *368* further affirmations about obscure and unknown matters which they arrived at only by probable conjectures; and then gradually attaching to such matters a complete faith, and mixing them indiscriminately with what is true and evident, they have finally grown unable to draw any conclusion that does not appear to depend on some such proposition, and so is not uncertain.

But in order that we may not fall into the same error, let us here enumerate all the acts of our intellect through which we can arrive at knowledge of things without any fear of error. We admit only two: namely, intuition and deduction.[3]

By *intuition* I understand neither the fleeting testimony of the senses nor the deceptive judgment of the imagination with its false constructions, but a conception of a pure and attentive mind, so easy and so distinct, that no doubt at all remains about what we understand. Or, what comes to the same thing, intuition is the indubitable conception of a pure and attentive mind arising from the light of reason alone; it is more certain even than deduction, because it is simpler, even though, as we noted above, people cannot err in deduction either. Thus everyone can intuit with his mind that he exists, that he is thinking, that a triangle is bounded by only three lines, a sphere by a single surface, and the like. Such things are much more numerous than most people think, because they disdain to turn their minds toward matters so easy.

369   But so that some may not be disturbed by the term intuition in this new sense, or still others by my being forced to depart in the same way from common meanings in the following pages, I add here the general warning: I do not in the least consider the way in which particular terms have been used in the schools recently, since it would have been very difficult to use the same words and inwardly to have such different thoughts. I consider only what each word means in Latin, so that when proper words are lacking I may transform whatever terms appear to me most suitable to fit my meaning.

This evidence and certainty of intuition is required, however, not only for single statements, but also for discursive reasoning of every kind. Thus, for example, given this conclusion: 2 and 2 amount to the same as 3 and 1, one must see by intuition not only that 2 and 2 make 4, and that 3 and 1 also make 4, but also that the third proposition is a necessary inference from the other two.

Thus there may now be some doubt as to why we should have added here another mode of knowledge besides intuition, that is, one proceeding by deduction, by which we understand all that is necessarily inferred from other things that are certainly known. But this procedure was necessary, since many things are known with certainty which nevertheless are not themselves evident, simply because they are deduced from true and known principles by the continuous and uninterrupted movement of a mind which clearly intuits each step. Thus we know that the last link of a long chain is connected with the first, even though we

370   do not take in with a single glance of the eyes all the intermediate links on which the connection depends—provided only that we run through them successively and remember that from first to last each one was attached to the one next to it. Therefore we distinguish here intuition from certain deduction by the fact that some movement or succession is conceived in the latter but not in the former.

---

3. The manuscript has *inductio*, but either *deductio* was intended or Descartes did not carefully differentiate between induction and deduction.

Moreover, evidence is not necessarily present for deduction, as it is for intuition, but deduction rather acquires its certainty, in a sense, from memory. From all this we may conclude that those propositions which follow immediately from first principles are known according to the way we look at it, now by intuition, now by deduction, but that the first principles themselves are known only by intuition, and the remote conclusions, in contrast, only by deduction.

These then are the two most certain paths to scientific knowledge. No others should be admitted by the mind, but all the rest rejected as suspect and liable to error. This does not, however, prevent our believing those matters which are divinely revealed to be more certain than all knowledge. For faith in these, although it concerns obscure matters, is not an act of intellect but of will, and if they have a basis in the intellect, they can and ought to be, more than all other things, discovered by one or the other of the two ways already mentioned, as we may perhaps indicate at greater length.

4. Method is necessary for the investigation of truth. *371*

Mortals are possessed by such blind curiosity that they often lead their minds through unknown paths, without any ground for hope, but simply venturing on the chance that what they seek might lie that way: as if a person is burning with so stupid a desire to find a treasure that he constantly roams about the streets to see if by chance he might find some article lost by a traveler. It is in this manner that almost all the chemists, most geometers, and not a few philosophers work. To be sure, I do not deny that they sometimes stray so fortunately as to find something true; still I do not therefore hold them more efficient, but only more fortunate. And it is much better never to think of investigating the truth of anything at all, than to do it without method. For it is very certain that through such disorderly studies and obscure meditations the natural light is obscured and our minds blinded. Thus all those who accustom themselves to walking in the dark weaken the acuteness of their eyes so much that afterward they cannot bear the light of the day. This is also confirmed by experience; for how often do we not see those who have never devoted themselves to letters judging much more solidly and clearly of the things that come their way than do those who have spent all their time in the schools? By method, then, I understand certain and simple rules such that if a person follows them exactly, he will never suppose any- *372* thing false to be true, and, spending no useless mental effort, but gradually and steadily increasing his knowledge, will arrive at true knowledge of all those things to which his powers are adequate.

Two things should be noted here: never to suppose true what is false, and to arrive at knowledge of all things. For if we are ignorant of some one of all the things that we can know, that happens only because we have never discovered any way that would lead us to such knowledge, or because we have slipped into the opposite error. But if the method explains correctly how the intuition of the mind is to be used, and how deductions are to be made, so that we may arrive at knowledge of all things, nothing more seems to me to be required to make it complete, since we have already said that there can be no scientific knowledge except through an intuition of the mind or through a deduction. Nor indeed must the method extend to showing how these operations themselves are to be conducted, since they are the first and simplest of all—so much so that, unless our intellect already knew how to use them, it could understand none of the precepts of the method itself, however simple. As to the other operations of the mind, moreover, which dialectic struggles to direct with the aid of these prior ones, they *373* are useless here—or rather they may be counted as obstructions, since nothing can be added to the pure light of reason without in some way obscuring it.

Since therefore the usefulness of this method is so great that it seems more harmful than useful to devote oneself to the study of the sciences without it, I am readily convinced that, doubtless with the sole guide of nature, the greatest minds have formerly perceived it in some fashion. For the human mind possesses an I-know-not-what that is divine, in which the first seeds of useful thoughts are scattered, so that often, though neglected and suffocated by perverse studies, they bear spontaneous fruit. We have experience of this in the simplest of the sciences, arithmetic and geometry; for we have sufficient evidence that the ancient geometers used a certain analysis, which they extended to the resolution of all problems, even though they begrudged it to posterity. And now there also exists a kind of arithmetic, called algebra, which does with numbers what the ancients did with figures. And these two are nothing but spontaneous fruits born of the innate principles of this method. Nor do I wonder that, with regard to the extremely simple objects of these arts, these fruits have developed more happily than in others, where greater obstacles usually stifle them. Even there, however, if only they are cultivated with the greatest care, they can without doubt arrive at full maturity.

This, then, is what I have principally undertaken to do in this treatise. Indeed, I should not make much of these rules, if they were adapted only to the solution of the vain problems with which logicians and geometers are accustomed to play at their leisure; for in that case I should think I had succeeded only in playing *374* with trifles perhaps more subtly than others had done. True, I shall often speak here of figures and of numbers (since one cannot expect from any other discipline examples so evident or so certain), yet whoever considers my meaning attentively will easily perceive that there is nothing of which I am thinking here less than of vulgar mathematics; but that I am expounding another discipline, of which these are the outer husks rather than the parts. This science should in fact contain the first rudiments of human reason, and should need only to extend itself in order to elicit truths on any subject whatsoever; and to speak freely, I am convinced that it is more powerful than all the other knowledge that mankind has taught us, because it is the source of all the rest. But I said outer husks, not because I want to wrap up this doctrine and hide it to keep the crowd away, but rather in order to decorate and ornament it, so that it may be more suitable for the human mind.

When I first applied my mind to the mathematical disciplines I began by reading most of those things that mathematical authors usually teach, and I paid most *375* attention to arithmetic and geometry, since they were said to be simplest and at the same time paths to the others. But in neither case did I at that time lay my hand on authors who fully satisfied me. I did indeed read in their works several statements about numbers which after making calculations I found to be true; and even with regard to figures, they set, so to speak, many things before my eyes, and inferred them from certain consequences. But they did not seem to my mind to exhibit satisfactorily why these matters stood thus, and how they had been discovered. So it did not surprise me that after tasting these arts, most persons of talent and knowledge at once set them aside as puerile and vain, or on the contrary are deterred at the very start from learning them because they appear so difficult and intricate. For indeed nothing is more futile than to occupy oneself with bare numbers and imaginary figures, in such a way as to appear willing to rest content with knowledge of such trifles; nor is anything more futile than so to attach oneself to those superficial demonstrations, which are more frequently discovered by chance than by art and have more to do with the eyes and the imagination than with the intellect, that one becomes in a sense unaccustomed to the use of reason. At the same time nothing is more complicated than to dispose in this manner of new difficulties hidden by the confusion of numbers. But then when I went on to think that those who first discovered philosophy long ago were unwilling to admit to the study of wisdom anyone untrained in mathematics, as if this discipline seemed to them the easiest and most necessary of all in training *376* minds and preparing them to understand other and higher sciences, I strongly suspected that they knew some mathematics very different from the vulgar mathematics of our age. Not that I think they knew it very perfectly, for their mad celebrations and thanksgivings for trifling discoveries indicate clearly how little advanced they were. Nor do certain of their machines that are celebrated by historians move me from my opinion; for although they were doubtless very simple, they could be praised to a degree of fame befitting miracles by the ignorant and astonished crowd. But I am convinced that the first seeds of truth, sown by nature in the human mind, but which we stifle in ourselves by reading and hearing every day so many errors of every kind, had such force in that crude and simple antiquity that, by the same light of the mind that made them see they ought to prefer virtue to pleasure and the good to the useful, although they were ignorant why it should be so, people had true ideas of philosophy and mathematics, although they had not yet been able to acquire perfectly these sciences themselves. In fact it seems to me that traces of that true mathematics are still visible in Pappus and Diophantus,[4] who, though not of the first age, still lived many centuries before our time. But this I believe was later suppressed, with a sort of evil cunning, by these authors themselves. For, as many artisans have done for their inventions, they feared perhaps that being very easy and simple their method might lose its price if given to the crowd. In order that we should admire them they preferred to give us instead of their discoveries a few sterile verities, subtly deduced, as the fruits of their art, rather than to teach the art itself, which would *377* clearly dispel the admiration. Finally there were some very ingenious persons who tried in this century to revive this art. For that art which is called by the barbarous name of algebra seems to be nothing else, provided only one could

---

4. Third- and fourth-century A.D. Alexandrian (Greek) mathematicians.

disentangle it from the multitudinous numerals and inexplicable figures with which it is encumbered, so that it might no longer lack that clarity and that supreme facility which ought, as we have said, to be present in true mathematics. When these thoughts had led me from the particular study of arithmetic and geometry to a general study of mathematics, I inquired first of all precisely what everyone means by this word, and why not only those two sciences of which we have already spoken, but also music, optics, mechanics, and several others are called parts of mathematics. For it is not enough in this case to consider the etymology of the word; since, as the term *mathesis* signifies simply science, the other sciences would have no less right than geometry itself to be called mathematics. Moreover, we see no one who, if he has so much as set foot in a school, fails to distinguish easily among those subject matters that are presented to him what belongs to mathematics and what belongs to other disciplines. And if one reflects on this matter more attentively, one finally observes

378   that all and only those subjects in which order and measurement are investigated are referred to mathematics, no matter whether such measure is sought in numbers, in figures, in stars, in sounds, or in some other object. One concludes, therefore, that there must be some general science explaining all that can be investigated concerning order and measure, without application to a particular material; and that this science is called, not by a strange name, but by a name already ancient and received by usage, *universal mathematics*, because it includes all that material by virtue of which other sciences are called parts of mathematics. How much it excels in usefulness and facility the sciences that depend on it is clear from the fact that it extends to all the objects which they treat and to many others; and that all the difficulties it involves are found also in the other sciences, accompanied in addition by many other difficulties, which arise from their particular objects, and which it for its part does not possess. But now, since everyone knows its name and knows what it deals with, even without applying it, how does it happen that most people try to learn the other sciences that depend on it, while no one takes the trouble to study it in itself? I should certainly be amazed at this, if I did not know that it is considered by everyone to be very simple, and if I had not observed long ago that the human mind, leaving aside what it thinks easy of attainment, hurries on to new and loftier things.

But I, conscious of my weakness, have decided constantly to observe in the

379   investigation of truth an order such that, always beginning with the simplest and easiest matters, I never proceed to others before it seems to me that nothing remains to be desired in the first. That is why I have cultivated up to now this universal mathematics to the best of my abilities; hence I believe that when I go on, as I hope to do soon, to deal in turn with higher sciences, my efforts will not be premature. But before I take this step I shall try to unite and to set in order all that I have found worthy of notice in my earlier studies—both in order to find them without trouble in this book, if need be, at a time when with increasing age my memory will fail, and in order to be able to carry a freer mind to other things, having discharged my memory of them.

5. All method consists in the order and disposition of those things toward which the eye of the mind must be directed if we are to discover any truth. And we follow this method exactly if we reduce involved and obscure propositions step by step to simpler ones, and then attempt to ascend by the same steps from the intuition of all those that are entirely simple to the cognition of all the others.

In this alone lies the sum total of human endeavor, and this must be followed no less carefully by one who would arrive at a knowledge of things than the   *380* thread of Theseus by him who would penetrate the labyrinth. But many people either do not reflect on what this precept teaches, or are completely ignorant of it, or suppose they do not need it. Hence they often examine the most difficult questions with so little order that they seem to me to behave as if they were trying to get from the bottom to the top of a building with one jump, either taking no account of the stairs intended for this use, or failing to notice them. That is what all the astrologers do, who, without knowing the nature of the heaven and without even having observed its motions adequately, hope to be able to indicate its effects. That is what many do, who study mechanics apart from physics, and rashly manufacture new instruments for the production of motions. That is also what those philosophers do, who neglect experience but think that truth will spring from their own brains, like Minerva from the head of Jupiter.

Indeed it is evident that all these err with respect to the present rule. But since the order required here is so obscure and intricate that not everyone can make out what it is, they can scarcely take enough care to avoid error, unless they diligently observe what is expounded in the following proposition.

6. To distinguish the simplest things from those which are complex, and to   *381* **follow them out in order, it is necessary, in every sequence of things in which we have directly deduced certain truths from others, to observe what constituent has the greatest simplicity, and in what way all the others are more or less or equally removed from it.**

Although this proposition appears to teach nothing new, it contains nevertheless the chief secret of this art, and there is no more useful proposition in all this treatise; for it counsels that all things can be arranged in certain sequences. Not indeed, that they can be so arranged insofar as they are referred to some genus of being, as the philosophers have divided them into their categories, but insofar as certain ones can be known through others. Thus, each time any difficulty occurs, we can see immediately whether it will be profitable to run through certain other matters first, and which ones, and in what order.

In order that this may be done correctly, however, it must first be noted that all things, to the degree to which they can be useful to our project (when we do not consider their natures in isolation but compare them with one another, in order that certain ones may be known through others), may be said to be either absolute or relative.

I call absolute everything that contains within itself the pure and simple nature in question: as all that is considered independent, cause, simple, universal, equal,
382   similar, straight, or the like; and I call this the simplest and easiest of all, so that we may use it for resolving questions.

The relative, on the other hand, is what participates in the same nature, or at least in something of it, in accordance with which it can be referred to the absolute, and deduced from it through some sequence, but which, in addition, involves in its conception other things I call relations. Such is all that is called dependent, effect, compounded, particular, many, unequal, dissimilar, oblique, etc. These relatives are removed from absolutes in proportion to the number of mutually subordinate relations they contain. And it is the necessity of distinguishing such relations that the present rule teaches. It also teaches the need of observing the pattern of interconnections between them and their natural order in such a fashion that we can proceed from the last of them to the most absolute, passing through all the rest.

And the secret of the whole art consists in this: that we notice carefully in all things what is most absolute in them. For some things are more absolute than others from one point of view, but more relative from another. Thus the universal is indeed more absolute than the particular, since it has a simpler nature, but at the same time one can say it is more relative since it depends on individuals for its existence. Again, there are sometimes things that are really more absolute than others, even though they are never the most absolute of all. Thus, if we consider individuals, the species is an absolute, and if we consider the genus, it is a relative; among measurable things, extension is an absolute, but among exten-
383   sions length is an absolute, etc. In the same way, finally, in order to make it clearer that we are here considering the sequences of things as objects of knowledge and not the nature of each one of them, we have purposely counted cause and equal among the absolutes, although their nature is really relative—for among the philosophers cause and effect are in fact correlatives. But here, if we are in fact inquiring into the nature of the effect, we must first know the cause, and not the reverse. Equals likewise correspond with one another; but we know unequals only by comparison with equals, and not the reverse, etc.

It should be noted, secondly, that there are only a few pure and simple natures, which we may intuit in themselves, independently of all others, whether in trials by experience, or by the light implanted in us. Moreover we declare that these must be painstakingly observed; for it is these we call the simplest in every sequence. All others, in contrast, can be perceived only insofar as they are deduced from these, either immediately or proximately, or through the mediation of two or three or more separate conclusions. And the number of these conclusions must also be noted, so that we may know if they are removed from the first and simplest propositions by a smaller or greater number of steps. And such is everywhere the nexus of consequences, from which arise those sequences of objects of investigation, to which every question is to be reduced in order that it
384   may be examined by a sure method. But because it is not easy to review them all, and since, besides, they do not need so much to be retained by the memory as distinguished by some insight of the mind, we must seek for something which

will form the mind so as to let it perceive these sequences whenever it needs to do so. For this purpose, I can say from experience, nothing is more effective than to reflect with some sagacity on the very smallest of those things we have already perceived.

Finally, it should be noted, in the third place, that we ought not to begin an inquiry with the investigation of difficult matters. Rather, before we set out to attack any definite questions, we must first collect indiscriminately all the truths that spontaneously present themselves, then gradually see if others can be deduced from them, and from these last yet others, and so on. That done, we must reflect attentively on the truths we have discovered, and consider carefully why we have been able to find some sooner and more easily than others, and which ones they are. This we do so that we may also be able to judge, when we begin some definite question, to what other inquiries we could profitably apply ourselves first. For example, if it occurred to me that 6 is the double of 3, I should look further for the double of 6, that is to say, 12; then I should look, if I liked, for the double of that, that is to say 24, and the double of that, that is 48, etc.; thus I should conclude, as it is easy to do, that there is the same proportion between 3 and 6 as between 6 and 12, and the same between 12 and 24, etc., and that consequently the numbers 3, 6, 12, 24, 48, etc., form a continuous proportion. Although all these things are so clear as to appear almost childish, I understand, on attentive reflection, in what way all questions are involved which can be 385 posed about proportions or the relations of things, and in what order they should be investigated: and this alone embraces the whole of the science of pure mathematics.

For first I observe, to begin with, that it is more difficult to find the double of 6 than the double of 3; and similarly, in every case, once we have found the proportion that exists between any two numbers, we can find other magnitudes in indefinite number having the same proportion to one another. And the nature of the difficulty does not change if we look for three or four or more, for the reason that we have to find each one separately and without taking account of the others. Further, I observe that although, given the magnitudes 6 and 3, you easily find the third in continuous proportion, namely, 12, it is nevertheless not so easy given the two extremes, that is, 3 and 12, to be able to find the mean proportional, that is, 6. If we look into the matter, we find that this is clearly a different kind of difficulty from the preceding, since, to find the mean proportional, we must attend at the same time to the two extremes and to the proportion that exists between them, so that something new is produced by their division. This is something very different from what is required, given two magnitudes, to find the third in some proportion. I go even further and ask whether, given the magnitudes 3 and 24, it would be as easy to find one of the two mean proportionals, namely, 6 and 12. Here we have yet another kind of problem, more involved than 386 previous ones, since here we have to attend, not to one or two, but to three things at the same time in order find a fourth. Let us go even further than this, and see whether, given only 3 and 48, it would be more difficult to find one of the three mean proportionals, namely, 6, 12, and 24. At first sight it does seem so. But then it occurs to us at once that this difficulty can be divided and diminished. Plainly, we first look for one main proportional between 3 and 48, namely, 12, and then we look for another mean proportional between 3 and 12, that is, 6, and another between 12 and 48, namely, 24. And in this way the difficulty is reduced to the second kind already discussed.

From all the above I observe, further, how the knowledge of one and the same thing can be pursued by different paths, which differ from one another considerably in difficulty and obscurity. For example, if we are to find the four proportionals, 3, 6, 12, 24, given any consecutive pairs, that is, 3 and 6, 6 and 12, or 12 and 24, in order to find the rest, that will be very easy to do. In that case we shall say that the proportion to be found is being examined directly. If, however, two are given alternately, namely, 3 and 12 or 6 and 24, and the others are to be found, then we shall say that the difficulty is examined indirectly to the first degree. If, finally, we suppose the two extremes, that is, 3 and 24, so that we are looking for

387   the two intermediates, 6 and 12, then this will be examined indirectly to the second degree. And I could go further and deduce many other things from this one example. But these are sufficient to let the reader observe what I mean when I say that some progression is deduced directly or indirectly, and to enable him to understand how it is that from some very simple things that are known first, many others also, in many disciplines, can be deduced by those who reflect attentively and inquire with sagacity.

7. In order to attain complete scientific knowledge, it is necessary to run through, one by one, in a movement of thought which is continuous and nowhere interrupted, all those matters which bear upon our undertaking; they must also be included in a sufficient and ordered enumeration.

The observation of what is propounded here is necessary for the admission among certain truths of those which, as we have said above, are not immediately deduced from first principles known through themselves. Sometimes, in fact, this deduction is made by a chain of consequences so long that, when we get to the end, we do not easily remember the whole path that has led us to this point; and that is why we said that it is necessary to aid the weakness of the memory by a continuous movement of thought. Thus if I have found out by separate operations, for example, what relation there is between the magnitudes A and B, next between B and C, and then between C and D, and finally between D and E, I do

388   not therefore see what relation there is between A and E, nor can I understand it with accuracy from the facts I have already learned, unless I remember them all. To remedy this, I should run over them several times with a continuous movement of the imagination that gives an intuition of every single one and at the same time passes to others, until I had learned to pass from the first to the last so rapidly that next to no part was left to memory, but I seemed to intuit the whole thing at once. For by this means, while it helps the memory, the sluggishness of the mind is corrected, and its capacity in a certain sense extended.

We add, moreover, that the movement must nowhere be interrupted. For often those who wish to deduce something too quickly and from distant principles do not run through the whole chain of intermediate propositions with sufficient care to prevent their rashly overlooking many points. But surely, wherever even the smallest point is omitted, the chain is immediately broken, and the whole certainty of the conclusion falls.

We say here, further, that enumeration is required for the complete attainment of scientific knowledge. To be sure, other precepts are of assistance in the solution of many questions; but only the aid of enumeration can bring it about that, to whatever question we may apply our minds, we would always make a true and certain judgment, and that therefore nothing at all would escape us, but we would appear to know something about everything.

This enumeration, then, or induction, is an inventory of everything that bears on any given question—an inventory so painstaking and accurate that we conclude from it with certainty and evidence that nothing has mistakenly been omitted by us. Thus every time we have used it, if the thing we are looking for escapes us, we are   *389* at least wiser in this respect: that we perceive with certainty that it can be found by no way known to us; and if perchance, as often happens, we have succeeded in reviewing all the ways to it open to men, we may boldly affirm that knowledge of it lies entirely beyond the reach of human intelligence.

It should be noted, further, that by sufficient enumeration or induction, we understand only the means by which truth is more certainly inferred than by any other kind of proof except simple intuition. As often as a cognition cannot be reduced to intuition, since we have thrown off all syllogistic fetters, there remains to us only this one way on which we should fasten all our faith. For whatever single propositions we have deduced immediately from others are already reduced to a true intuition if the inference was evident. If, however, we infer some one thing from many and disconnected facts, the capacity of our intellect is often insufficient to embrace them all in a single intuition, in which case the certitude of the present operation should suffice. In the same way we are unable to distinguish with a single glance of the eyes all the links of a very long chain; yet if we see the connection of each one to the next, that is enough to let us say that we have seen how the last is connected with the first.

I have said that this operation ought to be sufficient, because it can often be defective and in consequence liable to error. For sometimes, even though we review by enumeration a great number of things that are really evident, if never-   *390* theless we omit even the smallest point, the chain is broken, and the whole certainty of the conclusion falls. Sometimes, moreover, we embrace the whole with certainty in an enumeration, but we do not distinguish the single points from one another, and so know the whole only confusedly.

Besides, this enumeration should sometimes be complete, sometimes distinct, but sometimes neither is necessary; and that is why it has been stated only that it ought to be sufficient. For if I want to prove by enumeration how many genera of things are corporeal, or fall in some way under sense, I shall not declare that there are so many and no more, until I know for certain that I have included them all in my enumeration, and have distinguished each from the others. But if I wish to show by the same means that the rational soul is not corporeal, it will not be necessary for the enumeration to be complete, but it will be sufficient if I include all bodies at once in certain classes, in such a way as to demonstrate that the rational soul can be referred to none of them. And finally if I wish to show by enumeration that the area of the circle is greater than the area of other figures whose perimeter is equal, it is not necessary to review all the figures, but it is sufficient to demonstrate this of some particular figures, in order by induction to reach this same conclusion concerning all the others.

391   I have also added that enumeration should be ordered, not only because there is no better remedy for the defects already listed than to examine everything with order, but also because it often happens that, if it were necessary to examine separately every one of the things that bear on a given question, no human life would suffice for it, either because these things are too numerous, or because the same things would keep cropping up for renewed consideration. But if we dispose of all things in the best order, they will (for the most part) be (as far as possible) reduced to definite classes. It will then be enough to examine carefully either a single one of them, or something from each, or some rather than others; or at least we shall not review the same thing twice to no purpose. This procedure is so helpful that often because of a well-established order one traverses in a short time and with little effort a great many things which at first sight looked immense.

The order of things to be enumerated, however, can often vary, and it depends on the choice of each person. So, to grasp it more accurately, we must recall what was said in the fifth proposition. In the more trivial inventions of men, there are many things whose method of discovery consists entirely in disposing of things in this orderly way. Thus if you wish to construct a perfect anagram by transposing the letters of a name, there is no need to pass from the easy to the difficult, nor to distinguish absolute from relative. Here there is no place for these things; but it will be sufficient to adopt an order for transposing the letters under examination, such that one never comes twice to the same one, and that their number, for instance, is distributed in fixed classes so that where is the best hope of finding what is sought may immediately appear. In this fashion the work will often not take too long, but be mere child's play.

392   On the other hand, these three last propositions are not to be separated, because for the most part we must think of them at the same time, and because all concur equally in the perfection of our method. It did not make much difference which was given first; and we have explained them here briefly, because we have practically nothing left to do in the rest of the treatise, except to show in particular what we have considered here in general.

8. If in the series of things to be examined anything presents itself which our intellect is unable to intuit sufficiently well, we must stop there and should not examine what follows, but abstain from superfluous labor.

The three preceding rules prescribe order and explain it; this one shows when it is absolutely necessary and when it is only useful. Thus whatever constitutes a complete step in that series by which we must pass from relatives to some absolute or the reverse, must necessarily be examined before anything that follows it. If, however, as often happens, many things belong to the same step, it is indeed always useful to run through them all in order, but in this case we are not forced to observe order so strictly nor so rigidly. Often, although we do not know all these things clearly, but only a small number of them or just one, it is still possible to pass beyond them. *393*

This rule follows necessarily from the reasons given for the second rule. However it must not be supposed that it contains nothing new for the advancement of science, even though it appears only to keep us from the discussion of certain things and to propound no truth. As for beginners, indeed, it teaches them only not to waste their time, in almost the same way as the second rule. But to those who have perfectly learned the seven preceding rules, it shows how in any science whatsoever they can satisfy themselves so as to desire nothing further. For whoever has observed the preceding rules exactly in the solution of any difficulty and has nevertheless received from this rule the order to halt, will then know with certainty that he cannot by any device discover the knowledge he is seeking—and that not by the fault of his mind, but because the nature of the difficulty itself or the condition of humanity prevents him. This knowledge is science no less than is what exhibits the nature of the thing itself; and he would not appear of sound mind who should extend his curiosity further.

Let us illustrate this by one or two examples. If someone who studies only mathematics looks for that line which in dioptrics is called anaclastic, and in *394* which parallel lines are refracted in such fashion that all of them, after the refraction, meet in a single point, he will easily observe, according to rules five and six, that the determination of this line depends on the proportion of the angles of refraction to the angles of incidence. But as he will not be capable of investigating this matter, since it does not belong to mathematics but to physics, he will have to stop immediately. And it would be of no use to him if he wished to hear from the philosophers or draw from experience the knowledge of this truth; for he would be sinning against the third rule. Besides, this proposition is still composite and relative; but it is only in things that are perfectly simple and absolute that experience can be considered certain, as we shall show in the proper place. Moreover, it would be useless for him to postulate, between angles of this kind, some proportion he suspected to be truest of all; for then he would no longer be looking for the anaclastic line, but only for the line that should be a logical consequence of his supposition.

On the other hand, if someone who does not study mathematics alone, but who tries, according to the first rule, to look for the truth on any subject that presents itself, should fall into the same difficulty, he will go farther and discover that this proportion between the angles of incidence and the angles of refraction depends on the variation of these same angles in virtue of the difference of the media; that this variation in turn depends on the manner in which the ray penetrates into the transparent body; that knowledge of the property of penetrating into a body presupposes equally that the nature of illumination is known; and that finally to *395* understand illumination one must know what a natural power is in general—and this is the last and most absolute term in this whole sequence. Then when he has perceived this clearly by intuition, he will repeat the same steps, according to the fifth rule; and if in the second step he cannot at once recognize the nature of illumination, he will enumerate all the other natural powers, in accordance with the seventh rule, in order that, thanks to the knowledge of some one of them, he may understand it also, at least by analogy (of which I will speak later). This done, he will investigate the manner in which the ray penetrates the whole transparent body; and in this way he will run through the rest in order, until he has arrived at the anaclastic line itself. Although up to now this has been vainly attempted by many people, I see nothing to keep someone who makes perfect use of our method from evident knowledge of this line.

But let us give the most noble example of all. If a person proposes to himself the problem of examining all the truths for the knowledge of which human reason suffices—a task which should be undertaken at least once in his life, it seems to me, by anyone who is in all seriousness eager to attain excellence of mind— he will certainly discover by the rules given above that nothing can be known before the intellect, since the knowledge of all other things depends on this, and not the reverse. Then, when he has examined everything that follows immediately after the knowledge of the pure intellect, he will enumerate, among other things, all the other instruments of knowledge we possess besides the intellect;

396   and these are only two: namely, imagination and the senses. He will then devote all his care to distinguishing and examining these three modes of knowledge; and seeing that strictly speaking truth or falsity can exist only in the intellect, but that they often take their source from the other two as well, he will carefully attend to everything by which he can be deceived so that he may be on guard against it. And he will enumerate exactly all the paths to truth that are open to humans so that he may follow the sure one—for there are not so many that he cannot discover them all easily through a sufficient enumeration. And, what will seem marvelous and incredible to the inexperienced, as soon as he has distinguished, for each object, those cognitions which only fill and embellish the memory from those in virtue of which one may truly be said to be more learned, a distinction which it is also easy to make, [. . . .]⁵ he will feel that there is absolutely nothing of which he is ignorant through a defect of mind or art, and that nothing further can be known by any person which he is not also capable of knowing, provided only that he applies his mind to it as he ought. And although many things can often be proposed to him, the investigation of which are forbidden by this rule, he will nevertheless not think himself more ignorant for having clearly understood that they exceed the bounds of the human mind; but this knowledge itself, that no one can know the thing in question, will amply satisfy his curiosity if he is reasonable.

But that we may not always be uncertain what our mind is capable of, and that we may not labor wrongly and rashly, before we set ourselves to learn things in

397   detail; we ought to inquire carefully, once in our lives, of what knowledge human reason is capable. In order better to accomplish this task, among things that are equally simple we ought to investigate those which are more useful.

---

5. There is a gap in the original texts.

Indeed, this method resembles those of the mechanical arts which need no outside help, and which themselves teach us how to construct their instruments. Thus if one wished to practice one of them, the art of the blacksmith, for example, one would be forced at first to use as an anvil a hard stone or a rough lump of iron, to take a piece of rock in place of a hammer, to shape pieces of wood into tongs, and to collect other materials of this sort according to need. Thus equipped, one would not then at once try to forge swords or helmets or any object of iron for the use of others; but one would first of all manufacture hammers, an anvil, tongs, and the other things useful to oneself. This example teaches us that, if we have been able at the outset to find only some rough principles, which seem to be innate in our minds rather than prepared by art, we must not use them to try to settle immediately the controversies of the philosophers or to solve the puzzles of the mathematicians. We must rather use them first for seeking with the greatest care all that is more necessary for the examination of truth; since there is surely no reason why this should seem more difficult to discover than any of the questions usually propounded in geometry or physics or other disciplines.

Now nothing is more useful here than to inquire what human knowledge is and how far it extends. That is why we now embrace these problems in a single question, which we believe should be examined first in accordance with the rules previously started. This must be done once in his life by anyone who has even the faintest love for truth, since this inquiry contains the true instruments of knowledge and the whole of method. Nothing seems to me more absurd, on the other hand, than to argue boldly about the mysteries of nature, the influence of the heavens on our earth, the prediction of the future, and the like, as many do, and yet never to have inquired whether human reason is adequate for the discovery of these things. Nor should it seem arduous or difficult to determine the limits of the mind, which we feel within ourselves, since often we do not hesitate to make judgments on things outside us and quite foreign to us. Nor is it an immense task to attempt to embrace in thought all the things contained in this universe, in order that we may recognize how each one is subjected to the examination of our minds; for nothing can be so complex or so scattered that, by means of the enumeration with which we have been dealing, it cannot be circumscribed within definite limits and arranged under a certain number of headings. In order to have experience of this in the question at hand, we first divide everything that pertains to it into two parts; for it ought to be referred to either us, who are capable of knowledge, or to those things which can be known; and we discuss these two parts separately.

Now we notice in ourselves that the intellect alone is capable of scientific knowledge; but that it can be helped or hindered by three other faculties, namely by imagination, sense, and memory. We must therefore see, in order, in what respect each of these faculties can be a hindrance so that we may be on our guard; or in what respect each can be of use so that we may use all its resources. Thus this part shall be treated by a sufficient enumeration, as the following rule will make clear.

We must then proceed to the things themselves, which are to be examined only insofar as they are touched by the intellect. In this respect we divide them into

398

399

maximally simple natures and natures that are complex or composite. Simple natures must be either spiritual or corporeal, or related to both. Then among the composites the intellect experiences some to be complex before it judges that it can determine anything about them; but others it puts itself together. All this will be expounded at greater length in the twelfth rule, where it will be proved that there can be no falsity except in these last natures, which are put together by the intellect. That is why we distinguish them again into two kinds: those which are deduced from natures that are of the greatest simplicity and known through themselves, of which we shall treat in the following book; and those which likewise presuppose others which the facts themselves show us to be composite, for the exposition of which we intend the whole of the third book.

And, indeed, in all of this treatise we shall try to follow through with so much care and to make so easy all the paths that are open to humans for the knowledge of truth that anyone who has learned perfectly the whole of this method, however

400   mediocre his mind, may yet see that none of these paths is more closed to him than to others, and that he is no longer ignorant of anything through a defect of mind or art. But as often as he applies his mind to the knowledge of anything, either he will reach it entirely; or he will clearly understand that it depends on some experience not in his power, and then he will not blame his own mind, although he is forced to stop at that place; or, finally, he will demonstrate that what he is seeking exceeds the bounds of the human mind, and consequently he will not think himself more ignorant, because it is not a lesser thing to know this knowledge than any other thing.

9. We ought to turn the whole force of our minds to the smallest and simplest things, and to stop there for a long time, until we become accustomed to intuiting the truth clearly and distinctly.

We have now expounded the two operations of our intellect: intuition and deduction, which we have said are alone to be employed in learning the sciences. We continue in this and the next proposition to explain by what procedure we can become more skilled in using them and at the same time in developing the two principal faculties of our mind, perspicacity, in having a distinct intuition of each thing, and sagacity, in easily deducing certain facts from others.

In fact, we learn the manner in which mental intuition should be used by comparing it with vision. For whoever wishes to look at many objects at one time

401   with a single glance, sees none of them distinctly; and similarly whoever is used to attending to many objects at the same time in a single act of thought, is confused in mind. But those artisans who practice delicate operations, and are accustomed to direct the force of their eyes attentively to single points, acquire by use the ability to distinguish perfectly things as tiny and subtle as may be. In the same way, likewise, those who never disperse their thought among different objects at one time, but always occupy all its attention in considering the simplest and easiest matters, become perspicacious.

But it is a failing common to mortals to consider difficult things as more attractive. And most people think they know nothing when they find a cause for something that is really clear and simple, while they admire certain sublime and profound theories of the philosophers, although these rest for the most part on foundations never adequately examined by anyone. Poor fools, indeed, who prefer darkness to light! It should be noted, however, that those who really know discern the truth with equal facility whether they have drawn it from a simple or from an obscure subject. For they comprehend each truth by an act that is similar, single, and distinct, once they have arrived at it, but the whole difference is in the road, which should certainly be longer if it leads to a truth remote from the first and most absolute principles.

Thus we should all accustom ourselves to including in our thought, at one and the same time, matters so few and so simple that we cannot think we know anything at all unless we intuit it no less distinctly than we do those things that we know most distinctly of all. For this, indeed, some people are born much more *402* capable than others; but method and practice can also make minds much better at it. And if there is one point that must be stressed here, it seems to me, with more insistence than all the others, it is that the sciences, however hidden, can be deduced, not from great and obscure matters, but only from those that are easiest and most obvious.

So, for example, let us suppose that I want to inquire whether some natural power exists than can pass in the same instant to a distant place, while traversing all the intervening space. I shall not at once turn my mind to the power of the magnet, or to the influence of the stars, or even to the speed of light, in order to inquire whether perchance such actions take place in an instant. For to investigate this would be more difficult than the question I am asking. But I would rather reflect on the local motion of bodies, since nothing in this whole area is more accessible to the senses. And I would notice that a stone cannot pass from one place to another in an instant, since it is a body; but that a power similar to the one that moves the stone can pass in its bare state from one subject to another For instance, if I move one of the extremities of a stick, of any length whatever, I easily conceive that the power that sets that part of the stick in motion necessarily moves all the other parts as well in one and the same instant, since it is then communicated as a bare power, and does not reside in some body by which it is carried.

In the same way, if I should wish to know how contrary effects can be produced by the same cause, I shall not seek help from physicians whose drugs *403* expel certain humors and replace others. I shall not talk nonsense about the moon: that it heats by its light, and cools off by some occult quality. But instead I shall examine a scale, in which the same weight lifts one side at one and the same instant at which it depresses the other, and other examples of this kind.

10. In order that the mind may acquire sagacity, it is necessary to give it practice in investigating what has already been discovered by others; and it ought to traverse methodically even the most trifling inventions of men, but especially those which best explain or presuppose order.

 I confess that I was born with a mind such that I have always found the greatest pleasure of study, not in hearing the explanations of others, but in finding them by my own efforts. This alone attracted me, when I was young, to the study of the sciences. So whenever a book promised a new discovery by its title, before going farther I tried if by chance I could not succeed in finding something analogous by natural sagacity; and I took good care not to deprive myself of this innocent pleasure by a hasty reading. I succeeded in this so often that I finally noticed that I was no longer arriving at the truth of things, as others usually do, by vague and blind disquisitions, by the help of fortune rather than art, but that by long experience I had perceived certain rules, which are of great help in this study and which I afterward used to think out many others. And so I have diligently elaborated this whole method, and have become convinced from the start that I had followed the most useful mode of studying.

404

 But since not all minds are equally inclined by their nature to discover things of their own power, this proposition teaches that we should not occupy ourselves immediately with the more difficult and arduous matters, but should first discuss those disciplines which are easiest and simplest, and those above all in which order most prevails. Such are the arts of the craftsmen who make cloth and tapestries, those of women who embroider or make lace, as well as all the games with numbers, and all that relates to arithmetic, and the like. All these arts give the mind excellent practice, provided we do not learn them from others, but discover them ourselves. For since nothing in them remains hidden, and they are entirely adjusted to the capacity of human knowledge, they show us very distinctly innumerable arrangements, all different from one another and yet regular, in the scrupulous observation of which the whole of human sagacity consists.

 That is why we have warned that studies must be conducted with method. And method, in the more trivial cases, is usually nothing but the constant observation of order, whether existing in the thing itself or ingeniously thought out. For example, if we want to read something written in unknown characters, no order at all appears here, but nevertheless we invent one, in order to examine all the presumptions that can be held about each sign, each word or each phrase, so as to order these presumptions in such a way as to recognize by enumeration everything that can be deduced from them. And we must take the greatest care not to waste time in trying to guess at random and without method the solution of problems of this kind. For even if it often happens that we can solve them without method, and sometimes even more rapidly than with method, if we are lucky, in this way we would weaken the light of the mind and would accustom ourselves so thoroughly to childish vanities that we would be constantly held on the surface of things, without being able to penetrate more deeply. At the same time we should not fall into the error of those who occupy their minds wholly with serious and deeper things, of which after much labor they have acquired only confused knowledge, while they were wishing for profound insight. We must therefore first practice those easier matters, but with method, so that we may become accustomed, through simple and known paths, and as if in a game, to penetrating always to the inner core of things. For in this way, by a continuous progress, and more rapidly than we could have hoped, we shall find that we our-

405

selves can just as easily deduce from evident principles many progressions that appeared very difficult and complicated.

Perhaps, however, some may wonder that here, where we are looking for the means to make us more skillful in deducing one truth from another, we should omit all the precepts by which the dialecticians think to govern human reason. They prescribe to it certain forms of argument which conclude with such necessity that reason, if confined to them, although it does not take the trouble to consider the inference itself in an attentive and evident manner, can nevertheless *406* sometimes arrive, by virtue of the form, at a sure conclusion. The thing is that, as a matter of fact, we are aware that truth often escapes these fetters, while those, meanwhile, who have used them remain entangled. That does not happen so frequently to other men; and experience shows that ordinarily the subtlest sophisms hardly ever refute those who use only pure reason, but lead astray the sophists themselves.

That is why here, fearing above all things that our reason should take a vacation while we are examining the truth of some matter, we reject these forms of reasoning as contrary to our end, and search rather for all the aids by which our thought may be kept attentive, as we shall show in what follows. But that it may appear with even greater evidence that this method of argument is of no use for knowledge of the truth, it must be noted that the dialecticians can find by their art no syllogism that yields a true conclusion unless they first have the material for it, that is, unless they have already learned the truth itself which they are deducing in their syllogism. Hence it is clear that they themselves learn nothing new from such a form, and that vulgar dialectic is therefore entirely useless for those who wish to investigate the truth of things. On the contrary, its only use is that now and then it can expound more easily to others arguments already known; hence it should be transferred from philosophy to rhetoric.

11. After we have grasped by intuition a certain number of simple   *407*
propositions, if we wish to infer some other proposition from them, it is
useful to run over them in a continuous and uninterrupted movement of
thought in order to reflect on their relations to one another, and as far as
possible to conceive distinctly several at a time. For it is in this way that our
knowledge becomes much more certain and the power of our mind is greatly
increased.

This is the occasion to expound more clearly what has already been said of intuition in rules three and seven. For in one place we have contrasted it with deduction, and in another only with enumeration, which we have defined as an inference drawn from many and diverse things. But we said in the same place that the simple deduction of one thing from another is executed by intuition.

It was necessary to proceed in this way, because we demand two conditions of intuition: that the proposition be clearly and distinctly understood, and, further, that it be understood in its entirety at one time and not successively. Deduction, on the other hand, if we are thinking of its execution, as in rule three, does not seem to occur all at one time, but involves a certain movement of our mind,

which infers one thing from another. So we were right in distinguishing it from
408   intuition. But if we consider deduction as already accomplished, as in what we
said in rule seven, then it no longer designates any movement, but rather the end
of a movement. Therefore we suppose that it is seen by intuition when it is simple and clear, but not when it is complex and obscure. To the latter situation we
give the name of enumeration, or induction, because it cannot then be comprehended by the intellect all at one time, but its certainty depends to some extent
on memory, in which our judgments about the individual points enumerated must
be retained if some one single judgment is to be drawn from all of them.

All these distinctions were necessary for the interpretation of this rule. For
after the ninth rule had dealt with intuition alone, and the tenth with enumeration
alone, this one explains how these two operations mutually assist and complete
one another, to the point of seeming to merge into one by a certain movement of
thought which perceives each fact attentively by intuition and at the same time
passes to the others.

To this [cooperation] we assign a double advantage: namely, it promotes a
more certain knowledge of the conclusion with which we are concerned, and it
renders the mind more skillful in other discoveries. The fact is that memory (on
which, we have said, depends the certainty of conclusions that embrace more
than we can grasp in one intuition), though unstable and infirm, can be renewed
and strengthened by this continuous and repeated movement of thought. Thus if
by several operations I have first discovered the relation that exists between a
first and a second magnitude, then between the second and a third, then between
409   the third and a fourth, and finally between the fourth and a fifth, I do not therefore see what relation exists between the first and fifth, and I cannot deduce it
from the relations already known if I do not remember them all. That is why it is
necessary for me to run through them repeatedly in thought, until I have passed so
rapidly from the first to the last that practically no parts of the process are left to
memory, and I seem to grasp the whole thing at once by intuition.

Everyone must see that the sluggishness of the mind is corrected by this
scheme and its comprehension likewise enlarged. But it must be noted, further,
that the greatest utility of this rule consists in the fact that, in reflecting on the
mutual dependence of simple propositions, we get into the habit of distinguishing immediately what is more or less relative and by what degrees it is reduced
to the absolute. For example, if I run through several magnitudes that are in continuous proportion, I shall reflect on all the following facts: that it is by a similar
mental act—neither more nor less easy—that I recognize the relation that exists
between the first magnitude and the second, the second and the third, the third
and the fourth, and so on; but that I cannot grasp so easily what is the dependence of the second on the first and third at the same time; and that it is still more
difficult to grasp the dependence of the second on the first and fourth, and so on.
Hence I understand why I can easily find the third and fourth if only the first and
second are given, and so on: it is because this is accomplished by particular and
410   distinct conceptions. But if only the first and third are given, I do not so easily
learn the intermediate magnitude, because that can be done only by an effort of
thought which simultaneously embraces the two given magnitudes. If only the

first and the fourth are given, I shall have still more trouble in getting an intuitive grasp of the two intermediates, because here three concepts are simultaneously involved. Thus it would seem, in consequence, even more difficult to find the three intermediates between the first and fifth. But there is another scheme by which this can be achieved in a different way. Although four concepts are conjoined here, they can nevertheless be separated, since four can be divided by another number. Thus, I can look for the third by itself from the first and fifth, then the second from the first and third, and so on. Whoever accustoms himself to reflect on these and similar matters, every time he examines a new question, he immediately discovers the source of the difficulty, and what of all ways is the very simplest one for solving it, and this is a very great aid to knowledge of the truth.

12. Finally we ought to use all the aids of intellect, imagination, sense, and memory, partly in order to have a distinct intuition of simple propositions; partly to compare correctly what we seek with what we know so that we may recognize it; partly in order to discover those things which should be so compared with one another so that no human resources may be neglected.

This rule gives the conclusion of all that has been said above, and teaches in *411* general the points that had to be explained in particular, as follows.

In what concerns the knowledge of things, only two matters have to be considered: namely, ourselves who know and the objects themselves that are to be known. In us there are only four faculties that we can use for this purpose, namely, intellect, imagination, sense, and memory. To be sure, the intellect alone is capable of perceiving truth; but it must nevertheless be assisted by imagination, sense, and memory, if we are not to omit anything that lies in our power. On the side of the objects it is enough to examine three things: firstly, what presents itself spontaneously; secondly, how we learn one thing from another; and thirdly, what deductions we can make from each. This enumeration seems to me to be complete, and to omit nothing to which human powers can extend. [. . .]

13. If we understand a question perfectly, we must abstract it from every *430* **superfluous concept, simplify it as much as possible, and divide it by enumeration into the smallest possible parts. [. . .]**

14. The same question must be applied to the real extension of bodies, *438* **and represented in its entirety to the imagination by means of bare figures; for in this way it will be much more distinctly perceived by the understanding.**

If we wish also to use the aid of the imagination, we must notice that whenever we deduce something unknown from something else already known, we do not for all that discover a new genus of being; but it only happens that the knowledge we have is extended to the point of making us see that the thing sought after participates in one way or another in the nature of those things that are given in

the question. For example, if someone is blind from birth, we need not hope to bring it about by any argument that he should perceive true ideas of colors such as we have received from the senses. On the other hand, if someone has already seen the fundamental colors, but does not know the intermediate and mixed colors, it is possible for him by a sort of deduction to invent for himself the images
439   even of those he has not seen, according to their similarity with the others. In the same way, if there exists in the magnet some genus of being, to which our intellect has so far seen nothing similar, we need not hope ever to know it by reasoning. For that we should need either some new sense or a divine mind. All that the human mind can do in this matter, we shall think we have done if we see very distinctly the mixture of beings or of natures already known which produces the same effects that appear in the magnet.

In fact, whatever is the difference of subjects, it is by the same idea that we recognize all those beings already known, such as extension, figure, motion, and the like, which it is not the place to list here; and we do not imagine the shape of a crown differently, whether it is of silver or of gold. This common idea passes from one subject to another only by means of a simple comparison, through which we affirm that the thing sought after is, in one respect or another, similar, identical, or equal to the thing given, in such a way that in all ratiocination it is only by comparison that we know the truth with precision. For example in this: all A is B, all B is C, therefore all A is C: we compare with one another the thing sought after and the thing given, that is to say, A and C, with respect to the question whether either one is B, etc. But since, as we have often warned, the forms of the syllogisms are
440   of no help in perceiving the truth of things, it will be of advantage to the reader, if, after he has completely rejected them, he grasps the fact that every cognition whatsoever which is not gotten by a simple and pure intuition of one isolated object, is gotten by the comparison of two or more objects with one another. Indeed almost all the labor of human reason consists in preparing this operation; for, when it is open and simple, there is no need for any aid of art, but only of the light of nature alone, for the intuition of the truth that is gotten through it.

It must be noted that comparisons are not called simple and open except whenever the thing sought and the thing given participate equally in a certain nature; that all other comparisons, on the other hand, need preparation only because this common nature is not equally present in the one and the other, but with respect to other relations or proportions in which it is involved; and that the principal part of human contriving consists only in reducing these proportions in such a way as to see clearly an equality between what is sought and something known.

It must be noted, further, that nothing can be reduced to this equality except what admits of more and less, and that all this is comprised under the name of magnitude. Thus when the terms of the difficulty have been abstracted from every subject, according to the preceding rule, we understand that we have nothing further to occupy us except magnitudes in general.

But if we wish to imagine something more here, and to make use, not of the
441   pure intellect, but of the intellect aided by images depicted on the imagination, we must note, finally, that nothing is said about magnitudes in general which cannot also be referred to someone in particular.

Hence it is easy to conclude that there will be great advantage in transferring what we understand to be said about magnitudes in general to that species of magnitude which among all will be depicted most easily and most distinctly in our imagination. But, that this magnitude is the real extension of a body, abstracted from everything else but its figure, results from what has been said in rule twelve, where we have seen that imagination itself, with the ideas which exist in it, is only a true, real, extended, and figured body. This is also self-evident, because all the differences in proportion are not exhibited more distinctly in any other subject. For although one thing can be called more or less white than another, or again one sound more or less acute, and so of other things, still we cannot define exactly whether this more or less is in double or triple proportion, except by a certain analogy with the extension of a figured body. It remains sure and certain, therefore, that perfectly determined questions contain scarcely any difficulty beyond that which consists in resolving proportions into equalities; and that everything in which just this difficulty is discovered can and should be easily separated from every other subject, and then transferred to extension and figures, of which, for this reason, we shall later treat exclusively up to the twenty-fifth rule. [. . .]

15. It is also useful in many cases to describe these figures and to exhibit them to the external senses, in order that by this device our thought should more easily be kept attentive. [. . .]   *453*

16. As for the things which do not demand the immediate attention of the mind, although they are necessary for the conclusion it is better to designate them by very brief signs rather than by complete figures; for thus the memory cannot err, and meanwhile the thought will not be distracted for the purpose of retaining them, while it is applying itself to deducing other things. [. . .]   *454*

17. A given difficulty should be run through directly, in abstraction from the fact that some of its terms are known and others unknown, and with the intuition, obtained by taking the right road, of the mutual dependence of each term on the others. [. . .]   *459*

18. For this only four operations are required, addition, subtraction, multiplication, and division, among which the last two often do not need to be carried out here, as much to keep from complicating things needlessly as because they can be executed more easily later. [. . .]   *461*

19. By this method of ratiocination we should seek out as many magnitudes expressed in two different modes, as we suppose unknown terms directly bearing on the difficulty in place of known ones: for thus we shall have as many comparisons between two equals.   *468*

469 *20. When the equations have been found, we must finish the operations which we have left aside, never making use of multiplication whenever there is room for division.*

21. If there are several equations of this sort, we should reduce them all to a single one, that is to say, to the one whose terms will occupy the least number of degrees in the sequence of magnitudes in continuous proportion, according to which they are to be ordered.

To Mersenne, On the Eternal Truths (April 15, May 6, and May 27, 1630)

I, 143 [. . .] As for your theological question, although it exceeds the capacity of my
144 mind, nevertheless it does not seem to me to lie beyond my profession, since it in no way touches on what depends on revelation, that is, on what I call properly theology. Rather, it is metaphysical and is to be examined by human reason. Now I am of the opinion that all those to whom God has given the use of this reason are obliged to use it chiefly to try to know him and to know themselves. It is in this way that I have tried to begin my studies; and I will tell you that I would never have known how to discover the foundations of physics, if I had not sought them by that path. But this is the matter that I have studied above all others, and in which, by the grace of God, I have been in any way satisfied; at least I think that I have found out how one can demonstrate the truths of metaphysics in a way that is more evident than the demonstrations of geometry. I say this according to my own judgment, for I do not know if I will be able to persuade others of it. The first nine months I was in this country[6] I worked at nothing else, and I believe you have already heard me say that I had planned to put something of this in writing. But I do not consider it appropriate to do so until I have first seen how my physics will be received. If, however, the book of which you speak should be
145 something very well executed, and if it fell into my hands, I should feel myself obliged to reply to it on the spot, since it treats of matters that are very dangerous and I believe to be utterly false, if the report you have heard of it is true. But I shall not omit to touch on several metaphysical questions in my physics, and in particular the following. That the mathematical truths you call eternal have been established by God and depend entirely on him, just as much as all the rest of his creatures. It is in fact to speak of God as of a Jupiter or Saturn, and to subject him to the Styx and the Fates, to say that those truths are independent of him. Do not hesitate, I tell you, to avow and to proclaim everywhere, that it is God who has established the laws of nature, as a King establishes laws in his Kingdom.

Now there is no one law in particular that we cannot comprehend if our mind leads us to consider it, and they are *inborn in our minds,* as a King would establish his laws in the hearts of his subjects, if he had power enough to do so. On the other

---

6. The Netherlands.

hand, we cannot comprehend the greatness of God, even though we know it. But the very fact that we judge him to be incomprehensible makes us esteem him further, as a King has more majesty when he is less familiarly known to his subjects, provided, however, that they do not for all that consider themselves to be without a King, and that they know him well enough to have no doubt of it.

You will be told that if God has established these truths, he could also change them as a King changes his laws. To which it must be replied: yes, if his will can *146* change. But I understand them as eternal and immutable. And I judge the same of God. But his will is free. Yes, but his power is incomprehensible. And in general we can rest assured that God can do everything that we can comprehend, but not that he cannot do what we cannot comprehend. For it would be overly bold to think that our imagination has as great an extent as his power.

I hope to write this in my physics as soon as within the next two weeks. But for all that I do not in any way ask you to keep it secret. On the contrary, I urge you to say it as often as the occasion presents itself, provided that you do not mention my name. For I shall be happy to learn the objections that are brought against it, and also that the world become accustomed to hearing God spoken of with more dignity, as it seems to me, than the way the vulgar speak of him, who almost always imagine him to be a finite thing.

* * *

[…] As for the eternal truths, I say again that *they are true or possible insofar as* *I, 149* *God knows them as true or possible, but not, on the contrary, known to be true* *by God as though they were true independently of him.* And if people understood properly the meaning of their words, they could never say without blasphemy that the truth of something precedes the knowledge that God has of it, for in God willing and knowing are but one, in such a way that *from the very fact that he* *wills something, he therefore knows it, and it is only for that reason that such a* *thing is true.* Thus we must not say that *if God did not exist, nevertheless those* *150* *truths would be true;* for the existence of God is the first and the most eternal of all the truths there can be, and the only one from which all the others flow. But what makes it easy to be mistaken about this, is that most people do not consider God as an infinite and incomprehensible being, who is the sole author on whom all other things depend. Instead, they stop at the syllables of his name, and think that it is enough to know him if one knows that *Dieu* means the same thing in French as *Deus* in Latin, and that he is worshipped by men. Those who have no higher thoughts than this can easily become atheists, and since they understand mathematical truths perfectly, and not the truth of the existence of God, it is no wonder if they do not believe that the former truths depend on the latter. But they ought to judge, on the contrary, that since God is a cause whose power exceeds the limits of the human understanding, and the necessity of those [mathematical] truths by no means exceeds our knowledge, they are something lesser, and subject to that incomprehensible power. What you say about the production of the *Word* is not inconsistent, it seems to me, with what I am saying. But I do not wish to meddle in theology; I am even afraid that you may judge that my philosophy is too far emancipated for me to care to voice my opinion on such lofty matters.

* * *

I, 151   You ask me by what kind of cause God established the eternal truths. I reply to
152   you that it is *by the same kind of cause* by which he has created all things, that is
to say *as efficient and total cause.* For it is certain that he is the author of the
essence as well as of the existence of creatures. But that essence is nothing else
but those eternal truths, which I do not think of as emanating from God like the
rays of the sun; but I know that God is the author of all things, and that these
truths are something, and that consequently he is their author. I say that I know
this, and not that I conceive it or that I comprehend it. For we can know that God
is infinite and all-powerful, but that our soul, being finite, cannot comprehend or
conceive him, in the same way that we can touch a mountain with our hands, but
not embrace it as we would a tree, or whatever other thing you like that did not
exceed the length of our arms. For to comprehend is to embrace in thought; but
to know a thing it is sufficient to touch it with our thought. You also asked what
necessitated God to create the eternal truths. And I say that he was just as free to
bring it about that it is not true all the lines drawn from the center to the circum-
ference are equal, as he was not to create the world. And it is certain that these
truths are not more necessarily joined to his essence than are other creatures. You
ask what God has done to produce them. I say that *from the very fact that he
willed and understood them from eternity, he created them,* or rather (if you
153   attribute the term *created* only to the existence of things), *he established and made
them.* For in God it is the same thing to will, to understand, and to create, without
one of these taking precedence over the others, *even by a distinction of reason.*

2. As for the question *whether it is suitable to God's goodness to damn people
for eternity,* that is a question of theology; that is why you will allow me, if you
please, to say absolutely nothing about it. It is not because the arguments of the
libertines have any strength in this, for they seem frivolous and ridiculous to me,
but it is because I hold that to support only by human and probable reasons the
truths that depend on faith and that cannot be proven by natural demonstrations
would be to do wrong to them.

3. As for the one concerning God's freedom, I am in complete agreement with
the opinion you tell me was expounded by Father Gibieuf.[7] I did not know that
he had published on the subject, but I will try to have his treatise sent from Paris
at the earliest opportunity, so that I may see it. I am very pleased that my opinions follow his, because it assures me at least that they are not too extravagant to
be defended by an extremely able man.

XI, 3   *The World or Treatise on Light* [and *Man*] (1632)

CHAPTER 1: On the Difference Between Our Sensations and the
Things That Produce Them

In proposing to treat here the subject of light, the first thing I want to call your
attention to is that there can be a difference between the sensation we have of

---

7. Guillaume Gibieuf (c. 1591–1650) was an Oratorian priest, author of *De libertate Dei
et hominis* about free will.

light, that is, the idea of it formed in our imagination through the intermediary of our eyes, and what is in the objects that produces that sensation in us, that is, what is in the flame or in the Sun that is called by the name of light. For even though each person is commonly persuaded that the ideas we have in our thought are completely like the objects from which they proceed, nevertheless, I do not see any reason that assures us that this is so. I note, on the contrary, several experiences that should make us doubt it.   *4*

As you well know, words have no resemblance to the things they signify, yet they do not fail to make us conceive of the things, often even when we are not paying attention to the sound of the words or to their syllables. It can happen, in this way, that after we have heard a discourse whose meaning we have very well understood, we might not be able to say in what language it has been spoken. Now, if words, which signify nothing except by human convention, suffice to make us conceive of things to which they bear no resemblance, why could not nature have established a certain sign that makes us have the sensation of light, even though that sign does not have anything in itself similar to that sensation? Is it not thus that she has established laughter and tears, so that we may read joy and sadness on the face of men?

But perhaps you will say that our ears allow us to sense truly only the sounds of the words, and our eyes only the countenance of the person who laughs or cries, and that it is our mind which, having retained what those words and that countenance signify, represents the meaning to us at the same time. I could reply that, all the same, it is our mind that represents to us the idea of light, each time the action that signifies it touches our eye. But without wasting time debating this matter, I would rather bring forward another example.   *5*

Do you think that, even when we are not paying attention to the meaning of words and hear only their sound, the idea of this sound formed in our thought is something similar to the object that is its cause? A person opens his mouth, moves his tongue, pushes out his breath—I do not see anything in these actions that is not very different from the idea of sound they make us imagine. Most philosophers assure us that sound is nothing other than a certain vibration of air that strikes our ears. Thus, if the sense of hearing related the true image of its object to our thought, it would have to make us conceive the motion of the parts of air that is then vibrating against our ears, instead of making us conceive of the sound. But, perhaps not everyone will want to believe what the philosophers say; so I shall bring forward another example.

Of all our senses, touch is the one considered the least deceptive and the most certain, so that, if I show you that even touch makes us conceive of several ideas which in no way resemble the objects that produce them, I do not think you should find it strange if I say that sight can do the same. Now there is no one who does not know that the ideas of tickling and of pain, formed in our thought on the occasion of our being touched by external bodies, bear no resemblance to those   *6* sensations. You pass a feather lightly over the lips of a child who is falling asleep, and he senses that he is being tickled. Do you think that the idea of tickling he conceives of resembles something in this feather? A soldier returns from battle; during the heat of combat he could have been wounded without perceiving it. But now that he is beginning to cool off, he senses some pain and believes he has been wounded. A surgeon is called, the soldier's armor is removed, and he is examined. In the end it is discovered that what he was sensing was nothing but a buckle or a strap that was caught under his armor, which was pressing on him and making him feel uncomfortable. If his sense of touch, in making him feel this strap, had impressed its image on his thought, there would have been no need of a surgeon to tell him what he was sensing.

Now, I see no reason that requires us to believe that what is in the objects from which the sensation of light comes to us is any more similar to that sensation than the actions of a feather or of a strap are to tickling and to pain. And yet I did not bring forward these examples to make you believe absolutely that this light is different in the objects and in our eyes, but only so that you might feel doubtful about this matter, and could keep yourself from having a prepossession to the contrary, and you can now better examine with me what light is about.

7   ## Chapter 2: In What the Heat and Light of Fire Consists

I know of only two sorts of bodies in the world in which light is found, namely, the stars and flame or fire. And because the stars are no doubt less accessible to human knowledge than fire or a flame, I shall first try to explain what I observe regarding flame.

When a flame burns wood or some other similar material, we can see with our eyes that it moves the small parts of the wood and separates them from one another, thus transforming the subtlest parts into fire, air, or smoke, and leaving the coarsest as ashes. Others may, if they wish, imagine in this wood the form of fire, the quality of heat, and the action that burns as completely different things; in my case, since I am afraid of making a mistake by assuming in it something more than I see must necessarily be there, I am satisfied in conceiving of the motion of its parts. For you may posit fire and heat in the wood and you may make it burn as much as you please, if you do not also assume that any of its parts can move and detach itself from its neighboring parts, I could not imagine that it undergoes any alteration or change. On the contrary, if you remove the fire, remove the heat, prevent the wood from burning, as long as you grant me only that there is a power that puts the subtler parts into violent motion and separates

8   them from the coarser ones, I find that this alone will be able to bring about all the changes in the wood that we experience when it burns.

Given that it does not seem possible to conceive that a body can move another unless it itself is also moving, I conclude, as a result, that the body of the flame acting against the wood is composed of small parts that move independently of one another by very rapid and very violent motions. Moving in this way, they push and move with them the parts of the bodies they touch and those that do not offer them too much resistance. I say that its parts move independently of one another because, although several of them often work together and conspire to produce a single effect, we see, nevertheless, that each of them acts on its own against the bodies they touch. I say also that their motion is very rapid and very violent because, since they are so small that we cannot distinguish them by sight, they could not have enough force to act against the other bodies, if the rapidity of their motion did not compensate for their lack of size.

I add nothing about the direction in which each part moves. For if you consider that the power to move and the power to determine in what direction the motion must take place are two completely different things, one of which can exist with- *9* out the other (as I have explained in the *Dioptrics*),[8] you can easily judge that each one moves in the manner made less difficult by the disposition of the bodies surrounding it. In the same flame there may be parts going up and others going down, in straight lines, and in circles, and from all sides, without changing anything of its nature. As a result, if you see almost all of them tending upward, you must not think that this is for any other reason except that the other bodies touching them are almost always disposed to offer them more resistance in all the other directions.

But having recognized that the parts of the flame move in this manner, and that, to understand how it has the power to consume the wood and to burn, it suffices to conceive of their motions, let us please examine whether the same would not also suffice to make us understand how the flame heats us and how it illuminates us. For if we are able to discover this, it will no longer be necessary for the flame to have any other quality, and we could say that it is motion alone which is sometimes called heat and sometimes called light, according to the different effects it produces.

With respect to heat, I think, the sensation we have of it can be taken for a kind of pain, when it is a violent motion, and sometimes for a kind of tickling, when *10* it is a moderate motion. And since we have said that there is nothing outside our thought similar to the ideas of which we conceive in respect to tickling and pain, we can well believe also that there is nothing similar to the one we conceive of with respect to heat; rather, anything that can move differentially the small parts of our hands, or of some other place in our body, can arouse this sensation in us. This view is even supported by several experiences. For we can heat our hands merely by rubbing them together, and any other body can also be heated without being placed in contact with a fire, provided only that it is agitated and shaken in such a way that many of its small parts are moved and are therewith able to move the small parts of our hands.

With respect to light, we can also conceive that the same motion that is in the flame suffices to make us sense it. But because the principal part of my project consists in this, I want to try to explain it at some length and to resume my discussion from above.

CHAPTER 3: On Hardness and Liquidity [. . .]

CHAPTER 4: On the Void, and How It Happens That Our Senses *16* Do Not Perceive Certain Bodies

[. . .] I have recognized by various experiences that all the motions in the world *19* are in some way circular. That is, when a body leaves its place, it always enters

---

8. *Dioptrics*, AT VI, 88–90.

into the place of another body, and that other body into that of another, and that other into another still, and so on until the last body at the same instant occupies the place vacated by the first. Thus, there is not any more vacuum among bodies when they are moving than when they are at rest. And note here that it is not thereby necessary for all the parts of the bodies moving together to be disposed around exactly as in a true circle, nor even that they be of the same size and shape, for these inequalities can easily be compensated for by other inequalities in their speed.

We do not usually notice these circular motions when bodies move in the air, because we are accustomed to conceiving of the air only as a void space. But look at the fish swimming in the basin of a fountain. If they do not get too near the surface of the water, they do not make the surface move at all, even though they pass beneath it with great speed. From this it plainly appears that the water

20   the fish push before them does not push indifferently all the water of the basin, but pushes only the water that can better serve in perfecting the circle of their motion and can enter into the place they abandon.

This experience suffices to show how these circular motions are easy and familiar to nature. But I now wish to relate another experience to show that no motion ever takes place which is not circular. When the wine in a cask does not flow through an opening at the bottom because the top is completely closed, it is improper to say, as is ordinarily done, that this takes place because of fear of the void. We know well that the wine does not have a mind to fear anything; and even if it did, I do not know what reason it could have to be apprehensive of that void, which is in fact nothing but a chimera. Rather, we must say that it cannot leave the cask because outside everything is as full as it can be, and the part of the air whose place it would occupy, if it were to flow out, cannot find another place to occupy in the rest of the universe, unless an opening were made at the top of the cask, through which this air can rise by a circular path into its place.

For all that, I do not wish to say for certain that there is no void at all in nature. I fear that my treatise would become too long if I undertook to explain the mat-

21   ter at length, and the experiences of which I have spoken are not sufficient to prove it, although they are sufficient to persuade us that the spaces in which we sense nothing are filled with the same matter, and contain at least as much of that matter, as those occupied by bodies we sense. [. . .]

23   CHAPTER 5: On the Number of Elements and on Their Qualities

25   [. . .] If you find it strange that, in order to explain these [three] elements, I do not make use of the qualities called hot, cold, moist, and dry, as do the philoso-

26   phers, I shall say to you that these qualities seem to me to require explanation. And, unless I am mistaken, not only these four qualities, but also all others, and even all the forms of all inanimate bodies, can be explained without needing to assume anything in their matter other than the motion, size, shape, and arrangement of its parts. As a result, I shall easily make you understand why I do not accept other elements than the three I have described. For the difference between

the three elements and the other bodies the philosophers call mixed or composite consists in the forms of these mixed bodies always containing in themselves some qualities that oppose and counteract one another, or at least that do not tend to the conservation of one another. But the forms of the elements must be simple and must not have any qualities that do not accord so perfectly with one another that each tends to the conservation of all the others.

Now I could not find any such forms in the world except the three I have described. For the form I have attributed to the first element consists in its parts moving so extremely fast and being so small that there are no other bodies capable of stopping them; beyond that, they do not require any determinate size, shape, or situation. The form of the second element consists in its parts having a *27* motion and size so moderate that if there are several causes in the world that can increase their motion and decrease their size, there are just as many others that can do the opposite; and so they always remain as it were in balance in this same moderate state. And the form of the third element consists in its parts being so large or so joined together that they always have the force to resist the motion of other bodies.

Examine as much as you please all the forms that can be given to mixed bodies by the various motions, the various shapes and sizes, the various arrangements of parts of matter. I am sure that you would find none that does not have in itself qualities that tend to make it change and, in changing, to reduce it to one of the forms of the elements. [. . .]

CHAPTER 6: Description of a New World, and on the Qualities of *31*
the Matter of Which It Is Composed

Allow your thought to wander outside this world for a little time, then, so that you may come to see another, wholly different world, that I shall bring into existence before you in imaginary spaces. The philosophers tell us that these spaces are infinite, and they certainly should be believed, since they themselves have *32* constructed them. But, in order to keep this infinity from bothering and embarrassing us, let us try not to go all the way to the end; let us enter it only far enough to lose from view all the creatures God created five or six thousand years ago and, after stopping there in some determinate place, let us suppose that God creates anew so much matter around us that, whatever direction our imagination can be extended, it no longer perceives any place that is void.

Even though the sea is not infinite, those who are in its midst on some vessel can extend their view to infinity, it seems, and nevertheless, there is still water beyond what they see. Thus, even though our imagination seems to be able to extend to infinity, and this new matter is not assumed to be infinite, we can still assume, all the same, that it fills up much greater spaces than all the ones we have imagined. To insure that there is nothing in all this that you might find objectionable, let us not allow our imagination to extend even as far as it could, but let us purposely confine it in a determinate space, one not greater, for example, than the distance from the Earth to the principal stars of the firmament. And let us

33 suppose that the matter God has created extends well beyond that determinate space in all directions, to an indefinite distance. For it is much sounder, and we are much better able, to prescribe limits to the action of our thought than to the works of God.

Now, since we are taking the liberty of fashioning this matter according to our fancy, let us attribute to it, if you please, a nature in which there is nothing at all that anyone cannot know as perfectly as possible. To that end, let us expressly suppose that there is no form of earth, fire, or air, nor any other more particular form, such as the form of wood, stone, or metal. Nor does this matter have the qualities of being hot or cold, dry or wet, light or heavy, or having some taste, odor, sound, color, light, or similar quality in the nature of which it might be said that there is something that is not known manifestly by everyone.

On the other hand, let us not think that this matter is the prime matter of the philosophers, which has been so well stripped of all forms and qualities that nothing remains in it that can be clearly understood. But let us conceive it as a genuine, perfectly solid body, which equally fills all the length, depth, and breadth of this great space in the midst of which we have stopped our thought. Thus, each of its parts always occupies a part of this space truly proportionate to its size, such that it could not fill a larger space, nor be squeezed into a smaller, nor allow that another body might occupy its place while it remains in it.

34 Let us add, further, that this matter can be divided in all the parts and according to all the shapes we can imagine, and that each of its parts is capable of receiving in itself all the motions we can also conceive. Let us suppose, in addition, that God divides it truly into many such parts, some larger, others smaller, some of one shape, others of another, as it pleases us to fancy them. Not that God separates them from one another so that there is a void between them; let us think that the whole difference he places in them consists in the diversity of the motions he gives them. From the first instant they are created, he makes some move in one direction, others in another, some faster, others slower (or even, if you wish, not at all); and thereafter he makes them continue their motions according to the ordinary laws of nature. For God has so marvelously established those laws that even if we suppose that he has created nothing more than what I have said, and even if he imposes no order or proportion on it, but composes the most confused and disordered chaos the poets could describe, they are sufficient to make the parts of that chaos disentangle themselves and dispose themselves in

35 such good order that they will have the form of a most perfect world, one in which we would be able to see not only light, but also all the other things, both general and particular, that appear in the real world.

But before I explain this at greater length, stop again to consider this chaos a little, and note that it does not contain anything you do not know so perfectly that you could not even pretend to be ignorant of it. For, as regards the qualities I put into it, you may have noticed that I assumed them to be only such as you can imagine them. And, as regards the matter of which I have composed the chaos, there is nothing simpler, nor easier to know in inanimate creatures. The idea of that matter is so included in all the ideas our imagination can form that either you must necessarily conceive of it or you would never imagine anything.

Nevertheless, because philosophers are so subtle that they can find difficulties in things that seem extremely clear to other men, and because the memory of their prime matter—which they know to be rather hard to conceive of—could divert them from the knowledge of which I am speaking, I must tell them at this point that, unless I am mistaken, the whole difficulty they face in their matter derives only from their wanting to distinguish it from its own quantity and from its external extension, that is, from the property it has of occupying space. In this, however, I would like them to think that they are right, for I do not intend to stop and contradict them. But they should also not find it strange that I assume that the quantity of matter I have described does not differ from its substance any more than number differs from things numbered. Nor should they find it strange if I conceive of its extension, or the property it has of occupying space, not as an accident, but as its true form and its essence. For they could not deny that it is very easy to conceive of it in this way. And my design is not to explain things that are in fact in the real world, as they do, but only to invent, as I please, a world in which there is nothing other than what the crudest minds are capable of conceiving, and which nevertheless can be created along the lines I have invented. *36*

If I put into this world the least obscure thing, it could happen that, within that obscurity, there might be some hidden contradiction I had not perceived, and thus without thinking I would assume something impossible. Instead, since I am able to imagine distinctly everything I put into it, it is certain that even if there were nothing of this sort in the old world, God can nevertheless create it in the new world. For it is certain that he can create everything we can imagine.

CHAPTER 7: On the Laws of Nature of This New World

But I do not want to delay any longer in telling you by what means nature alone could untangle the confusion of the chaos I have spoken of, and what are the laws that God has imposed on it.

You should know, first, that by nature here I do not intend some goddess or some other sort of imaginary power. Rather, I make use of that word to signify matter itself, insofar as I consider it with all the qualities I have attributed to it taken all together, under the condition that God continues to conserve it in the same fashion in which he has created it. It follows necessarily, from the fact that he continues to conserve it in this way, that there must be several changes in its parts which cannot, it seems to me, be properly attributed to God's action—because that action never changes—and which I attribute to nature. And the rules by which these changes are brought about, I call the laws of nature. *37*

In order to understand this better, you should recall that among the qualities of matter we have assumed that its parts have had various motions from the moment they were created, and furthermore that they all touch each other from all sides without there being a void in between them. From this it follows necessarily that from then on, from the time they began to move, they also began to change and diversify their motions by colliding with one another. And thus if God conserves them subsequently in the same fashion as he has created them, he does not conserve them in the same state. That is, with God always acting the same, and consequently always producing the same substantial effect, there

38   would be, as if by accident, many differences in this effect. It is easy to believe that God, who is immutable, as everyone must know, always acts in the same fashion. But without involving myself further in these metaphysical considerations, I shall here set out two or three of the principal rules according to which it must be thought that God causes the nature of this new world to act, and which will suffice, I believe, to enable you to know all the others.

The first is that each particular part of matter always continues in the same state unless the collision with other bodies forces it to change that state. That is, if it has some size, it will never become smaller unless other bodies divide it. If it is round or square, it will never change that shape unless other bodies constrain it. If it is stopped in some place, it will never leave that place unless other bodies drive it out. And once it has begun to move, it will always continue to move with the same force until other bodies stop or retard it.

There is no one who does not believe that this same rule is observed in the old world with respect to size, shape, rest, and a thousand similar things. But the philosophers have exempted motion from it; and yet it is the thing that I desire most expressly to include in it. But do not think that I intend to contradict them in

39   this; the motion they speak of is so different from the one I conceive of, that it can easily happen that what is true of the one is not true of the other.

They themselves admit that the nature of their motion is very little understood. To render it intelligible in some way, they have not yet been able to explain it more clearly than in these terms: *Motus est actus entis in potentia, prout in potentia est.* For me these words are so obscure that I am compelled to leave them here in their language, because I cannot interpret them. (And, in fact, the words, "motion is the act of a being in potency, insofar as it is in potency," are not any clearer in translation.) On the contrary, the nature of the motion I intend to speak of here is so easy to know that the geometers themselves, who among all people are the most careful to conceive very distinctly the things they are studying, judged it simpler and more intelligible than the nature of their surfaces and of their lines. Thus it appears from the fact that they have explained the line by the motion of a point and the surface by the motion of a line.

The philosophers also suppose many motions they think can be accomplished without any body changing place, as those they call *motus ad formam, motus ad calorem, motus ad quantitatem* (motion with respect to form, motion with respect

40   to heat, motion with respect to quantity), and a thousand others. As for me, I do not know of any motion other than the one which is easier to conceive of than the geometers' lines, the motion that makes bodies pass from one place to another and occupy successively all the spaces in between.

In addition, the philosophers attribute to the least of these motions a being more solid and real than they attribute to rest, which they say is nothing other than the privation of motion. As for me, I also conceive of rest as a quality, one that must be attributed to matter while it remains in one place, just as motion is a quality attributed to it while it is changing place.

Finally, the motion of which they speak has a nature so strange that, instead of all things having as an end their perfection, and striving only to conserve themselves, it has no other end nor other aim than rest. And contrary to all laws of nature, it strives on its own to destroy itself. By contrast, the motion I suppose follows the same laws of nature as do generally all the dispositions and all the qualities found in matter, including those the scholars call *modos et entia rationis cum fundamento in re* (modes and beings of reason founded in things), [which they conceive of] as *qualitates reales*—their real qualities—though I frankly confess I can find no more reality in these than in their other beings.

I suppose as a second rule that when a body pushes another, it cannot give the other any motion unless it loses as much of its own motion at the same time, nor can it take any of the other body's motion away unless its own motion is increased by as much. This rule, together with the preceding, agrees very well with all the experiences in which we see one body begin or cease to move because it is pushed or stopped by another. For, having assumed the preceding rule, we are free from the difficulty the scholars find themselves in, when they want to explain why a stone continues to move for some time after leaving the hand of the person who threw it. We should ask instead: why does the stone not always continue to move? Yet the reason is easy to give; for who can deny that the air in which the stone moves offers some resistance to it? We hear the stone whistle when it divides the air. And if we move the air with a fan or some other very light and very extended body, we shall even be able to feel by the weight of our hand that the air impedes motion, instead of continuing it, as some have wanted to say. [. . .] *41*

Even if everything our senses ever experienced in the true world seemed manifestly contrary to what is contained in these two rules, the reasoning that has taught them to me seems to be so strong that I cannot help believing myself required to posit them in the new world I am describing to you. For what firmer and more solid foundation could you find to establish a truth, even if you wanted to choose it at will, than the very firmness and immutability which is in God? *43*

Now it is the case that these two rules follow manifestly from the mere fact that God is immutable and that, always acting in the same way, he always produces the same effect. For, supposing that he put a certain quantity of motion in all matter in general from the first instant he created it, we must either admit that he conserves it there always or not believe that he always acts in the same way. And, assuming in addition that, from this first instant, the various parts of matter in which these motions are unequally dispersed began to retain them or to transfer them from one another according to their power to do so, then we must necessarily think that God always makes them continue in the same way. And that is what these two rules contain.

I shall add as a third rule that, when a body is moving, even if its motion most often takes place along a curved line and can never take place along any line that is not in some way circular, as has been said before, nevertheless each of its parts individually tends always to continue its motion along a straight line. And thus their action, that is, the inclination they have to move, is different from their motion. *44*

For example, if a wheel is made to turn on its axle, even though all its parts go in a circle—because, being joined to one another they cannot do otherwise—nevertheless their inclination is to continue in a straight line, as it appears clearly if by chance one of them is detached from the others. For, as soon as it is free, its motion ceases to be circular and continues in a straight line.

Similarly, when a stone is whirled in a sling, not only does it go straight out as soon as it leaves the sling, but in addition, throughout the time it is in the sling, it presses against the middle of the sling and thus causes the cord to stretch. This clearly shows that it always has an inclination to go in a straight line and that it goes in a circle only under constraint.

This rule rests on the same foundation as the other two and depends only on God's conserving each thing by a continuous action, and consequently on his conserving it, not as it may have been some time earlier, but precisely as it is at the same instant he conserves it. Now, it is the case that, of all motions, only

45   straight line motion is entirely simple: its whole nature is understood in an instant. For, to conceive of it, it suffices to think that a body is in the act of moving in a certain direction, which is the case in each instant that can be determined during the time it moves. On the other hand, to conceive of circular motion, or of any other possible motion, we must consider at least two of its instants, or rather two of its parts and the relation between them. [. . .]

46   According to this rule, then, we must say that God alone is the author of all the motions in the world, insofar as they exist and are straight-line motions, but that the diverse dispositions of matter are what render the motions irregular and curved. The theologians teach us that God is also the author of all of our actions,

47   insofar as they exist and have some goodness, but that the various dispositions of our wills are what can render those actions evil.

I could set out here many additional rules for determining in detail when and by how much the motion of each body can be changed and increased or decreased by colliding with others, rules that summarize all the effects of nature. But I shall be content with showing you that, apart from the three laws I have explained, I wish to suppose no others but those that follow infallibly from the eternal truths on which mathematicians are used to support their most certain and most evident demonstrations—truths, I say, according to which God himself has taught us he disposed all things in number, weight, and measure. The knowledge of those laws is so natural to our souls that we cannot but judge them infallible when we conceive of them distinctly, nor can we doubt that, if God had created many worlds, the laws would be true in all of them as in this one. Those who are able to examine sufficiently the consequences of these truths and of our rules will be able to know effects by their causes. To explain myself in the terms of the schools, they will be able to have *a priori* demonstrations of everything that can be produced in this new world.

48   In order that no exception may prevent this, we shall, if you please, suppose in addition that God will never produce any miracle in the new world, and that intelligences or rational souls, which we might later be able to suppose in this world, will in no way disturb the ordinary course of nature. Nonetheless, in consequence of this, I do not promise to set out here exact demonstrations of all the things I shall say. It will be enough that I open for you the path by which you will be able to find them yourself, when you take the trouble to look for them. Most minds lose interest when things are made too easy for them. And to present a picture that pleases you, I must use shadow as well as bright colors. Thus, I shall be content to pursue the description I have begun, as if I had no other design than to tell you a fable.

CHAPTER 8: On the Formation of the Sun and Stars of This New World [. . .]

Like us, these men[10] will be composed of a soul and of a body. I must describe to you first the body by itself, and the soul, also by itself, and finally I must show 120 you how these two natures must be joined and united to constitute people who resemble us.

I assume that the body is nothing other than a statue or earthen machine, which God forms expressly to make it as much as possible like us, so that not only does he give it externally the color and shape of all our members, but also he puts

---

9. Chapters 16 and 17 of *The World* are unknown. Chapter 18 was published separately as the *Treatise on Man,* in Latin translation at Leyden, 1662, and in French at Paris, 1664 and 1677.

10. That is, the men of the new world Descartes is describing.

within it all the parts necessary to make it walk, eat, breathe, and ultimately imitate all those of our functions that may be imagined to proceed from matter and to depend only on the arrangement of organs.

We see clocks, artificial fountains, mills, and other similar machines, which, although they are made only by men, are not without the power of moving themselves in many different ways. And it seems to me that I could imagine many different kinds of motions in the machine I am assuming to be made by the hands of God, and I could not attribute it so much artistry that you would have no reason to think there could not be more.

Now, I shall not stop to describe to you the bones, nerves, muscles, veins, arteries, stomach, liver, spleen, heart, brain, nor all the other different parts of which the machine must be composed. For I assume them to be wholly similar to those parts of our own body with the same names. These you can have shown
121   to you by any learned anatomist (at least the parts that are large enough to be seen), if you do not already know them well enough yourself. And, as for the parts too small to be seen, I can make you understand them more easily and clearly by speaking of the motions that depend on them, so that it is only necessary here to explain these motions in order, and to tell you by the same means which of our functions they represent. [. . .]
129   As for the particles of blood that penetrate as far as the brain, they serve not only to nourish and support its substance, but chiefly also to produce there a certain very fine wind or, rather, a very active and very pure flame called the *animal spirits*. For it must be understood that the arteries carrying them from the heart, after being divided into an infinity of small branches making up the small tissues which are spread like tapestries at the base of the cavities of the brain, collect about a certain small *gland* located around the middle of the substance of the brain, just at the entrance of its cavities; the arteries have a great number of small openings there, through which the finest particles of the blood can flow into this gland, but these openings are so narrow that they cannot admit the larger particles. [. . .]
130   Now, in proportion as these spirits enter the cavities of the brain, they pass from there into the pores of its substance, and from these pores into the nerves. There, depending on how they enter, or even only on how they tend to enter, in greater or lesser degree into some nerves rather than into others, they have the power to change the shape of the muscles into which their nerves are connected, and by this means to make all the members move. This is similar to what you may have seen in the grottos and fountains of the royal gardens, that the mere force with which the water moves as it emerges from the spring is enough to move the various machines, and even to make them play on certain instruments, or utter certain words, according to the different arrangement of the tubes through which the water is conducted.

And, indeed, the nerves of the machine I am describing to you may very well
131   be compared to the tubes of the machinery of these fountains, its muscles and its tendons to various other devices and springs that serve to move them, its animal spirits to the water that sets them in motion, of which the heart is the source and the cavities of the brain the outlets. Moreover, respiration and other such func-

tions as are natural and usual to it, which depend on the course of the spirits, are like the movements of a clock or a mill, which the regular flow of water can render continuous. External objects which, by their mere presence, act upon its sense organs, and thus determine them to move in many different ways, according to the arrangement of the parts of its brain, are like visitors who enter some of the grottos of these fountains and unintentionally cause the motions that occur in their presence. For they cannot enter without stepping on certain tiles of the pavement so arranged that, for example, if they approach a Diana bathing, they make her hide in the reeds, and if they move forward in pursuit of her, they cause a Neptune to appear and threaten them with his trident, or if they turn in some other direction, they will make a sea monster come out and squirt water in their faces—or something similar according to the whim of the engineers who constructed the fountains. And finally, when the *rational soul* is present in this machine, it will have its principal seat in the brain, and it will be there like the fountain keeper who must be stationed at the openings where all the tubes of these machines are discharged, if he wants to start, stop, or change their movements in any way. [. . .]   *132*

I should like you to consider next all the functions I have attributed to this   *201*
machine—such as the digestion of food, the beating of the heart and arteries, the   *202*
nourishment and growth of the members, respiration, walking, and sleeping; the reception of light, sounds, odors, tastes, heat, and other such qualities by the external sense organs; the impression of their ideas on the organs of the common sense and the imagination; the retention of the impression of the ideas upon the memory; the internal motions of the appetites and passions; and, finally, the external motions of all the members, which so suitably follow the actions of objects that present themselves to sense as the passions and impressions found in memory, that they imitate in the most perfect manner possible those of a real man. I should like you to consider that all these functions follow naturally in this machine simply from the arrangement of its organs, no more or less than the movements of a clock or other automaton follow from that of its counterweights and wheels, so that it is not at all necessary for their explanation to conceive in it any other soul, vegetative or sensitive, or any other principle of motion and life other than its blood and its spirits, set in motion by the heat of the fire that burns continually in its heart, and which is of a nature no different from all fires in inanimate bodies.

To Mersenne, **About Galileo's Condemnation (April 1634)**

I learn from your letters that the last letters I wrote to you were lost, although I   *I, 285*
thought I had addressed them quite reliably. I told you at length the reason that had prevented me from sending you my treatise, a reason that I do not doubt you would find so legitimate, that, rather than blaming me for resolving never to show it to anyone, on the contrary, you would be the first to exhort me, if I had not already fully made up my mind about this.

You doubtless know that Galileo has recently been censured by the Inquisitors of the Faith, and that his opinion concerning the motion of the earth has been condemned as heretical. Now I must tell you that all the things I explained in my treatise, which included that opinion about the motion of the earth, were so completely dependent on one another, that the knowledge that one of them is false is sufficient for the recognition that all the arguments I made use of are worthless. And although I thought that they were supported by very certain and very evident demonstrations, nevertheless I would not for anything in the world maintain them against the authority of the church. I know very well that it could be said that everything that the Inquisitors of Rome have decided is not for all that automatically an article of faith, and that it is first necessary for the Council to pass on it. But I am not so much in love with my own opinions as to want to make use of such exceptions, in order to have the means of maintaining them. And the desire that I have to live in peace and to continue the life I have embarked on, taking as my device the motto: *he lives well who hides well*, means that I am happy to be freed from the fear I had of acquiring, by means of my writing, more knowledge than I desire, rather than angry at having lost the time and the trouble I used in composing it. [. . .]

286

As for the experimental results of Galileo you tell me of, I deny them all,[11] but I do not thereby judge that the motion of the earth is any less probable. It is not that I do not admit that the motion of a chariot, a boat, or a horse, remains in some fashion in the stone after it has been thrown from them; but there are other arguments that prevent its remaining so large. And as for the cannon ball shot from the top of a tower, it must take much longer to descend than if it were let fall from the top to the base. For it meets more air on its path, which not only prevents it from moving in parallel to the horizon, but also from descending.

287

288

As for the motion of the earth, I am astonished that a man of the church dares to write of it, however he excuses himself. For I have seen letters patent for the condemnation of Galileo, printed at Liege on September 20, 1633, in which are the words *"although he pretended that he was putting it forward only hypothetically."* Thus they seem even to be forbidding the use of that hypothesis in astronomy. This prevents me from daring to communicate to him any of my thoughts

---

11. Descartes's general opinion of Galileo's work can be read in his letter to Mersenne of October 11, 1638. Commenting on Galileo's methodology and theories in the *Two New Sciences,* Descartes states:

> I find in general that he philosophizes much better than common people insofar as he avoids as much as possible the errors of the Schools, and attempts to examine physical matters by means of mathematical reasons. In that I entirely agree with him, and hold that there is no other means to discover the truth. But it seems to me that he is greatly deficient in that he digresses continually and does not stop to explain fully a subject; this shows that he has not examined them in orderly fashion, and has sought for the reasons of some particular effects without having considered the first causes of nature, and thus, he has built without foundation. But, to the extent that his method of philosophizing is closer to the true one, we can more easily know his faults, in the same way that we can more easily recognize of those who sometimes follow the right path that they have strayed away, than we can of those who never follow the right path. (AT II, 380)

on this subject. Moreover, since I do not yet see that this censure has been authorized by the Pope or by the Council, but only by a particular congregation of the Cardinal Inquisitors, I do not wholly lose hope that the same thing will happen in this case that happened with the antipodes, which were formerly condemned in pretty much the same manner, and thus that, with time, my *World* will be able to see the light. But in that case I will myself need to use my arguments.

II

DISCOURSE ON THE METHOD FOR CONDUCTING ONE'S REASON WELL AND FOR SEEKING THE TRUTH IN THE SCIENCES (1637)

[Author's Preface]

If this discourse seems too long to be read at one time, it may be divided into six parts. In the first part, you will find various considerations concerning the sciences; in the second part, the chief rules of the method which the author has sought; in the third part, some of the rules of morality which he has derived from this method; in the fourth part, the arguments by which he proves the existence of God and of the human soul, which are the foundations of his metaphysics; in the fifth part, the order of the questions in physics that he has investigated, and particularly the explanation of the movement of the heart and of other difficulties that pertain to medicine, as well as the difference between our soul and that of beasts; and in the final part, what things the author believes are required in order to advance further in the investigation of nature than the author has done, and what reasons have made him write.

PART ONE

Good sense is the best distributed thing in the world, for everyone thinks himself to be so well endowed with it that even those who are the most difficult to please in everything else are not at all wont to desire more of it than they have. It is not likely that everyone is mistaken in this. Rather, it provides evidence that the power of judging well and of distinguishing the true from the false (which is, properly speaking, what people call "good sense" or "reason") is naturally equal in all men, and that the diversity of our opinions does not arise from the fact that some people are more reasonable than others, but solely from the fact that we lead our thoughts along different paths and do not take the same things into consideration. For it is not enough to have a good mind; the main thing is to apply it well. The greatest souls are capable of the greatest vices as well as of the greatest virtues. And those who proceed only very slowly can make much greater progress, provided they always follow the right path, than do those who hurry and stray from it.

For myself, I have never presumed that my mind was in any respect more perfect than that of ordinary men. In fact, I have often desired to have as quick a

---

Selections on pp. 46–82 reprinted from *René Descartes: Discourse on Method*, 3rd ed., translated by Donald Cress (Indianapolis: Hackett Publishing Company, 1998). Reprinted by permission of the publisher with minor changes by permission of the translator.

wit, or as keen and distinct an imagination, or as full and responsive a memory as some other people. And other than these I know of no qualities that serve in the perfecting of the mind, for as to reason or sense, inasmuch as it alone makes us men and distinguishes us from the beasts, I prefer to believe that it exists whole and entire in each of us, and in this to follow the opinion commonly held by the philosophers, who say that there are differences of degree only between *accidents,* but not at all between *forms* or natures of individuals of the same *species.*   *3*

But I shall have no fear of saying that I think I have been rather fortunate to have, since my youth, found myself on certain paths that have led me to considerations and maxims from which I have formed a method by which, it seems to me, I have the means to increase my knowledge by degrees and to raise it little by little to the highest point which the mediocrity of my mind and the short duration of my life will be able to allow it to attain. For I have already reaped from it such a harvest that, although I try, in judgments I make of myself, always to lean more on the side of diffidence than of presumption, and although, looking with a philosopher's eye at the various actions and enterprises of all men, there is hardly one of them that does not seem to me vain and useless, I cannot but take immense satisfaction in the progress that I think I have already made in the search for truth, and I cannot but envisage such hopes for the future that if, among the occupations of men purely as men, there is one that is solidly good and important, I dare to believe that it is the one I have chosen.

All the same, it could be that I am mistaken, and what I take for gold and diamonds is perhaps nothing but a bit of copper and glass. I know how much we are prone to err in what affects us, and also how much the judgments made by our friends should be distrusted when these judgments are in our favor. But I will be very happy to show in this discourse what paths I have followed and to represent   *4* my life in it as if in a picture, so that everyone may judge it for himself; and that, learning from the common response the opinions one will have of it, this may be a new means of teaching myself, which I shall add to those that I am accustomed to using.

Thus my purpose here is not to teach the method that everyone ought to follow in order to conduct his reason well, but merely to show how I have tried to conduct my own. Those who take it upon themselves to give precepts must regard themselves as more competent than those to whom they give them; and if they are found wanting in the least detail, they are to blame. But putting forward this essay merely as a story or, if you prefer, as a fable in which, among some examples one can imitate, one will perhaps also find many others which one will have reason not to follow, I hope that it will be useful to some without being harmful to anyone, and that everyone will be grateful to me for my frankness.

I have been nourished on letters since my childhood, and because I was convinced that by means of them one could acquire a clear and assured knowledge of everything that is useful in life, I had a tremendous desire to master them. But as soon as I had completed this entire course of study, at the end of which one is ordinarily received into the ranks of the learned, I completely changed my mind. For I found myself confounded by so many doubts and errors that it seemed to

me that I had not gained any profit from my attempt to teach myself, except that
5   more and more I had discovered my ignorance. And yet I was at one of the most
renowned schools of Europe, where I thought there must be learned men, if in
fact any such men existed anywhere on earth. There I had learned everything the
others were learning; and, not content with the disciplines we were taught there,
I had gone through all the books I could lay my hands on that treated those disciplines considered the most curious and most unusual. Moreover, I knew what
judgments the others were making about me; and I did not at all see that I was
rated inferior to my fellow students, even though there already were some among
them who were destined to take the place of our teachers. And finally our age
seemed to me to be just as flourishing and as fertile in good minds as any of the
preceding ones. This made me feel free to judge all others by myself, and to think
that there was no doctrine in the world that was of the sort that I had previously
been led to hope for.

  I did not, however, cease to hold in high regard the academic exercises with
which we occupy ourselves in the schools. I knew that the languages learned
there are necessary for the understanding of classical texts; that the charm of
fables awakens the mind; that the memorable deeds recounted in histories uplift
it, and, if read with discretion, aid in forming one's judgment; that the reading of
all good books is like a conversation with the most honorable people of past ages,
who were their authors, indeed, even like a set conversation in which they reveal
to us only the best of their thoughts; that oratory has incomparable power and
6   beauty; that poetry has quite ravishing delicacy and sweetness; that mathematics
has some very subtle stratagems that can serve as much to satisfy the curious as
to facilitate all the arts and to lessen men's labor; that writings dealing with
morals contain many lessons and many exhortations to virtue that are very useful; that theology teaches one how to reach heaven; that philosophy provides the
means of speaking plausibly about all things and of making oneself admired by
the less learned; that jurisprudence, medicine, and the other sciences bring hon-
ors and riches to those who cultivate them; and, finally, that it is good to have
examined all these disciplines, even the most superstition-ridden and the most
false of them, in order to know their true worth and to guard against being
deceived by them.

  But I believed I had already given enough time to languages, and also to the
reading of classical texts, both to their histories and to their fables. For conversing with those of other ages is about the same thing as traveling. It is good to
know something of the customs of various peoples, so as to judge our own more
soundly and so as not to think that everything that is contrary to our ways is
ridiculous and against reason, as those who have seen nothing have a habit of
doing. But when one takes too much time traveling, one eventually becomes a
stranger in one's own country; and when one is too curious about what commonly took place in past ages, one usually remains quite ignorant of what is taking place in one's own country. Moreover, fables make one imagine many events
7   to be possible which are not so at all. And even the most accurate histories, if
they neither alter nor exaggerate the significance of things in order to render
them more worthy of being read, almost always at least omit the baser and less

noteworthy details. Consequently the rest do not appear as they really are, and those who govern their own conduct by means of examples drawn from these texts are liable to fall into the extravagances of the knights of our romances and to conceive plans that are beyond their powers.

I held oratory in high regard and was enamored of poetry, but I thought both were gifts of the mind, rather than fruits of study. Those who possess the strongest reasoning and who best order their thoughts in order to make them clear and intelligible can always best persuade others of what they are proposing, even if they were to speak only Low Breton[1] and had never learned rhetoric. And those who have the most pleasing rhetorical devices and who know how to express themselves with the most embellishment and sweetness would not fail to be the greatest poets, even if the art of poetry were unknown to them.

I delighted most of all in mathematics because of the certainty and the evidence of its reasonings. But I did not yet notice its true use, and, thinking that it was of service merely to the mechanical arts, I was astonished by the fact that no one had built anything more noble upon its foundations, given that they were so solid and firm. On the other hand, I compared the writings of the ancient pagans that deal with morals to very proud and very magnificent palaces that were built on nothing but sand and mud. They place virtues on a high plateau and make them appear to be valued more than anything else in the world, but they do not sufficiently instruct us about how to recognize them; and often what they call by so fine-sounding a name is nothing more than a kind of insensibility, pride, desperation, or parricide.

I revered our theology, and I desired as much as anyone else to reach heaven; but having learned as something very certain that the road to heaven is open no less to the most ignorant than to the most learned, and that the revealed truths guiding us there are beyond our understanding, I would not have dared to submit them to the frailty of my reasonings. And I thought that, in order to undertake an examination of these truths and to succeed in doing so, it would be necessary to have some extraordinary assistance from heaven and to be more than a man.

Concerning philosophy I shall say only that, seeing that it has been cultivated for many centuries by the most excellent minds that have ever lived and that, nevertheless, there still is nothing in it about which there is not some dispute, and consequently nothing that is not doubtful, I was not at all so presumptuous as to hope to fare any better there than the others; and that, considering how many opinions there can be about the very same matter that are held by learned people without there ever being the possibility of more than one opinion being true, I deemed everything that was merely probable to be well nigh false.

Then, as for the other sciences, I judged that, insofar as they borrow their principles from philosophy, one could not have built anything solid upon such unstable foundations. And neither the honor nor the monetary gain they promised was sufficient to induce me to master them for I did not perceive myself, thank God, to be in a condition that obliged me to make a career out of science in order to

8

9

---

1. This dialect was considered rather barbarous and hardly suitable for sophisticated literary endeavors.

enhance my fortune. And although I did not make a point of rejecting glory after the manner of a Cynic, nevertheless I placed very little value on the glory that I could not hope to acquire except through false pretenses. And finally, as to the false doctrines, I thought I already knew well enough what they were worth, so as not to be liable to be deceived either by the promises of an alchemist, the predictions of an astrologer, the tricks of a magician, or the ruses or boasts of any of those who profess to know more than they do.

That is why, as soon as age permitted me to emerge from the supervision of my teachers, I completely abandoned the study of letters. And resolving to search for no knowledge other than what could be found within myself, or else in the great book of the world, I spent the rest of my youth traveling, seeing courts and armies, mingling with people of diverse temperaments and circumstances, gathering various experiences, testing myself in the encounters that fortune offered me, and everywhere engaging in such reflection upon the things that presented themselves that I was able to derive some profit from them. For it seemed to me that I could find much more truth in the reasonings that each person makes concerning matters that are important to him, and whose outcome ought to cost him dearly later on if he has judged badly, than in those reasonings engaged in by a man of letters in his study, which touch on speculations that produce no effect and are of no other consequence to him except perhaps that, the more they are removed from common sense, the more pride he will take in them, for he will have to employ that much more wit and ingenuity in attempting to render them plausible. And I have always had an especially great desire to learn to distinguish the true from the false, in order to see my way clearly in my actions, and to go forward with confidence in this life.

It is true that, so long as I merely considered the customs of other men, I found hardly anything there about which to be confident, and that I noticed there was about as much diversity as I had previously found among the opinions of philosophers. Thus the greatest profit I derived from this was that, on seeing many things that, although they seem to us very extravagant and ridiculous, do not cease to be commonly accepted and approved among other great peoples, I learned not to believe anything too firmly of which I had been persuaded only by example and custom; and thus I little by little freed myself from many errors that can darken our natural light and render us less able to listen to reason. But after I had spent some years thus studying in the book of the world and in trying to gain some experience, I resolved one day to study within myself too and to spend all the powers of my mind in choosing the paths that I should follow. In this I had much more success, it seems to me, than had I never left either my country or my books.

PART TWO

I was then in Germany, where the occasion of the wars which are not yet over there[2] had called me; and as I was returning to the army from the coronation of

2. Thirty Years' War (1618–1648).

the emperor, the onset of winter detained me in quarters where, finding no conversation to divert me and fortunately having no worries or passions to trouble me, I remained for an entire day shut up by myself in a stove-heated room,[3] where I was completely free to converse with myself about my thoughts. Among them, one of the first was that it occurred to me to consider that there is often not as much perfection in works composed of many pieces and made by the hands of various master craftsmen as there is in those works on which but a single individual has worked. Thus one sees that buildings undertaken and completed by a single architect are usually more attractive and better ordered than those which many architects have tried to patch up by using old walls that had been built for other purposes. Thus those ancient cities that were once mere villages and in the course of time have become large towns are usually so poorly laid out, compared to those well-ordered places that an engineer traces out on a vacant plain as it suits his fancy, that even though, upon considering each building one by one in the former sort, one often finds as much, if not more art, than one finds in those of the latter, still, upon seeing how the buildings are arranged—here a large one, there a small one—and how they make the streets crooked and uneven, one would say that it is chance rather than the will of some men using reason that has arranged them thus. And if one considers that there have nevertheless always been officials responsible for seeing that private buildings contribute to the attractiveness of public areas, one will well understand that it is difficult to make things that are very finely crafted by laboring only on the works of others. Thus I imagined that peoples who, having once been half-savages and having been civilized only little by little, have made their laws only to the extent that the inconvenience due to crimes and quarrels have forced them to do so, could not be as well ordered as those who, from the very beginning of their coming together, have followed the fundamental precepts of some prudent legislator. Likewise, it is quite certain that the state of the true religion, whose ordinances were made by God alone, must be incomparably better ordered than all the others. And, speaking of things human, I believe that if Sparta was at one time very flourishing, this was not because of the goodness of each one of its laws taken by itself, seeing that many of them were very strange and even contrary to good morals, but because, having been devised by a single individual, they all tended toward the same end. And thus I thought that book learning, at least the kind whose reasonings are merely probable and that do not have any demonstrations, having been composed and enlarged little by little from the opinions of many different persons, does not draw nearly so close to the truth as the simple reasonings that a man of good sense can naturally make about the things he encounters. And thus, too, I thought that, because we were all children before being men and because for a long time it was necessary for us to be governed by our appetites and our teachers (which were frequently in conflict with one another, and of

12

13

---

3. There is no need to allege that Descartes sat in or on a stove. A poêle is simply a room heated by an earthenware stove. See Etienne Gilson, *Discours de la méthode: texte et commentaire* (Paris: Vrin, 1967), p. 157.

which perhaps neither always gave us the best advice), it is nearly impossible for our judgments to be as pure or as solid as they would have been if we had had the full use of our reason from the moment of our birth and if we had always been guided by it alone.

It is true that we never see anyone pulling down all the houses in a city for the sole purpose of rebuilding them in a different style and of making the streets more attractive; but one does see very well that many people tear down their own houses in order to rebuild them, and that in some cases they are even forced to do so when their houses are in danger of collapsing and when the foundations are not very secure. This example persuaded me that it would not really be at all reasonable for a single individual to plan to reform a state by changing everything in it from the foundations up and by toppling it in order to set it up again; nor even also to reform the body of the sciences or the order established in the schools for teaching them; but that, as regards all the opinions to which I had until now given credence, I could not do better than to try to get rid of them once and for all, in order to replace them later on, either with other ones that are bet-

14   ter, or even with the same ones once I had reconciled them to the level of reason. And I firmly believed that by this means I would succeed in conducting my life much better than if I were to build only upon old foundations and if I were to rely only on the principles of which I had allowed myself to be persuaded in my youth without ever having examined whether they were true. For although I noticed various difficulties in this undertaking, still they were not irremediable, nor were they comparable to those difficulties occurring in the reform of the least things that affect the public. These great bodies are too difficult to raise up once they have been knocked down, or even to hold up once they have been shaken; and their fall can only be very violent. Moreover, as to their imperfections, if they have any (and the mere fact of the diversity that exists among them suffices to assure one that many do have imperfections), custom has doubtless greatly mitigated them and has even prevented or imperceptibly corrected many of them, against which prudence could not provide so well. And finally, these imperfections are almost always more tolerable than changing them would be; similarly, the great roads that wind through mountains little by little become so smooth and so convenient by dint of being frequently used, that it is much better to follow them than to try to take a more direct route by climbing over rocks and descending to the bottom of precipices.

That is why I could in no way approve of those trouble-making and restless personalities who, called neither by their birth nor by their fortune to manage

15   public affairs, are forever coming up with an idea for some new reform in this matter. And if I thought there were in this writing the slightest thing by means of which one might suspect me of such folly, I would be very sorry to permit its publication. My plan has never gone beyond trying to reform my own thoughts and building upon a foundation which is completely my own. And if, my work having pleased me sufficiently, I here show you a model of it, it is not for the reason that I would wish to advise anyone to imitate it. Perhaps those with whom God has better shared his graces will have more lofty plans; but I fear that even this one here may already be too daring for many. The single resolution to rid

oneself of all the opinions to which one has heretofore given credence is not an example that everyone ought to follow; and the world consists almost exclusively of two kinds of minds for whom it is not at all suitable. First, there are those who, believing themselves more capable than they are, are unable to avoid being hasty in their judgments or have enough patience to conduct all their thoughts in an orderly manner; as a result, if they have once taken the liberty of doubting the principles they had accepted and of straying from the common path, they could never keep to the path one must take in order to go in a more straightforward direction, and they would remain lost all their lives. Second, there are those who have enough reason or modesty to judge that they are less capable of distinguishing the true from the false than certain others by whom they can be instructed; such people should content themselves more with following the opinions of these others than with looking for better ones themselves.

And as for myself, I would unquestionably have been counted among these latter persons if I had always had only one master or if I had not known at all the differences that have always existed among the opinions of the most learned. But I had learned in my college days that one cannot imagine anything so strange or so little believable that it has not been said by one of the philosophers, and since then, I had recognized in my travels that all those who have sentiments quite contrary to our own are not for that reason barbarians or savages, but that many of them use their reason as much as or more than we do. And I considered how one and the same man with the very same mind, were he brought up from infancy among the French or the Germans, would become different from what he would be had he always lived among the Chinese or the cannibals; and how, even down to the styles of our clothing, the same thing that pleased us ten years ago, and that perhaps will again please us ten years hence, now seems to us extravagant and ridiculous. Thus it is more custom and example that persuades us than any certain knowledge; and yet the majority opinion is worthless as a proof of truths that are at all difficult to discover, since it is much more likely that one man would have found them than a whole multitude of people. Hence I could not choose anyone whose opinions seemed to me preferable over those of the others, and I found myself, as it were, constrained to try to guide myself on my own. *16*

But, like a man who walks alone and in the dark, I resolved to go so slowly and to use so much circumspection in all things that, if I advanced only very slightly, at least I would effectively keep myself from falling. Nor did I want to begin to reject totally any of the opinions that had once been able to slip into my head without having been introduced there by reason, until I had first spent sufficient time planning the work I was undertaking and seeking the true method for arriving at the knowledge of everything of which my mind would be capable. *17*

When I was younger, I had studied, among the parts of philosophy, a little logic, and among those of mathematics, a bit of geometrical analysis and algebra—three arts or sciences that, it seemed, ought to contribute something to my plan. But in examining them, I noticed that, in the case of logic, its syllogisms and the greater part of its other lessons served more to explain to someone else the things one knows, or even, like the art of Lully,[4] to speak without judgment concerning matters about which one is ignorant, than to learn them. And although, in effect, it might well contain many very true and very good precepts, nevertheless there are so many others mixed up with them that are either harmful or superfluous, that it is almost as difficult to separate the latter precepts from the former as it is to draw a Diana or a Minerva from a block of marble that has not yet been hewn. Then, as to the analysis of the ancients and the algebra of the moderns, apart from the fact that they apply only to very abstract matters and seem to be of no use, the former is always so closely tied to the consideration of figures that it cannot exercise the understanding without greatly fatiguing the imagination; and in the case of the latter, one is so subjected to certain rules and to certain symbols, that out of it there results a confused and obscure art that encumbers the mind, rather than a science that cultivates it. That is why I thought it necessary to search for some other method embracing the advantages of these three yet free from their defects. And since the multiplicity of laws often provides excuses for vices, so that a state is much better ruled when it has but very few laws and when these are very strictly observed; likewise, in place of the large number of precepts of which logic is composed, I believed that the following four rules would be sufficient for me, provided I made a firm and constant resolution not even once to fail to observe them:

The first was never to accept anything as true that I did not plainly know to be such; that is to say, carefully to avoid hasty judgment and prejudice; and to include nothing more in my judgments than what presented itself to my mind so clearly and so distinctly that I had no occasion to call it in doubt.

The second, to divide each of the difficulties I would examine into as many parts as possible and as was required in order better to resolve them.

The third, to conduct my thoughts in an orderly fashion, by commencing with those objects that are simplest and easiest to know, in order to ascend little by little, as by degrees, to the knowledge of the most composite things, and by supposing an order even among those things that do not naturally precede one another.

And the last, everywhere to make enumerations so complete and reviews so general that I was assured of having omitted nothing.

Those long chains of utterly simple and easy reasonings that geometers commonly use to arrive at their most difficult demonstrations had given me occasion to imagine that all the things that can fall within human knowledge follow from one another in the same way, and that, provided only that one abstain from accepting any of them as true that is not true, and that one always adheres to the order one must follow in deducing the ones from the others, there cannot be any that are so remote that they are not eventually reached nor so hidden that they are

---

4. Lully, that is, Ramon Lull (c. 1236–1315), was a Catalan philosopher and Franciscan who wrote in defense of Christianity against the Moors by attempting to demonstrate the articles of faith by means of logic. Descartes seems to have encountered a Lullist in Dordrecht who could hold forth on any subject whatever for long periods of time. This encounter, more than any direct contact with the writings of Lull, seems to have colored Descartes's understanding of the "art of Lully." See Gilson, pp. 185–6.

not discovered. And I was not very worried about trying to find out which of them it would be necessary to begin with; for I already knew that it was with the simplest and easiest to know. And considering that, of all those who have hitherto searched for the truth in the sciences, only the mathematicians have been able to find any demonstrations, that is to say, certain and evident reasonings, I did not at all doubt that it was with these same things that they had examined [that I should begin]; although I expected from them no other utility but that they would accustom my mind to nourish itself on truths and not to be content with false reasonings. But it was not my plan on that account to try to learn all those particular sciences commonly called "mathematical"; and seeing that, even *20* though their objects differed, these sciences did not cease to be all in accord with one another in considering nothing but the various relations or proportions which are found in their objects, I thought it would be more worthwhile for me to examine only these proportions in general, and to suppose them to be only in subjects that would help me make the knowledge of them easier, and without at the same time in any way restricting them to those subjects, so that later I could apply them all the better to everything else to which they might pertain. Then, having noted that, in order to know these proportions, I would sometimes need to consider each of them individually, and sometimes only to keep them in mind, or to grasp many of them together, I thought that, in order better to consider them in particular, I ought to suppose them to be relations between lines, since I found nothing more simple, or nothing that I could represent more distinctly to my imagination and to my senses; but that, in order to keep them in mind or to grasp many of them together, I would have to explicate them by means of certain symbols, the briefest ones possible; and that by this means I would be borrowing all that is best in geometrical analysis and algebra, and correcting all the defects of the one by means of the other.

In fact, I dare say the strict adherence to these few precepts I had chosen gave me such facility for disentangling all the questions to which these two sciences extend, that, in the two or three months I spent examining them, having begun with the simplest and most general, and each truth that I found being a rule that *21* later helped me to find others, not only did I arrive at a solution of many problems that I had previously judged very difficult, but also it seemed to me toward the end that, even in those instances where I was ignorant, I could determine by what means and how far it was possible to resolve them. In this perhaps I shall not seem to you to be too vain, if you will consider that, there being but one truth with respect to each thing, whoever finds this truth knows as much about a thing as can be known; and that, for example, if a child who has been instructed in arithmetic has made an addition following its rules, he can be assured of having found everything regarding the sum he was examining that the human mind would know how to find. For ultimately, the method that teaches one to follow the true order and to enumerate exactly all the circumstances of what one is seeking, contains everything that gives certainty to the rules of arithmetic.

But what pleased me most about this method was that by means of it I was assured of using my reason in everything, if not perfectly, at least as well as was in my power; and in addition that I felt that in practicing this method my mind

was little by little getting into the habit of conceiving its objects more rigorously and more distinctly and that, not having restricted the method to any particular subject matter, I promised myself to apply it as usefully to the problems of the other sciences as I had to those of algebra. Not that, on this account, I would have dared at the outset to undertake an examination of all the problems that presented themselves; for that would itself have been contrary to the order prescribed by the method. But having noted that the principles of these sciences must all be
22   derived from philosophy, in which I did not yet find any that were certain, I thought it was necessary for me first of all to try to establish some there; and that, this being the most important thing in the world, and the thing in which hasty judgment and prejudice were most to feared, I should not try to accomplish that objective until I had reached a much more mature age than that of merely twenty-three, which I was then, and until I had first spent a great deal of time preparing myself for it, as much in rooting out from my mind all the wrong opinions that I had accepted before that time as in accumulating many experiences, in order for them later to be the subject matter of my reasonings, and in always practicing the method I had prescribed for myself so as to strengthen myself more and more in its use.

Part Three

And finally, just as it is not enough, before beginning to rebuild the house where one is living, simply to pull it down, and to make provision for materials and architects or to train oneself in architecture, and also to have carefully drawn up the building plans for it; but it is also necessary to be provided with someplace else where one can live comfortably while working on it; thus, too, in order not to remain irresolute in my actions while reason required me to be so in my judg-ments, and in order not to cease to live as happily as possible during this time, I formulated a provisional code of morals, which consisted of but three or four maxims, which I very much want to share with you.
23   The first was to obey the laws and the customs of my country, constantly hold-ing on to the religion in which, by God's grace, I had been instructed from my childhood, and governing myself in everything else according to the most mod-erate opinions and those furthest from excess—opinions that were commonly accepted in practice by the most judicious of those with whom I would have to live. For, beginning from then on to count my own opinions as nothing because I wished to submit them all to examination, I was assured that I could not do bet-ter than to follow those of the most judicious. And although there may perhaps be people among the Persians or the Chinese just as judicious as there are among ourselves, it seemed to me that the most useful thing was to rule myself in accor-dance with those with whom I had to live, and that, in order to know what their opinions truly were, I ought to pay attention to what they did rather than to what they said, not only because in the corruption of our morals there are few people who are willing to say everything they believe, but also because many do not know what they believe; for, given that the action of thought by which one

believes something is different from that by which one knows that one believes
it, the one often occurs without the other. And among many opinions that are
equally accepted, I would choose only the most moderate, not only because they
are always the most suitable for practical affairs and probably the best (every
excess usually being bad), but also so as to stray less from the true path, in case
I should be mistaken, than if I had chosen one of the two extremes when it was
the other one I should have followed. And in particular I counted among the   *24*
excesses all the promises by which one curtails something of one's freedom. Not
that I disapproved of laws that, to remedy the inconstancy of weak minds, permit someone, when he has a good plan or even, for the security of commerce,
some plan that is merely indifferent, to make vows or contracts that oblige him
to persevere in it; but because I saw nothing in the world that always remained
in the same state, and because, for my part, I promised myself to improve my
judgments more and more, and never to make them worse, I would have thought
I committed a grave indiscretion against good sense if, having once approved
of something, I had obliged myself to take it as good again later, when perhaps
it might have stopped being so or when I might have stopped considering it
as such.

My second maxim was to be as firm and resolute in my actions as I could, and
to follow the most doubtful opinions, once I had decided on them, with no less
constancy than if they had been very well assured. In this I would be imitating
travelers who, finding themselves lost in some forest, should not wander about
turning this way and that, nor, worse still, stop in one place, but should always
walk in as straight a line as they can in one direction and never change it for feeble reasons, even if at the outset it had perhaps been only chance that made them
choose it; for by this means, even if they are not going exactly where they wish,
at least they will eventually arrive somewhere where they will probably be bet-   *25*
ter off than in the middle of a forest. And thus the actions of life often tolerating
no delay, it is a very certain truth that, when it is not in our power to discern the
truest opinions, we must follow the most probable; and even if we notice no more
probability in some than in others, nevertheless we must settle on some, and
afterwards no longer regard them as doubtful, insofar as they relate to practical
matters, but as very true and very certain, because the reason that made us decide
on them appears so. And from then on this was able to free me from all the regret
and remorse that usually agitate the consciences of those frail and irresolute
minds that allow themselves inconstantly to go about treating as if good, things
they later judge to be bad.

My third maxim was always to try to conquer myself rather than fortune, and
to change my desires rather than the order of the world; and generally to accustom myself to believing that there is nothing that is completely within our power
except our thoughts, so that, after we have done our best regarding things external to us, everything that is lacking for us to succeed, is, from our point of view,
absolutely impossible. And this alone seemed to me sufficient to prevent me in
the future from desiring anything but what I was to acquire, and thus to make me
contented. For, our will tending by nature to desire only what our understanding   *26*
represents to it as somehow possible, it is certain that, if we consider all the

goods that are outside us as equally beyond our power, we will have no more regrets about lacking those that seem owed to us as our birthright when we are deprived of them through no fault of our own, than we have in not possessing the kingdoms of China or Mexico; and that, making a virtue of necessity, as they say, we shall no more desire to be healthy if we are sick, or to be free if we are in prison, than we now do to have a body made of a material as incorruptible as diamonds, or wings to fly like birds. But I admit that long exercise is needed as well as frequently repeated meditation, in order to become accustomed to looking at everything from this point of view; and I believe that it is principally in this that the secret of those philosophers consists, who in earlier times were able to free themselves from fortune's domination and who, despite sorrows and poverty, could rival their gods in happiness. For occupying themselves ceaselessly with considering the limits prescribed to them by nature, they so perfectly persuaded themselves that nothing was in their power but their thoughts, that this alone was sufficient to prevent them from having any affection for other things, and they controlled their thoughts so absolutely that in this they had some reason for reckoning themselves richer, more powerful, freer, and happier 27 than any other men who, not having this philosophy, never thus controlled everything they wished to control, however favored by nature and fortune they might be.

Finally, to conclude this code of morals, I took it upon myself to review the various occupations that men have in this life, in order to try to choose the best one; and, not wanting to say anything about the occupations of others, I thought I could not do better than to continue in that very one in which I found myself, that is to say, spending my whole life cultivating my reason and advancing, as far as I could, in the knowledge of the truth, following the method I had prescribed to myself. I had met with such extreme contentment since the time I had begun to make use of this method, that I did not believe one could obtain any sweeter or more innocent contentment in this life; and, discovering every day by its means some truths that to me seemed quite important and commonly ignored by other men, the satisfaction I had from them so filled my mind that nothing else was of any consequence to me. In addition, the three preceding maxims were founded solely on the plan I had of continuing to instruct myself; for since God has given each of us some light to distinguish the true from the false, I would not have believed I ought to rest content for a single moment with the opinions of others, had I not proposed to use my own judgment to examine them when there would be time; and I would not have been able to free myself of scruples in following these opinions, had I not hoped that I would not, on that account, lose any 28 opportunity of finding better ones, in case there were any. And finally, I could not have limited my desires or have been content, had I not followed a path by which, thinking I was assured of acquiring all the knowledge of which I was capable, I thought I was assured by the same means of the knowledge of all the true goods that would ever be in my power. For, given that our will tends not to pursue or flee anything unless our understanding represents it to the will as either good or bad, it suffices to judge well in order to do well, and to judge as best one can, in order also to do one's very best, that is to say, to acquire all the virtues and in general all the other goods that one could acquire; and, when one is certain that this is the case, one could not fail to be contented.

When I had thus assured myself of these maxims and put them to one side along with the truths of the faith, which have always held first place among my beliefs, I judged that, as for the rest of my opinions, I could freely undertake to rid myself of them. And inasmuch as I hoped to be able to reach my goal better by conversing with men than by staying shut up any longer in the stove-heated room where I had had all these thoughts, the winter was not yet over when I set out again on my travels. And in all the nine years that followed I did nothing but wander here and there in the world, trying to be more a spectator than an actor in all the comedies that are played out there; and reflecting particularly in each matter on what might render it suspect and give us occasion for erring, I meanwhile rooted out from my mind all the errors that had previously been able to slip   *29* into it. Not that, in order to do this, I was imitating the skeptics who doubt merely for the sake of doubting and put on the affectation of being perpetually undecided; for, on the contrary, my entire plan tended simply to give me assurance and to cast aside the shifting earth and sand in order to find the rock or clay. In this I was quite successful, it seems to me, inasmuch as, trying to discover the falsity or the uncertainty of the propositions I was examining, not by feeble conjectures but by clear and certain reasonings, I never found any that was so doubtful that I could not draw from it some quite certain conclusion, even if it had been merely that it contained nothing certain. And just as in tearing down an old house, one usually saves the wreckage for use in building a new one, similarly, in destroying all those opinions of mine that I judged to be poorly founded, I made various observations and acquired many experiences that have since served me in establishing more certain opinions. Moreover, I continued to practice the method I had prescribed for myself; for, besides taking care generally to conduct all my thoughts according to its rules, from time to time I set aside some hours that I spent particularly in applying it to mathematical problems, or even also to some other problems that I could make as it were similar to those of mathematics, by detaching them from all the principles of the other sciences, which I did not find to be sufficiently firm, as you will see I have done in many problems that are explained in this volume.[5] And thus, without living any differently in outward appearance than do those who, having no task but to live a sweet and innocent   *30* life, make a point of separating pleasures from vices, and who, in order to enjoy their leisure without becoming bored, involve themselves in all sorts of honest diversions, I did not cease to carry out my plan and to progress in the knowledge of the truth, perhaps more than if I had done nothing but read books or keep company with men of letters.

Nevertheless, those nine years slipped by before I had as yet taken any stand regarding the difficulties commonly debated among learned men, or had begun to seek the foundations of any philosophy that was more certain than the commonly accepted one. And the example of many excellent minds, who had previously had

---

5. Descartes also published treatises on optics, geometry, and meteorology in this same volume.

this plan and had not, it seemed to me, succeeded in it, made me imagine so much difficulty in it that perhaps I would not have dared to undertake it so soon again, if I had not seen that some had already spread the rumor that I had achieved my goal. I cannot say on what they based this opinion; and if I have contributed something to it by my conversation, this must have been because I confessed that of which I was ignorant more ingenuously than those who have studied only a little are in the habit of doing, and perhaps also because I showed the reasons I had for doubting many things that other people regard as certain, rather than because I was boasting of any learning. But having a good enough heart not to want someone to take me for something other than I was, I thought it necessary to try by every means to render myself worthy of the reputation that was bestowed on me. And it is exactly eight years ago that this desire made me resolve to take my leave of all those places where I might have acquaintances, and to retire here, to a country where the long duration of the war has led to the establishment of such well-ordered discipline that the armies quartered here seem to serve only to make one enjoy the fruits of peace with even greater security, and where in the midst of the crowd of a great and very busy people who are more concerned with their own affairs than they are curious about those of others, I have been able, without lacking any of the amenities to be found in the most bustling cities, to live as solitary and as withdrawn a life as I could in the remotest deserts.

31

PART FOUR

I do not know whether I ought to tell you about the first meditations I engaged in there; for they are so metaphysical and so out of the ordinary that perhaps they will not be to everyone's liking. And yet, in order that it should be possible to judge whether the foundations I have laid are sufficiently firm, I find myself in some sense forced to talk about them. For a long time I had noticed that in matters of morality one must sometimes follow opinions that one knows to be quite uncertain, just as if they were indubitable, as has been said above; but because I then desired to devote myself exclusively to the search for the truth, I thought it necessary that I do exactly the opposite, and that I reject as absolutely false everything in which I could imagine the least doubt, in order to see whether, after this process, something in my beliefs remained that was entirely indubitable. Thus, because our senses sometimes deceive us, I wanted to suppose that nothing was exactly as they led us to imagine. And because there are men who make mistakes in reasoning, even in the simplest matters in geometry, and who commit paralogisms, judging that I was just as prone to err as any other, I rejected as false all the reasonings that I had previously taken for demonstrations. And finally, considering the fact that all the same thoughts we have when we are awake can also come to us when we are asleep, without any of them being true, I resolved to pretend that all the things that had ever entered my mind were no more true than the illusions of my dreams. But immediately afterward I noticed that, while I wanted thus to think that everything was false, it necessarily had to

32

be the case that I, who was thinking this, was something. And noticing that this truth—*I think, therefore I am*—was so firm and so assured that all the most extravagant suppositions of the skeptics were incapable of shaking it, I judged that I could accept it without scruple as the first principle of the philosophy I was seeking.

Then, examining with attention what I was, and seeing that I could pretend that I had no body and that there was no world nor any place where I was, I could not pretend, on that account, that I did not exist at all; and that, on the contrary, from the very fact that I thought of doubting the truth of other things, it followed very evidently and very certainly that I existed; whereas, on the other hand, had I simply stopped thinking, even if all the rest of what I had ever imagined had been *33* true, I would have had no reason to believe that I had existed. From this I knew that I was a substance the whole essence or nature of which is simply to think, and which, in order to exist, has no need of any place nor depends on any material thing. Thus this "I," that is to say, the soul through which I am what I am, is entirely distinct from the body and is even easier to know than the body, and even if there were no body at all, it would not cease to be all that it is.

After this, I considered in general what is needed for a proposition to be true and certain; for since I had just found one of them that I knew to be such, I thought I ought also to know in what this certitude consists. And having noticed that there is nothing at all in this *I think, therefore I am* that assures me that I am speaking the truth, except that I see very clearly that, in order to think, it is necessary to exist, I judged that I could take as a general rule that the things we conceive very clearly and very distinctly are all true, but that there is merely some difficulty in properly discerning which are those that we distinctly conceive.

Following this, reflecting upon the fact that I doubted and that, as a consequence, my being was not utterly perfect (for I saw clearly that it is a greater perfection to know than to doubt), I decided to search for the source from which I had learned to think of something more perfect than I was; and I plainly knew that this had to be from some nature that was in fact more perfect. As to those *34* thoughts I had of many other things outside me, such as the heavens, the earth, light, heat, and a thousand others, I had no trouble at all knowing where they came from, because, noticing nothing in them that seemed to me to make them superior to me, I could believe that, if they were true, they were dependencies of my nature, insofar as it had some perfection; and that, if they were not true, I obtained them from nothing, that is to say, they were in me because I had some defect. But the same could not hold for the idea of a being more perfect than my own, for it is a manifest contradiction to receive this idea from nothing; and because it is no less a contradiction that something more perfect should follow from and depend upon something less perfect than that something should come from nothing, I could not obtain it from myself. It thus remained that this idea had been placed in me by a nature truly more perfect than I was and that it even had within itself all the perfections of which I could have any idea, that is to say, to explain myself in a single word, that it was God. To this I added that, since I knew of some perfections that I did not at all possess, I was not the only being that existed (here, if you please, I shall freely use the terminology of the School), but that of necessity there must be something else more perfect, upon which I depended, and from which I had acquired all that I had. For, had I been alone and *35* independent of everything else, so that I had had from myself all that small amount of perfection in which I participated in the perfect being, I would have been able, for the same reason, to have from myself everything else I knew I lacked; and thus to be myself infinite, eternal, unchanging, all-knowing, all-powerful; in short, to have all the perfections I could observe to be in God. For, following the reasonings I have just gone through, in order to know the nature of God, so far as my own nature was capable of doing so, I had only to consider, regarding all the things of which I found in myself some idea, whether or not it was a perfection to possess them, and I was assured that none of those that indicated any imperfection were in God, but that all others were in him. Thus I saw that doubt, inconstancy, sadness, and the like could not be in God, since I myself would have been happy to be exempt from them. Then, besides this, I had ideas of a number of sensible and corporeal things; for even if I were to suppose that I was dreaming and that everything I saw or imagined was false, I still could not deny that the ideas of these things were not truly in my thought. But since I had already recognized very clearly in myself that intelligent nature is distinct from corporeal nature, taking into consideration that all composition attests to dependence and that dependence is manifestly a defect, I judged from this that being composed of these two natures could not be a perfection in God and that, as a consequence, God was not thus composed; but that, if there are bodies in the world, or even intelligences, or other natures that were not at all entirely perfect, *36* their being had to depend on God's power in such a way that they could not subsist without God for a single moment.

After this, I wanted to search for other truths, and, having set before myself the object dealt with by geometers, which I conceived of as a continuous body or a space indefinitely extended in length, breadth, and height or depth, divisible into various parts which could have various shapes and sizes and which may be moved or transposed in all sorts of ways—for the geometers assume all this in their object—I went through some of their simplest demonstrations. And, having noted that the great certitude that everyone attributes to these demonstrations is founded exclusively on the fact that they are plainly conceived, following the rule that I mentioned earlier, I also noted that there was nothing at all in them that assured me of the existence of their object. For I saw very well that by supposing, for example, a triangle, it was necessary for its three angles to be equal to two right angles; but I did not see anything in all this to assure me that there was any triangle existing in the world. On the other hand, returning to examine the idea I had of a perfect being, I found that existence was contained in it in the same way in which the equality of its three angles to two right angles is contained in the idea of a triangle, or that the equidistance of all its parts from its center is contained in the idea of a sphere, or even more plainly still; and that, consequently, it is, at the very least, just as certain that God, who is this perfect being, is or exists, as any demonstration in geometry could be.

37   But what brings it about that there are many people who are persuaded that it is difficult to know this and also even to know what their soul is, is that they never lift their minds above sensible things and that they are so accustomed to consider nothing except by imagining it (which is a way of thinking appropriate for material things), that everything unimaginable seems to them unintelligible. This is obvious enough from the fact that even the philosophers take it as a maxim in the schools that there is nothing in the understanding that has not first been in the senses, where it is nevertheless certain that the ideas of God and the soul have never been. And it seems to me that those who want to use their imagination in order to grasp these ideas are doing the very same thing as if, in order to hear sounds or to smell odors, they wanted to use their eyes. There is just this difference: the sense of sight assures us no less of the truth of its objects than do the senses of smell or hearing, whereas neither our imagination nor our senses could ever assure us of anything if our understanding did not intervene.

Finally, if there still are men who have not been sufficiently persuaded of the existence of God and of their soul by means of the reasons I have brought forward, I very much want them to know that all the other things of which they think themselves perhaps more assured, such as having a body, that there are stars and an earth, and the like, are less certain. For although one might have a moral assurance about these things, which is such that it seems one cannot doubt them 38 without being extravagant, still when it is a question of metaphysical certitude, it seems unreasonable for anyone to deny that there is not a sufficient basis for one's being completely assured about them, when one observes that while asleep one can, in the same fashion, imagine that one has a different body and that one sees different stars and a different earth, without any of these things being the case. For how does one know that the thoughts that come to us in dreams are any more false than the others, given that they are often no less vivid and explicit? And even if the best minds study this as much as they please, I do not believe they can give any reason sufficient to remove this doubt, unless they presuppose the existence of God. For first of all, even what I have already taken for a rule, namely that the things we very clearly and very distinctly conceive are all true, is assured only for the reason that God is or exists, and that he is a perfect being, and that all that is in us comes from him. It follows from this that our ideas or notions, being real things and coming from God, cannot, in all that is clear and distinct in them, be anything but true. Thus, if we quite often have ideas that contain some falsity, this can only be the case with respect to things that have something confused or obscure about them, because in this respect they participate in nothing; that is, they are thus confused in us only because we are not perfect. And it is evident that it is no less a contradiction that falsity or imperfection as such 39 proceeds from God, than that truth or perfection proceeds from nothing. But if we did not know that all that is real and true in us comes from a perfect and infinite being, however clear and distinct our ideas were, we would have no reason that assured us that they had the perfection of being true.

But once the knowledge of God and the soul has thus made us certain of this rule, it is very easy to know that the dreams we imagine while asleep ought in no way to make us doubt the truth of the thoughts we have while awake. For if it did happen, even while asleep, that one had a very distinct idea (as, for example, if a geometer found some new demonstration), one's being asleep would not prevent its being true. And as to the most common error of our dreams, which consists in the fact that they represent to us various objects in the same way as our external senses do, it does not matter that it gives us occasion to question the truth of such ideas, since they can also deceive us quite often without our being asleep, such as when those with jaundice see everything as yellow, or when the stars or other very distant bodies appear to us much smaller than they are. For finally, whether awake or asleep, we should never allow ourselves to be persuaded except by the evidence of our reason. And it is to be observed that I say "of our reason," and not "of our imagination," or "of our senses." Even though we see the sun very clearly, we should not on that account judge that it is only as large as we see it; and we can well imagine distinctly the head of a lion grafted onto the body of a goat, without having to conclude for that reason that there is a chimera in the world; for reason does not at all dictate to us that what we thus see or imagine is true. But it does dictate to us that all our ideas or notions must have some foundation of truth; for it would not be possible that God, who is all perfect and all truthful, would have put them in us without that. And because our reasonings are never so evident nor so complete while we are asleep as they are while we are awake, even though our imaginings while we are asleep are sometimes just as vivid and explicit as those we have while we are awake, or even more so, reason also dictates to us that our thoughts cannot all be true, since we are not all-perfect; what truth there is in them must infallibly be encountered in those we have when we are awake rather than in those we have in our dreams.

Part Five

I would be quite happy to continue and to show here the whole chain of other truths that I have deduced from these first ones. But because, in order to do this, it would now be necessary for me to speak about many questions that are a matter of controversy among the learned, with whom I have no desire to get into any quarrel, I believe it will be better for me to abstain from this and to state only in a general way what these questions are, in order to let those who are wiser judge whether it would be useful for the public to be more particularly informed about them. I have always remained firm in the resolution I had made not to suppose any principle but the one I have just used to demonstrate the existence of God and of the soul, and not to accept anything as true that did not seem to me clearer and more certain than the demonstrations of the geometers had hitherto seemed. And, nevertheless, I dare say not only that have I found a means of satisfying myself within a short time regarding all the principal difficulties commonly treated in philosophy, but also that I have noted certain laws that God has so established in nature, and of which he has impressed in our souls such notions, that, after having reflected sufficiently on these matters, we cannot doubt that they are strictly adhered to in everything that exists or occurs in the world. Moreover, in considering the consequences of these laws, it seems to me that I have discovered many truths more useful and more important than all that I had previously learned or even hoped to learn.

But because I have tried to explain the principal ones among these truths in a treatise that certain considerations prevented me from publishing,[6] I could not make them better known than by stating here in summary form what the treatise contains. I had intended to include in it everything that I thought I knew, before writing it down, concerning the nature of material things. But just as painters, who are unable to represent equally well on a flat surface all the various sides of a solid body, choose one of the principal sides to place alone facing the light of day, and, by darkening the rest with shadows, make them appear only as they can *42* be seen by someone who is looking at the principal side; just so, fearing I could not put into my discourse everything I had in mind about it, I undertook in it merely to speak at length about what I conceived with respect to light; then, at the proper time, to add something about the sun and the fixed stars, because light proceeds almost entirely from them; something about the heavens, because they transmit light; about the planets, comets, and the earth because they reflect light; and, in particular, about all terrestrial bodies, because they are either colored, or transparent, or luminous; and finally, about man, because he is the observer of these things. All the same, to cast all these things a little in shadow and to be able to say more freely what I judged about them without being obliged either to follow or to refute the opinions that are accepted among the learned, I resolved to leave this entire world here to their disputes, and to speak only of what would happen in a new world, were God now to create enough matter to compose it, somewhere in imaginary spaces, and were he to agitate in various ways and without order the different parts of this matter, so that he composed from it a chaos as confused as any the poets could concoct and that later he did no more than apply his ordinary concurrence to nature, and let nature act in accordance with the laws he had established. Thus, first, I described this matter and tried to represent it in such a way that there is nothing in the world, it seems to me, clearer and more intelligible, with the exception of what has already been said about God and the soul; for I even explicitly supposed that in this matter there were *43* none of those forms or qualities about which disputes occur in the schools, nor generally anything the knowledge of which was not so natural to our souls that one could not even pretend to be ignorant of it. Moreover, I showed what the laws of nature were; and, without supporting my reasons on any other principle but the infinite perfections of God, I tried to demonstrate all those laws about which one might have been able to have any doubt and to show that they are such that, even if God had created many worlds, there could not be any of them in which these laws failed to be observed. After that, I showed how, as a consequence of these laws, the greater part of the matter of this chaos had to be disposed and arranged in a certain way, which made it similar to our heavens; how, at the same time, some of its parts had to compose an earth; others, planets and comets; and still others, a sun and fixed stars. And here, dwelling on the subject of light, I explained at some length what this light was that had to be found in the sun and the stars, and how from thence it traveled in an instant across the

---

6. Descartes's *Le Monde (The World)*. One of the considerations preventing the publication of *Le Monde* was the trial in 1633 of Galileo by the Holy Office in Rome.

immense spaces of the heavens, and how it was reflected from the planets and comets to the earth. To this I added also a number of things touching on the sub-stance, position, motions, and all the various qualities of these heavens and these stars; and as a result, I thought I said enough on these matters to show that there is nothing to be observed in the things of this world which should not, or at least

44   could not, have appeared entirely similar in those of the world I was describing. From there, I went on to speak in particular about the earth: how, although I had expressly supposed that God had not put any weight[7] in the matter out of which the earth was composed, none of its parts ceased to tend precisely toward its cen-ter; how, there being water and air on its surface, the disposition of the heavens and of the stars, principally of the moon, had to cause there an ebb and flow sim-ilar in all respects to what we observe in our seas, and, in addition, a certain coursing, as much of the water as of the air, from east to west, such as is also observed between the tropics; how mountains, seas, springs, and rivers could nat-urally be formed there, and how metals could make their way into mines there; how plants could grow naturally in the fields there, and generally how all the bodies called "mixed" or "composed" could be engendered there. And, among other things, because apart from the stars I know of nothing else in the world that would produce light except fire, I tried to make very clearly understood all that belonged to its nature: how it is made, how it is nourished, how sometimes it has only heat but no light, and sometimes only light but no heat; how it can introduce various colors and various other qualities into various bodies; how it melts some bodies and hardens others; how it can consume nearly all of them or turn them into ashes and smoke; and finally, how from these ashes, merely by the force of

45   its action, it produces glass; for since this transmutation of ashes into glass seemed to me to be as awesome as any other that occurs in nature, I took partic-ular pleasure in describing it.

Yet I did not want to infer from all these things that this world has been cre-ated in the manner I was proposing, for it is much more likely that, from the beginning, God made it such as it had to be. But it is certain (and this is an opin-ion commonly accepted among theologians) that the action by which God pre-serves the world is precisely the same as that by which he created it; so that, even if, in the beginning, he had never given it any other form at all but that of a chaos, provided he established the laws of nature and bestowed his concurrence in order for nature to function just as it does ordinarily, one can believe, without doing injustice to the miracle of creation, that by this means alone all the things that are purely material could over time have been rendered such as we now see them. And their nature is much easier to conceive, when one sees them coming to be little by little in this manner, than when one considers them only in their com-pleted state.

From the description of inanimate bodies and plants I passed to that of animals and in particular to that of human beings. But because I did not yet have sufficient

---

7. Gilson, p. 388, observes that *pesanteur* here means the same thing as *gravitas*, a scholastic term referring to the tendency of terrestrial objects always to tend downwards. Gilson also directs the reader to *The World,* chapter xi: "On Weight."

knowledge of them to speak of them in the same manner as I did of the rest, that is to say, by demonstrating effects from causes and by showing from what seeds and in what manner nature must produce them, I contented myself with supposing that God formed the body of a man exactly like one of ours, as much in the *46* outward shape of its members as in the internal arrangement of its organs, without composing it out of any material but the type I had described, and without putting into it, at the start, any rational soul, or anything else to serve there as a vegetative or sensitive soul, but merely kindled in the man's heart one of those fires without light which I had already explained and which I did not at all conceive to be of a nature other than what heats hay when it has been stored before it is dry, or which makes new wines boil when they are left to ferment after crushing. For on examining the functions that could, as a consequence, be in this body, I found there precisely all those things that can be in us without our thinking about them, and hence, without our soul's contributing to them, that is to say, that part distinct from the body of which it has been said previously that its nature is only to think. And these are all the same features in which one can say that animals lacking reason resemble us. But I could not on that account find there any of those functions, which, being dependent on thought, are the only ones that belong to us as men, although I did find them all later on, once I had supposed that God created a rational soul and joined it to this body in a particular manner that I described.

But in order that one might be able to see how I treated this matter there, I want to place here the explanation of the movement of the heart and of the arteries; because, this being the first and most general movement that one observes in animals, on the basis of it one will easily judge what one ought to think about all the *47* others. And, in order that there might be less difficulty in understanding what I shall say on the matter, I would like those who are not at all versed in anatomy to take the trouble, before reading this, to have dissected in their presence the heart of some large animal that has lungs (for such a heart is in all respects sufficiently similar to that of a man), and to be shown the two chambers or cavities that are in it. First, there is the one on the right side of the heart, into which two very large tubes lead, namely the vena cava, which is the principal receptacle of the blood, and which is like the trunk of a tree of which the other veins of the body are the branches, and the arterial vein (which has thus been rather ill-named, because it is, in effect, an artery), which, taking its origin from the heart, divides up after leaving the heart into many branches that go on to be spread throughout the lungs. Then there is the chamber or cavity on the left side, into which two tubes lead in the same fashion, which are as large or larger than the preceding ones: namely, the venous artery (which has also been ill-named, since it is nothing but a vein), which comes from the lungs, where it is divided into many branches interlaced with those of the arterial vein and with those in the passageway called the "windpipe," through which the air one breathes enters; and the great artery, which, on leaving the heart, sends its branches throughout the body. I would also like those who are not versed in anatomy to be carefully shown the eleven little membranes that, like so many little doors, open and shut the four openings in the two cavities: namely, three at the entrance to the vena *48* cava, where they are so disposed that they cannot in any way prevent the blood it contains from flowing into the right cavity of the heart, and yet completely prevent it from being able to leave it; three at the entrance to the arterial vein, which, being arranged totally in the other direction, readily permit the blood in this cavity to pass into the lungs, but do not permit any blood in the lungs to return there; likewise, two others at the entrance to the venous artery, which let blood flow from the lungs into the left cavity of the heart but block its return; and three at the entrance to the great artery, which permit blood to leave the heart but prevent it from returning there. And there is no need at all to search for any other reason for the number of membranes except that the opening of the venous artery, being oval-shaped because of its location, can conveniently be closed with two, while the other openings, being round, can better be closed with three. Further, I would like to make them consider that the great artery and the arterial vein are of a much harder and firmer constitution than the venous artery and the vena cava; and that these latter two become enlarged before entering the heart and there form, as it were, sacks, called the "auricles" of the heart, which are made of flesh similar to that of the heart; and that there is always more heat in the heart than anywhere else in the body; and, finally, that this heat is able to bring it about that,

49   if a drop of blood enters its cavities, it promptly expands and is dilated, just as all liquids generally do when one lets them fall drop by drop into some vessel that is very hot.

For, after that, I have no need to say anything else in order to explain the movement of the heart, except that, when its cavities are not full of blood, blood necessarily flows from the vena cava into the right cavity and from the venous artery into the left cavity, given that these two vessels are always full of blood, and their openings, which face the heart, cannot then be closed. But as soon as two drops of blood have thus entered the heart, one into each of its cavities, these drops, which can only be very large because the openings through which they enter are very wide and the vessels from whence they come are quite full of blood, are rarefied and dilated because of the heat they find there, by means of which, making the whole heart inflate, they push and close the five little doors that are at the entrances to the two vessels from whence they come, thus preventing any more blood from descending into the heart; and, continuing to become more and more rarefied, they push and open the six other little doors which are at the entrances to the other two vessels by which they leave. By this means they inflate all the branches of the arterial vein and the great artery, almost at the same instant as the heart; immediately afterward the heart contracts, as do these arteries as well, because the blood that has entered them gets cooled and their six little doors close again, and the five doors of the vena cava and the

50   venous artery reopen and grant passage to two other drops of blood, which immediately make the heart and the arteries inflate exactly as before. And, because the blood that thus enters the heart passes through the two sacks called its "auricles," it follows from this that their movement is contrary to that of the heart, and that they are deflated while the heart is inflated. As for the rest (in order that those who do not know the force of mathematical demonstrations and are not accustomed to distinguishing true reasons from probable ones should not

venture to deny this without examining it), I want to put them on notice that this movement which I have just been explaining follows just as necessarily from the mere disposition of the organs that can be seen in the heart by the naked eye, and from the heat that can be felt with the fingers, and from the nature of blood, which can be known through observation, as does the movement of a clock from the force, placement, and shape of its counterweights and wheels.

But if one asks how it is that the blood in the veins is not at all dissipated in flowing thus continually into the heart, and how the arteries are never overly full of blood, since all the blood that flows through the heart is going to flow into them, to this I need give no other answer than what has already been written by an English physician,[8] to whom homage must be paid for having broken the ice in this area, and for being the first to have taught that there are many small passages at the extremities of the arteries through which the blood they receive enters into the small branches of the veins, from which it flows immediately to the heart, so that its course is merely a perpetual circulation. He proves this very *51* effectively from the common experience of surgeons, who, on binding an arm moderately tightly above the spot where they open the vein, cause the blood to flow out in even greater abundance than if they had not bound the arm at all. And just the opposite would happen if they bound the arm below, between the hand and the opening, or even if they bound it very tightly above the opening, for it is obvious that a moderately tight tourniquet, being able to prevent the blood that is already in the arm from returning to the heart through the veins, does not on that account prevent new blood from coming in through the arteries, because they are located below the veins, and their membranes, being harder, are less easy to press, and also because the blood coming from the heart tends to pass through the arteries toward the hand with greater force than it does in returning from these to the heart through the veins. And since this blood leaves the arm through the opening in one of the veins, there must necessarily be some passages below the tourniquet, that is to say, toward the extremities of the arm, through which it could come from the arteries. He also proves quite effectively what he says regarding the circulation of blood by referring to certain small membranes that are so disposed in various places along the length of the veins that they do not at all permit blood to pass from the middle of the body toward the extremities, but only to return from the extremities toward the heart; and further, by means of the experiment that shows that all the blood that is in the body can flow out of it in a very short time through just one artery when it is cut open, even if the artery is very tightly bound quite close to the heart, and cut open between the heart and the tourniquet, so that one would have no basis for imagining that the *52* blood that flowed out came from somewhere else.

---

8. William Harvey (1578–1657), an English physiologist who demonstrated the function of the heart and the complete circulation of blood throughout the body. His most important work is *Anatomical Exercises on the Motion of the Heart and Blood* (1628). Descartes accepted Harvey's account of how blood circulated, but not his account of the heart's motion.

But there are many other things that attest to the fact that the true cause of this movement of blood is as I have said. First, the difference that one notices between the blood leaving the veins and the blood leaving the arteries can result only from the fact that the blood is rarefied and, as it were, distilled, in passing through the heart; it is thinner, livelier, and warmer just after having left the heart, that is to say, while it is in the arteries, than it is shortly before it enters the heart, that is to say, while it is in the veins. And if one takes note of it, one will find that this difference is more readily apparent near the heart and not at all so much in those places furthest removed from the heart. Then the hardness of the membranes of which the arterial vein and the great artery are composed shows well enough that the blood beats against them with more force than it does against the veins. And why would the left cavity of the heart and the great artery be larger and wider than the right cavity and the arterial vein, unless it is because the blood in the venous artery, having been only in the lungs after having passed through the heart, is thinner and is more forcefully and easily rarefied than what comes immediately from the vena cava? And what can physicians divine from taking the pulse, if they do not know that, as the blood changes its nature, it can be rarefied by the heat of the heart more or less strongly, and more or less quickly than before? And if one examines how this heat is communicated to the other mem-
53   bers, must one not admit that it is by means of the blood, which, on passing through the heart, is reheated there and from there is spread throughout the whole body? It follows from this that if one removes the blood from some part of the body, one thereupon also removes the heat; and even if the heart were as hot as a piece of glowing iron, it would not be enough to reheat the feet and hands as much as it does, if it did not continuously send new blood to them. Then, too, it is also evident from this that the true function of respiration is to bring enough fresh air into the lungs to cause the blood which comes there from the right cavity of the heart, where it has been rarefied and, as it were, changed into vapors, immediately to be condensed and to be converted once again into blood before returning to the left cavity; without this process the blood could not properly aid in feeding the fire that is in the heart. This is confirmed because one sees that animals without lungs have but one single cavity in their hearts, and that children who cannot use their lungs while enclosed within their mother's womb have an opening through which blood flows from the vena cava into the left cavity of the heart, as well as a tube through which blood goes from the arterial vein to the great artery without passing through the lungs. Next, how would digestion take place in the stomach if the heart did not send heat there through the arteries, and with it some of the most fluid parts of the blood, which help dissolve the food that has gone there? And is it not easy to understand the action that changes the juice of this food into blood, if one considers that, in passing and repassing through the heart, it is distilled perhaps more than one or two hundred times a
54   day? And is anything else needed to explain nutrition and the production of the various humors that are in the body, except to say that the force with which the blood, in being rarefied, passes from the heart toward the extremities of the arteries, makes some of its parts stop in those parts of the members where they are found and there take the place of others that they expel from there; and that,

according to the situation or the shape or the smallness of the pores they encounter, some of the parts of the blood tend to go certain places rather than others, in just the same way that anyone can have seen various sieves of different fineness serve to separate out different grains from one another? And finally what is most remarkable in all this is the generation of the animal spirits, which are like a very subtle wind, or rather, like a very pure and lively flame that rises continuously in great abundance from the heart to the brain, and from there goes through the nerves into the muscles, and gives movement to all the members. The parts of the blood that are the most agitated and penetrating and are thus the best suited to compose these spirits are going to move toward the brain rather than elsewhere; and there is no need to imagine any other reason for this other than that the arteries that carry these parts of the blood there are those that come from the heart in the straightest line of all, and that, according to the laws of mechanics (which are the same as those of nature), when a number of things tend to move together in the same direction, where there is not enough room for all of them, as when the parts of the blood leaving the left cavity of the heart tend toward the brain, the weakest and least agitated must be pushed aside by the *55* strongest, which by this means arrive there alone.

I had provided a sufficiently detailed explanation for all these things in the treatise that I had previously intended to publish.[9] And then I had shown what the constitution of the nerves and muscles of the human body must be in order to make the animal spirits within them have the force to move its members, as when one observes that heads, shortly after being severed, still move about and bite the earth, even though they are no longer alive. I had also shown what changes must take place in the brain in order to cause wakefulness, sleep, and dreams; how light, sounds, odors, tastes, heat, and all the other qualities of external objects can imprint various ideas there through the mediation of the senses; how hunger, thirst, and the other internal passions can also send their ideas there; what part of them needs to be taken there for the common sense, where these ideas are received; for the memory, which preserves them; and for the imagination, which can change them in various ways and compose new ones out of them, and, by the same means, distributing the animal spirits into the muscles, make the members of this body move in as many different ways (and in a manner appropriate to the objects that present themselves to the senses and to the internal passions that are in the body) as our own bodies can, without their being guided by the will. This will in no way seem strange to those who are cognizant of how many different automata or moving machines the ingenuity of men can make, without using, in *56* doing so, but a very small number of parts, in comparison with the great multitude of bones, muscles, nerves, arteries, veins, and all the other parts which are in the body of each animal. For they will regard this body as a machine which, having been made by the hands of God, is incomparably better ordered and has within itself movements far more wondrous than any of those that can be invented by men.

---

9. Again, this is a reference to *The World,* of which the *Treatise on Man* was a part.

I paused here in particular in order to show that, if there were such machines having the organs and the shape of a monkey or of some other animal that lacked reason, we would have no way of recognizing that they were not entirely of the same nature as these animals; whereas, if there were any such machines that bore a resemblance to our bodies and imitated our actions as far as this is practically feasible, we would always have two very certain means of recognizing that they were not at all, for that reason, true men. The first is that they could never use words or other signs, or put them together as we do in order to declare our thoughts to others. For one can well conceive of a machine being so made that it utters words, and even that it utters words appropriate to the bodily actions that will cause some change in its organs (such as, if one touches it in a certain place, it asks what one wants to say to it, or, if in another place, it cries out that one is hurting it, and the like). But it could not arrange its words differently so as to

57   respond to the sense of all that will be said in its presence, as even the dullest men can do. The second means is that, although they might perform many tasks very well or perhaps better than any of us, such machines would inevitably fail in other tasks; by this means one would discover that they were acting, not through knowledge, but only through the disposition of their organs. For while reason is a universal instrument that can be of help in all sorts of circumstances, these organs require some particular disposition for each particular action; consequently, it is for all practical purposes impossible for there to be enough different organs in a machine to make it act in all the contingencies of life in the same way as our reason makes us act.

Now by these two means one can also know the difference between men and beasts. For it is rather remarkable that there are no men so dull and so stupid (excluding not even the insane), that they are incapable of arranging various words together and of composing from them a discourse by means of which they might make their thoughts understood; and that, on the other hand, there is no other animal at all, however perfect and pedigreed it may be, that does the like. This does not happen because they lack the organs, for one sees that magpies and parrots can utter words just as we can, and yet they cannot speak as we do, that is to say, by testifying to the fact that they are thinking about what they are saying; on the other hand, men born deaf and dumb, who are deprived just as much

58   as, or more than, beasts of the organs that aid others in speaking, are wont to invent for themselves various signs by means of which they make themselves understood to those who, being with them on a regular basis, have the time to learn their language. And this attests not merely to the fact that the beasts have less reason than men but that they have none at all. For it is obvious it does not need much to know how to speak; and since we notice as much inequality among animals of the same species as among men, and that some are easier to train than others, it is unbelievable that a monkey or a parrot that is the most perfect of its species would not equal in this respect one of the most stupid children or at least a child with a disordered brain, if their soul were not of a nature entirely different from our own. And we should not confuse words with the natural movements that attest to the passions and can be imitated by machines as well as by animals. Nor should we think, as did some of the ancients, that beasts speak, although we

do not understand their language; for if that were true, since they have many organs corresponding to our own, they could make themselves as well understood by us as they are by their fellow creatures. It is also a very remarkable phenomenon that, although there are many animals that show more skill than we do in some of their actions, we nevertheless see that they show none at all in many other actions. Consequently, the fact that they do something better than we do does not prove that they have any intelligence; for were that the case, they would have more of it than any of us and would excel us in everything. But rather it proves that they have no intelligence at all, and that it is nature that acts in them, according to the disposition of their organs—just as we see that a clock composed exclusively of wheels and springs can count the hours and measure time more accurately than we can with all our carefulness.

    After that, I described the rational soul and showed that it can in no way be derived from the potentiality of matter, as can the other things I have spoken of, but rather that it must be expressly created; and how it is not enough for it to be lodged in the human body like a pilot in his ship, unless perhaps in order to move its members, but rather that it must be more closely joined and united to the body in order to have, in addition to this, feelings and appetites similar to our own, and thus to constitute a true man. As to the rest, I elaborated here a little on the subject of the soul because it is of the greatest importance; for, after the error of those who deny the existence of God (which I think I have sufficiently refuted), there is none at all that puts weak minds at a greater distance from the straight path of virtue than to imagine that the soul of beasts is of the same nature as ours, and that, as a consequence, we have nothing to fear or to hope for after this life any more than do flies and ants. On the other hand, when one knows how different they are, one understands much better the arguments which prove that our soul is of a nature entirely independent of the body, and consequently that it is not subject to die with it. Then, since we do not see any other causes at all for its destruction, we are naturally led to judge from this that it is immortal.

PART SIX

But it is now three years since I arrived at the end of the treatise that contains all these things and began to review it in order to put it into the hands of a printer, when I learned that some people to whom I defer and whose authority over my actions can hardly be less than that of my reason over my thoughts, had disapproved of an opinion in physics, published a short time earlier by someone else,[10] concerning which I do not want to say that I was in agreement, but rather that I

---

10. Galileo Galilei (1564–1642), Italian astronomer, mathematician, and physicist. His *Dialogue . . . on the Two Chief Systems of the World* (1632), in which he advanced the theory of the movement of the earth, occasioned the Inquisitors of the Holy Office to conduct a trial in Rome and to extort a retraction of that theory from Galileo. Descartes, who also advocated a theory of terrestrial motion, was not about to let Rome sin twice against philosophy. See Gilson, pp. 439–42; see also the letter *To Mersenne,* About Galileo's Condemnation (April 1634), AT I, 285–8, above.

had not noticed anything in it, before their censuring of it, that I could imagine to be prejudicial either to religion or to the state, nor, as a consequence, had I found anything that would have prevented me from writing it, had reason persuaded me of it; and this made me fear that there might likewise be found among my opinions one in which I had been mistaken, not withstanding the great care that I have always taken never to accept into my beliefs any new opinions for which I did not have very certain demonstrations and never to write anything that could turn to anyone's disadvantage. This was sufficient to make me change the resolution I had had to publish my opinions. For although the reasons for which I had earlier made the resolution were very strong, my inclination, which has always made me hate the business of writing books, immediately made me find enough other reasons to excuse me from it. And these reasons, both for and against, are such that not only do I have some interest in stating them here, but perhaps also the public has some interest in knowing them.

61   I had never made much of the things that came from my mind, and so long as I had reaped no other fruits from the method I am using except my own satisfaction regarding certain problems that pertain to the speculative sciences, or else my attempt at governing my moral conduct by means of the reasons which the method taught me, I believed I was under no obligation whatever to write anything about it. For as to moral conduct, everyone is so very full of his own viewpoint, that it would be possible to find as many reformers as heads, if anyone other than those God has established as rulers over his peoples or even those to whom he has given sufficient grace and zeal to be prophets were permitted to try to change anything here. And although my speculations pleased me very much, I believed that others also had their own, which perhaps pleased them more. But as soon as I had acquired some general notions regarding physics, and, beginning to test them in various particular difficulties, I had noticed where they could lead and how much they differ from the principles that have been in use up to the present, I believed I could not keep them hidden away without sinning grievously against the law that obliges us to procure, as much as is in our power, the common good of all men. For these notions made me see that it is possible to arrive at knowledge that would be very useful in life and that, in place of that specula-

62   tive philosophy taught in the schools, it is possible to find a practical philosophy, by means of which, knowing the force and the actions of fire, water, air, the stars, the heavens, and all the other bodies that surround us, just as distinctly as we know the various skills of our craftsmen, we might be able, in the same way, to use them for all the purposes for which they are appropriate, and thus render ourselves, as it were, masters and possessors of nature. This is desirable not only for the invention of an infinity of devices that would enable one to enjoy trouble-free the fruits of the earth and all the goods found there, but also principally for the maintenance of health, which unquestionably is the first good and the foundation of all the other goods of this life; for even the mind depends so greatly on the temperament and on the disposition of the organs of the body that, if it is possible to find some means to render men generally more wise and more adroit than they have been up until now, I believe that one should look for it in medicine. It is true that the medicine currently practiced contains few things

whose usefulness is so noteworthy; but without intending to ridicule it, I am sure there is no one, not even among those who make a profession of it, who would not admit that everything known in medicine is practically nothing in comparison with what remains to be known, and that one could rid oneself of an infinity of maladies, as much of the body as of the mind, and even perhaps also the frailty of old age, if one had a sufficient knowledge of their causes and of all the remedies that nature has provided us. For, having the intention of spending my entire   63
life in the search for so indispensable a science, and having found a path that seems to me such that, by following it, one ought infallibly to find this science, unless one is prevented from doing so either by the brevity of life or by a lack of experiments,[11] I judged there to be no better remedy against these two obstacles than to communicate faithfully to the public the entirety of what little I had found and to urge good minds to try to advance beyond this by contributing, each according to his inclination and ability, to the experiments that must be performed and also by communicating to the public everything they might learn, in order that, with subsequent inquirers beginning where their predecessors had left off, and thus, joining together the lives and labors of many, we might all advance together much further than a single individual could do on his own.

Moreover, I noticed, in regard to experiments, that they are the more necessary as one is more advanced in knowledge. For in the beginning it is better to make use only of those observations which present themselves to our senses of their own accord and which we could not ignore, provided we reflect, however so little, on them, rather than to search for unusual and contrived experiments. The reason for this is that these more unusual experiments often deceive one when one does not know yet the causes of the more common ones, and that the circumstances on which the unusual ones depend are almost always so particular and so minute that it is very difficult to notice them. But the order I have held to has been the following. First, I have tried to find in general the principles or first   64
causes of all that is or can be in the world, without considering anything but God alone, who created the world, and without deriving these principles from any other source but from certain seeds of truths that are naturally in our souls. After that I examined what were the first and most ordinary effects that could be deduced from these causes; and it seems to me that by this means I had found the heavens, stars, an earth, and even, on the earth, water, air, fire, minerals, and other such things that are the most common of all and the simplest, and, as a consequence, the easiest to know. Then, when I wanted to descend to those things which were more particular, so many different ones were presented to me that I did not believe it possible for the human mind to distinguish the forms or species of bodies that are on the earth from an infinity of others that could have been there had it been the will of God to have put them there, nor, as a consequence, to make them serviceable to us, unless we advance to the causes through the effects and make use of many particular observations. After this, passing my

---

11. *Expérience* is used by Descartes to refer to a wide range of activities, from simple observations to sophisticated scientific experiments. *Expérience* will be translated as "observations" or as "experiments," depending on the context.

mind again over all the objects that have ever presented themselves to my senses, I dare say I did not notice anything in them that I could not explain easily enough by means of the principles I had found. But I must also admit that the power of nature is so ample and so vast, and these principles are so simple and so general, that I notice hardly any particular effect without at once knowing that it can be
65   deduced in many different ways from them, and that ordinarily my greatest difficulty is to find in which of these ways it depends on them. For, to this end, I know of no other expedient at all except to search once more for some experiments which are such that their outcomes are not the same, if it is in one of these ways rather than in another that one ought to explain the outcome. As to the rest, I am now at the point where, it seems to me, I see quite well what approach one must take in order to make most of the experiments that can serve this purpose; but I also see that they are of such a kind and of so great a number that neither my adroitness nor my financial resources (even if I had a thousand times more than I have) would suffice for all of them; so that, according as I henceforth have the opportunity to perform more or fewer experiments, I shall also advance more or less in the knowledge of nature. That is what I meant to make known through the treatise I had written, and to show there so clearly the utility that the public could gain from such knowledge that I would oblige all those who desire the general well-being of men (that is to say, all those who really are virtuous, not just appearing to be so through false pretenses or merely by reputation) both to communicate those experiments they have already performed and to assist me in the search for those that remain to be made.

But since then other reasons have made me change my mind and think that I really ought to continue to write about all the things I judged to be of some importance, to the extent that I discovered the truth with respect to them, and to take the same care in regard to them as I would take if I wanted to have them
66   published. I did this as much to have all the more of an occasion to examine them well (since without doubt one always looks more carefully at what one believes must be seen by many than at what one does only for oneself; and often the things that have seemed to me to be true when I began to conceive them, have appeared false to me when I wanted to put them on paper), as in order not to lose any occasion to benefit the public, if I am able, and in order that, if my writings are worth anything, those who will have them after my death can thus use them as will be most fitting. But I must not in any way consent to their being published during my lifetime, so that neither the hostilities and the controversies to which they might be subject, nor even such reputation as they could gain for me, would give me any occasion for losing the time I have intended to use in instructing myself. For although it may be true that each man is obliged to secure as best he can the good of others, and that to be useful to no one is, strictly speaking, to be worthless, still it is also true that our concerns ought to extend further than to the present time, and that it is well to omit things that perhaps would yield some profit to those who are alive, when it is with the intention of doing other things that would yield even more profit to our posterity. In any event, I very much want people to understand that what little I have learned up until now is almost nothing in comparison to what I do not know and to what I do not despair of being

able to learn; for it is almost the same with those who little by little discover the truth in the sciences as it is with those who, upon beginning to acquire wealth, have less trouble making large acquisitions than they had had before, when they were poorer, in making very small ones. Or indeed, one can compare them to army commanders whose forces typically grow in proportion to their victories and who need more skill to maintain themselves after losing a battle than they do to take cities or provinces when they have won one. For it is truly to engage in battle, when one tries to overcome all the difficulties and errors that prevent us from arriving at the knowledge of the truth; and it is truly to lose a battle, when one accepts a false opinion touching on a matter that is at all general and important. And afterwards it requires much more skill to recover one's former position than to make great progress when one already has principles that are assured. For myself, if I have already found some truths in the sciences (and I hope the things contained in this volume will make people judge that I have found some of them), I can say that these are only things that result from and depend on five or six principal difficulties that I have surmounted and that I count as so many battles in which I have had fortune on my side. I will not even fear to say that I think I need to win only two or three more battles like them in order to succeed entirely in my plans, and that my age is not at all so advanced that, in the ordinary course of nature, I might not still have enough time to bring this about. But I believe I am all the more obliged to manage well the time remaining to me, the more hope I have of being able to use it well; and doubtless I would have many opportunities to lose time, had I published the foundations of my physics. For although they are nearly all so evident that it is necessary only to understand them in order to believe them, and although there has not been a single one for which I did not believe I could give demonstrations, nevertheless, because it is impossible for them to be in agreement with all the diverse opinions of other men, I foresee that I would often be distracted by the disputes they would engender.

One could say that these disputes might be useful, as much in order that I be made aware of my faults, as in order that, if I had anything worthwhile to say, others would by this means have greater understanding of it, and that, since many can see more than one man alone, these others, by beginning right now to use it, might also help me with their discoveries. But, although I recognize that I am extremely prone to err and that I almost never rely on the first thoughts that come to me, still the experience I have of the objections that can be made against me prevents me from expecting any profit from them. For I have already often put to the test the judgments of those I took to be my friends, as well as of some others whom I took to be indifferent, and even of those too whose maliciousness and envy I knew would try hard enough to discover what affection would hide from my friends. But it has rarely happened that an objection has been raised against me that I had not at all foreseen, unless it was very far removed from my subject; thus I have almost never found any critic of my opinions who did not seem to me to be either less rigorous or less unbiased than myself. Nor have I ever observed that, through the method of disputations practiced in the schools, any truth has been discovered that had until then been unknown. For, so long as each person in the dispute aims at winning, he is more concerned with making much out of probability than with weighing the arguments on each side; and those who have long been good advocates are not, on that account, afterwards better judges.

As to the utility that others might gain from the communication of my thoughts, it could not be so very great, given that I have not yet at all taken them so far that there is no need to add many things to them before applying them to actual practice. And I think I can say without vanity that, if there is anyone who is capable of doing this, it must be myself rather than someone else: not that there could not be in the world many minds incomparably greater than mine, but because one cannot conceive a thing so well and make it one's own when one learns it from someone else as one can when one discovers it for oneself. This is so true in this matter that, although I have often explained some of my opinions to people with good minds, who, while I spoke to them, seemed to understand them quite distinctly, nevertheless, when they repeated them, I noticed that they had almost always changed them in such a way that I could no longer acknowl-
70   edge them as mine. In this connection, I am very happy here to ask our descendants never to believe the things people tell them came from me, unless I myself have divulged them. And I am in no way surprised by the extravagances attributed to all those ancient philosophers whose writings we do not have; nor do I judge, for that reason, that their thoughts have been so very unreasonable, given that they were the greatest minds of their time, but only that their thoughts have been poorly reported to us. For one also sees that it has almost never happened that any of their followers had ever surpassed them; and I am sure that the most impassioned of those who now follow Aristotle would believe themselves fortunate, if they had as much knowledge of nature as he had, even if it were on the condition that they would never have any more. They are like ivy, which never stretches any higher than the trees supporting it, and which often even descends again after it has reached their tops; for it seems to me that they too are redescending, that is, they are making themselves somehow less knowledgeable than if they abstained from studying; not content with knowing all that is intelligibly explained in their author, they want in addition to find the solutions there to many difficulties about which he says nothing and about which he has perhaps never thought. Still, their manner of philosophizing is very convenient for those who have only very mediocre minds, for the obscurity of the distinctions and the principles they make use of is the reason why they can speak about all things as
71   boldly as if they knew them, and why they can uphold everything they say against the most subtle and the most adroit, without anyone's having the means of convincing them that they are mistaken. In this they seem to me like a blind man, who, in order to fight without a disadvantage against someone who is sighted, had made his opponent go into the depths of some very dark cellar. And I may say that these people have an interest in my refraining from publishing the principles of the philosophy I use; for my principles being as very simple and very evident as they are, I would, by publishing them, be doing almost the same as if I were to open some windows and make some daylight enter that cellar they had gone into in order to fight. But even the best minds have no reason for wanting to know these principles; for if they want to know how to speak about all things and to acquire the reputation for being learned, they will achieve their

objective more easily by contenting themselves with probability, which can be found without great difficulty in all sorts of matters, than by seeking the truth, which can only be discovered little by little in some and which, when it is a question of speaking about other matters, obliges one to confess frankly that one is ignorant of them. But if they prefer the knowledge of some few truths to the vanity of appearing to be ignorant of nothing, as no doubt it is really preferable to do, and if they want to follow a plan similar to mine, they do not, on that score, need me to say anything more except what I have already said in this discourse. For, if they are capable of advancing further than I have, then *a fortiori* they are also capable of finding for themselves all that I think I have found. Inasmuch as I have never examined anything except in an orderly manner, it is certain that what still remains for me to discover is of itself more difficult and more hidden   72
than what I have heretofore been able to discover; and they would take much less pleasure in learning it from me than from themselves. Moreover, the habit they will acquire of seeking first the easy things and then of passing little by little by degrees to other more difficult ones, will serve them better than all my instructions could do. As for myself, I am convinced that, if I had been taught from my youth all the truths for which I have since then sought demonstrations, and if I had not had any difficulty in learning them, I might perhaps have never known any other truths, and at least I would never have acquired the habit and facility I think I have for always finding new truths, to the extent that I apply myself in searching for them. And, in a word, if there is any task in the world that could not be accomplished so well by anyone else but the same person who began it, it is the one on which I am working.

It is true that, with respect to experiments that can help here, one man alone cannot suffice to perform them all, but neither can he usefully employ hands other than his own, except those of craftsmen, or such people as he could pay and whom the hope of gain, which is a very effective means, would cause to do precisely what he ordered them to do. For, as to volunteers, who, out of curiosity or a desire to learn, might offer themselves in order perhaps to help him (aside from the fact that they usually make more promises than they produce achievements, and merely make fine proposals, none of which will come to anything), they would inevitably want to be paid by the explanation of various difficulties, or at   73
least by compliments and useless conversations, which could not cost him so little time that he would not lose by it. And as to the experiments that others have already performed, even if these people did want to communicate them to him (something those who call them "secrets" would never do), they are for the most part composed of so many details and superfluous ingredients that it would be very hard for him to discern the truth in them; besides, he would find almost all of them to be so badly explained or even so false, because those who have done them strove to make them appear to be in conformity with their principles, that, if there were among them some experiments that might serve him, they could not be worth the time he would need to spend in selecting them. In this way, if there were someone in the world whom one assuredly knows to be capable of finding the greatest things and the things as beneficial to the public as possible, and whom, for this cause, other men were to exert themselves to help in every way

to succeed in his plans, I do not see that they could do a thing for him except to make a donation toward the expenses of the experiments he would need and, for the rest, to prevent his leisure from being wasted by the importunity of anyone. But, although I do not presume so much of myself as to want to promise anything out of the ordinary, or feast on such vain thoughts as to imagine that the public ought to be especially interested in my plans, I do not have so base a soul that I *74* would want to accept from anyone any favor that one might believe I had not deserved.

All these considerations taken together were the reason why, three years ago, I did not at all want to divulge the treatise I had on hand, and even why I had made a resolution not to make public during my lifetime any other treatise which was so general or on the basis of which one could understand the foundations of my physics. But since then there have been yet again two other reasons that have obliged me to place here certain particular essays and to render to the public some account of my actions and my plans. The first is that, if I failed to do so, many who knew of the intention I once had to have certain writings published could imagine that the reasons for which I am abstaining from doing so were more to my disadvantage than they are. For although I do not love glory excessively—indeed, if I dare say so, I hate it inasmuch as I judge it to be contrary to the tranquillity I esteem above all things—still, I have also never tried to hide my actions as if they were crimes, nor have I taken many precautions so as not to be known. This is the case as much because I would have believed I would be doing myself an injustice, as because it would have given me a certain kind of disquiet, which again would have been contrary to the perfect peace of mind I am seeking. And because, having always been thus indifferent about the concern over being known or not known, I could not prevent my acquiring some type of reputation, I thought I ought to do my best at least to spare myself from having a bad *75* one. The other reason that has obliged me to write this is as follows: I saw more and more every day the delay that the plan I have of self-instruction is suffering because of an infinity of experiments of which I have need and which it is impossible for me to perform without the help of others. And although I do not flatter myself so much as to hope that the public will become greatly taken with my interests, still I also do not want to fail myself so much as to give those who will survive me cause to reproach me one day on the grounds that I could have left them many far better things than I had done, if I had not so badly neglected making them understand how they could contribute to my plans.

And I thought that it was easy to choose certain matters that, without being subjected to much controversy or obliging me to declare more of my principles than I desire, would nevertheless allow me to show quite clearly what I can or cannot do in the sciences. I cannot say whether I have been successful in this, and I do not at all want to prejudice the judgments of anyone in speaking for myself about my writings; but I shall be very happy if they are examined, and, in order to have more of an opportunity to do this, I am imploring all who have any objections to make against them to take the trouble to send them to my publisher, and, on being advised about them by him, I shall try at the same time to append my reply to the objections; and by this means, seeing both of them together, readers will judge the truth all the more easily. For I promise never to make long replies to them, but only to admit my errors very candidly, if I recognize them, or, even *76* if I cannot perceive any, to say simply what I believe to be required for the defense of what I have written, without adding to it an explanation of any new material, in order not to become endlessly involved in one issue after another.

And, if any of those things about which I have spoken at the beginning of the *Dioptrics* and the *Meteors* are shocking at first glance because I call them "suppositions" and seem to lack the inclination to prove them, I entreat the reader to have the patience to read the whole thing with attention; and I hope he will find himself satisfied with it. For it seems to me that the reasonings follow each other there in such a way that, just as the last are demonstrated by means of the first, which are their causes, so these first are reciprocally demonstrated by means of the last, which are their effects. And one must not imagine that I am here committing the fallacy that logicians call a "circle"; for, experience rendering the majority of these effects very certain, the causes from which I deduce these effects serve not so much to prove them as to explain them; on the contrary, it is rather the case that the causes are what is proved by the effects. And I have called them "suppositions" only to make it understood that I think I can deduce them from these first truths that I have explained above. But I wanted expressly not to do so, in order to prevent certain minds, who imagine that they know in one day all that someone else has thought about for twenty years as soon as he has said but two or three words to them about it, and who are the more subject to error and the less capable of truth, the more penetrating and lively they are, from being able to take this occasion to build some extravagant philosophy on what they *77* believe are my principles, and in order to prevent me from being blamed for it. For as to the opinions that are entirely mine, I do not apologize for their being new, since, if one considers well the arguments for them, I am sure that one will find them so simple and so in conformity with common sense that they will seem less extraordinary and less strange than any others one could have on the same subjects. Nor do I pride myself at all on being the first discoverer of any of them; rather, I pride myself on never having accepted them because they have or have not been said by others, but only because reason has persuaded me of them.

If craftsmen cannot immediately carry out the invention explained in the *Dioptrics*,[12] I do not believe one could say, on that account, that it is bad; for, inasmuch as skill and practice are needed to make and adjust the machines I have described, without any detail being overlooked there, I would be no less astonished if they were to succeed on the first try than if someone were able to learn in one day to play the lute with distinction simply because he had been given a good score. And if I write in French, the language of my country, rather than in Latin, the language of my teachers, it is because I am hoping that those who use only their natural reason in all its purity will judge my opinions better than those who believe only in old books. And as to those who combine good sense with study, whom alone I wish to have as my judges, they will not at all, I am sure, be *78*

12. This is a reference to Descartes's method of cutting lenses in the *Dioptrics*, Discourse 10, AT VI, 211–27.

so partial to Latin that they refuse to listen to my reasons because I explain them in the vernacular.

As to the rest, I do not at all want to speak here in detail about the future progress I hope to make in the sciences, or to involve vis-à-vis the public in any promise that I am not assured of keeping; rather I shall say simply that I have resolved to spend the rest of my life on nothing but trying to acquire some knowledge of nature which is such that one could draw from it rules for medicine that are more reliable than those we have had to the present; and that my inclination puts me at such a great distance from all other sorts of plans, principally from those that can be useful to some only by being harmful to others, that if circumstances were to force me to busy myself with them, I do not at all believe I could succeed. About this I am here making a declaration which I know very well cannot serve to make me eminent in the world, but I also have no desire to be so; and I shall always hold myself obliged more to those by whose favor I enjoy my leisure without hindrance than to those who might offer me the most honorable positions on earth.

END

III

CORRESPONDENCE (1637–1641)

To Silhon,[1] Existence of God and of the Soul (March 1637)

I confess that, as you have remarked, there is a great weakness in the writing you $I, 353$
have seen, and that I have not sufficiently developed the arguments by which I
think I prove that there is nothing in the world in itself more evident and more
certain than the existence of God and of the human soul, so as to make them simple for everyone. But I did not dare to attempt to do this, since I would have had
to explain at great length the strongest arguments of the skeptics, in order to show
that there is no material thing of whose existence we can be assured, and by the
same means to accustom the reader to detach his thought from sensible things.
Then I would have had to show that whoever thus doubts everything material,
cannot at the same time doubt his own existence. From this it follows that he, that
is to say, the soul, is a being or substance which is in no way corporeal, and
whose nature is only to think, and also that the soul is the first thing we can know
with certainty. If you spend long enough time on this meditation, you acquire little by little a very clear, and if I may say so, an intuitive knowledge of intellectual nature in general, the idea of which, considered without limitation, is what
represents God to us, or when limited, is the idea of an angel or a human mind.
But it is not possible to understand fully what I said afterward about the existence
of God, if you have not begun in this way, as I have made sufficiently plain on
page 38.[2]

But I was afraid that this approach, which would at first have seemed to intro- 354
duce the opinion of the skeptics, would trouble weaker minds, chiefly because I
was writing in the vernacular. So I did not dare to say even the little that is on
page 32[3] without some warning. And as for you, sir, and your like, who are more
intelligent, I hoped that if such people took the trouble, not only to read, but also
to meditate in order on the same things that I said I had meditated on, stopping
long enough on each point, to see whether or not I had been mistaken, they would
draw the same conclusions I had drawn. I will be happy, at the first moment of
leisure I have, to make an effort to try to clarify this matter further.

Selections on pp. 83–96 translated by Marjorie Grene and Roger Ariew.

1. Jean de Silhon (1596–1667), a French statesman and moralist, was a friend of
Descartes. Along with their friendship, Descartes and de Silhon shared an anti-skeptical
apologetic program. In his 1626 treatise, *Les deux vérités (The Two Truths)*, de Silhon
combated skepticism by attempting to establish that God exists and that our souls are
immortal. An English translation of relevant selections from the work is available in
Ariew, Cottingham, and Sorell, pp. 176–200.

2. *Discourse on Method,* AT VI, 37.

3. *Discourse on Method,* AT VI, 31.

To Plempius for Fromondus,[4] Atomism and Mechanism (October 3, 1637)

I, 413 The very distinguished and learned Dr. Fromondus most opportunely reminds me at the beginning of his objections of the fable of Ixion.[5] He not only does well to warn me of embracing useless and obscure opinions in the place of truth— which insofar as I am able, I profess I wish to do and have always done until now—but he also does well in that he himself, when he claims to be impugning my philosophy, is only refuting that inane philosophy conflated of atoms and the void, usually ascribed to Democritus and Epicurus, and others like it, which have nothing to do with me.

And first, when he says about pp. 46 and 47[6] that "such noble actions as vision and the like could not be produced by so ignoble and brutish a cause as heat," he supposes me to think that brutes see exactly as we do, that is, in being aware of and knowing that they see; this is believed to have been the opinion of Epicurus and is even now the common opinion of almost everyone. However, all the way up to p. 60,[7] I expressly showed that brutes do not see as we do when we are aware that we are seeing. Rather, they see as we do when our mind has been diverted; yet the images of external objects are painted on the retinas of our eyes, and furthermore the impressions made by these on our optic nerves

414 may determine our members to certain movements, although we are utterly unaware of them. Moreover, in this case we move in no other way than do automata, about which no one would say that heat did not suffice in initiating their movements. [. . .]

416 When he says about p. 50[8] that "there would be no less heat required in the heart than in a furnace, so that the drops of blood would be rarefied rapidly enough to make the heart expand," it seems he has not noticed how milk, oil, and almost all other fluids that are placed on the fire at first expand very slowly. But when they reach a certain degree of heat, they boil up in an instant, so that unless they are removed from the heat, or at least the vessel containing them is uncovered, allowing the spirits that are the principal cause of that rarefaction to escape, the greatest part of them overflows and escapes into the ashes. And the degree of heat can be different, according to the differing nature of the fluid, so that there are even some that are rarefied although they are scarcely tepid. If he had observed that, he could easily have judged that the blood contained in the veins of each animal could easily reach nearly the degree of heat that it would have to acquire in the heart, if it were to be rarefied instantaneously there.

---

4. Libertius Fromondus (1587–1653) and Plempius Vopiscus (1601–1671) were professors (of philosophy and of medicine, respectively) at the University of Louvain.

5. Fromondus had referred to the story of Ixion, who thought he was holding Juno in his arms when he was embracing only a cloud.

6. AT VI, 46.

7. AT VI, 60.

8. AT VI, 50.

But nowhere does he show more plainly that he has embraced the clouds of Democritean philosophy, instead of grasping my Juno, than in his note to p. 4 of the *Dioptrics*[9] where he denies that I am explaining correctly "how a luminous body transmits its rays in an instant, by comparing this with a blind man's stick, since," he says, "the ray which leaves the solar body should rather be compared *417* with an arrow shot from a bow, which traverses the air successively, not in an instant." Now isn't he here taking Leucippus or Epicurus instead of me—or certainly Lucretius, who, if memory does not fail me, speaks somewhere in his poem of "the shafts of the sun"? As for me, since I never suppose a vacuum anywhere, but on the contrary have explicitly said that all the spaces from the sun to our bodies are full of a body that is indeed very fluid, but for that very reason more continuous (and which I have called subtle matter), I do not see what can be objected to the comparisons either with the stick or with the vat of pressed grapes, both of which I used to explain the instantaneous transmission of rays. And if he calls my philosophy "crude and gross" because I think that some body can easily penetrate the pores of a pane of glass, he ought to pardon me if I answer that I consider much crasser, and yet much less solid, that philosophy which denies that there are any pores in glass, because [those pores] are impervious to sound. For we see that, when curtains are placed in its way, sound is, if not wholly extinguished, at least greatly diminished and dulled. [. . .]

He is astonished that on p. 30[10] I do not recognize any sensation but that which *420* takes place in the brain. But all the physicians and surgeons will help me to persuade him of that: for they know that those who have recently had a limb amputated often continue to feel pain in those parts they no longer have. I once knew a girl who had a serious injury in her hand. When the surgeon came, they used to blindfold her, so that she would be treated more easily. The whole arm was amputated because of creeping gangrene, and bandages were put in its place, so that for several weeks afterward she did not know she had lost it. Still in the meantime she complained of various pains, now in the fingers, now in the wrist, now in the forearm, all of which she lacked. This was plainly due to the brachial nerves which formerly descended to those parts from the brain. Certainly this would not have happened if the sense of pain, or the sensation, as it is called, took place anywhere else than in the brain.

I do not understand what he is objecting to concerning pp. 159 and 163.[11] For if my philosophy seems too "crass" to him because, like mechanics, it considers only shapes and magnitudes and motions, he is condemning what I believe is to be most praiseworthy. That is what I myself prefer about my philosophy and what *421* I am proudest of, namely, that I use the kind of philosophizing in which there is no argument that is not mathematical and evident, and whose conclusions are confirmed by true experiments. Thus whatever I have concluded can be done, on the basis of my principles, really can be done, so long as actives are appropriately

9. AT VI, 85–6.

10. *Dioptrics*, AT VI, 110.

11. *Meteors*, AT VI, 233.

applied to passives. I am surprised he himself has not noticed that what has been practiced until now, mechanics, is nothing but a part of the true physics, which, because it could find no place with the vulgar philosophy, withdrew to the mathematicians. Thus this part of philosophy remains truer and less corrupt than others, since, because it relates to use and practice, those who make mistakes in it usually suffer by the loss of their expenses: so that if he condemns my style of philosophizing for its similarity to mechanics, this seems to me the same thing as if he were to condemn it because it is true.

To Vatier,[12] **On the** *Discourse* **(February 22, 1638)**

I, 558 I am delighted by the kindness you have done me, in examining so carefully my book of essays, and of letting me know your opinions with so much evidence of good will. In sending it to you I would have enclosed a letter, and would have taken that occasion of assuring you of my very humble service, had it not been that I hoped to let it pass anonymously. But since this plan did not succeed, I can only believe that it is rather the affection you have for the father than the merit of the child that causes the favorable reception it has had from you. And I am most particularly obliged to thank you. I do not know if it is because I flatter

559 myself in view of several things very much to my advantage that are contained in the two letters I have received from you, but I will tell you frankly, that of all those who have obliged me by letting me know the judgment they made of my writings, there has been no one, it seems to me, who has done me as much justice as you have, I mean, so favorable, without bias, and with more pertinent knowledge. Incidentally, I am surprised that your two letters could follow one another so quickly; for I received them almost at the same time, and seeing the first, I was persuaded that I would have to wait for the second until after your vacation on Saint Luke's Day.

But in order to reply punctually to your letters, I will say first, that my plan was not at all to teach the whole of my method in the discourse in which I propose it, but only to say enough about it to permit the judgment that the new opinions that would be found in the *Dioptrics* and in the *Meteors* had not been conceived frivolously, and that they were perhaps worth the trouble of being examined. Nor could I show the use of that method in the three treatises that I included, since it prescribes an order of investigation which is different enough from the order I believed I must use in order to explain them. However, I have given a sample of it in describing the rainbow,[13] and if you take the trouble to reread it, I hope that it will satisfy you better than it did the first time. For the topic is difficult enough in itself. But what made me append the three treatises to

560 the discourse that precedes them is that I thought they might suffice to bring it about that those who examined them carefully and compared them with what had

---

12. Antoine Vatier (1596–1659) was a French Jesuit and professor at the College of La Flèche.

13. *Meteors*, Discourse 8, AT VI, 325–44.

previously been written on the same topics, would judge that I was using some method other than the common one, and that it was not among the worst.

It is true that I was too obscure in what I wrote about the existence of God in the treatise *On Method,* and though it is the most important, I confess that it is the least worked out section in the whole work. This comes in part from the fact that I had not decided to add it until the end, and when the publisher was pressing me. But the chief reason for its obscurity comes from the fact that I did not dare to expound in detail the arguments of the skeptics, or to say all the things that are necessary *to lead the mind away from the senses.* For it is not possible to know well the certainty and evidence of the arguments that I use to prove the existence of God, except by recalling distinctly those that make us notice the uncertainty of all the knowledge we have of material things. And these thoughts do not seem to me proper to include in a book I wanted to be intelligible in some way even to women, and yet to have more subtle minds also provided with sufficient matter to command their attention. I also admit that, as you have rightly noticed, this obscurity comes in part from the fact that I assumed that certain notions which the habit of thought has made familiar and evident to me, must be so to everyone. For example, that since our ideas cannot receive their forms or *561* their being except from some external objects or from ourselves, they cannot represent any reality or perfection not in those objects or else in us—and other similar notions. I have decided to give some clarification of these points in a second printing.

I did indeed think that what I said I had put in my treatise *On Light*[14] concerning the creation of the universe would be incredible. For only ten years ago I would not myself have wanted to believe that the human mind could have achieved such knowledge, if anyone else had written it. But my conscience, and the force of truth, have prevented me from fearing to advance a topic that I thought I could not omit without betraying my own cause, and for which I already have sufficient witnesses. Moreover, if the part of my physics that was finished and prepared for publication some time ago should ever see the light of day, I hope that our descendants will not be able to doubt what I say.

I am under obligation to you for the care you have taken in examining my opinion about the movement of the heart. If your physician has some objections to make, I shall be happy to receive them, and will not fail to reply. It is not yet a week since I received seven or eight objections from a professor of medicine at Louvain, who is a friend of mine.[15] I have sent him two sheets of replies, and I should hope that I could receive more of them in the same way, touching on all the difficulties that come up in which I have tried to explain. I would not fail to reply to them carefully, and I am convinced that I could do that without dis- *562* obliging any of those who had proposed them to me. It is something that several people together could do more easily than an individual, and there is no one who could do it better than those of your Society. I should take it as a very great honor

---

14. That is, *The World or Treatise on Light.*
15. Namely, Plempius.

and favor if they would take the trouble to do it. It would be without doubt the shortest way to discover all the errors or the truths of my writings.

As for what concerns light, if you attend to the third page of the *Dioptrics*,[16] you will see that I have there said expressly that I will speak only hypothetically. And in fact, because the treatise that contains the whole body of my physics bears the title *On Light,* and since that is the thing that I explain the most fully and the most ingeniously of all, I did not want to treat further the same things I had dealt with there, but only to give some idea of it by comparisons and hints, insofar as that seemed necessary for the subject of the *Dioptrics.*

I am obliged to you for saying that you are glad I have not let myself be anticipated by others in the publication of my thought. But that is something I have never had any fear of. For apart from the fact that I care very little whether I am the first or the last to describe the things I write, provided only that they are true, all my opinions are so closely joined together and depend so heavily on one another that it would not be possible to appropriate any of them without knowing them all. I beg you not to defer telling me of the difficulties you find in what
563   I have written about refraction, or anything else. For to wait for my more particular opinions about light to be published might perhaps be to wait a long time. As to what I supposed at the beginning of my *Meteors,* I could not demonstrate it *a priori* without giving the whole of my physics. But the observations I have deduced necessarily from it, and which cannot be deduced in the same way from any other principles, seem to me to demonstrate it well enough *a posteriori.* I had indeed foreseen that this way of writing would at first shock the readers, and I believe that I could easily have remedied this simply by removing the title of assumptions from the things I first talked about, and stating them only to the extent that I could give some arguments to prove them. But I will tell you frankly that I have chosen this way of proposing my thoughts because, believing that I could deduce them in order from the first principles of my metaphysics, I wanted to neglect all other sorts of proofs. Besides, I wanted to try whether the mere exposition of the truth would suffice to induce persuasion, without mixing in any disputes or refutations of contrary opinions. Those of my friends who have read most carefully my treatises on dioptrics and on the meteors assure me that I have succeeded in this. For although at the start they found no less difficulty than did others, nevertheless after they had read and reread the treatises three or four times, they said they no longer found anything that seemed able to be called into doubt. To be sure, it is not always necessary to have *a priori* arguments to per-
564   suade people of a truth. And Thales, or whoever it was, who first said that the moon receives its light from the sun, no doubt gave no other proof than this: that by assuming it, one very easily explains all the different phases of the moon's light. This was sufficient to bring it about that, since then, this opinion has spread without contradiction throughout the world. And the interconnection of my thoughts is such that I dare to hope my principles will be found to be as well proved by the consequence I draw from them, once they have been sufficiently

---

16. AT VI, 83.

noticed to become familiar, and to be considered all together, as the borrowed light of the moon is proved by its increases and decreases.

I have no further reply to make to you except about the publication of my physics and metaphysics, concerning which I can tell you in one word, that I desire it as much as or more than anyone, but nevertheless subject to conditions without which it would be imprudent to desire it. And I will also tell you that I do not fear at all, basically, that anything contrary to the faith can be found there. For, on the contrary, I flatter myself that the faith has never been so strongly supported by human arguments—particularly transubstantiation, which the Calvinists consider impossible to explain by ordinary philosophy, and is very easy to explain by mine. But I do not see any sign that the conditions which can oblige me to do this are coming about, at least for a long time. And being content on my side to do all that I consider to be my duty, I submit myself for the rest to the providence that rules the world. For, knowing that it is providence that has given me the small beginnings of which you have seen the essays, I hope that *565* it will give me the grace to finish, if that is useful for its glory, and if it is not, I wish to abstain from desiring it. For the rest, I assure you that the sweetest fruit I have received until now from what I have had printed is the approbation that you were kind enough to give me in your letter. For it is particularly dear and agreeable to me, since it comes from a person of your merit and of your cloth, and from the very place where I have had the happiness of receiving all the instructions of my youth, and which is the home of my masters, toward whom I will never be lacking in gratitude.

To Regius,[17] Knowledge of the Infinite (May 24, 1640)

I am most indebted to you and M. Emilius for reading and amending the writing *III, 63* I sent you.[18] For I see that you did not even refuse to correct the punctuation and orthography. But you would have made me even more indebted to you, if you had corrected something in the words and thoughts. For however small these had *64* been, I would have entertained the hope that what was left was less faulty. But now I fear that you may have withheld your criticism because too much criticism was needed or the whole needed to be deleted.

As to your objections: in the first you say: "that it is from the fact that there is in us some wisdom, power, goodness, quantity, etc., that we form the idea of infinite, or at least of indefinite, wisdom, power, goodness and the other perfections that are attributed to God, as well as the idea of an infinite quantity." I readily concede all of this, and am entirely convinced that there is in us no idea of God not formed in this manner. But the whole force of my argument is that I claim I cannot be of such a nature that, by thinking, I can extend to infinity those perfections,

---

17. Henricus Regius (1598–1679), professor of medicine at the University of Utrecht (1638 on), was one of Descartes's first followers.

18. Antonius Emilius (1589–1666) was a Dutch natural philosopher. The writing Descartes sent to Regius and Emilius was a manuscript of the *Meditations*.

which in me are minute, unless we have our origin from a being, in whom they are actually infinite. Nor, from the inspection of a very small quantity, or of a finite body, could I conceive of an indefinite quantity unless the world were indeed, or at least could be, of indefinite magnitude.

In your second objection you say: "The truth of axioms that are clearly and distinctly understood is manifest in itself." This too I concede, while they are clearly and distinctly understood, since mind is of such a nature, that it cannot refrain from assenting to what is clearly understood. But since we often remember conclusions that we have deduced from such premises, even if we are not attending to the premises themselves, I say that then, if we are ignorant of God, we can imagine that these are uncertain, even though we recall that they were deduced from clear principles. For perhaps our nature is such that we err even in what is most evident. Hence, even at the time when we deduced them from those principles, we did not have *scientific knowledge* of them, but only a *conviction.* These two I distinguish as follows: it is *conviction*, when there remains any reason whatsoever that could impel us to doubt it; but *scientific knowledge* is an opinion produced by reason, so strong that it could never be shaken by any stronger conviction. Those who are ignorant of God have no such knowledge. However, as for one who has understood clearly the arguments that persuade us that God exists, and that he cannot be a deceiver, even if he is no longer attending to those arguments, as long as he remembers this conclusion: *God is not a deceiver*, there will remain in him not only the conviction, but true scientific knowledge of this, as well as of all other conclusions, the arguments for which he recalls having once clearly perceived.

Further, you say in your last objections (which, when I received them yesterday, reminded me that I ought to reply to the earlier ones): "all the rashness of hasty judgment depends on the temperament of the body, whether acquired or innate." This I can in no way admit, since it would undermine freedom and the amplitude of our will, which can correct such rashness. Or if it does not do this, the error that arises in this way is a certain privation with respect to us, but with respect to God a mere negation. [. . .]

65

To Colvius,[19] On Augustine and the *Cogito* (November 14, 1640)

III, 247   You have obliged me by bringing to my notice the passage of Saint Augustine which bears some relation to my "I think, therefore I am."[20] Today I have been to read it at the library of this city,[21] and I do indeed find that he makes use of it to prove the certainty of our being, and then to show that there is in us a kind of image of the Trinity, in that we exist, we know that we exist, and we love this

---

19. Andreas Colvius (1596–1676) was a Dutch minister.

20. Augustine, *The City of God,* 11, chap. 26.

21. Leiden.

being and the knowledge that is in us. On the other hand, I use it to make it known that this *I* who is thinking is an *immaterial substance*, and has nothing in it that is corporeal. These are two very different things. It is something so simple   *248* and natural in itself to infer that one exists from the fact that one is doubting, that it might have come from anybody's pen. But I am still glad to have come together with Saint Augustine, if only to shut the mouths of the little minds who have tried to quibble with that principle. The little I have written on metaphysics is already on its way to Paris, where I hope it will be printed. What I have here is a rough copy so full of crossings out that I could barely read it myself. That is why I cannot offer it to you. But as soon as it is printed, I will take pains to send you one of the first copies, since it pleases you to do me the favor of wishing to read it, and I will be very glad to learn your judgment of it.

To Mersenne, Immortality of the Soul (December 24, 1640)

I received your letters an hour or two before the messenger was to return. That is   *III, 263* why I will not be able to reply punctually to everything this time. But since the difficulty that you propose about the *conarium*[22] seems to be the most pressing, and since the honor afforded me by the person who wants to defend publicly what I have touched on in my *Dioptrics*[23] obliges me to try to satisfy him, I do not wish to wait for the next trip to tell you that the pituitary gland does indeed have some relation to the pineal gland, in that it is also situated between the carotids and in the straight line by which the spirits come from the heart to the brain. But for all that there is no reason to suspect that it has the same use, since it is not, like the pineal gland, in the brain, but beneath it, and entirely separate from the mass of the brain in a concavity of the spheroid bone specially made to receive it, even below the *dura mater,* if I remember correctly. Besides, it is entirely immobile, and we experience, when we imagine, that the seat of the common sense, that is to say the part of the brain in which the soul exercises all its principal operations, must be mobile. But it is no wonder that the pituitary gland is found where it is, between the heart and the *conarium,* since there it encounters a sufficient quantity of small arteries, which make up the *plexus*   *264* *mirabilis,* and which do not at all reach to the brain. For it is, so to speak, a general rule through the whole body that there are glands where several branches of veins or arteries meet. Nor is it any wonder that the carotids send out several branches in that place. For this is necessary in order to nourish the bones and other parts, and also to separate the heavier parts of the blood from the more subtle parts, which are the only ones that rise through the straightest branches of the carotids, right into the brain, where the *conarium* is. You must not in the least conceive of this separation as occurring otherwise than *by mechanical means,*

---

22. That is, the pineal gland.

23. AT VI, 129. The person referred to is Christophe Villiers (1595–1661), a physician from Sens who wrote some comments about the pineal gland that Mersenne transmitted to Descartes.

just as we see that if reeds and foam are floating in a torrent that divides somewhere into two branches, all the reeds and foam will go into the branch in which
the water flows less in a straight line. But there is good reason that the *conarium*
resembles a gland, since the principal office of all the glands is to receive the subtlest parts of the blood emitted by the surrounding vessels, and its office is to
receive the animal spirits in the same way. And since there is no solid part in the
whole brain that is single, it follows necessarily that it is the seat of the common
sense, that is to say, of thought, and consequently of the soul. For the one cannot
be separated from the other. Or else we would have to maintain that the soul is
not immediately united to any solid part of the body, but only to the animal spirits that are in its concavities, and that they enter and leave continually like the
265   water of a river—and that would be considered too absurd. Further, the situation
of the *conarium* is such that we can easily understand how the images that come
from the two eyes, or the sounds that enter the two ears, etc., can be united at the
place where it is. They could not do this in the concavities, except in the middle
one, or in the passage under the *conarium*. But that would not suffice, since these
concavities are in no way distinct from the others, in which the images are necessarily double. If I can do anything else for the person who proposed this, I beg
you to assure him that I will do all I can to satisfy him.

As to my metaphysics, you put me under great obligation by the care you are
taking of it, and I leave it entirely to you to correct or alter anything you judge
appropriate there. But I am astonished that you promise me the objections of various theologians in a week, since I am convinced that it would take much more
time to notice all that there is in it. And the person who made the objections at
the end thought the same. He is a priest of Alkmaar who does not want to be
named.[24] That is why if his name occurs anywhere I ask you to delete it. It will
also be necessary, if you please, to instruct the printer to change the numbers in
his objections, where the pages of the *Meditations* are cited, in order to make
them agree with the printed pages.

266   As to what you say, that I have not included a word on the immortality of the
soul, you should not be astonished. For I would not know how to demonstrate
that God cannot annihilate the soul, but only that it is of a nature entirely distinct
from that of the body, and consequently that it is not naturally subject to die with
it, which is all that is required to establish religion. And that is also all that I set
myself to prove.

Nor should you find it strange that I do not prove, in my Second Meditation,
that the soul is really distinct from the body, and that I am satisfied with making
it conceived of without the body, since I do not yet have at that point the premises from which one could draw that conclusion. But I prove it afterward, in the
Sixth Meditation.

And it is to be noted, in all that I write, that I do not follow the order of the
topics, but only that of the arguments. That is to say, I do not in the least undertake to say in one and the same place all that pertains to a topic, since it would

---

24. Caterus, author of the *First Set of Objections*.

be impossible for me to prove it well, there being arguments that have to be elicited, from one another, much further on. But in reasoning in order from *the simpler to the more difficult,* I deduce what I can, now for one topic, now for another. This is, in my view, the true path for finding and explaining the truth. And as for the order of topic, it is good only for those whose arguments are all isolated, and can be used as well for one difficulty as for another. Thus I do not   *267* consider it in any way appropriate, or even possible, to insert in my *Meditations* the reply to the objections that can be made to them. For that would interrupt their sequence, and would even remove the force of my arguments, which depend principally on the ability to turn one's thought away from sensible things, from which most of the objections would be drawn. But I have put those of Caterus at the end, in order to show the place where others could also be, if any arrive.

But I will be happy if people take their time making objections; for it does not matter much if this treatise is not published for two or three years. And since the copy of it is very badly written, and can be seen only by one person at a time, it seems to me that it would not be bad if twenty or thirty exemplars were printed in advance. I will be happy to pay whatever that costs. I would have had it done here, but for the fact that there is no publisher I can trust, and because I did not want the ministers of this country to see it before our theologians.

As for the style, I should be glad if it were better than it is. But, except for faults of grammar, if there are any, or what may sound like Gallicisms, as in *in dubium ponere* [to place in doubt] for *revocare* [to revoke or retract], I am afraid nothing can be changed without changing the sense—as in these words: *nempe quicquid hactenus et maxime verum admisis, vel a sensibus vel per sensus accepi* [whatever I had admitted until now as most true I received either from the senses or through the senses], if *falsum esse* [to be false] were added, as you suggest, that would change the sense entirely, which is that all I received from the sense,   *268* or through the senses, was all that till now I believed to be the most true. To put *erutis fundamentis* in place of *suffosis* would not do great harm, since both are Latin and have pretty much the same meaning.[25] But it still seems to me that the latter, having no meaning except the one in which I took it, is also much better than the other expression, which has several meanings.

In a week I will possibly send you an abstract of the principal points that touch on God and the soul. This can be printed ahead of the *Meditations,* so that people can see where they will find these. For otherwise I do see that some will be annoyed at not finding in one single place everything they are looking for. I will be glad if M. Desargues[26] is also one of my judges, if he wishes to take the trouble, and I have more trust in him than in three theologians. Nor will it displease me at all if a number of objections are made to me, for I promise myself that they will help to make the truth better known, and, by the grace of God, I am not afraid of not being able to answer them satisfactorily. The time constrains me to finish.

---

25. They both mean demolishing or undermining the foundations.

26. Girard Desargues (1593–1662) was a geometer.

To Mersenne, The Aim of the *Meditations* and the Context for the *Principles* (December 31, 1640)

III, 271   I did not receive any of your letters on this delivery; but because I did not have the time last week to reply to everything, I will add here what I had omitted. And first, I am sending you an abstract of my Metaphysics which, if you approve, can be placed ahead of the six Meditations. After the preceding words *"will draw the*

272   *same conclusions from them that I do,"* should be added: *"but because in the following six Meditations etc."* In the abstract it will be possible to see everything I have proved about the immortality of the soul, and everything I can add to it in publishing my physics. And without perverting the order, I could not prove that the soul is distinct from the body before proving the existence of God.

    What you say, "that we do not know if the idea of a very perfect being is not at all the same as that of the corporeal world," is easy to answer, through the very same argument which proves that the soul is distinct from the body, that is, because we conceive of an entirely different thing in the one case and in the other. But for this purpose it is necessary to form distinct ideas of the things of which we wish to judge—something ordinary people do not do. And that is principally what I try to teach through my *Meditations*. But I do not pause further over these objections, since you promise to send me shortly all those that can be put forward. On this matter I ask you only that they should not hurry. For those who do not pay attention to everything, and who are satisfied with reading the Second Meditation to know what I write about the soul, or the Third to know what I write about God, will easily raise objections that I have already answered. [. . .]

274   As to the mystery of the Trinity, I judge, with Saint Thomas, that it is purely a matter of faith, and cannot be known by natural light. I do not in the least deny that there are things in God we do not understand, just as there are even in a triangle some properties that no mathematician will ever know, although for all that we do not fail to know what a triangle is.

    It is certain that there is nothing in the effect *"that is not contained formally or eminently in the EFFICIENT and TOTAL cause"*—two words that I expressly added. Thus neither the sun nor the rain are in any way the total cause of the animals they engender.

    I was finishing this when I received your last letter, and that reminds me to ask

275   you to write to me if you know the reason why you did not receive my Metaphysics on the trip on which I sent it to you, or even at the same time as the letters I wrote you a week later, and whether the package had been opened—for I had given it to the same messenger. [. . .]

276   As for the rest, except for what concerns my metaphysics, to which I will not fail to reply as soon as you send it to me, I will be happy to have as few distractions as possible, at least for this year, which I have resolved to use for writing my philosophy in such an order that it can easily be taught. And the first part, which I am now working on, contains almost the same things as the *Meditations* that you have, except that it is in an entirely different style, and that what is said at length in the one is more abridged in the other, and vice versa. [. . .]

To Mersenne, On J.-B. Morin's[27] Proof for the Existence of God (January 28, 1641)

III, 293

This note is just to tell you that I have not yet been able to send you my reply to the objections,[28] partly because I have had other occupations, which have scarcely left me a day free, and partly also because those who made them seem to have understood nothing at all of what I have written, and to have read it only posthaste, so that they only give me occasion to repeat what I have already said. And that troubles me more than if they proposed difficulties that gave more exercise to my mind. Let this be said between us, since I would be very sorry to disoblige them. And you will see by the trouble I take in replying to them, that I consider myself in their debt, both as to the earlier ones and also to the one that I received lately, and which I did not receive until last Tuesday.[29] That is why I said no more about it in my last, since our messenger leaves on Monday.

I have read through Mr. Morin's booklet.[30] Its chief defect is that he treats of the infinite everywhere as if his mind were above it and he could comprehend its properties. That is a common fault with nearly everyone. I have tried with care to avoid it, for I have never treated the infinite except to submit myself to it, and not in the least to determine what it is and what it is not. Further, before explaining anything that is in controversy, in his sixteenth theorem, where he begins to 294 try to prove that God exists, he bases his reasoning on the fact that he claims to have refuted the motion of the earth, and on the fact that heaven rotates around it, which he has by no means proved. And he also supposes that there cannot be an infinite number, and so on, which he could not prove either. And thus all that he says right up to the end is far removed from the geometrical evidence and certitude that he would seem to be promising at the beginning. Let this, too, be said, if you please, between us, since I do not want to displease him at all. [. . .]

I am very much obliged to you for all the good advice you have given me 295 about my metaphysics and about other things.

I claim that we have ideas not only of all that is in our intellect, but even of all that is in our will. For we could not will anything without knowing that we are willing it, nor could we know this except through an idea; but I do not assert that the idea is different from the act itself.

There will be no difficulty, it seems to me, in accommodating theology to my manner of philosophizing. For I do not see anything to change except for transubstantiation, which is very clear and easy on my principles. And I will be 296 obliged to explain it in my physics, along with the first chapter of Genesis. I pro-

---

27. Jean-Baptiste Morin (1583–1656) was professor of mathematics at the Collège de France from 1629 until his death; his interests included physics and astronomy, as well as mathematics.

28. This is a reference to the *Second Set of Objections*, collected by Mersenne.

29. This is a reference to the *Third Set of Objections*, by Thomas Hobbes.

30. Jean-Baptiste Morin, *Quod Deus Sit (That God Exists)* (Paris 1635). An English translation of the work is available in Ariew, Cottingham, and Sorell, pp. 230–51.

pose to send this, too, to the Sorbonne,[31] so that it can be examined before it is printed. If you find that there are other things that merit writing a whole course of theology, and if you would undertake it, I will consider it a favor and will assist you in any way I can. [. . .]

297   I will be very happy to have people make as many and as strong objections as possible, for I hope that the truth will appear so much the better. But I beg you to show my reply and the objections that you have already sent me to those who want to make new objections, so that they do not propose anything to which I have already replied.

    I have proved quite explicitly that God was the creator of all things, and all his other attributes at the same time. For I demonstrated his existence from the idea that we have of him; and even because, having that idea in us, we must have been created by him.

    But I see that people take more account of the titles that are in books than of all the rest. This makes me think that to the title of the Second Meditation, *Of the Human Mind,* one can add, *that it is better known than the body,* so that it will not be thought that I wanted to prove its immortality there. And afterward, in the third, *Of God—that he exists.* In the fifth, *Of the essence of material things—and again, of God, that he exists.* In the sixth, *Of the existence of material things,— and of the real distinction of mind from body.* For these are the things to which I want people to pay most attention. But I think I have included many other things;

298   I will tell you, between us, that these six meditations contain all the foundations of my physics. But it will not do to say this, if you please; for those who favor Aristotle would perhaps find it more difficult to approve of them. And I hope that those who read them will accustom themselves insensibly to my principles, and will recognize the truth before noticing that they destroy those of Aristotle.

---

31. The faculty of theology of the University of Paris.

IV

MEDITATIONS ON FIRST PHILOSOPHY (1641) AT VII, 1

[Letter of Dedication]

To those Most Wise and Distinguished Men,
the Dean and Doctors of the Faculty of Sacred Theology of Paris
René Descartes Sends Greetings

So right is the cause that impels me to offer this work to you, that I am confident you too will find it equally right and thus take up its defense, once you have understood the plan of my undertaking; so much is this the case that I have no better means of commending it here than to state briefly what I have sought to achieve in this work.

I have always thought that two issues—namely, God and the soul—are chief among those that ought to be demonstrated with the aid of philosophy rather than theology. For although it suffices for us believers to believe by faith that the human soul does not die with the body, and that God exists, certainly no unbe- 2 lievers seem capable of being persuaded of any religion or even of almost any moral virtue, until these two are first proven to them by natural reason. And since in this life greater rewards are often granted to vices than to virtues, few would prefer what is right to what is useful, if they neither feared God nor anticipated an afterlife. Granted, it is altogether true that we must believe in God's existence because it is taught in the Holy Scriptures, and, conversely, that we must believe the Holy Scriptures because they have come from God. This is because, of course, since faith is a gift from God, the very same one who gives the grace that is necessary for believing the rest can also give the grace to believe that he exists. Nonetheless, this reasoning cannot be proposed to unbelievers because they would judge it to be circular. In fact, I have observed that not only do you and all other theologians affirm that one can prove the existence of God by natural reason, but also that one may infer from Sacred Scripture that the knowledge of him is easier to achieve than the many things we know about creatures, and is so utterly easy that those without this knowledge are blameworthy. For this is clear from Wisdom, chapter 13 where it is said: "They are not to be excused, for if their capacity for knowing were so great that they could think well of this world, how is it that they did not find the Lord of it even more easily?" And in Romans, chapter 1, it is said that they are "without excuse." And again in the same passage it appears we are being warned with the words: "What is known of God is manifest in them," that everything that can be known about God can be shown by reasons

Selections on pp. 97–141 reprinted from *René Descartes: Meditations on First Philosophy*, 3rd ed., translated by Donald Cress (Indianapolis: Hackett Publishing Company, 1993). Reprinted by permission of the publisher with minor changes by permission of the translator.

drawn exclusively from our own mind. For this reason, I did not think it unbecoming for me to inquire how this may be the case, and by what path God may be known more easily and with greater certainty than the things of this world.

3   And as to the soul, there are many who have regarded its nature as something into which one cannot easily inquire, and some have even gone so far as to say that human reasoning convinces them that the soul dies with the body, while it is by faith alone that they hold the contrary position. Nevertheless, because the Lateran Council held under Leo X, in Session 8, condemned such people and expressly enjoined Christian philosophers to refute their arguments and to use all their powers to demonstrate the truth, I have not hesitated to undertake this task as well.

Moreover, I know that there are many irreligious people who refuse to believe that God exists and that the human mind is distinct from the body—for no other reason than their claim that up until now no one has been able to demonstrate these two things. By no means am I in agreement with these people; on the contrary, I believe that nearly all the arguments which have been brought to bear on these questions by great men have the force of a demonstration, when they are adequately understood, and I am convinced that hardly any arguments can be given that have not already been discovered by others. Nevertheless, I judge that there is no greater task to perform in philosophy than assiduously to seek out, once and for all, the best of all these arguments and to lay them out so precisely and plainly that henceforth all will take them to be true demonstrations. And finally, I was strongly urged to do this by some people who knew that I had developed a method for solving all sorts of problems in the sciences—not a new one, mind you, since nothing is more ancient than the truth, but one they had seen me use with some success in other areas. Accordingly, I took it to be my task to attempt something on this subject.

4   This treatise contains all that I have been able to accomplish. Not that I have attempted to gather together in it all the various arguments that could be brought forward as proof of the very same conclusions, for this does not seem worthwhile, except where no one proof is sufficiently certain. Rather, I have sought out the primary and chief arguments, so that I now make bold to propose these as most certain and evident demonstrations. Moreover, I will say in addition that these arguments are such that I believe there is no way open to the human mind whereby better ones could ever be found. For the urgency of the cause, as well as the glory of God, to which this entire enterprise is referred, compel me here to speak somewhat more freely on my own behalf than is my custom. But although I believe these arguments to be certain and evident, still I am not thereby convinced that they are suited to everyone's grasp. In geometry there are many arguments developed by Archimedes, Apollonius, Pappus, and others, which are taken by everyone to be evident and certain because they contain absolutely nothing which, considered by itself, is not quite easily known, and in which what follows does not square exactly with what has come before. Nevertheless they are rather lengthy and require a particularly attentive reader; thus only a small handful of people understand them. Likewise, although the arguments I use here do, in my opinion, equal or even surpass those of geometry in certitude and obviousness,

nevertheless I am fearful that many people will not be capable of adequately perceiving them, both because they too are a bit lengthy, with some of them depending on still others, and also because, first and foremost, they demand a mind that is quite free from prejudices and that can easily withdraw itself from association with the senses. Certainly there are not to be found in the world more people with an aptitude for metaphysical studies than those with an aptitude for geometry. Moreover, there is the difference that in geometry everyone is of a mind that usually nothing is put down in writing without there being a sound demonstration for it; thus the inexperienced more frequently err on the side of assenting to what is false, wanting as they do to give the appearance of understanding it, than on the side of denying what is true. But it is the reverse in philosophy: since it is believed that there is no issue that cannot be defended from either side, few look for the truth, and many more prowl about for a reputation for profundity by arrogantly challenging whichever arguments are the best. 5

And therefore, regardless of the force of my arguments, because they are of a philosophical nature I do not anticipate that what I will have accomplished through them will be very worthwhile unless you assist me with your patronage. Your faculty is held in such high esteem in the minds of all, and the name of the Sorbonne has such authority that not only in matters of faith has no association, with the exception of the councils of the Church, been held in such high regard as yours, but even in human philosophy nowhere is there thought to be greater insightfulness and solidity, or greater integrity and wisdom in rendering judgments. Should you deign to show any interest in this work, I do not doubt that, first of all, its errors would be corrected by you (for I am mindful not only of my humanity but also, and most especially, of my ignorance, and thus do not claim that there are no errors in it); second, what is lacking would be added, or what is not sufficiently complete would be perfected, or what is in need of further discussion would be expanded upon more fully, either by yourselves or at least by me, after you have given me your guidance; and finally, after the arguments contained in this work proving that God exists and that the mind is distinct from the body have been brought (as I am confident they can be) to such a level of lucidity that these arguments ought to be regarded as the most precise of demonstrations, you may be of a mind to make such a declaration and publicly attest to it. Indeed, should this come to pass, I have no doubt that all the errors that have ever been entertained regarding these issues would shortly be erased from the minds of men. For the truth itself will easily cause other men of intelligence and learning to subscribe to your judgment. Your authority will cause the atheists, who more often than not are dilettantes rather than men of intelligence and learning, to put aside their spirit of contrariness, and perhaps even to defend the arguments which they will come to know are regarded as demonstrations by all who are discerning, lest they appear not to understand them. And finally, everyone else will readily give credence to so many indications of support, and there no longer will be anyone in the world who would dare call into doubt either the existence of God or the real distinction between the soul and the body. Just how great the usefulness of this thing might be, you yourselves, in virtue of your singular wisdom, are in the best position of anyone to 6 judge; nor would it behoove me to commend the cause of God and religion at any greater length to you, who have always been the greatest pillar of the Catholic Church.

7   Preface to the Reader

I have already touched briefly on the issues of God and the human mind in my *Discourse on the Method for Conducting One's Reason Well and for Seeking the Truth in the Sciences*, published in French in 1637. The intent there was not to provide a precise treatment of them, but only to offer a sample and to learn from the opinions of readers how these issues should be treated in the future. For they seemed to me to be so important that I judged they ought to be dealt with more than once. And the path I follow in order to explain them is so little trodden and so far removed from the one commonly taken that I did not think it useful to hold forth at greater length in a work written in French and designed to be read indiscriminately by everyone, lest weaker minds be in a position to think that they too ought to set out on this path.

In the *Discourse* I asked everyone who might find something in my writings worthy of refutation to do me the favor of making me aware of it. As for what I touched on regarding these issues, only two objections were worth noting, and I will respond briefly to them here before undertaking a more precise explanation of them.

8   The first is that, from the fact that the human mind, when turned in on itself, does not perceive itself to be anything other than a thinking thing, it does not follow that its nature or *essence* consists only in its being a thinking thing, such that the word *only* excludes everything else that also could perhaps be said to belong to the nature of the soul. To this objection I answer that in that passage I did not intend my exclusion of those things to reflect the order of the truth of the matter (I was not dealing with it then), but merely the order of my perception. Thus what I had in mind was that I was aware of absolutely nothing that I knew belonged to pertain to my essence, save that I was a thinking thing, that is, a thing having within itself the faculty of thinking. Later on, however, I will show how it follows, from the fact that I know of nothing else belonging to my essence, that nothing else really does belong to it.

The second objection is that it does not follow from the fact that I have within me an idea of a thing more perfect than me, that this idea is itself more perfect than me, and still less that what is represented by this idea exists. But I answer that there is an equivocation here in the word "idea." For "idea" can be taken either materially, for an operation of the intellect (in which case it cannot be said to be more perfect than me), or objectively, for the thing represented by means of that operation. This thing, even if it is not presumed to exist outside the intellect, can nevertheless be more perfect than me by reason of its essence. I will explain in detail in the ensuing remarks how, from the mere fact that there is within me an idea of something more perfect than me, it follows that this thing really exists.

In addition, I have seen two rather lengthy treatises, but these works, utilizing as they do arguments drawn from atheist commonplaces, focused their attack not so much on my arguments regarding these issues, as on my conclusions.[1] Moreover, arguments of this type exercise no influence over those who understand my arguments, and the judgments of many people are so preposterous and feeble that they are more likely to be persuaded by the first opinions to come along, however false and contrary to reason they may be, than by a true and firm refutation of them which they hear subsequently. Accordingly, I have no desire to respond here to these objections, lest I first have to state what they are. I will only say in general that all the objections typically bandied about by the atheists to assail the existence of God always depend either on ascribing human emotions to God, or on arrogantly claiming for our minds such power and wisdom that we attempt to determine and grasp fully what God can and ought to do. Hence these objections will cause us no difficulty, provided we but remember that our minds are to be regarded as finite, while God is to be regarded as incomprehensible and infinite.

But now, after having, to some degree, conducted an initial review of the judgments of men, here I begin once more to treat the same questions about God and the human mind, together with the starting points of the whole of first philosophy, but not in a way that causes me to have any expectation of widespread approval or a large readership. On the contrary, I do not advise anyone to read these things except those who have both the ability and the desire to meditate seriously with me, and to withdraw their minds from the senses as well as from all prejudices. I know all too well that such people are few and far between. As to those who do not take the time to grasp the order and linkage of my arguments, but will be eager to fuss over statements taken out of context (as is the custom for many), they will derive little benefit from reading this work. Although perhaps they might find an occasion for quibbling in several places, still they will not find it easy to raise an objection that is either compelling or worthy of response.

But because I do not promise to satisfy even the others on all counts the first time around, and because I do not arrogantly claim for myself so much that I believe myself capable of anticipating all the difficulties that will occur to someone, I will first of all narrate in the *Meditations* the very thoughts by means of which I seem to have arrived at a certain and evident knowledge of the truth, so that I may determine whether the same arguments that persuaded me can be useful in persuading others. Next, I will reply to the objections of a number of very gifted and learned gentlemen, to whom these *Meditations* were forwarded for their examination prior to their being sent to press. For their objections were so

9

10

---

1. One of the objectors to which Descartes is referring is Pierre Petit (c. 1594–1677), a French engineer and mathematician; the other is unknown. For an analysis of Petit's objections and Descartes's replies, see Jean-Luc Marion, "The Place of the *Objections* in the Development of Cartesian Metaphysics," in *Descartes and His Contemporaries*, eds. Roger Ariew and Marjorie Grene, pp. 7–20.

many and varied that I have dared to hope that nothing will readily occur to anyone, at least nothing of importance, which has not already been touched upon by
these gentlemen. And thus I earnestly entreat the readers not to form a judgment
regarding the *Meditations* until they have deigned to read all these objections and
the replies I have made to them.

12 Synopsis of the Following Six Meditations

In the First Meditation the reasons are given why we can doubt all things, especially material things, so long, that is, as, of course, we have no other foundations
for the sciences than the ones which we have had up until now. Although the utility of so extensive a doubt is not readily apparent, nevertheless its greatest utility lies in freeing us of all prejudices, in preparing the easiest way for us to
withdraw the mind from the senses, and finally, in making it impossible for us to
doubt any further those things that we later discover to be true.

   In the Second Meditation the mind, through the exercise of its own freedom,
supposes the nonexistence of all those things about whose existence it can have
even the least doubt. In so doing the mind realizes that it is impossible for it not
to exist during this time. This too is of the greatest utility, since by means of it
the mind easily distinguishes what things belong to it, that is, to an intellectual
nature, from what things belong to the body. But because some people will perhaps expect to see proofs for the immortality of the soul in this Meditation, I
13 think they should be put on notice here that I have attempted to write only what
I have carefully demonstrated. Therefore the only order I could follow was the
one typically used by geometers, which is to lay out everything on which a given
proposition depends, before concluding anything about it. But the first and principal prerequisite for knowing that the soul is immortal is that we form a concept
of the soul that is as lucid as possible and utterly distinct from every concept of
a body. This is what has been done here. Moreover, there is the additional
requirement that we know that everything that we clearly and distinctly understand is true, in exactly the manner in which we understand it; however, this
could not have been proven prior to the Fourth Meditation. Moreover, we must
have a distinct concept of corporeal nature, and this is formulated partly in the
Second Meditation itself, and partly in the Fifth and Sixth Meditations. From all
this one ought to conclude that all the things we clearly and distinctly conceive
as different substances truly are substances that are really distinct from one
another. (This, for example, is how mind and body are conceived). This conclusion is arrived at in the Sixth Meditation. This same conclusion is also confirmed in this Meditation in virtue of the fact that we cannot understand a body
to be anything but divisible, whereas we cannot understand the mind to be anything but indivisible. For we cannot conceive of half a mind, as we do for any
body whatever, no matter how small. From this we are prompted to acknowledge
that the natures of mind and body not only are different from one another, but
even, in a manner of speaking, are contraries of one another. However, I have not
written any further on the matter in this work, both because these considerations
suffice for showing that the annihilation of the mind does not follow from the

decaying of the body (and thus these considerations suffice for giving mortals hope in an afterlife), and also because the premises from which the immortality of the mind can be inferred depend upon an account of the whole of physics. First, we need to know that absolutely all substances, that is, things that must be   *14* created by God in order to exist, are by their very nature incorruptible, and can never cease to exist, unless, by the same God's denying his concurrence to them, they be reduced to nothingness. Second, we need to realize that body, taken in a general sense, is a substance and hence it too can never perish. But the human body, insofar as it differs from other bodies, is composed of merely a certain configuration of members, together with other accidents of the same sort. But the human mind is not likewise composed of any accidents, but is a pure substance. For even if all its accidents were changed, so that it understands different things, wills different things, senses different things, and so on, the mind itself does not on that score become something different. On the other hand, the human body does become something different, merely as a result of the fact that a change in the shape of some of its parts has taken place. It follows from these considerations that a body can very easily perish, whereas the mind by its nature is immortal.

In the Third Meditation I have explained at sufficient length, it seems to me, my principal argument for proving the existence of God. Nevertheless, since my intent was to draw the minds of readers as far as possible from the senses, I had no desire to draw upon comparisons based upon corporeal things. Thus many obscurities may perhaps have remained; but these, I trust, will later be entirely removed in my *Replies* to the *Objections*. One such point of contention, among others, is the following: how can the idea that is in us of a supremely perfect being have so much objective reality that it can only come from a supremely perfect cause? This is illustrated in the *Replies* by a comparison with a very perfect machine, the idea of which is in the mind of some craftsman.[2] For, just as the objective ingeniousness of this idea ought to have some cause (say, the knowledge possessed by the craftsman or by someone else from whom he received this knowledge), so too, the idea of God which is in us must have God himself as its   *15* cause.

In the Fourth Meditation it is proved that all that we clearly and distinctly perceive is true, and it is also explained what constitutes the nature of falsity. These things necessarily need to be known both to confirm what has preceded as well as to help readers understand what remains. (But here one should meanwhile bear in mind that in that Meditation there is no discussion whatsoever of sin, that is, the error committed in the pursuit of good and evil, but only the error that occurs in discriminating between what is true and what is false. Nor is there an examination of those matters pertaining to the faith or to the conduct of life, but merely of speculative truths known exclusively by the means of the light of nature.)[3]

---

2. See *Replies I*, AT VII, 103 et seq.

3. The parenthetical passage was added by Descartes following upon Arnauld's objections (see AT VII, 215–6). Descartes asked Mersenne to make the changes and to enclose them in brackets, "so that it can be known that I have deferred to his judgment, and so that others, seeing how ready I am to take advice, would tell me more frankly whatever reasons they might have against me, and be less stubborn in wanting to contradict me without reason," AT III, 334–5.

In the Fifth Meditation, in addition to an explanation of corporeal nature in general, the existence of God is also demonstrated by means of a new proof. But again several difficulties may arise here; however, these are resolved later in my *Replies* to the *Objections*. Finally, it is shown how it is true that the certainty of even geometrical demonstrations depends upon the knowledge of God.

Finally, in the Sixth Meditation the understanding is distinguished from the imagination and the marks of this distinction are described. The mind is proved to be really distinct from the body, even though the mind is shown to be so closely joined to the body that it forms a single unit with it. All the errors commonly arising from the senses are reviewed; an account of the ways in which these errors can be avoided is provided. Finally, all the arguments on the basis of which we may infer the existence of material things are presented—not because

16   I believed them to be very useful for proving what they prove, namely, that there really is a world, that men have bodies, and the like (things which no one of sound mind has ever seriously doubted), but rather because, through a consideration of these arguments, one realizes that they are neither so firm nor so evident as the arguments leading us to the knowledge of our mind and of God, so that, of all the things that can be known by the human mind, these latter are the most certain and the most evident. Proving this one thing was for me the goal of these Meditations. For this reason I will not review here the various issues that are also to be treated in these Meditations as the situation arises.

17   ## Meditations on First Philosophy in Which the Existence of God and the Distinction Between the Soul and the Body Are Demonstrated

MEDITATION ONE: Concerning Those Things
That Can Be Called into Doubt

Several years have now passed since I first realized how numerous were the false opinions that in my youth I had taken to be true, and thus how doubtful were all those that I had subsequently built upon them. And thus I realized that once in my life I had to raze everything to the ground and begin again from the original foundations, if I wanted to establish anything firm and lasting in the sciences. But the task seemed enormous, and I was waiting until I reached a point in my life that was so timely that no more suitable time for undertaking these plans of action would come to pass. For this reason, I procrastinated for so long that I would henceforth be at fault, were I to waste the time that remains for carrying out the project by brooding over it. Accordingly, I have today suitably freed my

18   mind of all cares, secured for myself a period of leisurely tranquillity, and am withdrawing into solitude. At last I will apply myself earnestly and unreservedly to this general demolition of my opinions.

Yet to bring this about I will not need to show that all my opinions are false, which is perhaps something I could never accomplish. But reason now persuades me that I should withhold my assent no less carefully from opinions that are not completely certain and indubitable than I would from those that are patently false. For this reason, it will suffice for the rejection of all of these opinions, if I find in each of them some reason for doubt. Nor therefore need I survey each opinion individually, a task that would be endless. Rather, because undermining the foundations will cause whatever has been built upon them to crumble of its own accord, I will attack straightaway those principles which supported everything I once believed.

Surely whatever I had admitted until now as most true I received either from the senses or through the senses. However, I have noticed that the senses are sometimes deceptive; and it is a mark of prudence never to place our complete trust in those who have deceived us even once.

But perhaps, even though the senses do sometimes deceive us when it is a question of very small and distant things, still there are many other matters concerning which one simply cannot doubt, even though they are derived from the very same senses: for example, that I am sitting here next to the fire, wearing my winter dressing gown, that I am holding this sheet of paper in my hands, and the like. But on what grounds could one deny that these hands and this entire body are mine? Unless perhaps I were to liken myself to the insane, whose brains are   *19* impaired by such an unrelenting vapor of black bile that they steadfastly insist that they are kings when they are utter paupers, or that they are arrayed in purple robes when they are naked, or that they have heads made of clay, or that they are gourds, or that they are made of glass. But such people are mad, and I would appear no less mad, were I to take their behavior as an example for myself.

This would all be well and good, were I not a man who is accustomed to sleeping at night, and to experiencing in my dreams the very same things, or now and then even less plausible ones, as these insane people do when they are awake. How often does my evening slumber persuade me of such ordinary things as these: that I am here, clothed in my dressing gown, seated next to the fireplace—when in fact I am lying undressed in bed! But right now my eyes are certainly wide awake when I gaze upon this sheet of paper. This head which I am shaking is not heavy with sleep. I extend this hand consciously and deliberately, and I feel it. Such things would not be so distinct for someone who is asleep. As if I did not recall having been deceived on other occasions even by similar thoughts in my dreams! As I consider these matters more carefully, I see so plainly that there are no definitive signs by which to distinguish being awake from being asleep. As a result, I am becoming quite dizzy, and this dizziness nearly convinces me that I am asleep.

Let us assume then, for the sake of argument, that we are dreaming and that such particulars as these are not true: that we are opening our eyes, moving our head, and extending our hands. Perhaps we do not even have such hands, or any such body at all. Nevertheless, it surely must be admitted that the things seen during slumber are, as it were, like painted images, which could only have been produced in the likeness of true things, and that therefore at least these general things—eyes, head, hands, and the whole body—are not imaginary things, but   *20* are true and exist. For indeed when painters themselves wish to represent sirens and satyrs by means of especially bizarre forms, they surely cannot assign to them utterly new natures. Rather, they simply fuse together the members of various animals. Or if perhaps they concoct something so utterly novel that nothing like it has ever been seen before (and thus is something utterly fictitious and false), yet certainly at the very least the colors from which they fashion it ought to be true. And by the same token, although even these general things—eyes, head, hands and the like—could be imaginary, still one has to admit that at least certain other things that are even more simple and universal are true. It is from these components, as if from true colors, that all those images of things that are in our thought are fashioned, be they true or false.

This class of things appears to include corporeal nature in general, together with its extension; the shape of extended things; their quantity, that is, their size and number; as well as the place where they exist; the time through which they endure, and the like.

Thus it is not improper to conclude from this that physics, astronomy, medicine, and all the other disciplines that are dependent upon the consideration of composite things are doubtful, and that, on the other hand, arithmetic, geometry, and other such disciplines, which treat of nothing but the simplest and most general things and which are indifferent as to whether these things do or do not in fact exist, contain something certain and indubitable. For whether I am awake or asleep, 2 plus 3 make 5, and a square does not have more than 4 sides. It does not seem possible that such obvious truths should be subject to the suspicion of being false.

21   Be that as it may, there is fixed in my mind a certain opinion of long standing, namely that there exists a God who is able to do anything and by whom I, such as I am, have been created. How do I know that he did not bring it about that there is no earth at all, no heavens, no extended thing, no shape, no size, no place, and yet bringing it about that all these things appear to me to exist precisely as they do now? Moreover, since I judge that others sometimes make mistakes in matters that they believe they know most perfectly, may I not, in like fashion, be deceived every time I add 2 and 3 or count the sides of a square, or perform an even simpler operation, if that can be imagined? But perhaps God has not willed that I be deceived in this way, for he is said to be supremely good. Nonetheless, if it were repugnant to his goodness to have created me such that I be deceived all the time, it would also seem foreign to that same goodness to permit me to be deceived even occasionally. But we cannot make this last assertion.

Perhaps there are some who would rather deny so a powerful a God, than believe that everything else is uncertain. Let us not oppose them; rather, let us grant that everything said here about God is fictitious. Now they suppose that I came to be what I am either by fate, or by chance, or by a connected chain of events, or by some other way. But because deceived and being mistaken appear to be a certain imperfection, the less powerful they take the author of my origin to be, the more probable it will be that I am so imperfect that I am always deceived. I have nothing to say in response to these arguments. But eventually I am forced to admit that there is nothing among the things I once believed to be true which it is not permissible to doubt—and not out of frivolity or lack of forethought, but for valid and considered arguments. Thus I must be no less careful to withhold assent henceforth even from these beliefs than I would from *22* those that are patently false, if I wish to find anything certain.

But it is not enough simply to have realized these things; I must take steps to keep myself mindful of them. For long-standing opinions keep returning, and, almost against my will, they take advantage of my credulity, as if it were bound over to them by long use and the claims of intimacy. Nor will I ever get out of the habit of assenting to them and believing in them, so long as I take them to be exactly what they are, namely, in some respects doubtful, as has just now been shown, but nevertheless highly probable, so that it is much more consonant with reason to believe them than to deny them. Hence, it seems to me I would do well to deceive myself by turning my will in completely the opposite direction and pretend for a time that these opinions are wholly false and imaginary, until finally, as if with prejudices weighing down each side equally, no bad habit should turn my judgment any further from the correct perception of things. For indeed I know that meanwhile there is no danger or error in following this procedure, and that it is impossible for me to indulge in too much distrust, since I am now concentrating only on knowledge, not on action.

Accordingly, I will suppose not a supremely good God, the source of truth, but rather an evil genius, supremely powerful and clever, who has directed his entire effort at deceiving me. I will regard the heavens, the air, the earth, colors, shapes, sounds, and all external things as nothing but the bedeviling hoaxes of my dreams, with which he lays snares for my credulity. I will regard myself as not *23* having hands, or eyes, or flesh, or blood, or any senses, but as nevertheless falsely believing that I possess all these things. I will remain resolute and steadfast in this meditation, and even if it is not within my power to know anything true, it certainly is within my power to take care resolutely to withhold my assent to what is false, lest this deceiver, however powerful, however clever he may be, have any effect on me. But this undertaking is arduous, and a certain laziness brings me back to my customary way of living. I am not unlike a prisoner who enjoyed an imaginary freedom during his sleep, but, when he later begins to suspect that he is dreaming, fears being awakened and nonchalantly conspires with these pleasant illusions. In just the same way, I fall back of my own accord into my old opinions, and dread being awakened, lest the toilsome wakefulness which follows upon a peaceful rest must be spent thenceforward not in the light but among the inextricable shadows of the difficulties now brought forward.

Meditation Two: Concerning the Nature of the Human Mind: That It Is Better Known Than the Body

Yesterday's meditation has thrown me into such doubts that I can no longer ignore them, yet I fail to see how they are to be resolved. It is as if I had suddenly *24* fallen into a deep whirlpool; I am so tossed about that I can neither touch bottom with my foot, nor swim up to the top. Nevertheless I will work my way up and will once again attempt the same path I entered upon yesterday. I will accomplish

this by putting aside everything that admits of the least doubt, as if I had discovered it to be completely false. I will stay on this course until I know something
certain, or, if nothing else, until I at least know for certain that nothing is certain.
Archimedes sought but one firm and immovable point in order to move the entire
earth from one place to another. Just so, great things are also to be hoped for if I
succeed in finding just one thing, however slight, that is certain and unshaken.

Therefore I suppose that everything I see is false. I believe that none of what
my deceitful memory represents ever existed. I have no senses whatever. Body,
shape, extension, movement, and place are all chimeras. What then will be true?
Perhaps just the single fact that nothing is certain.

But how do I know there is not something else, over and above all those things
that I have just reviewed, concerning which there is not even the slightest occasion for doubt? Is there not some God, or by whatever name I might call him,
who instills these very thoughts in me? But why would I think that, since I
myself could perhaps be the author of these thoughts? Am I not then at least
something? But I have already denied that I have any senses and any body. Still
25   I hesitate; for what follows from this? Am I so tied to a body and to the senses
that I cannot exist without them? But I have persuaded myself that there is
absolutely nothing in the world: no sky, no earth, no minds, no bodies. Is it then
the case that I too do not exist? But doubtless I did exist, if I persuaded myself
of something. But there is some deceiver or other who is supremely powerful and
supremely sly and who is always deliberately deceiving me. Then too there is no
doubt that I exist, if he is deceiving me. And let him do his best at deception, he
will never bring it about that I am nothing so long as I shall think that I am something. Thus, after everything has been most carefully weighed, it must finally be
established that this pronouncement "I am, I exist" is necessarily true every time
I utter it or conceive it in my mind.

But I do not yet understand sufficiently what I am—I, who now necessarily
exist. And so from this point on, I must be careful lest I unwittingly mistake
something else for myself, and thus err in that very item of knowledge that I
claim to be the most certain and evident of all. Thus, I will meditate once more
on what I once believed myself to be, prior to embarking upon these thoughts.
For this reason, then, I will set aside whatever can be weakened even to the
slightest degree by the arguments brought forward, so that eventually all that
remains is precisely nothing but what is certain and unshaken.

What then did I formerly think I was? A man, of course. But what is a man?
Might I not say a "rational animal"? No, because then I would have to inquire
what "animal" and "rational" mean. And thus from one question I would slide
into many more difficult ones. Nor do I now have enough free time that I want
to waste it on subtleties of this sort. Instead, permit me here to focus here on what
26   came spontaneously and naturally into my thinking whenever I pondered what I
was. Now it occurred to me first that I had a face, hands, arms, and this entire
mechanism of bodily members: the very same as are discerned in a corpse, and
which I referred to by the name "body." It next occurred to me that I took in food,
that I walked about, and that I sensed and thought various things; these actions I
used to attribute to the soul. But as to what this soul might be, I either did not

think about it or else I imagined it a rarefied I-know-not-what, like a wind, or a fire, or ether, which had been infused into my coarser parts. But as to the body I was not in any doubt. On the contrary, I was under the impression that I knew its nature distinctly. Were I perhaps tempted to describe this nature such as I conceived it in my mind, I would have described it thus: by "body," I understand all that is capable of being bounded by some shape, of being enclosed in a place, and of filling up a space in such a way as to exclude any other body from it; of being perceived by touch, sight, hearing, taste, or smell; of being moved in several ways, not, of course, by itself, but by whatever else impinges upon it. For it was my view that the power of self-motion, and likewise of sensing or of thinking, in no way belonged to the nature of the body. Indeed I used rather to marvel that such faculties were to be found in certain bodies.

But now what am I, when I suppose that there is some supremely powerful and, if I may be permitted to say so, malicious deceiver who deliberately tries to fool me in any way he can? Can I not affirm that I possess at least a small measure of all those things which I have already said belong to the nature of the body? 27 I focus my attention on them, I think about them, I review them again, but nothing comes to mind. I am tired of repeating this to no purpose. But what about those things I ascribed to the soul? What about being nourished or moving about? Since I now do not have a body, these are surely nothing but fictions. What about sensing? Surely this too does not take place without a body; and I seemed to have sensed in my dreams many things that I later realized I did not sense. What about thinking? Here I make my discovery: thought exists; it alone cannot be separated from me. I am; I exist—this is certain. But for how long? For as long as I am thinking; for perhaps it could also come to pass that if I were to cease all thinking I would then utterly cease to exist. At this time I admit nothing that is not necessarily true. I am therefore precisely nothing but a thinking thing; that is, a mind, or intellect, or understanding, or reason—words of whose meanings I was previously ignorant. Yet I am a true thing and am truly existing; but what kind of thing? I have said it already: a thinking thing.

What else am I? I will set my imagination in motion. I am not that concatenation of members we call the human body. Neither am I even some subtle air infused into these members, nor a wind, nor a fire, nor a vapor, nor a breath, nor anything I devise for myself. For I have supposed these things to be nothing. The assumption still stands; yet nevertheless I am something. But is it perhaps the case that these very things which I take to be nothing, because they are unknown to me, nevertheless are in fact no different from that me that I know? This I do not know, and I will not quarrel about it now. I can make a judgment only about things that are known to me. I know that I exist; I ask now who is this "I" whom I know? Most certainly, in the strict sense the knowledge of this "I" does not depend upon things whose existence I do not yet know. Therefore it is not 28 dependent upon any of those things that I simulate in my imagination. But this word "simulate" warns me of my error. For I would indeed be simulating were I to "imagine" that I was something, because imagining is merely the contemplating of the shape or image of a corporeal thing. But I now know with certainty that I am and also that all these images—and, generally, everything belonging to the nature of the body—could turn out to be nothing but dreams. Once I have realized this, I would seem to be speaking no less foolishly were I to say: "I will use my imagination in order to recognize more distinctly who I am," than were I to say: "Now I surely am awake, and I see something true; but since I do not yet see it clearly enough, I will deliberately fall asleep so that my dreams might represent it to me more truly and more clearly." Thus I realize that none of what I can grasp by means of the imagination pertains to this knowledge that I have of myself. Moreover, I realize that I must be most diligent about withdrawing my mind from these things so that it can perceive its nature as distinctly as possible.

But what then am I? A thing that thinks. What is that? A thing that doubts, understands, affirms, denies, wills, refuses, and that also imagines and senses.

Indeed it is no small matter if all of these things belong to me. But why should they not belong to me? Is it not the very same "I" who now doubts almost everything, who nevertheless understands something, who affirms that this one thing is true, who denies other things, who desires to know more, who wishes not to be deceived, who imagines many things even against my will, who also notices many things which appear to come from the senses? What is there in all of this that is not every bit as true as the fact that I exist—even if I am always asleep or even if my creator makes every effort to mislead me? Which of these things is distinct from my thought? Which of them can be said to be separate from myself? For it is so obvious that it is I who doubt, I who understand, and I who will, that there is nothing by which it could be explained more clearly. But indeed it is also the same "I" who imagines; for although perhaps, as I supposed before, absolutely nothing that I imagined is true, still the very power of imagining really does exist, and constitutes a part of my thought. Finally, it is this same "I" who senses or who is cognizant of bodily things as if through the senses. For example, I now see a light, I hear a noise, I feel heat. These things are false, since I am asleep. Yet I certainly do seem to see, hear, and feel warmth. This cannot be false. Properly speaking, this is what in me is called "sensing." But this, precisely so taken, is nothing other than thinking.

From these considerations I am beginning to know a little better what I am. But it still seems (and I cannot resist believing) that corporeal things—whose images are formed by thought, and which the senses themselves examine—are much more distinctly known than this mysterious "I" which does not fall within the imagination. And yet it would be strange indeed were I to grasp the very things I consider to be doubtful, unknown, and foreign to me more distinctly than what is true, what is known—than, in short, myself. But I see what is happening: my mind loves to wander and does not yet permit itself to be restricted within the confines of truth. So be it then; let us just this once allow it completely free rein, so that, a little while later, when the time has come to pull in the reins, the mind may more readily permit itself to be controlled.

Let us consider those things which are commonly believed to be the most distinctly grasped of all: namely the bodies we touch and see. Not bodies in general, mind you, for these general perceptions are apt to be somewhat more confused, but one body in particular. Let us take, for instance, this piece of wax. It has been taken quite recently from the honeycomb; it has not yet lost all the honey flavor.

It retains some of the scent of the flowers from which it was collected. Its color, shape, and size are manifest. It is hard and cold; it is easy to touch. If you rap on it with your knuckle it will emit a sound. In short, everything is present in it that appears needed to enable a body to be known as distinctly as possible. But notice that, as I am speaking, I am bringing it close to the fire. The remaining traces of the honey flavor are disappearing; the scent is vanishing; the color is changing; the original shape is disappearing. Its size is increasing; it is becoming liquid and hot; you can hardly touch it. And now, when you rap on it, it no longer emits any sound. Does the same wax still remain? I must confess that it does; no one denies it; no one thinks otherwise. So what was there in the wax that was so distinctly grasped? Certainly none of the aspects that I reached by means of the senses. For whatever came under the senses of taste, smell, sight, touch, or hearing has now changed; and yet the wax remains.

Perhaps the wax was what I now think it is: namely that the wax itself never really was the sweetness of the honey, nor the fragrance of the flowers, nor the whiteness, nor the shape, nor the sound, but instead was a body that a short time ago manifested itself to me in these ways, and now does so in other ways. But just what precisely is this thing that I thus imagine? Let us focus our attention on this and see what remains after we have removed everything that does not belong   *31* to the wax: only that it is something extended, flexible, and mutable. But is it to be flexible and mutable? Is it what my imagination shows it to be: namely, that this piece of wax can change from a round to a square shape, or from the latter to a triangular shape? Not at all; for I grasp that the wax is capable of innumerable changes of this sort, even though I am incapable of running through these innumerable changes by using my imagination. Therefore this insight is not achieved by the faculty of imagination. What is it to be extended? Is this thing's extension also unknown? For it becomes greater in wax that is beginning to melt, greater in boiling wax, and greater still as the heat is increased. And I would not judge correctly what the wax is if I did not believe that it takes on an even greater variety of dimensions than I could ever grasp with the imagination. It remains then for me to concede that I do not grasp what this wax is through the imagination; rather, I perceive it through the mind alone. The point I am making refers to this particular piece of wax, for the case of wax in general is clearer still. But what is this piece of wax which is perceived only by the mind? Surely it is the same piece of wax that I see, touch, and imagine; in short it is the same piece of wax I took it to be from the very beginning. But I need to realize that the perception of the wax is neither a seeing, nor a touching, nor an imagining. Nor has it ever been, even though it previously seemed so; rather it is an inspection on the part of the mind alone. This inspection can be imperfect and confused, as it was before, or clear and distinct, as it is now, depending on how closely I pay attention to the things in which the piece of wax consists.

But meanwhile I marvel at how prone my mind is to errors. For although I am considering these things within myself silently and without words, nevertheless   *32* I seize upon words themselves and I am nearly deceived by the ways in which people commonly speak. For we say that we see the wax itself, if it is present, and not that we judge it to be present from its color or shape. Whence I might conclude straightaway that I know the wax through the vision had by the eye, and not through an inspection on the part of the mind alone. But then were I perchance to look out my window and observe men crossing the square, I would ordinarily say I see the men themselves just as I say I see the wax. But what do I see aside from hats and clothes, which could conceal automata? Yet I judge them to be men. Thus what I thought I had seen with my eyes, I actually grasped solely with the faculty of judgment, which is in my mind.

But a person who seeks to know more than the common crowd ought to be ashamed of himself for looking for doubt in common ways of speaking. Let us then go forward, inquiring on when it was that I perceived more perfectly and evidently what the piece of wax was. Was it when I first saw it and believed I knew it by the external sense, or at least by the so-called "common" sense, that is, the power of imagination? Or do I have more perfect knowledge now, when I have diligently examined both what the wax is and how it is known? Surely it is absurd to be in doubt about this matter. For what was there in my initial perception that was distinct? What was there that any animal seemed incapable of possessing? But indeed when I distinguish the wax from its external forms, as if stripping it of its clothing, and look at the wax in its nakedness, then, even though there can be still an error in my judgment, nevertheless I cannot perceive it thus without a human mind.

33   But what am I to say about this mind, that is, about myself? For as yet I admit nothing else to be in me over and above the mind. What, I ask, am I who seem to perceive this wax so distinctly? Do I not know myself not only much more truly and with greater certainty, but also much more distinctly and evidently? For if I judge that the wax exists from the fact that I see it, certainly from this same fact that I see the wax it follows much more evidently that I myself exist. For it could happen that what I see is not truly wax. It could happen that I have no eyes with which to see anything. But it is utterly impossible that, while I see or think I see (I do not now distinguish these two), I who think am not something. Likewise, if I judge that the wax exists from the fact that I touch it, the same outcome will again obtain, namely that I exist. If I judge that the wax exists from the fact that I imagine it, or for any other reason, plainly the same thing follows. But what I note regarding the wax applies to everything else that is external to me. Furthermore, if my perception of the wax seemed more distinct after it became known to me not only on account of sight or touch, but on account of many reasons, one has to admit how much more distinctly I am now known to myself. For there is not a single consideration that can aid in my perception of the wax or of any other body that fails to make even more manifest the nature of my mind. But there are still so many other things in the mind itself on the basis of which my knowledge of it can be rendered more distinct that it hardly seems worth enumerating those things which emanate to it from the body.

34   But lo and behold, I have returned on my own to where I wanted to be. For since I now know that even bodies are not, properly speaking, perceived by the senses or by the faculty of imagination, but by the intellect alone, and that they are not perceived through their being touched or seen, but only through their being understood, I manifestly know that nothing can be perceived more easily and more evidently than my own mind. But since the tendency to hang on to long-held beliefs cannot be put aside so quickly, I want to stop here, so that by the length of my meditation this new knowledge may be more deeply impressed upon my memory.

MEDITATION THREE: Concerning God, That He Exists

I will now shut my eyes, stop up my ears, and withdraw all my senses. I will also blot out from my thoughts all images of corporeal things, or rather, since the latter is hardly possible, I will regard these images as empty, false, and worthless. And as I converse with myself alone and look more deeply into myself, I will attempt to render myself gradually better known and more familiar to myself. I am a thing that thinks, that is to say, a thing that doubts, affirms, denies, understands a few things, is ignorant of many things, wills, refrains from willing, and also imagines and senses. For as I observed earlier, even though these things that I sense or imagine may perhaps be nothing at all outside me, nevertheless I am certain that these modes of thinking, which are cases of what I call sensing and imagining, insofar as they are merely modes of thinking, do exist within me.   *35*

In these few words, I have reviewed everything I truly know, or at least what so far I have noticed that I know. Now I will ponder more carefully to see whether perhaps there may be other things belonging to me that up until now I have failed to notice. I am certain that I am a thinking thing. But do I not therefore also know what is required for me to be certain of anything? Surely in this first instance of knowledge, there is nothing but a certain clear and distinct perception of what I affirm. Yet this would hardly be enough to render me certain of the truth of a thing, if it could ever happen that something that I perceived so clearly and distinctly were false. And thus I now seem able to posit as a general rule that everything I very clearly and distinctly perceive is true.

Be that as it may, I have previously admitted many things as wholly certain and evident that nevertheless I later discovered to be doubtful. What sort of things were these? Why, the earth, the sky, the stars, and all the other things I perceived by means of the senses. But what was it about these things that I clearly perceived? Surely the fact that the ideas or thoughts of these things were hovering before my mind. But even now I do not deny that these ideas are in me. Yet there was something else I used to affirm, which, owing to my habitual tendency to believe it, I used to think was something I clearly perceived, even though I actually did not perceive it all: namely, that certain things existed outside me, things from which those ideas proceeded and which those ideas completely resembled. But on this point I was mistaken; or, rather if my judgment was a true one, it was not the result of the force of my perception.

But what about when I considered something very simple and easy in the areas   *36* of arithmetic or geometry, for example that 2 plus 3 make 5, and the like? Did I not intuit them at least clearly enough so as to affirm them as true? To be sure, I did decide later on that I must doubt these things, but that was only because it occurred to me that some God could perhaps have given me a nature such that I might be deceived even about matters that seemed most evident. But whenever this preconceived opinion about the supreme power of God occurs to me, I cannot help admitting that, were he to wish it, it would be easy for him to cause me to err even in those matters that I think I intuit as clearly as possible with the eyes of the mind. On the other hand, whenever I turn my attention to those very things that I think I perceive with such great clarity, I am so completely persuaded by them that I spontaneously blurt out these words: "let him who can deceive me; so long as I think that I am something, he will never bring it about that I am nothing. Nor will he one day make it true that I never existed, for it is true now that I do exist. Nor will he even bring it about that perhaps 2 plus 3 might equal more or less than 5, or similar items in which I recognize an obvious contradiction." And certainly, because I have no reason for thinking that there is a God who is a deceiver (and of course I do not yet sufficiently know whether there even is a God), the basis for doubting, depending as it does merely on the above hypothesis, is very tenuous and, so to speak, metaphysical. But in order to remove even this basis for doubt, I should at the first opportunity inquire whether there is a God, and, if there is, whether or not he can be a deceiver. For if I am ignorant of this, it appears I am never capable of being completely certain about anything else.

37   However, at this stage good order seems to demand that I first group all my thoughts into certain classes, and ask in which of them truth or falsity properly resides. Some of these thoughts are like images of things; to these alone does the word "idea" properly apply, as when I think of a man, or a chimera, or the sky, or an angel, or God. Again there are other thoughts that take different forms: for example, when I will, or fear, or affirm, or deny, there is always some thing that I grasp as the subject of my thought, yet I embrace in my thought something more than the likeness of that thing. Some of these thoughts are called volitions or affects, while others are called judgments.

Now as far as ideas are concerned, if they are considered alone and in their own right, without being referred to something else, they cannot, properly speaking, be false. For whether it is a she-goat or a chimera that I am imagining, it is no less true that I imagine the one than the other. Moreover, we need not fear that there is falsity in the will itself or in the affects, for although I can choose evil things or even things that are utterly nonexistent, I cannot conclude from this that it is untrue that I do choose these things. Thus there remain only judgments in which I must take care not to be mistaken. Now the principal and most frequent error to be found in judgments consists in the fact that I judge that the ideas which are in me are similar to or in conformity with certain things outside me. Obviously, if I were to consider these ideas merely as certain modes of my thought, and were not to refer them to anything else, they could hardly give me any subject matter for error.

38   Among these ideas, some appear to me to be innate, some adventitious, and some produced by me. For I understand what a thing is, what truth is, what thought is, and I appear to have derived this exclusively from my very own nature. But say I am now hearing a noise, or looking at the sun, or feeling the fire; up until now I judged that these things proceeded from certain things

outside me, and finally, that sirens, hippogriffs, and the like are made by me. Or perhaps I can even think of all these ideas as being adventitious, or as being innate, or as fabrications, for I have not yet clearly ascertained their true origin.

But here I must inquire particularly into those ideas that I believe to be derived from things existing outside me. Just what reason do I have for believing that these ideas resemble those things? Well, I do seem to have been so taught by nature. Moreover, I do know from experience that these ideas do not depend upon my will, nor consequently upon myself, for I often notice them even against my will. Now, for example, whether or not I will it, I feel heat. It is for this reason that I believe this feeling or idea of heat comes to me from something other than myself, namely from heat of the fire by which I am sitting. Nothing is more obvious than the judgment that this thing is sending its likeness rather than something else into me.

I will now see whether these reasons are powerful enough. When I say here "I have been so taught by nature," all I have in mind is that I am driven by a spontaneous impulse to believe this, and not that some light of nature is showing me that it is true. These are two very different things. For whatever is shown me by this light of nature, for example, that from the fact that I doubt, it follows that I am, and the like, cannot in any way be doubtful. This is owing to the fact that there can be no other faculty that I can trust as much as this light and which could teach that these things are not true. But as far as natural impulses are concerned, *39* in the past I have often judged myself to have been driven by them to make the poorer choice when it was a question of choosing a good; and I fail to see why I should place any greater faith in them in other matters.

Again, although these ideas do not depend upon my will, it does not follow that they necessarily proceed from things existing outside me. For just as these impulses about which I spoke just now seem to be different from my will, even though they are in me, so too perhaps there is also in me some other faculty, one not yet sufficiently known to me, which produces these ideas, just as it has always seemed up to now that ideas are formed in me without any help from external things when I am asleep.

And finally, even if these ideas did proceed from things other than myself, it does not therefore follow that they must resemble those things. Indeed it seems I have frequently noticed a vast difference in many respects. For example, I find within myself two distinct ideas of the sun. One idea is drawn, as it were, from the senses. Now it is this idea which, of all those that I take to be derived from outside me, is most in need of examination. By means of this idea the sun appears to me to be quite small. But there is another idea, one derived from astronomical reasoning, that is, it is elicited from certain notions that are innate in me, or else is fashioned by me in some other way. Through this idea the sun is shown to be several times larger than the earth. Both ideas surely cannot resemble the same sun existing outside me; and reason convinces me that the idea that seems to have emanated from the sun itself from so close is the very one that least resembles the sun.

All these points demonstrate sufficiently that up to this point it was not a well- *40* founded judgment, but only a blind impulse that formed the basis of my belief that things existing outside me send ideas or images of themselves to me through the sense organs or by some other means.

But still another way occurs to me for inquiring whether some of the things of which there are ideas in me do exist outside me: insofar as these ideas are merely modes of thought, I see no inequality among them; they all seem to proceed from me in the same manner. But insofar as one idea represents one thing and another idea another thing, it is obvious that they do differ very greatly from one another. Unquestionably, those ideas that display substances to me are something more and, if I may say so, contain within themselves more objective reality than those which represent only modes or accidents. Again, the idea that enables me to understand a supreme deity, eternal, infinite, omniscient, omnipotent, and creator of all things other than himself, clearly has more objective reality within it than do those ideas through which finite substances are displayed.

Now it is indeed evident by the light of nature that there must be at least as much [reality] in the efficient and total cause as there is in the effect of that same cause. For whence, I ask, could an effect get its reality, if not from its cause? And how could the cause give that reality to the effect, unless it also possessed that reality? Hence it follows that something cannot come into being out of nothing, and also that what is more perfect (that is, what contains in itself more reality)

41 cannot come into being from what is less perfect. But this is manifestly true not merely for those effects whose reality is actual or formal, but also for ideas in which only objective reality is considered. For example, not only can a stone which did not exist previously not now begin to exist unless it is produced by something in which there is, either formally or eminently, everything that is in the stone; nor heat be introduced into a subject which was not already hot unless it is done by something that is of at least as perfect an order as heat—and the same for the rest—but it is also true that there can be in me no idea of heat, or of a stone, unless it is placed in me by some cause that has at least as much reality as I conceive to be in the heat or in the stone. For although this cause conveys none of its actual or formal reality to my idea, it should not be thought for that reason that it must be less real. Rather, the very nature of an idea is such that of itself it needs no formal reality other than what it borrows from my thought, of which it is a mode. But that a particular idea contains this as opposed to that objective reality is surely owing to some cause in which there is at least as much formal reality as there is objective reality contained in the idea. For if we assume that something is found in the idea that was not in its cause, then the idea gets that something from nothing. Yet as imperfect a mode of being as this is by which a thing exists in the intellect objectively through an idea, nevertheless it is plainly not nothing; hence it cannot get its being from nothing.

Moreover, even though the reality that I am considering in my ideas is merely objective reality, I ought not on that account to suspect that there is no need for

42 the same reality to be formally in the causes of these ideas, but that it suffices for it to be in them objectively. For just as the objective mode of being belongs to ideas by their very nature, so the formal mode of being belongs to the causes of ideas, at least to the first and preeminent ones, by their very nature. And although one idea can perhaps issue from another, nevertheless no infinite

regress is permitted here; eventually some first idea must be reached whose cause is a sort of archetype that contains formally all the reality that is in the idea merely objectively. Thus it is clear to me by the light of nature that the ideas that are in me are like images that can easily fail to match the perfection of the things from which they have been drawn, but which can contain nothing greater or more perfect.

And the longer and more attentively I examine all these points, the more clearly and distinctly I know they are true. But what am I ultimately to conclude? If the objective reality of any of my ideas is found to be so great that I am certain that the same reality was not in me, either formally or eminently, and that therefore I myself cannot be the cause of the idea, then it necessarily follows that I am not alone in the world, but that something else, which is the cause of this idea, also exists. But if no such idea is found in me, I will have no argument whatsoever to make me certain of the existence of anything other than myself, for I have conscientiously reviewed all these arguments, and so far I have been unable to find any other.

Among my ideas, in addition to the one that displays me to myself (about which there can be no difficulty at this point), are others that represent God, corporeal and inanimate things, angels, animals, and finally other men like myself.   *43*

As to the ideas that display other men, or animals, or angels, I easily understand that they could be fashioned from the ideas that I have of myself, of corporeal things, and of God—even if no men (except myself), no animals, and no angels existed in the world.

As to the ideas of corporeal things, there is nothing in them that is so great that it seems incapable of having originated from me. For if I investigate them thoroughly and examine each one individually in the way I examined the idea of wax yesterday, I notice that there are only a very few things in them that I perceive clearly and distinctly: namely, size, or extension in length, breadth, and depth; shape, which arises from the limits of this extension; position, which various things possessing shape have in relation to one another; and motion, or alteration in position. To these can be added substance, duration, and number. But as for the remaining items, such as light and colors, sounds, odors, tastes, heat and cold, and other tactile qualities, I think of these only in a very confused and obscure manner, to the extent that I do not even know whether they are true or false, that is, whether the ideas I have of them are ideas of things or ideas of non-things. For although a short time ago I noted that falsity properly so called (or "formal" falsity) is to be found only in judgments, nevertheless there is another kind of falsity (called "material" falsity) which is found in ideas whenever they represent a non-thing as if it were a thing. For example, the ideas I have of heat and cold fall so far short of being clear and distinct that I cannot   *44* tell from them whether cold is merely the privation of heat or whether heat is the privation of cold, or whether both are real qualities, or whether neither is. And because ideas can only be, as it were, of things, if it is true that cold is merely the absence of heat, then an idea that represents cold to me as something real and positive, will not inappropriately be called false. The same holds for other similar ideas.

Assuredly I need not assign to these ideas an author distinct from myself. For if they were false, that is, if they were to represent non-things, I know by the light of nature that they proceed from nothing; that is, they are in me for no other reason than that something is lacking in my nature, and that my nature is not entirely perfect. If, on the other hand, these ideas are true, then because they exhibit so little reality to me that I cannot distinguish it from a non-thing, I see no reason why they cannot get their being from me.

As for what is clear and distinct in the ideas of corporeal things, it appears I could have borrowed some of these from the idea of myself: namely, substance, duration, number, and whatever else there may be of this type. For instance, I think that a stone is a substance, that is to say, a thing that is suitable for existing in itself; and likewise I think that I too am a substance. Despite the fact that I conceive myself to be a thinking thing and not an extended thing, whereas I conceive of a stone as an extended thing and not a thinking thing, and hence there is the greatest diversity between these two concepts, nevertheless they seem to agree with one another when considered under the rubric of substance. Furthermore, I perceive that I now exist and recall that I have previously existed for some time. And I have various thoughts and know how many of them there 45   are. It is in doing these things that I acquire the ideas of duration and number, which I can then apply to other things. However, none of the other components out of which the ideas of corporeal things are fashioned (namely extension, shape, position, and motion) are contained in me formally, since I am merely a thinking thing. But since these are only certain modes of a substance, whereas I am a substance, it seems possible that they are contained in me eminently.

Thus there remains only the idea of God. I must consider whether there is anything in this idea that could not have originated from me. I understand by the name "God" a certain substance that is infinite, independent, supremely intelligent and supremely powerful, and that created me along with everything else that exists—if anything else exists. Indeed all these are such that, the more carefully I focus my attention on them, the less possible it seems they could have arisen from myself alone. Thus, from what has been said, I must conclude that God necessarily exists.

For although the idea of substance is in me by virtue of the fact that I am a substance, that fact is not sufficient to explain my having the idea of an infinite substance, since I am finite, unless this idea proceeded from some substance which really was infinite.

Nor should I think that I do not perceive the infinite by means of a true idea, but only through a negation of the finite, just as I perceive rest and darkness by means of a negation of motion and light. On the contrary, I clearly understand that there is more reality in an infinite substance than there is in a finite one. Thus the perception of the infinite is somehow prior in me to the perception of the finite, that is, my perception of God is prior to my perception of myself. For how 46   would I understand that I doubt and that I desire, that is, that I lack something and that I am not wholly perfect, unless there were some idea in me of a more perfect being, by comparison with which I might recognize my defects?

Nor can it be said that this idea of God is perhaps materially false and thus can originate from nothing, as I remarked just now about the ideas of heat and cold, and the like. On the contrary, because it is the most clear and distinct and because it contains more objective reality than any other idea, no idea is in and of itself truer and has less of a basis for being suspected of falsehood. I maintain that this idea of a being that is supremely perfect and infinite is true in the highest degree. For although I could perhaps pretend that such a being does not exist, nevertheless I could not pretend that the idea of such a being discloses to me nothing real, as was the case with the idea of cold which I referred to earlier. It is indeed an idea that is utterly clear and distinct; for whatever I clearly and distinctly perceive to be real and true and to involve some perfection is wholly contained in that idea. It is no objection that I do not comprehend the infinite or that there are countless other things in God that I can in no way either comprehend or perhaps even touch with my thought. For the nature of the infinite is such that it is not comprehended by a being such as I, who am finite. And it is sufficient that I understand this very point and judge that all those things that I clearly perceive and that I know to contain some perfection—and perhaps even countless other things of which I am ignorant—are in God either formally or eminently. The result is that, of all the ideas that are in me, the idea that I have of God is the most true, the most clear and distinct.

But perhaps I am something greater than I myself understand. Perhaps all these perfections that I am attributing to God are somehow in me potentially, although they do no yet assert themselves and are not yet actualized. For I now *47* observe that my knowledge is gradually being increased, and I see nothing standing in the way of its being increased more and more to infinity. Moreover, I see no reason why, with my knowledge thus increased, I could not acquire all the remaining perfections of God. And, finally, if the potential for these perfections is in me already, I see no reason why this potential would not suffice to produce the idea of these perfections.

Yet none of these things can be the case. First, while it is true that my knowledge is gradually being increased and that there are many things in me potentially that are not yet actual, nevertheless, none of these pertains to the idea of God, in which there is nothing whatever that is potential. Indeed this gradual increase is itself a most certain proof of imperfection. Moreover, although my knowledge may always increase more and more, nevertheless I understand that this knowledge will never by this means be actually infinite, because it will never reach a point where it is incapable of greater increase. On the contrary, I judge God to be actually infinite, so that nothing can be added to his perfection. Finally, I perceive that the objective being of an idea cannot be produced by a merely potential being (which, strictly speaking, is nothing), but only by an actual or formal being.

Indeed there is nothing in all these things that is not manifest by the light of nature to one who is conscientious and attentive. But when I am less attentive, and the images of sensible things blind the mind's eye, I do not so easily recall why the idea of a being more perfect than me necessarily proceeds from a being

48   that really is more perfect. This being the case, it is appropriate to ask further whether I myself who have this idea could exist, if such a being did not exist.

From what source, then, do I derive my existence? Why, from myself, or from my parents, or from whatever other things there are that are less perfect than God. For nothing more perfect than God, or even as perfect as God, can be thought or imagined.

But if I got my being from myself, I would not doubt, nor would I desire, nor would I lack anything at all. For I would have given myself all the perfections of which I have some idea; in so doing, I myself would be God! I must not think that the things I lack could perhaps be more difficult to acquire than the ones I have now. On the contrary, it is obvious that it would have been much more difficult for me (that is, a thing or substance that thinks) to emerge out of nothing than it would be to acquire the knowledge of many things about which I am ignorant (these items of knowledge being merely accidents of that substance). Certainly, if I got this greater thing from myself, I would not have denied myself at least those things that can be had more easily. Nor would I have denied myself any of those other things that I perceive to be contained in the idea of God, for surely none of them seem to me more difficult to bring about. But if any of them were more difficult to bring about, they would certainly also seem more difficult to me, even if the remaining ones that I possess I got from myself, since it would be on account of them that I would experience that my power is limited.

Nor am I avoiding the force of these arguments, if I suppose that perhaps I have always existed as I do now, as if it then followed that no author of my exis-
49   tence need be sought. For because the entire span of one's life can be divided into countless parts, each one wholly independent of the rest, it does not follow from the fact that I existed a short time ago that I must exist now, unless some cause, as it were, creates me all over again at this moment, that is to say, which preserves me. For it is obvious to one who pays close attention to the nature of time that plainly the same force and action are needed to preserve anything at each individual moment that it lasts as would be required to create that same thing anew, were it not yet in existence. Thus conservation differs from creation solely by virtue of a distinction of reason; this too is one of those things that are manifest by the light of nature.

Therefore I must now ask myself whether I possess some power by which I can bring it about that I myself, who now exist, will also exist a little later on. For since I am nothing but a thinking thing—or at least since I am now dealing simply and precisely with that part of me which is a thinking thing—if such a power were in me, then I would certainly be aware of it. But I observe that there is no such power; and from this very fact I know most clearly that I depend upon some being other than myself.

But perhaps this being is not God, and I have been produced either by my parents or by some other causes less perfect than God. On the contrary, as I said before, it is obvious that there must be at least as much in the cause as there is in the effect. Thus, regardless of what it is that eventually is assigned as my cause, because I am a thinking thing and have within me a certain idea of God, it must be granted that what caused me is also a thinking thing and it too has an idea of all the perfections which I attribute to God. And I can again inquire of this cause whether it got its existence from itself or from another cause. For if it got its existence from itself, it is evident from what has been said that it is itself God, because, having the power of existing in and of itself, it unquestionably also has *50* the power of actually possessing all the perfections of which it has in itself an idea—that is, all the perfections that I conceive to be in God. However, if it got its existence from another cause, I will once again inquire in similar fashion about this other cause: whether it got its existence from itself or from another cause, until finally I arrive at the ultimate cause, which will be God. For it is apparent enough that there can be no infinite regress here, especially since I am not dealing here merely with the cause that once produced me, but also and most especially with the cause that preserves me at the present time.

Nor can one fancy that perhaps several partial causes have concurred in bringing me into being, and that I have taken the ideas of the various perfections I attribute to God from a variety of causes, so that all of these perfections are found somewhere in the universe, but not all joined together in a single being—God. On the contrary, the unity, the simplicity, that is, the inseparability of all those features that are in God is one of the chief perfections that I understand to be in him. Certainly the idea of the unity of all his perfections could not have been placed in me by any cause from which I did not also get the ideas of the other perfections; for neither could some cause have made me understand them joined together and inseparable from one another, unless it also caused me to recognize what they were.

Finally, as to my parents, even if everything that I ever believed about them were true, still it is certainly not they who preserve me; nor is it they who in any way brought me into being, insofar as I am a thinking thing. Rather, they merely placed certain dispositions in the matter which I judged to contain me, that is, a mind, which now is the only thing I take myself to be. And thus there can be no *51* difficulty here concerning my parents. Indeed I have no choice but to conclude that the mere fact of my existing and of there being in me an idea of a most perfect being, that is, God, demonstrates most evidently that God too exists.

All that remains for me is to ask how I received this idea of God. For I did not draw it from the senses; it never came upon me unexpectedly, as is usually the case with the ideas of sensible things when these things present themselves (or seem to present themselves) to the external sense organs. Nor was it made by me, for I plainly can neither subtract anything from it nor add anything to it. Thus the only option remaining is that this idea is innate in me, just as the idea of myself is innate in me.

To be sure, it is not astonishing that in creating me, God should have endowed me with this idea, so that it would be like the mark of the craftsman impressed upon his work, although this mark need not be something distinct from the work itself. But the mere fact that God created me makes it highly plausible that I have somehow been made in his image and likeness, and that I perceive this likeness, in which the idea of God is contained, by means of the same faculty by which I perceive myself. That is, when I turn the mind's eye toward myself, I understand not only that I am something incomplete and dependent upon another, something

aspiring indefinitely for greater and greater or better things, but also that the being on whom I depend has in himself all those greater things—not merely indefinitely and potentially, but infinitely and actually, and thus that he is God. The whole force of the argument rests on the fact that I recognize that it would
52   be impossible for me to exist, being of such a nature as I am (namely, having in me the idea of God), unless God did in fact exist. God, I say, that same being the idea of whom is in me: a being having all those perfections that I cannot comprehend, but can somehow touch with my thought, and a being subject to no defects whatever. From these considerations it is quite obvious that he cannot be a deceiver, for it is manifest by the light of nature that all fraud and deception depend on some defect.

    But before examining this idea more closely and at the same time inquiring into other truths that can be gathered from it, at this point I want to spend some time contemplating this God, to ponder his attributes and, so far as the eye of my darkened mind can take me, to gaze upon, to admire, and to adore the beauty of this immense light. For just as we believe by faith that the greatest felicity of the next life consists solely in this contemplation of the divine majesty, so too we now experience that from the same contemplation, although it is much less perfect, the greatest pleasure of which we are capable in this life can be perceived.

MEDITATION FOUR: Concerning the True and the False

Lately I have become accustomed to withdrawing my mind from the senses, and
53   I have carefully taken note of the fact that very few things are truly perceived regarding corporeal things, although a great many more things are known regarding the human mind, and still many more things regarding God. The upshot is that I now have no difficulty directing my thought away from things that can be imagined to things that can be grasped only by the understanding and are wholly separate from matter. In fact the idea I clearly have of the human mind—insofar as it is a thinking thing, not extended in length, breadth, or depth, and having nothing else from the body—is far more distinct than the idea of any corporeal thing. And when I take note of the fact that I doubt, or that I am a thing that is incomplete and dependent, there comes to mind a clear and distinct idea of a being that is independent and complete, that is, an idea of God. And from the mere fact that such an idea is in me, or that I who have this idea exist, I draw the obvious conclusion that God also exists, and that my existence depends entirely upon him at each and every moment. This conclusion is so obvious that I am confident that the human mind can know nothing more evident or more certain. And now I seem to see a way by which I might progress from this contemplation of the true God, in whom, namely, are hidden all the treasures of the sciences and wisdom, to the knowledge of other things.

    To begin with, I acknowledge that it is impossible for God ever to deceive me, for trickery or deception are always indicative of some imperfection. And although the ability to deceive seems to be an indication of cleverness or power, the will to deceive undoubtedly attests to maliciousness or weakness. Accordingly, deception is incompatible with God.

Next I experience that there is in me a certain faculty of judgment, which, like everything else that is in me, I undoubtedly received from God. And since he *54* does not wish to deceive me, he assuredly has not given me the sort of faculty with which I could ever make a mistake, when I use it properly.

No doubt regarding this matter would remain, but for the fact that it seems to follow from this that I am never capable of making a mistake. For if everything that is in me I got from God, and he gave me no faculty for making mistakes, it seems I am incapable of ever erring. And thus, so long as I think exclusively about God and focus my attention exclusively on him, I discern no cause of error or falsity. But once I turn my attention back on myself, I nevertheless experience that I am subject to countless errors. As I seek a cause of these errors, I notice that passing before me is not only a real and positive idea of God (that is, of a supremely perfect being), but also, as it were, a certain negative idea of nothingness (that is, of what is at the greatest possible distance from any perfection), and that I have been so constituted as a kind of middle ground between God and nothingness, or between the supreme being and non-being. Thus insofar as I have been created by the supreme being, there is nothing in me by means of which I might be deceived or be led into error; but insofar as I participate in nothingness or non-being, that is, insofar as I am not the supreme being and lack a great many things, it is not surprising that I make mistakes. Thus I certainly understand that error as such is not something real that depends upon God, but rather is merely a defect. And thus there is no need to account for my errors by positing a faculty given to me by God for the purpose. Rather, it just so happens that I make mistakes because the faculty of judging the truth, which I got from God, is not, in my case, infinite.

Still this is not yet altogether satisfactory; for error is not a pure negation, but *55* rather a privation or a lack of some knowledge that somehow ought to be in me. And when I attend to the nature of God, it seems impossible that he would have placed in me a faculty that is not perfect in its kind or that is lacking some perfection it ought to have. For if it is true that the more expert the craftsman, the more perfect the works he produces, what can that supreme creator of all things make that is not perfect in all respects? No doubt God could have created me such that I never erred. No doubt, again, God always wills what is best. Is it then better that I should be in error rather than not?

As I mull these things over more carefully, it occurs to me first that there is no reason to marvel at the fact that God should bring about certain things the reasons for which I do not understand. Nor is his existence therefore to be doubted because I happen to experience other things of which I fail to grasp why and how he made them. For since I know now that my nature is very weak and limited, whereas the nature of God is immense, incomprehensible, and infinite, this is sufficient for me also to know that he can make innumerable things whose causes escape me. For this reason alone the entire class of causes which people customarily derive from a thing's "end," I judge to be utterly useless in physics. It is not without rashness that I think myself capable of inquiring into the ends of God.

It also occurs to me that whenever we ask whether the works of God are perfect, we should keep in view not simply some one creature in isolation from the rest, but the universe as a whole. For perhaps something might rightfully appear very imperfect if it were all by itself; and yet be most perfect, to the extent that it has the status of a part in the universe. And although subsequent to having decided to doubt everything, I have come to know with certainty only that I and God exist, nevertheless, after having taken note of the immense power of God, I cannot deny that many other things have been made by him, or at least could have been made by him. Thus I may have the status of a part in the universal scheme of things.

Next, as I focus more closely on myself and inquire into the nature of my errors (the only things that are indicative of some imperfection in me), I note that these errors depend on the simultaneous concurrence of two causes: the faculty of knowing that is in me and the faculty of choosing, that is, the free choice of the will, in other words, simultaneously on the intellect and will. Through the intellect alone I merely perceive ideas, about which I can render a judgment. Strictly speaking, no error is to be found in the intellect when properly viewed in this manner. For although perhaps there may exist countless things about which I have no idea, nevertheless it must not be said that, strictly speaking, I am deprived of these ideas but only that I lack them in a negative sense. This is because I cannot adduce an argument to prove that God ought to have given me a greater faculty of knowing than he did. No matter how expert a craftsman I understand him to be, still I do not for that reason believe he ought to have bestowed on each one of his works all the perfections that he can put into some. Nor, on the other hand, can I complain that the will or free choice I have received from God is insufficiently ample or perfect, since I experience that it is limited by no boundaries whatever. In fact, it seems to be especially worth noting that no other things in me are so perfect or so great but that I understand that they can be still more perfect or greater. If, for example, I consider the faculty of understanding, I immediately recognize that in my case it is very small and quite limited, and at the very same time I form an idea of another much greater faculty of understanding—in fact, an understanding which is consummately great and infinite; and from the fact that I can form an idea of this faculty, I perceive that it pertains to the nature of God. Similarly, were I to examine the faculties of memory or imagination, or any of the other faculties, I would understand that in my case each of these is without exception feeble and limited, whereas in the case of God I understand each faculty to be boundless. It is only the will or free choice that I experience to be so great in me that I cannot grasp the idea of any greater faculty. This is so much the case that the will is the chief basis for my understanding that I bear a certain image and likeness of God. For although the faculty of willing is incomparably greater in God than it is in me, both by virtue of the knowledge and power that are joined to it and that render it more resolute and efficacious and by virtue of its object inasmuch as the divine will stretches over a greater number of things, nevertheless, when viewed in itself formally and precisely, God's faculty of willing does not appear to be any greater. This is owing to the fact that willing is merely a matter of being able to do or not do the same thing, that is, of being able to affirm or deny, to pursue or to shun; or better still, the will consists solely in the fact that when something is proposed to us by our intellect either to affirm or deny, to pursue or to shun, we are moved in such a way that we sense that we are determined to it by no external force. In order to be free I need not be capable of being moved in each direction; on the contrary, the more I am inclined toward one direction—either because I clearly understand that there is in it an aspect of the good and the true, or because God has thus disposed the inner recesses of my thought—the more freely do I choose that direction. Nor indeed does divine grace or natural knowledge ever diminish one's freedom; rather, they increase and strengthen it. However, the indifference that I experience when there is no reason moving me more in one direction than in another is the lowest grade of freedom; it is indicative not of any perfection in freedom, but rather of a defect, that is, a certain negation in knowledge. Were I always to see clearly what is true and good, I would never deliberate about what is to be judged or chosen. In that event, although I would be entirely free, I could never be indifferent.

    But from these considerations I perceive that the power of willing, which I got from God, is not, taken by itself, the cause of my errors, for it is most ample as well as perfect in its kind. Nor is my power of understanding the cause of my errors. For since I got my power of understanding from God, whatever I understand I doubtless understand rightly, and it is impossible for me to be deceived in this. What then is the source of my errors? They are owing simply to the fact that, since the will extends further than the intellect, I do not contain the will within the same boundaries; rather, I also extend it to things I do not understand. Because the will is indifferent in regard to such matters, it easily turns away from the true and the good; and in this way I am deceived and I sin.

    For example, during these last few days I was examining whether anything in the world exists, and I noticed that, from the very fact that I was making this examination, it obviously followed that I exist. Nevertheless, I could not help judging that what I understood so clearly was true; not that I was coerced into making this judgment because of some external force, but because a great light in my intellect gave way to a great inclination in my will, and the less indifferent I was, the more spontaneously and freely did I believe it. But now, in addition to my knowing that I exist, insofar as I am a certain thinking thing, I also observe a certain idea of corporeal nature. It happens that I am in doubt as to whether the thinking nature which is in me, or rather which I am, is something different from this corporeal nature, or whether both natures are one and the same thing. And I assume that as yet no consideration has occurred to my intellect to convince me of the one alternative rather than the other. Certainly in virtue of this very fact I am indifferent about whether to affirm or to deny either alternative, or even whether to make no judgment at all in the matter.

    Moreover, this indifference extends not merely to things about which the intellect knows absolutely nothing, but extends generally to everything of which the intellect does not have a clear enough knowledge at the very time when the will is deliberating on them. For although probable guesses may pull me in one direction, the mere knowledge that they are merely guesses and not certain and indubitable proofs is all it takes to push my assent in the opposite direction. These last few days have provided me with ample experience on this point. For all the beliefs that I had once held to be most true I have supposed to be utterly false, and for the sole reason that I determined that I could somehow raise doubts about them.

But if I hold off from making a judgment when I do not perceive what is true with sufficient clarity and distinctness, it is clear that I am acting properly and am not committing an error. But if instead I were to make an assertion or a denial, then I am not using my freedom properly. Were I to select the alternative that is false, then obviously I will be in error. But were I to embrace the other alternative, it will be by sheer luck that I happen upon the truth; but I will still not be without fault, for it is manifest by the light of nature that a perception on the part of the intellect must always precede a determination on the part of the will. Inherent in this incorrect use of free will is the privation that constitutes the very essence of error: the privation, I say, present in this operation insofar as the operation proceeds from me, but not in the faculty given to me by God, nor even in its operation insofar as it depends upon him.

Indeed I have no cause for complaint on the grounds that God has not given me a greater power of understanding or a greater light of nature than he has, for it is of the essence of a finite intellect not to understand many things, and it is of the essence of a created intellect to be finite. Actually, instead of thinking that he has withheld from me or deprived me of those things that he has not given me, I ought to thank God, who never owed me anything, for what he has bestowed upon me.

Again, I have no cause for complaint on the grounds that God has given me a will that has a wider scope than my intellect. For since the will consists of merely one thing, something indivisible, as it were, it does not seem that its nature could withstand anything being removed from it. Indeed, the more ample the will is, the more I ought to thank the one who gave it to me.

Finally, I should not complain because God concurs with me in eliciting those acts of the will, that is those judgments, in which I am mistaken. For insofar as those acts depend on God, they are absolutely true and good; and in a certain sense, there is greater perfection in me in being able to elicit those acts than in not being able to do so. But privation, in which alone the defining characteristic of falsehood and wrongdoing is to be found, has no need whatever for God's concurrence, since a privation is not a thing, nor, when it is related to God as its cause, is it to be called a privation, but simply a negation. For it is surely no imperfection in God that he has given me the freedom to give or withhold my assent in those instances where he has not placed a clear and distinct perception in my intellect. But surely it is an imperfection in me that I do not use my freedom well and that I make judgments about things I do not properly understand. Nevertheless, I see that God could easily have brought it about that, while still being free and having finite knowledge, I should nonetheless never make a mistake. This result could have been achieved either by his endowing my intellect

with a clear and distinct perception of everything about which I would ever deliberate, or by simply impressing the following rule so firmly upon my memory that
I could never forget it: I should never judge anything that I do not clearly and distinctly understand. I readily understand that, considered as a totality, I would
have been more perfect than I am now, had God made me that way. But I cannot
therefore deny that it may somehow be a greater perfection in the universe as a
whole that some of its parts are not immune to error, while others are, than if all
of them were exactly alike. And I have no right to complain that the part God has
wished me to play is not the principal and most perfect one of all.

Furthermore, even if I cannot abstain from errors in the first way mentioned
above, which depends upon a clear perception of everything about which I must
deliberate, nevertheless I can avoid error in the other way, which depends solely
on my remembering to abstain from making judgments whenever the truth of a   62
given matter is not apparent. For although I experience a certain infirmity in
myself, namely that I am unable to keep my attention constantly focused on one
and the same item of knowledge, nevertheless, by attentive and often repeated
meditation, I can bring it about that I call this rule to mind whenever the situation calls for it, and thus I would acquire a certain habit of not erring.

Since herein lies the greatest and chief perfection of man, I think today's meditation, in which I investigated the cause of error and falsity, was quite profitable.
Nor can this cause be anything other than the one I have described; for as often
as I restrain my will when I make judgments, so that it extends only to those matters that the intellect clearly and distinctly discloses to it, it plainly cannot happen that I err. For every clear and distinct perception is surely something, and
hence it cannot come from nothing. On the contrary, it must necessarily have
God for its author: God, I say, that supremely perfect being to whom it is repugnant to be a deceiver. Therefore the perception is most assuredly true. Today I
have learned not merely what I must avoid so as never to make a mistake, but at
the same time what I must do to attain truth. For I will indeed attain it, if only I
pay enough attention to all the things that I perfectly understand, and separate
them off from the rest, which I apprehend more confusedly and more obscurely.
I will be conscientious about this in the future.

MEDITATION FIVE: Concerning the Essence of Material Things,   *63*
and Again Concerning God, That He Exists

Several matters remain for me to examine concerning the attributes of God and
myself, that is, concerning the nature of my mind. But perhaps I will take these
up at some other time. For now, since I have noted what to avoid and what to do
in order to attain the truth, nothing seems more pressing than that I try to free
myself from the doubts into which I fell a few days ago, and that I see whether
anything certain is to be had concerning material things.

Yet, before inquiring whether any such things exist outside me, I surely ought
to consider the ideas of these things, insofar as they exist in my thought, and see
which ones are distinct and which ones are confused.

I do indeed distinctly imagine the quantity that philosophers commonly call "continuous," that is, the extension of this quantity, or rather of the thing quantified in length, breadth, and depth. I enumerate the various parts in it. I ascribe to these parts any sizes, shapes, positions, and local movements whatever; to these movements I ascribe any durations whatever.

Not only are these things manifestly known and transparent to me, viewed thus in a general way, but also, when I focus my attention on them, I perceive countless particulars concerning shapes, number, movement, and the like. Their truth
64   is so open and so much in accord with my nature that, when I first discover them, it seems I am not so much learning something new as recalling something I knew beforehand. In other words, it seems as though I am noticing things for the first time that were in fact in me for a long while, although I had not previously directed a mental gaze upon them.

What I believe must be considered above all here is the fact that I find within me countless ideas of certain things, that, even if perhaps they do not exist anywhere outside me, still cannot be said to be nothing. And although, in a sense, I think them at will, nevertheless they are not something I have fabricated; rather they have their own true and immutable natures. For example, when I imagine a triangle, even if perhaps no such figure exists outside my thought anywhere in the world and never has, the triangle still has a certain determinate nature, essence, or form which is unchangeable and eternal, which I did not fabricate, and which does not depend on my mind. This is evident from the fact that various properties can be demonstrated regarding this triangle: namely, that its three angles are equal to two right angles, that its longest side is opposite its largest angle, and so on. These are properties I now clearly acknowledge, whether I want to or not, even if I previously had given them no thought whatever when I imagined the triangle. For this reason, then, they were not fabricated by me.

It is irrelevant for me to say that perhaps the idea of a triangle came to me from external things through the sense organs because of course I have on occasion seen triangle-shaped bodies. For I can think of countless other figures, concerning which there can be no suspicion of their ever having entered me through the
65   senses, and yet I can demonstrate various properties of these figures, no less than I can those of the triangle. All these properties are patently true because I know them clearly, and thus they are something and not merely nothing. For it is obvious that whatever is true is something, and I have already demonstrated at some length that all that I know clearly is true. And even if I had not demonstrated this, certainly the nature of my mind is such that nevertheless I cannot refrain from assenting to these things, at least while I perceive them clearly. And I recall that even before now, when I used to keep my attention glued to the objects of the senses, I always took the truths I clearly recognized regarding figures, numbers, or other things pertaining to arithmetic, geometry, or, in general, to pure and abstract mathematics to be the most certain of all.

But if, from the mere fact that I can bring forth from my thought the idea of something, it follows that all that I clearly and distinctly perceive to belong to that thing really does belong to it, then cannot this too be a basis for an argument proving the existence of God? Clearly the idea of God, that is, the idea of a supremely perfect being, is one I discover to be no less within me than the idea of any figure or number. And that it belongs to God's nature that he always exists is something I understand no less clearly and distinctly than is the case when I demonstrate in regard to some figure or number that something also belongs to the nature of that figure or number. Thus, even if not everything that I have meditated upon during these last few days were true, still the existence of God ought to have for me at least the same degree of certainty that truths of mathematics   *66* had until now.

However, this point is not wholly obvious at first glance, but has a certain look of a sophism about it. Since in all other matters I have become accustomed to distinguishing existence from essence, I easily convince myself that it can even be separated from God's essence, and hence that God can be thought of as not existing. But nevertheless, it is obvious to anyone who pays close attention that existence can no more be separated from God's essence than its having three angles equal to two right angles can be separated from the essence of a triangle, or than the idea of a valley can be separated from the idea of a mountain. Thus it is no less[4] contradictory to think of God (that is, a supremely perfect being) lacking existence (that is, lacking some perfection), than it is to think of a mountain without a valley.

But granted I can no more think of God as not existing than I can think of a mountain without a valley, nevertheless it surely does not follow from the fact that I think of a mountain without a valley that a mountain exists in the world. Likewise, from the fact that I think of God as existing, it does not seem to follow that God exists, for my thought imposes no necessity on things. And just as one may imagine a winged horse, without there being a horse that has wings, in the same way perhaps I can attach existence to God, even though no God exists.

But there is a sophism lurking here. From the fact that I am unable to think of a mountain without a valley, it does not follow that a mountain or a valley exists   *67* anywhere, but only that, whether they exist or not, a mountain and a valley are inseparable from one another. But from the fact that I cannot think of God except as existing, it follows that existence is inseparable from God, and that for this reason he really exists. Not that my thought brings this about or imposes any necessity on anything; but rather the necessity of the thing itself, namely of the existence of God, forces me to think this. For I am not free to think of God without existence, that is, a supremely perfect being without a supreme perfection, as I am to imagine a horse with or without wings.

Further, it should not be said here that even though I surely need to assent to the existence of God once I have asserted that God has all perfections and that existence is one of these perfections, nevertheless that earlier assertion need not have been made. Likewise, I need not believe that all four-sided figures can be inscribed in a circle; but given that I posit this, it would then be necessary for me to admit that a rhombus can be inscribed in a circle. Yet this is obviously false. For although it is not necessary that I should ever happen upon any thought of

---

4. A literal translation of the Latin text *(non magis)* is "no more." This is obviously a misstatement on Descartes's part, since it contradicts his own clearly stated views.

God, nevertheless whenever I am of a mind to think of a being that is first and supreme, and bring forth the idea of God as it were from the storehouse of my mind, I must of necessity ascribe all perfections to him, even if I do not at that time enumerate them all or take notice of each one individually. This necessity plainly suffices so that afterwards, when I realize that existence is a perfection, I rightly conclude that a first and supreme being exists. In the same way, there is no necessity for me ever to imagine a triangle, but whenever I do wish to consider a rectilinear figure having but three angles, I must ascribe to it those prop-
68   erties on the basis of which one rightly infers that the three angles of this figure are no greater than two right angles, even though I do not take note of this at the time. But when I inquire as to the figures that may be inscribed in a circle, there is absolutely no need whatever for my thinking that all four-sided figures are of this sort; for that matter, I cannot even fabricate such a thing, so long as I am of a mind to admit only what I clearly and distinctly understand. Consequently, there is a great difference between false assumptions of this sort and the true ideas that are inborn in me, the first and chief of which is the idea of God. For there are a great many ways in which I understand that this idea is not an invention that is dependent upon my thought, but is an image of a true and immutable nature. First, I cannot think of anything aside from God alone to whose essence existence belongs. Next, I cannot understand how there could be two or more Gods of this kind. Again, once I have asserted that one God now exists, I plainly see that it is necessary that he has existed from eternity and will endure for eternity. Finally, I perceive many other features in God, none of which I can remove or change.

But, whatever type of argument I use, it always comes down to the fact that the only things that fully convince me are those that I clearly and distinctly perceive. And although some of these things I thus perceive are obvious to everyone, while others are discovered only by those who look more closely and inquire carefully, nevertheless, once they have been discovered, they are considered no less certain than the others. For example, in the case of a right triangle,
69   although it is not so readily apparent that the square of the hypotenuse is equal to the sum of the squares of the other two sides as it is that the hypotenuse is opposite the largest angle, nevertheless, once the former has been ascertained, it is no less believed. However, as far as God is concerned, if I were not overwhelmed by prejudices and if the images of sensible things were not besieging my thought from all directions, I would certainly acknowledge nothing sooner or more easily than him. For what, in and of itself, is more manifest than that a supreme being exists, that is, that God, to whose essence alone existence belongs, exists?

And although I needed to pay close attention in order to perceive this, nevertheless I now am just as certain about this as I am about everything else that seems most certain. Moreover, I observe also that certitude about other things is so dependent on this, that without it nothing can ever be perfectly known.

For I am indeed of such a nature that, while I perceive something very clearly and distinctly, I cannot help believing it to be true. Nevertheless, my nature is also such that I cannot focus my mental gaze always on the same thing, so as to perceive it clearly. Often the memory of a previously made judgment may return when I am no longer attending to the arguments on account of which I made such a judgment. Thus, other arguments can be brought forward that would easily make me change my opinion, were I ignorant of God. And thus I would never have true and certain knowledge about anything, but merely fickle and changeable opinions. Thus, for example, when I consider the nature of a triangle, it appears most evident to me, steeped as I am in the principles of geometry, that its three angles are equal to two right angles. And so long as I attend to its demonstration I cannot help believing this to be true. But 70 no sooner do I turn the mind's eye away from the demonstration, than, however much I still recall that I had observed it most clearly, nevertheless, it can easily happen that I entertain doubts about whether it is true, were I ignorant of God. For I can convince myself that I have been so constituted by nature that I might occasionally be mistaken about those things I believe I perceive most evidently, especially when I recall that I have often taken many things to be true and certain, which other arguments have subsequently led me to judge to be false.

But once I perceived that there is a God, and also understood at the same time that everything else depends on him, and that he is not a deceiver, I then concluded that everything that I clearly and distinctly perceive is necessarily true. Hence even if I no longer attend to the reasons leading me to judge this to be true, so long as I merely recall that I did clearly and distinctly observe it, no counterargument can be brought forward that might force me to doubt it. On the contrary, I have a true and certain knowledge of it. And not just of this one fact, but of everything else that I recall once having demonstrated, as in geometry, and so on. For what objections can now be raised against me? That I have been made such that I am often mistaken? But I now know that I cannot be mistaken in matters I plainly understand. That I have taken many things to be true and certain which subsequently I recognized to be false? But none of these were things I clearly and distinctly perceived. But I was ignorant of this rule for determining the truth, and I believed these things perhaps for other reasons, which I later discovered were less firm. What then remains to be said? That perhaps I am dreaming, as I recently objected against myself, in other words, that everything I am now thinking of is no truer than what occurs to someone who is asleep? Be that as it may, this changes nothing; for certainly, even if I were dreaming, if anything is evident to my intellect, then it is entirely true. 71

And thus I see plainly that the certainty and truth of every science depends exclusively upon the knowledge of the true God, to the extent that, prior to my becoming aware of him, I was incapable of achieving perfect knowledge about anything else. But now it is possible for me to achieve full and certain knowledge about countless things, both about God and other intellectual matters, as well as about the entirety of that corporeal nature which is the object of pure mathematics.

MEDITATION SIX: Concerning the Existence of Material Things, and the Real Distinction between Mind and Body

It remains for me to examine whether material things exist. Indeed I now know that they can exist, at least insofar as they are the object of pure mathematics, since I clearly and distinctly perceive them. For no doubt God is capable of bringing about everything that I am capable of perceiving in this way. And I have never judged that God was incapable of something, except when it was incompatible with my perceiving it distinctly. Moreover, from the faculty of imagination, which I notice I use while dealing with material things, it seems to follow that they exist. For to anyone paying very close attention to what imagination is,
72   it appears to be simply a certain application of the knowing faculty to a body intimately present to it, and which therefore exists.

To make this clear, I first examine the difference between imagination and pure intellection. So, for example, when I imagine a triangle, I not only understand that it is a figure bounded by three lines, but at the same time I also envisage with the mind's eye those lines as if they were present; and this is what I call "imagining." On the other hand, if I want to think about a chiliagon, I certainly understand that it is a figure consisting of a thousand sides, just as well as I understand that a triangle is a figure consisting of three sides, yet I do not imagine those thousand sides in the same way, or envisage them as if they were present. And although in that case, because of force of habit I always imagine something whenever I think about a corporeal thing, I may perchance represent to myself some figure in a confused fashion, nevertheless this figure is obviously not a chiliagon. For this figure is really no different from the figure I would represent to myself, were I thinking of a myriagon or any other figure with a large number of sides. Nor is this figure of any help in knowing the properties that differentiate a chiliagon from other polygons. But if the figure in question is a pentagon, I surely can understand its figure, just as was the case with the chiliagon, without the help of my imagination. But I can also imagine a pentagon by turning the mind's eye both to its five sides and at the same time to the area bounded by those sides. At this point I am manifestly aware that I am in need of a pecu-
73   liar sort of effort on the part of the mind in order to imagine, one that I do not employ in order to understand. This new effort on the part of the mind clearly shows the difference between imagination and pure intellection.

Moreover, I consider that this power of imagining that is in me, insofar as it differs from the power of understanding, is not required for my own essence, that is, the essence of my mind. For were I to be lacking this power, I would nevertheless undoubtedly remain the same entity I am now. Thus it seems to follow that the power of imagining depends upon something distinct from me. And I readily understand that, were a body to exist to which a mind is so joined that it may apply itself in order, as it were, to look at it any time it wishes, it could happen that it is by means of this very body that I imagine corporeal things. As a result, this mode of thinking may differ from pure intellection only in the sense that the mind, when it understands, in a sense turns toward itself and looks at one of the ideas that are in it; whereas when it imagines, it turns toward the body, and intuits in the body something that conforms to an idea either understood by the mind or perceived by sense. To be sure, I easily understand that the imagination can be actualized in this way, provided a body does exist. And since I can think of no other way of explaining imagination that is equally appropriate, I make a probable conjecture from this that a body exists. But this is only a probability. And even though I may examine everything carefully, nevertheless I do not yet see how the distinct idea of corporeal nature that I find in my imagination can enable me to develop an argument which necessarily concludes that some body exists.

But I am in the habit of imagining many other things, over and above that cor- *74* poreal nature which is the object of pure mathematics, such as colors, sounds, tastes, pain, and the like, though not so distinctly. And I perceive these things better by means of the senses, from which, with the aid of the memory, they seem to have arrived at the imagination. Thus I should pay the same degree of attention to the senses, so that I might deal with them more appropriately. I must see whether I can obtain any reliable argument for the existence of corporeal things from those things that are perceived by the mode of thinking that I call "sense."

First of all, to be sure, I will review here all the things I previously believed to be true because I had perceived them by means of the senses and the causes I had for thinking this. Next I will assess the causes why I later called them into doubt. Finally, I will consider what I must now believe about these things.

So first, I sensed that I had a head, hands, feet, and other members that comprised this body which I viewed as part of me, or perhaps even as the whole of me. I sensed that this body was found among many other bodies, by which my body can be affected in various beneficial or harmful ways. I gauged what was opportune by means of a certain sensation of pleasure, and what was inopportune by a sensation of pain. In addition to pain and pleasure, I also sensed within me hunger, thirst, and other such appetites, as well as certain bodily tendencies toward mirth, sadness, anger, and other such affects. And externally, besides the extension, shapes, and motions of bodies, I also sensed their hardness, heat, and *75* other tactile qualities. I also sensed light, colors, odors, tastes, and sounds, on the basis of whose variety I distinguished the sky, the earth, the seas, and the other bodies, one from the other. Now given the ideas of all these qualities that presented themselves to my thought, and which were all that I properly and immediately sensed, still it was surely not without reason that I thought I sensed things that were manifestly different from my thought, namely, the bodies from which these ideas proceeded. For I knew by experience that these ideas came upon me utterly without my consent, to the extent that, wish as I may, I could not sense any object unless it was present to a sense organ. Nor could I fail to sense it when it was present. And since the ideas perceived by sense were much more vivid and explicit and even, in their own way, more distinct than any of those that I deliberately and knowingly formed through meditation or that I found impressed on my memory, it seemed impossible that they came from myself. Thus the remaining alternative was that they came from other things. Since I had no knowledge

of such things except from those same ideas themselves, I could not help enter-
taining the thought that they were similar to those ideas. Moreover, I also
recalled that the use of the senses antedated the use of reason. And since I saw
that the ideas that I myself fashioned were not as explicit as those that I perceived
through the faculty of sense, and were for the most part composed of parts of the
latter, I easily convinced myself that I had absolutely no idea in the intellect that
I did not have beforehand in the sense faculty. Not without reason did I judge that
76   this body, which by a certain special right I called "mine," belongs more to me
than did any other. For I could never be separated from it in the same way I could
be from other bodies. I sensed all appetites and feelings in and on behalf of it.
Finally, I noticed pain and pleasurable excitement in its parts, but not in other
bodies external to it. But why should a certain sadness of spirit arise from some
sensation or other of pain, and why should a certain elation arise from a sensation of excitement, or why should that peculiar twitching in the stomach, which
I call hunger, warn me to have something to eat, or why should dryness in the
throat warn me to take something to drink, and so on? I plainly had no explanation other than that I had been taught this way by nature. For there is no affinity
whatsoever, at least none I am aware of, between this twitching in the stomach
and the will to have something to eat, or between the sensation of something
causing pain and the thought of sadness arising from this sensation. But nature
also seems to have taught me everything else as well that I judged concerning the
objects of the senses, for I had already convinced myself that this was how things
were, prior to my assessing any of the arguments that might prove it.

   Afterwards, however, many experiences gradually weakened any faith that I
had in the senses. Towers that had seemed round from afar occasionally appeared
square at close quarters. Very large statues mounted on their pedestals did not
seem large to someone looking at them from ground level. And in countless other
such instances I determined that judgments in matters of the external senses were
77   in error. And not just the external senses, but the internal senses as well. For what
can be more intimate than pain? But I had sometimes heard it said by people
whose leg or arm had been amputated that it seemed to them that they still occasionally sensed pain in the very limb they had lost. Thus, even in my own case it
did not seem to be entirely certain that some bodily member was causing me
pain, even though I did sense pain in it. To these causes for doubt I recently added
two quite general ones. The first was that everything I ever thought I sensed
while awake I could believe I also sometimes sensed while asleep, and since I do
not believe that what I seem to sense in my dreams comes to me from things
external to me, I saw no reason why I should hold this belief about those things
I seem to be sensing while awake. The second was that, since I was still ignorant
of the author of my origin (or at least pretended to be ignorant of it), I saw nothing to prevent my having been so constituted by nature that I should be mistaken
even about what seemed to me most true. As to the arguments that used to convince me of the truth of sensible things, I found no difficulty responding to them.
For since I seemed driven by nature toward many things about which reason tried
to dissuade me, I did not think that what I was taught by nature deserved much
credence. And even though the perceptions of the senses did not depend on my

will, I did not think that we must therefore conclude that they
distinct from me, since perhaps there is some faculty in me, a.
me, that produces these perceptions.

But now, having begun to have a better knowledge of myself an.
my origin, I am of the opinion that I must not rashly admit everythin,
to derive from the senses; but neither, for that matter, should I call
into doubt.

First, I know that all the things that I clearly and distinctly understand can be
made by God such as I understand them. For this reason, my ability clearly and
distinctly to understand one thing without another suffices to make me certain
that the one thing is different from the other, since they can be separated from
each other, at least by God. The question as to the sort of power that might effect
such a separation is not relevant to their being thought to be different. For this
reason, from the fact that I know that I exist, and that at the same time I judge
that obviously nothing else belongs to my nature or essence except that I am a
thinking thing, I rightly conclude that my essence consists entirely in my being
a thinking thing. And although perhaps (or rather, as I shall soon say, assuredly)
I have a body that is very closely joined to me, nevertheless, because on the one
hand I have a clear and distinct idea of myself, insofar as I am merely a thinking
thing and not an extended thing, and because on the other hand I have a distinct
idea of a body, insofar as it is merely an extended thing and not a thinking thing,
it is certain that I am really distinct from my body, and can exist without it.

Moreover, I find in myself faculties for certain special modes of thinking,
namely the faculties of imagining and sensing. I can clearly and distinctly understand myself in my entirety without these faculties, but not vice versa: I cannot
understand them clearly and distinctly without me, that is, without a substance
endowed with understanding in which they inhere, for they include an act of
understanding in their formal concept. Thus I perceive them to be distinguished
from me as modes from a thing. I also acknowledge that there are certain other
faculties, such as those of moving from one place to another, of taking on various shapes, and so on, that, like sensing or imagining, cannot be understood apart
from some substance in which they inhere, and hence without which they cannot
exist. But it is clear that these faculties, if in fact they exist, must be in a corporeal or extended substance, not in a substance endowed with understanding. For
some extension is contained in a clear and distinct concept of them, though certainly not any understanding. Now there clearly is in me a passive faculty of
sensing, that is, a faculty for receiving and knowing the ideas of sensible things;
but I could not use it unless there also existed, either in me or in something else,
a certain active faculty of producing or bringing about these ideas. But this faculty surely cannot be in me, since it clearly presupposes no act of understanding,
and these ideas are produced without my cooperation and often even against my
will. Therefore the only alternative is that it is in some substance different from
me, containing either formally or eminently all the reality that exists objectively
in the ideas produced by that faculty, as I have just noted above. Hence this substance is either a body, that is, a corporeal nature, which contains formally all that
is contained objectively in the ideas, or else it is God, or some other creature

.ے noble than a body, which contains eminently all that is contained objec- tively in the ideas. But since God is not a deceiver, it is patently obvious that he does not send me these ideas either immediately by himself, or even through the mediation of some creature that contains the objective reality of these ideas not formally but only eminently. For since God has given me no faculty whatsoever for making this determination, but instead has given me a great inclination to believe that these ideas issue from corporeal things, I fail to see how God could be understood not to be a deceiver, if these ideas were to issue from a source other than corporeal things. And consequently corporeal things exist. Nevertheless, per- haps not all bodies exist exactly as I grasp them by sense, since this sensory grasp is in many cases very obscure and confused. But at least they do contain everything I clearly and distinctly understand—that is, everything, considered in a general sense, that is encompassed in the object of pure mathematics.

80

As far as the remaining matters are concerned, which are either merely partic- ular (for example, that the sun is of such and such a size or shape, and so on) or less clearly understood (for example, light, sound, pain, and the like), even though these matters are very doubtful and uncertain, nevertheless the fact that God is no deceiver (and thus no falsity can be found in my opinions, unless there is also in me a faculty given me by God for the purpose of rectifying this falsity) offers me a definite hope of reaching the truth even in these matters. And surely there is no doubt that all that I am taught by nature has some truth to it; for by "nature," taken generally, I understand nothing other than God himself or the ordered network of created things which was instituted by God. By my own par- ticular nature I understand nothing other than the combination of all the things bestowed upon me by God.

There is nothing that this nature teaches me more explicitly than that I have a body that is ill-disposed when I feel pain, that needs food and drink when I suf- fer hunger or thirst, and the like. Therefore, I should not doubt that there is some truth in this.

81

By means of these sensations of pain, hunger, thirst, and so on, nature also teaches that I am present in my body not merely in the way a sailor is present in a ship, but that I am most tightly joined and, so to speak, commingled with it, so much so that I and the body constitute one single thing. For if this were not the case, then I, who am only a thinking thing, would not sense pain when the body is injured; rather, I would perceive the wound by means of the pure intellect, just as a sailor perceives by sight whether anything in his ship is broken. And when the body is in need of food or drink, I should understand this explicitly, instead of having confused sensations of hunger and thirst. For clearly these sensations of thirst, hunger, pain, and so on are nothing but certain confused modes of think- ing arising from the union and, as it were, the commingling of the mind with the body.

Moreover, I am also taught by nature that various other bodies exist around my body, some of which are to be pursued, while others are to be avoided. And to be sure, from the fact that I sense a wide variety of colors, sounds, odors, tastes, levels of heat, and grades of roughness, and the like, I rightly conclude that in the bodies from which these different perceptions of the senses proceed there are differences corresponding to the different perceptions—though perhaps the latter do not resemble the former. And from the fact that some of these perceptions are pleasant while others are unpleasant, it is plainly certain that my body, or rather my whole self, insofar as I am comprised of a body and a mind, can be affected by various beneficial and harmful bodies in the vicinity.

Granted, there are many other things that I seem to have been taught by nature; nevertheless it was not really nature that taught them to me but a certain habit of making reckless judgments. And thus it could easily happen that these judgments are false: for example, that any space where there is absolutely nothing happening to move my senses is empty; or that there is something in a hot body that bears an exact likeness to the idea of heat that is in me; or that in a white or green body there is the same whiteness or greenness that I sense; or that in a bitter or sweet body there is the same taste, and so on; or that stars and towers and any other distant bodies have the same size and shape that they present to my senses, and other things of this sort. But to ensure that my perceptions in this matter are sufficiently distinct, I ought to define more precisely what exactly I mean when I say that I am "taught something by nature." For I am taking "nature" here more narrowly than the combination of everything bestowed on me by God. For this combination embraces many things that belong exclusively to my mind, such as my perceiving that what has been done cannot be undone, and everything else that is known by the light of nature. That is not what I am talking about here. There are also many things that belong exclusively to the body, such as that it tends to move downward, and so on. I am not dealing with these either, but only with what God has bestowed on me insofar as I am composed of mind and body. Accordingly, it is this nature that teaches me to avoid things that produce a sensation of pain and to pursue things that produce a sensation of pleasure, and the like. But it does not appear that nature teaches us to conclude anything, besides these things, from these sense perceptions unless the intellect has first conducted its own inquiry regarding things external to us. For it seems to belong exclusively to the mind, and not to the composite of mind and body, to know the truth in these matters. Thus, although a star affects my eye no more than does the flame from a small torch, still there is no real or positive tendency in my eye toward believing that the star is no larger than the flame. Yet, ever since my youth, I have made this judgment without any reason for doing so. And although I feel heat as I draw closer to the fire, and I also feel pain upon drawing too close to it, there is not a single argument that persuades me that there is something in the fire similar to that heat, any more than to that pain. On the contrary, I am convinced only that there is something in the fire that, regardless of what it finally turns out to be, causes in us those sensations of heat or pain. And although there may be nothing in a given space that moves the senses, it does not therefore follow that there is no body in it. But I see that in these any many other instances I have been in the habit of subverting the order of nature. For admittedly I use the perceptions of the senses (which are properly given by nature only for signifying to the mind what things are useful or harmful to the composite of which it is a part, and to that extent they are clear and distinct enough), as reliable rules for immediately discerning what is the essence of bodies located outside us. Yet they signify nothing about that except quite obscurely and confusedly.

82

83

I have already examined in sufficient detail how it could happen that my judgments are false, despite the goodness of God. But a new difficulty now arises regarding those very things that nature shows me are either to be sought out or avoided, as well as the internal sensations where I seem to have detected errors, as for example, when someone is deluded by a food's pleasant taste to eat the
84   poison hidden inside it. In this case, however, he is driven by nature only toward desiring the thing in which the pleasurable taste is found, but not toward the poison, of which he obviously is unaware. I can only conclude that this nature is not omniscient. This is not remarkable, since man is a limited thing, and thus only what is of limited perfection befits him.

But we not infrequently err even in those things to which nature impels us. Take, for example, the case of those who are ill and who desire food or drink that will soon afterwards be injurious to them. Perhaps it could be said here that they erred because their nature was corrupt. However, this does not remove our difficulty, for a sick man is no less a creature of God than a healthy one, and thus it seems no less inconsistent that the sick man got a deception-prone nature from God. And a clock made of wheels and counterweights follows all the laws of nature no less closely when it has been badly constructed and does not tell time accurately than it does when it completely satisfies the wish of its maker. Likewise, I might regard a man's body as a kind of mechanism that is outfitted with and composed of bones, nerves, muscles, veins, blood, and skin in such a way that, even if no mind existed in it, the man's body would still exhibit all the same motions that are in it now except for those motions that proceed either from a command of the will or, consequently, from the mind. I easily recognize that it would be natural for this body, were it, say, suffering from dropsy and experiencing dryness in the throat (which typically produces a thirst sensation in the mind), and also so disposed by its nerves and other parts to take something to drink, the result of which would be to exacerbate the illness. This is as natural as
85   for a body without any such illness to be moved by the same dryness in the throat to take something to drink that is useful to it. And given the intended purpose of the clock, I could say that it deviates from its nature when it fails to tell the right time. And similarly, considering the mechanism of the human body in terms of its being equipped for the motions that typically occur in it, I may think that it too is deviating from its nature, if its throat were dry when having something to drink is not beneficial to its conservation. Nevertheless, I am well aware that this last use of "nature" differs greatly from the other. For this latter "nature" is merely a designation dependent on my thought, since it compares a man in poor health and a poorly constructed clock with the ideas of a healthy man and of a well-made clock, a designation extrinsic to the things to which it is applied. But by "nature" taken in the former sense, I understand something that is really in things, and thus is not without some truth.

When we say, then, in the case of the body suffering from dropsy, that its "nature" is corrupt, given the fact that it has a parched throat and yet does not need something to drink, "nature" obviously is merely an extrinsic designation. Nevertheless, in the case of the composite, that is, of a mind joined to such a body, it is not a mere designation, but a true error of nature that this body should be thirsty when having something to drink would be harmful to it. It therefore remains to inquire here how the goodness of God does not prevent "nature," thus considered, from being deceptive.

Now my first observation here is that there is a great difference between a mind and a body, in that a body, by its very nature, is always divisible. On the other hand, the mind is utterly indivisible. For when I consider the mind, that is, 86 myself insofar as I am only a thinking thing, I cannot distinguish any parts within me; rather, I understand myself to be manifestly one complete thing. Although the entire mind seems to be united to the entire body, nevertheless, were a foot or an arm or any other bodily part to be amputated, I know that nothing has been taken away from the mind on that account. Nor can the faculties of willing, sensing, understanding, and so on be called "parts" of the mind, since it is one and the same mind that wills, senses, and understands. On the other hand, there is no corporeal or extended thing I can think of that I may not in my thought easily divide into parts; and in this way I understand that it is divisible. This consideration alone would suffice to teach me that the mind is wholly diverse from the body, had I not yet known it well enough in any other way.

My second observation is that my mind is not immediately affected by all the parts of the body, but only by the brain, or perhaps even by just one small part of the brain, namely, by that part where the "common" sense is said to reside. Whenever this part of the brain is disposed in the same manner, it presents the same thing to the mind, even if the other parts of the body are able meanwhile to be related in diverse ways. Countless experiments show this, none of which need be reviewed here.

My next observation is that the nature of the body is such that whenever any of its parts can be moved by another part some distance away, it can also be moved in the same manner by any of the parts that lie between them, even if this more distant part is doing nothing. For example, in the cord ABCD, if the final 87 part D is pulled, the first part A would be moved in exactly the same manner as it could be, if one of the intermediate parts B or C were pulled, while the end part D remained immobile. Likewise, when I feel a pain in my foot, physics teaches me that this sensation took place by means of nerves distributed throughout the foot, like stretched cords extending from the foot all the way to the brain. When these nerves are pulled in the foot, they also pull on the inner parts of the brain to which they extend, and produce a certain motion in them. This motion has been constituted by nature so as to affect the mind with a sensation of pain, as if it occurred in the foot. But because these nerves need to pass through the shin, thigh, loins, back, and neck, to get from the foot to the brain, it can happen that even if it is not the part in the foot, but merely one of the intermediate parts that is being struck, the very same movement will occur in the brain that would occur, were the foot badly injured. The inevitable result will be that the mind feels the same pain. The same opinion should hold for any other sensation.

My final observation is that, since any given motion occurring in that part of the brain immediately affecting the mind produces but one sensation in it, I can think of no better arrangement than that it produces the one sensation that, of all the ones it is able to produce, is most especially and most often conducive to the

maintenance of a healthy man. Moreover, experience shows that all the sensations bestowed on us by nature are like this. Hence there is absolutely nothing to
be found in them that does not bear witness to God's power and goodness. Thus,

88   for example, when the nerves in the foot are agitated in a violent and unusual
manner, this motion of theirs extends through the marrow of the spine to the
inner reaches of the brain, where it gives the mind the sign to sense something,
namely, the pain as if it is occurring in the foot. This provokes the mind to do its
utmost to move away from the cause of the pain, since it is seen as harmful to the
foot. But the nature of man could have been so constituted by God that this same
motion in the brain might have indicated something else to the mind: for example, either the motion itself as it occurs in the brain, or in the foot, or in some
place in between, or something else entirely different. But nothing else would
have served so well the maintenance of the body. Similarly, when we need something to drink, a certain dryness arises in the throat that moves the nerves in the
throat, and, by means of them, the inner parts of the brain. And this motion
affects the mind with a sensation of thirst, because in this entire affair nothing is
more useful for us to know than that we need something to drink in order to
maintain our health; the same holds in the other cases.

From these considerations it is utterly apparent that, notwithstanding the
immense goodness of God, the nature of man, insofar as it is composed of mind
and body, cannot help being sometimes mistaken. For if some cause, not in the
foot but in some other part through which the nerves extend from the foot to the
brain, or perhaps even in the brain itself, were to produce the same motion that
would normally be produced by a badly injured foot, the pain will be felt as if it
were in the foot, and the senses will naturally be deceived. For since an identical
motion in the brain can only bring about an identical sensation in the mind, and
it is more frequently the case that this motion is wont to arise on account of a
cause that harms the foot than on account of some other thing existing elsewhere,

89   it is reasonable that the motion should always show pain to the mind as something belonging to the foot rather than to some other part. And if dryness in the
throat does not arise, as is normal, from drink's contributing to bodily health, but
from a contrary cause, as happens in the case of someone with dropsy, then it is
far better that it should deceive on that occasion than that it should always be
deceptive when the body is in good health. The same holds for the other cases.

This consideration is most helpful, not only for my noticing all the errors to
which my nature is liable, but also for enabling me to correct or avoid them without difficulty. To be sure, I know that all the senses set forth what is true more
frequently than what is false regarding what concerns the welfare of the body.
Moreover, I can nearly always make use of several of them in order to examine
the same thing. Furthermore, I can use my memory, which connects current hap-
penings with past ones, and my intellect, which now has examined all the causes
of error. Hence I should no longer fear that those things that are daily shown me
by the senses are false. On the contrary, the hyperbolic doubts of the last few
days ought to be rejected as ludicrous. This goes especially for the chief reason
for doubting, which dealt with my failure to distinguish being asleep from being
awake. For I now notice that there is a considerable difference between these

two; dreams are never joined by the memory with all the other actions of life, as is the case with those actions that occur when one is awake. For surely, if, while I am awake, someone were suddenly to appear to me and then immediately disappear, as occurs in dreams, so that I see neither where he came from nor where he went, it is not without reason that I would judge him to be a ghost or a phantom conjured up in my brain, rather than a true man. But when these things happen, and I notice distinctly where they come from, where they are now, and when they come to me, and when I connect my perception of them without interruption with the whole rest of my life, I am clearly certain that these perceptions have happened to me not while I was dreaming but while I was awake. Nor ought I have even the least doubt regarding the truth of these things, if, having mustered all the senses, in addition to my memory and my intellect, in order to examine them, nothing is passed on to me by one of these sources that conflicts with the others. For from the fact that God is no deceiver, it follows that I am in no way mistaken in these matters. But because the need to get things done does not always permit us the leisure for such a careful inquiry, we must confess that the life of man is apt to commit errors regarding particular things, and we must acknowledge the infirmity of our nature.

V

OBJECTIONS BY SOME LEARNED MEN TO THE PRECEDING MEDITATIONS, WITH REPLIES BY THE AUTHOR (1641)

First Set of Objections

Gentlemen:[1]

When I[2] realized that you were absolutely resolved that I should examine more deeply the writings of M. Descartes, I could not help complying in this matter with men who have been so particularly friendly to me. I am complying with this request both so that you may see how great is my esteem for you and so that it may be apparent how much my powers and acumen fall short, with the result that you might both give me greater support in the future, if I need it, and hold me less accountable, if I am not up to the task.

As I see it, M. Descartes is clearly a man whose intelligence is without match and whose moderation is unrivaled—traits that even Momus[3] would cherish, were he alive today. I think, says M. Descartes, therefore I exist. In fact, I am that
92   very thought or mind. So be it. Moreover, in thinking, I have the ideas of things within me, and, above all, an idea of a most perfect and infinite being. I will grant this as well. But I, who do not equal the objective reality of this idea, am not the cause of this idea. Therefore the cause of this idea is something more perfect than me. Hence there exists something other than myself. There exists something more perfect than me. There exists someone who is a being not in some restricted fashion or other, but who embraces in himself all being equally and without qualification or limitation, and is, as it were, an anticipatory cause, as Dionysius[4] declares in his *On Divine Names,* chapter eight.

Selections on pp.142–206 translated by Donald Cress.

1. This set of objections is addressed to two friends of Descartes, Ban (Bannius in Latin) and Bloemaert. Both of these individuals were canons of the chapter of Harlem. More information on the objectors, with analyses of their objections and Descartes's replies, can be found in the various essays collected in Ariew and Grene.

2. Johan de Kater (1590–1655), whose latinized name was Johannes Caterus, was a Catholic priest and theologian at Alkmaar, Holland. Bannius and Bloemaert had forwarded to Caterus prepublication copies of Descartes's *Meditations on First Philosophy* together with the request that he provide comments and objections, which Descartes would publish along with his replies.

3. Greek god of censure and mockery.

4. A late neo-Platonic writer whose works were for a long time mistakenly thought to be those of the Dionysius the Areopagite mentioned in Acts 17:34; hence this writer is often referred to as (the) Pseudo-Dionysius.

But I am compelled to stop here for a short while, lest I become utterly exhausted. For, just like the billowing Euripus,[5] my mind is in a whirl. I affirm, I deny, I approve, and again I disapprove. I do not want to disagree with the man, yet I cannot agree with him. Indeed, I ask, what cause does an idea require? Or what, pray, is an idea? It is the very thing thought insofar as it exists objectively in the intellect. But what is it to exist objectively in the intellect? I was once taught that to exist objectively is to terminate the act of the intellect after the manner of an object. This characterization is surely an extrinsic denomination and it has no bearing on the thing itself. For just as being seen is simply an act of seeing terminating in me, so, being thought or existing objectively in the intellect is an act of thinking on the part of the mind stopping at and terminating in itself. This process can occur whether the thing be motionless or unchanged, nay even nonexistent. Why, therefore, do I seek the cause of what is not actual, of what is a mere denomination, of what is nothing?

Nevertheless, this great genius declares "that this idea contains this as opposed to that objective reality is surely owing to some cause. . ."[6] In point of fact, it gets it from no cause at all, for objective reality is just a pure denomination and is nothing actual, whereas a cause imparts a real and actual influence. What is not actual does not receive anything and thus does not undergo the actual influence of a cause, nor does it need to. Thus I grant that I have ideas but not that ideas have a cause, let alone a cause that is greater than me and infinite. 93

But if you do not grant that ideas have a cause, then at least state some reason why this idea has this objective reality rather than that objective reality. A point well taken, for I am not in the habit of being tightfisted with friends; on the contrary, I am quite openhanded. I declare universally with respect to all ideas what M. Descartes has said elsewhere regarding the triangle: ". . . even if perhaps," he says, "no such figure exists outside my thought anywhere in the world and never has, the triangle still has a certain determinate nature, essence, or form which is immutable and eternal. . ." It is, to be sure, an eternal truth, which requires no cause. A boat is a boat and not something else; Davus is Davus and not Oedipus.[7] If, however, you insist on a reason, it is the imperfection of our intellect, which is not infinite. For since our intellect does not comprehend the entire universe all at once in a single grasp, the intellect divides and separates every good; and thus, what it cannot bring forth whole it conceives by degrees, or, as they also say, "inadequately."

The gentleman continues further: "Yet as imperfect a mode of being as this is by which a thing exists in the intellect objectively through an idea, nevertheless

---

5. A narrow strait in the Aegean Sea between the island of Euboea and the Greek mainland. Its strong tidal currents change directions several times a day.

6. When a passage is cited verbatim or nearly verbatim, quotation marks are used. Quotation marks are not used when a passage is merely paraphrased.

7. Caterus gilds the lily somewhat in alluding to Terence, *Andria*, Act I, Scene ii, line 194. In this passage the slave Davus, vexed by a somewhat enigmatic question, declares in frustration that "I am Davus, not Oedipus"—his point being that he is neither a mind reader nor a guesser of riddles.

it is plainly not nothing; hence it cannot get its being from nothing." There is an equivocation here. For if "nothing" means the same thing as a being that is not actual, then it is absolutely nothing, because it is not actual and thus is from nothing, that is, it is not derived from some cause. But if "nothing" means something conjured up in the mind (that is, something traditionally called a "being of reason"), then it is not nothing, but something real that is distinctly conceived. Nevertheless, though it can indeed be conceived, it can hardly be caused, since it is merely conceived and is not actual.

But ". . . it is appropriate to ask further whether I myself who have this idea could exist, if such a being did not exist, namely the source from which proceeds the idea of a being more perfect than myself," as he states just prior to this. "From what source, then," he says, "do I derive my existence? Why, from myself, or from my parents, or from whatever other things . . . But if I got my being from myself, I would not doubt, I would not hope, nor would I lack anything at all. For I would have given myself all the perfections of which I have some idea; in so doing, I would myself be God!" But if I am derived from something else, I would eventually arrive at something that is derived from itself. Now precisely the same line of reasoning applies to it as applies to me. This is precisely the very same way that St. Thomas[8] follows and which he calls his way "from the causality of the efficient cause."[9] He picked this up from the Philosopher;[10] however, neither of them is concerned with the causes of ideas. And perhaps there was no need for such concern. After all, should I not advance by a straight and narrow way? I think, therefore I am—to the extent that I am a mind and an act of thinking. However, this mind, this act of thinking, is derived either from itself or from something else. If the latter, from what further source is that something else derived? If it is derived from itself, then it is God, for what is derived from itself would easily confer all things upon itself.

I implore and entreat the gentleman not to hide himself from a reader who is eager and is perhaps of inferior intellect. "From itself" is understood in two senses. The first is the positive sense, namely "from itself as from a cause." Thus what is derived from itself would give its own existence to itself. If by a prior choice it should give itself whatever it wanted, then it undoubtedly would give itself everything, and would thus be God. In the second sense, "from itself" is taken negatively; it means the same thing as "by itself" or "not from another." And, as I recall, everyone understands "from itself" in this latter sense.

But if something is derived from itself (that is to say, not from something else), how am I to prove that it encompasses all things and that it is infinite? For I do not follow you now when you say: if it is derived from itself, it would easily have

94

95

8. St. Thomas Aquinas (1225?–1274), sometimes referred to as the "Doctor Angelicus" for his writings on the theology of angels. Dominican theologian and philosopher who is one of the principal figures in medieval thought. Even during his lifetime, no little controversy arose in response to Aquinas's extensive use of newly translated writings of Aristotle to help explicate Christian beliefs.

9. *Summa Theologiae* I, Q. 2, a. 3, corpus.

10. Aristotle.

given itself all things. For neither is it derived from itself as from a cause, nor did it exist prior to itself in such a way that it would chose beforehand what it would later be. I know I once heard Suárez[11] declare that every limitation is derived from a cause. Thus a thing is limited and finite because its cause either could not or would not give anything greater and more perfect. If, therefore, something is derived from itself and not from a cause, it is truly unlimited and infinite.

But I am not really in total agreement with this. For what if the limitation were derived from intrinsic constitutive principles, that is to say, from the very form and essence—which you nevertheless have not yet proved to be infinite, even if the thing is derived from itself, that is to say, not from something else? Clearly something hot (if you suppose that there is something hot) will be hot—and not cold—by virtue of intrinsic constitutive principles, even if you were to imagine that the very object itself which exists is derived from nothing. I have every confidence that M. Descartes is not without arguments to support what others perhaps have not established with sufficient clarity.

At last there is agreement between myself and the gentleman. He declares the following as a general rule: whatever I clearly and distinctly know is obviously a true being.[12] Indeed whatever I think is true. For almost from our youth we   96 banned all chimeras and any being of reason. For no power can deviate from its proper object: if the will is moved, it tends toward the good. Nor indeed do the senses themselves err, for sight sees what it sees and the ear hears what it hears. If you see brass, you see rightly; but you are mistaken when in your judgment you decide that what you see is gold. Thus M. Descartes most appropriately attributes every error to judgment and to the will.

But I now gather from this rule what you had in mind. I clearly and distinctly know an infinite being; therefore it is a true being and is something. But someone will ask: do you clearly and distinctly know an infinite being? What then does he make of the traditional commonplace that "the infinite qua infinite is unknown"? For if, when I think about a chiliagon and confusedly represent to myself some figure, I do not distinctly imagine or know a chiliagon, because I do not distinctly intuit its thousand sides, surely that same person will ask: how is it that he thinks distinctly and not merely confusedly of the infinite as such, if he cannot see clearly the infinite perfections that constitute it, as if it were before his very eyes?

Perhaps this is what St. Thomas had in mind, for when he denied that the proposition "God exists" is self-evident, he brought to bear against himself a text

---

11. Francisco Suárez (1548–1617). Spanish Jesuit theologian of the counter-Reformation who was perhaps best known for his treatises in political philosophy. In addition to lengthy commentaries on Aquinas's *Summa Theologiae,* Suárez also wrote the *Metaphysical Disputations.* The manner of exposition employed in this latter work marked a substantial innovation in philosophical style. A selection from the *Disputations,* of particular relevance to Descartes, can be found in Ariew, Cottingham, and Sorell, pp. 29–50.

12. The text cited actually says: "everything I very clearly and distinctly perceive is true."

from St. John Damascene:[13] "the knowledge that God exists has been naturally implanted in everyone; therefore it is self-evident that God exists."[14] And to this St. Thomas replies: "it is naturally implanted in us to know that God exists in some general sense and in a certain confused manner, that is to say, insofar as
97   God is man's beatitude . . . . But this," he says, "is not to know without qualification that God exists; just as knowing that someone is approaching is not the same thing as knowing that it is Peter, even though it is Peter who is approaching . . ."[15] St. Thomas seems to be saying that God is known under a general rubric—either as ultimate end or as first and most perfect being—or ultimately under the rubric of something that embraces all things in a confused and common manner, but not under the precise rubric of his being, for God is infinite and unknown to us. I know that M. Descartes will respond with ease to anyone who asks such a question. Nevertheless, I believe that because of these matters, which I bring up simply for the sake of argument, he will call to mind the dictum of Boethius:[16] "There are certain common conceptions in the mind which are self-evident only to the wise. . . ."[17] Hence there is no cause for wonder if those who are desirous of understanding more ask a lot of questions and if they dwell for a long time upon those matters which they know have been laid down as the primary foundation for the whole enterprise, and which they still do not understand without a great deal of investigation.

Let us then grant that someone has a clear and distinct idea of a supreme and most perfect being. Where do you go from there? Namely to the conclusion that this infinite being exists; and this conclusion is so certain that "I ought to be at least as certain of the existence of God as I have hitherto been about the truths of mathematics," so "it is no less contradictory[18] to think of God (that is, a supremely perfect being) lacking existence (that is, lacking some perfection), than it is to think of a mountain without a valley." The whole argument hinges on this; whoever makes a concession at this point must admit defeat. Because I am dealing with someone stronger than myself, I would like to skirmish for a
98   short while, so that, since I must eventually be defeated, I might nevertheless delay what I cannot avoid.

---

13. St. John Damascene or St. John of Damascus (c. 675–749), a Greek theologian perhaps most famous for his polemical writings against the iconoclasts.

14. *Summa Theologiae* I, Q. 2, a. 1, obj. 1. Aquinas is citing John Damascene's *De Fide Orthodoxa* I.1.

15. Caterus's citation of Aquinas contains a slight transposition.

16. Anicius Manlius Severimus Boethius (c. 470–524), Roman scholar and Christian theologian and philosopher, perhaps best known for his *On the Consolation of Philosophy,* a somewhat neo-Platonic treatise in which the search for wisdom and the love of God are judged to be the keys to human happiness. Boethius is sometimes referred to as "the last of the Romans and the first of the Scholastics."

17. *Summa Theologiae* I, Q. 2, a. 1, corpus. Aquinas is paraphrasing Boethius's *De Hebdomadibus (Quomodo Substantiae Bonae Sint),* principle 1.

18. A literal translation of the Latin text *(non magis)* is "no more." This is obviously a misstatement on Descartes's part, since it contradicts his own clearly stated views.

First, although we are proceeding not merely on the basis of authority, but rather on the basis of reason alone, still, lest I seem arbitrarily to resist such a great mind, let us listen instead to St. Thomas himself. He urges the following objection against himself: "once one understands what is signified by the word 'God,' one immediately grasps the fact that God exists; for we signify by the word 'God' something than which a greater cannot be signified. But what exists in reality and in the intellect is greater than what exists in the intellect alone. Thus it follows that God also exists in reality, because, upon understanding the word 'God,' God exists in the intellect."[19] I put this argument in proper logical form thus: God is something than which a greater cannot be signified. But something than which a greater cannot be signified includes existence. Therefore existence is included in the very word "God" or in the concept of God. Thus God can neither be nor be conceived without existence. Now please tell me, is this not the argument of M. Descartes? St. Thomas defines God thus: that than which a greater cannot be signified. M. Descartes calls God a being who is supremely perfect. Clearly nothing greater than this being can be signified. St. Thomas states the following minor premise: that than which a greater cannot be signified includes existence, otherwise something greater than it can be signified, namely, that which is also signified as including existence. But does not M. Descartes seem to state the same minor premise? God, he says, is a supremely perfect being; but a supremely perfect being includes existence, otherwise it would not be supremely perfect. St. Thomas concludes: therefore, since the word "God" is immediately in the intellect once it is understood, it follows that God also exists in reality. In other words, from the very fact that existence is involved in the essential concept of a being than which a greater cannot be signified, it follows that this very being exists. M. Descartes draws the same conclusion: "But," he says, "from the fact that I cannot think of God except as existing, it follows that existence is inseparable from God; and thus he truly exists."[20] But then let St. Thomas reply to himself and to M. Descartes: "Granted," he says, "everyone understands that what is signified . . . by this word 'God' is what it is said to signify, namely something than which a greater cannot be thought. Still it does not follow on account of this that one understands that what is signified by the word exists in reality, but only that it exists in the apprehension of the intellect. Nor can one argue that it exists in reality, unless one grants that there exists in reality something than which a greater cannot be thought—a point not granted by those who claim that God does not exist."[21] On the basis of this argument, my reply is surely a brief one: even if it be granted that a "supremely perfect being" entails existence in its very defining formula, still it does not follow that that existence is something actual and real, but only that the concept of existence is inseparably joined to the concept of a supreme being. From this it follows that you do not infer that the existence of God is something actual, unless

99

---

19. *Summa Theologiae* I, Q. 2, a. 1, obj. 2.

20. Caterus's citation of Descartes is nearly but not quite verbatim.

21. *Summa Theologiae* I, Q. 2, a. 1, ad 2.

you presuppose that this supreme being actually exists, for then it will actually include all perfections, and surely the perfection of real existence.

Forgive me, gentlemen, for I am weary and will engage in a slight bit of frivolity. The compound "existing lion" includes both lion and the mode of existence, and it surely includes them essentially. For if you remove either of the two elements, it will not be this very same compound. But then, has not God throughout all eternity known this compound clearly and distinctly? And does not the idea of this compound, precisely as a compound, essentially involve each part of it? That is to say, is it not the case that existence is of the very essence of this compound "existing lion"? And yet a distinct knowledge on the part of God—a distinct knowledge, I say, on the part of God throughout all eternity—does not necessarily require that either of the parts of this compound exists, unless one supposes that the compound itself exists, for then it involves all its essential perfections, and thus it also involves actual existence. Consequently, even if I distinctly know a supreme being, and although a being that is supremely perfect may include existence in its essential concept, nevertheless it does not follow that its existence is anything actual, unless you presume that this supreme being exists; for then, since it includes all its perfections, it will also include this actual existence. But then we must prove by some other means that this supremely perfect being exists.

I shall say a little bit about the essence of the soul and about the distinction between the soul and the body. For I confess that this great genius has already so tired me out that I can scarcely go on any further. He seems to prove the distinction (if that is what it is) between the soul and the body by the fact that they can be conceived distinctly and separately. Here I leave the very learned gentleman with Duns Scotus,[22] who declares that, for one thing to be conceived distinctly and separately from another, it suffices that there be a distinction which he calls "formal and objective," which he claims to be midway between a real distinction and a distinction of reason.[23] And thus Scotus distinguishes between God's justice and his mercy; "for," he says, "before every operation of the intellect these attributes have formally diverse meanings, so that even then the one is not the other. Nevertheless, it does not follow, from the fact that God's justice can be conceived separately from his mercy, that God's justice therefore exists separately."[24]

But I see that I have totally exceeded the conventions of a letter. These are the points regarding the matter before us that I observed to be in need of discussion. But you, gentlemen, must select what you judge to be of superior quality. If you

100

101

---

22. John Duns Scotus (1266?–1308), sometimes referred to as "Doctor Subtilis," was a major figure in the Franciscan school of philosophy.
23. For accounts of Scotus's doctrine of formal distinctions, see Maurice J. Grajewski, *The Formal Distinction of Duns Scotus: A Study in Metaphysics* (Washington, DC: Catholic University of America, Ph.D. thesis, 1944) and Michael J. Jordan, *Duns Scotus on the Formal Distinction* (New Brunswick, NJ: Rutgers University, Ph.D. thesis, 1984).
24. *Ordinatio* I, Dist. 8, part 1, q. 4. The topic of q. 4 is the simplicity of God.

support me, we will easily overcome M. Descartes with friendship, lest in the future he have any bad feelings toward me, were I to have contradicted him a little. If you support him, I surrender, I am conquered; and I readily admit as much, lest I be vanquished yet again. I send you my greetings.

Reply by the Author to the First Set of Objections

Gentlemen:[25]

You have certainly stirred up against me a mighty adversary, whose wit and learning could have given me a great deal of trouble, were it not for the fact that, being a theologian who is both pious and thoroughly civilized, he preferred championing the cause of God and any of its defenders, to making a serious attack upon it. But though this minor trickery is a very fine trait in him, nonetheless, such collusion on my part would not warrant praise. And so I prefer here to expose his ruse for aiding me, rather than to respond to him as if he were an adversary.

First of all, he has brought together in a few words my chief argument for proving the existence of God, so that it might better remain in the reader's memory. And, having briefly indicated his assent to what he judged to be demonstrated with sufficient clarity, and having thus strengthened them with his own authority, he inquired into that single matter upon which the main difficulty rests, namely, what we are to understand here by the word "idea" and what cause an   *102* idea requires.

I have written that "an idea is the very thing thought, insofar as it exists objectively in the intellect," but he pretends to understand these words in a sense quite different from that in which I meant them, so that he can provide me an opportunity to explain them more clearly. ". . . to exist objectively in the intellect," he says, "is to terminate the act of the intellect after the manner of an object. This characterization is surely an extrinsic denomination and it has no bearing on the thing itself." Note that he is referring to the thing itself insofar as it exists outside the intellect. Seen in this light, it certainly is an extrinsic denomination for the thing to exist objectively in the intellect. But I was talking about an idea which is never outside the intellect, and thus "objective existence" merely means that the thing exists in the intellect in just the way that objects normally exist in the intellect. Thus, for example, were a person to ask what happens to the sun as a result of its existing objectively in my intellect, the best answer would be that nothing happens to it except an extrinsic denomination, to wit, that the sun terminates the operation of the intellect after the manner of an object. But were one to ask what the idea of the sun is and were the answer that it is the very thing thought insofar as it exists objectively in the intellect, no one would take it to be the very sun itself insofar as that extrinsic denomination is in it. Nor will "objective existence in the intellect" signify that it terminates the

---

25. Again Descartes is addressing Bannius and Bloemaert.

operation of the intellect after the manner of an object, but rather that it is in the intellect in the manner in which its objects normally exist in it—surely not for-

103   mally, as it is in the heavens, but objectively, that is, in the way in which objects normally exist in the intellect. Clearly this mode of existence is definitely far less perfect than that mode of existence by which things exist outside the intellect; but it is not for that reason simply nothing, as I have already written.

And when this most learned theologian declares that there is an "equivocation" in these words, he seems to have wanted to warn me about what I have just now noted, lest perhaps I not be mindful of it. For he says first that a thing existing thus in the intellect through an idea is not an "actual being," that is, it is not something existing outside the intellect. This is true. Then he also says that objective being is not something conjured up in the mind or a being or reason, but something real which is distinctly conceived. With these words he admits all that I have assumed. But he still makes the further point that "since it is merely conceived and is not actual" (that is, because it is merely an idea and not something existing outside the intellect), "though it can indeed be conceived, it can hardly be caused" (that is, it does not need a cause in order to exist outside the intellect). I grant this; but it clearly does need a cause in order to be conceived, and the point at issue is with respect to this cause alone. Thus, were one to have in one's intellect an idea of a machine devised with the greatest of skill, one indeed could with justification ask what the cause is of that idea. Now it will not suffice for one to declare that the idea is nothing outside of the mind and thus cannot be caused but only conceived; for all that is asked for here is what the cause is in virtue of which it is conceived. Nor again will it suffice to say that the intellect is itself the cause, insofar as it is the cause of its operation. For regarding this cause there can be no doubt, but only regarding the cause of the "objective skill" which is in the idea. For it ought to be the result of some cause that

104   this idea of a machine contains this "objective skill" rather than some other, and the "objective skill" of this idea of the machine is in the same relationship to the idea of the machine as the objective reality of the idea of God is to the idea of God. And surely various things could be reckoned to be the cause of this skill: either some such real machine has been seen beforehand, in accordance with whose likeness the idea has been formed, or a great knowledge of mechanics, which is in this intellect, or perhaps a great subtlety of mind by which one might even invent the machine without any previous knowledge. Note that all the skill that exists merely objectively in this idea ought necessarily to exist either formally or eminently in its cause, whatever that cause finally turns out to be—be it a formal cause or an eminent cause. And the same thing is to be reckoned even with respect to the objective reality which is in the idea of God. But in what will such a reality thus exist, except in a God who really exists? But the insightful gentleman has seen all these things quite well and therefore admits that one can ask ". . . why a given idea has this objective reality rather than that one." To this question he responds first that what I wrote regarding the triangle holds for all ideas, namely that, even if perhaps the triangle exists nowhere in the world, still its determinate nature, essence, or form is immutable and eternal. Indeed he declares that this requires no cause. But this reply does not seem satisfactory; for although the nature of the triangle is immutable and eternal, nevertheless it is not therefore any less incumbent upon us to ask why the idea of a triangle is in us. Thus he added by way of a postscript that if I insist upon a reason, it is the imperfection of our intellect, and so on. By this answer he seems to have wanted to show merely that those who wished to disagree with me in this matter offer no answer that has any semblance of truth about it. For it is certainly no more prob- *105* able that the reason why there exists in us an idea of God is the imperfection of our intellect, than that the lack of experience in mechanics is the cause of our imagining some very skillfully made machine rather than some other less perfect machine. On the contrary, were one to have an idea of a machine in which every conceivable skill is contained, the most appropriate inference is that this idea issued from some cause in which every conceivable skill really existed, even though in the idea it existed only objectively. And for the same reason, since we have in us an idea of God in which every conceivable perfection is contained, it can then most manifestly be concluded that this idea depends upon some cause in which there is also all this perfection, namely in a God who really exists. Nor does there seem more difficulty in the one case than in the other: just as not all are experts in mechanics and thus cannot have ideas of very skillfully produced machines, so too not all have the same power of conceiving the idea of God. However, since this idea has been implanted in the minds of all in the same way and since we never observe that it comes to us from anywhere but ourselves, we assume that it pertains to the nature of our intellect. Surely none of this is incorrect, but we are leaving out something else that is especially in need of consideration, something on which the whole force and lucidity of this argument depend, namely, that this power of having within oneself the idea of God could not be in our intellect, were this intellect merely a finite being (as in fact it is) and *106* did it not have God as its cause. And thus I inquired further whether I could exist if God did not exist—not so much to offer a proof different from the preceding one, but rather to explain the very same proof more fully.

But here the gentleman, by being excessively obliging, has placed me in an awkward position, for he compares my argument with another one drawn from St. Thomas and Aristotle, with the result that he seems to demand a reason, when I set out on the same path as these two, why I did not follow it in all respects. But I beg him to allow me to give an account of those things which I myself have written and to be silent about what others have written.

And so, first of all, I have not based my argument on my having observed a certain order or succession of efficient causes in the realm of sensible things. For one thing, I thought it much more evident that God exists than that any sensible things exist; for another thing, the only conclusion I seemed able to arrive at was that I ought to acknowledge the imperfection of my intellect, given that admittedly I could not comprehend how an infinite number of such causes succeeded one another in such a way that none of them was first. For certainly from the fact that I could not comprehend this it does not follow that one of them ought to be first cause, any more than it follows from the fact that I cannot also comprehend the infinite divisions in a finite quantity that there is a final division, such that it cannot be divided further. All that follows is that my intellect, which is finite, *107* does not grasp the infinite. Thus I preferred to use my own existence as the foundation of my argument, since my existence depends on no series of causes and is so well known to me that nothing else could be more well known. And, in order to free myself from the whole problem of the succession of causes, I asked concerning myself not so much what the cause was by which I was at one time produced, as the cause by which I am being conserved at the present time.

Next, I inquired about the cause of myself, not insofar as I am composed of mind and body, but only and precisely insofar as I am a thing that thinks. I believe that this is quite relevant to the matter at hand; for in so doing I have been able to free myself much more effectively from prejudices, to attend to the light of nature, to question myself, and to affirm as certain that there cannot be anything within me of which I am not somehow aware. This approach is clearly different from seeing that I was begotten by my father and concluding from this that he in turn was begotten by my grandfather, and from putting an end to my search by declaring that some cause is first, because in seeking the parents of parents I could not go on to infinity.

Moreover, I inquired about the cause of myself, not merely insofar as I am a thing that thinks, but, most especially and primarily, insofar as I observe that, among my other thoughts, there is within me the idea of a supremely perfect being. On this one point hangs the entire force of my demonstration. First, because in this idea is contained what God is, at least insofar as he can be understood by me; and, according to the rules of the true logic, one should never ask whether something exists unless one first understands what it is. Second, because it is this very idea which gives me the opportunity to examine whether I am derived from myself or from something else, as well as to acknowledge my defects. And lastly, because this idea is what teaches not only that something is the cause of me but also that in this cause are contained all perfections, and hence that this cause is God.

108

Finally, I did not say that it is impossible for something to be the efficient cause of itself. For although this obviously is the case when the term "efficient cause" is restricted to those causes which are temporally prior to their effects or are different from them, still it does not seem that such a restriction is appropriate in this inquiry. First, the inquiry would be pointless (for who does not know that the same thing can neither exist prior to itself nor be different from itself?). Second, the light of nature does not stipulate that the nature of an efficient cause requires that it be temporally prior to its effect. On the contrary, a thing does not bear the trademark of a cause except during the time it is producing an effect, and thus it is not prior to the effect. However, the light of nature does surely stipulate that there exists nothing about which it is inappropriate to ask why it exists or to inquire into its efficient cause, or, if it has none, to demand to know why it does not need one. Thus, if I believed that nothing could in any respect stand in relation to itself the way an efficient cause stands to its effect, it is utterly out of the question that I should then conclude that something is the first cause. On the contrary, I should again ask for the cause of what was called the "first cause," and thus I would never arrive at anything that was the first cause of all things. But I do readily admit that there could exist something in which there is such a great

109

and inexhaustible power that it never needs the help of anything in order to exist. Nor again does it now need a cause in order to be conserved. Thus, in a manner of speaking, it is the cause of itself. And I understand God to be such a cause. For even if I had existed from all eternity and thus nothing existed prior to me, nevertheless, considering the fact that the parts of time can be separated one from another (and thus from the fact that I now exist it does not follow that I will exist in the future unless some cause were, so to speak, to remake me over and over at each individual moment in time), I would not hesitate to call that cause which conserves me an "efficient cause." Thus, even though there has never been a time when God did not exist, nevertheless, because it is he who truly conserves himself, it does not seem wholly inappropriate to call God the cause of himself. Still, we should note here that by "conservation" we do not mean the sort of conservation that takes place through any positive influence on the part of an efficient cause, but only that the very essence of God is such that God must always exist.

On the basis of these considerations it will be easy for me to reply to the distinction drawn with respect to the expression "derived from itself," an expression, the very learned theologian warns me, that requires an explanation. For some people, attending only to the strict and literal meaning of "efficient cause," think it impossible for something to be the efficient cause of itself, and do not discern here a place for any other type of cause analogous to an efficient cause. When these people say that something is "derived from itself," they are in the habit of understanding only that it has no cause. Nevertheless, if these very same people were of a mind to pay more attention to the facts than to words, they would easily observe that the negative rendering of the expression "derived from itself" proceeds merely from the imperfection of the human intellect and has no foundation in reality. But there is another rendering, a positive one, which has been sought from the truth of things and from which alone my argument proceeds. For were one to believe, for example, that some body were derived from itself, one may simply mean that it has no cause. Now it is not the case that one affirms this on the basis of some positive consideration, but only negatively, in the sense that one fails to recognize the cause of the body. But this is a certain imperfection in oneself, as one will easily come to find out for oneself later when one considers that the parts of time do not depend one upon another. Thus, the fact that this body is presumed up until the present time to have been derived from itself (that is, it has no cause) does not suffice to make it also exist in the future, unless there is in it some power which, as it were, continuously "remakes" it. For then, seeing that no such power is contained in the idea of a body, one immediately gathers from this that this body is not derived from itself, taking the expression, "derived from itself," in a positive sense. In like manner, when we say that God is derived from himself, we surely can also understand this negatively, that is, such that the entire meaning of the expression is that he has no cause. But if we have previously asked why God exists or why he continues to exist, and, on noting the immense and incomprehensible power which is contained in the idea of God, we acknowledged that this power is so overwhelming that it is clearly the cause of God's continuing to exist and that nothing but this can be the cause, then we are saying that God is derived from himself—this no

longer in a negative sense but in a thoroughly positive sense. For although we
111 need not say that God is the efficient cause of himself (lest perhaps we be argu-
ing about words), still, because we perceive that his being derived from himself
or his having no cause different from himself is itself derived not from nothing
but from a real immensity of power, it is wholly fitting for us to think that God
stands in the same relationship to himself as an efficient cause does to its effect,
and thus that God is derived from himself positively. And it is also fitting for each
person to ask himself whether he is derived from himself in the same sense. On
finding in himself no power sufficient to conserve him through even a moment
of time, he rightly concludes that he is derived from another, and this is surely
derived from something else which is derived from itself, because this inquiry
cannot go on to infinity, since it is a question here of the present and not of the
past or the future. In fact, I will also add here something I have not put in writing before, namely, that it is not even a secondary cause at which one arrives, but
certainly that cause in which there is enough power to conserve something existing outside it and *a fortiori* conserves itself by its own power, and thus is derived
from itself.

However, when it is said that "every limitation is derived from a cause," I
believe something true is being understood, but it is not expressed in very appropriate terms and the difficulty is not resolved. For, strictly speaking, limitation is
merely the negation of a further perfection; and this negation is not derived from
a cause, but is the very thing being limited. However, even if it were true that
everything is limited by a cause, still it is not self-evident, but must be proved
some other way, for, as the subtle theologian very well replies, anything can be
112 thought to be limited either in the way just mentioned or in virtue of the fact that
it pertains to its nature, just as it is of the nature of the triangle that it is composed
of no more than three lines. However, what does seem self-evident to me is that
everything that exists is derived either from a cause or from itself as from a
cause. For since we understand not only existence but also the negation of existence, we cannot pretend that anything is derived from itself without there being
some reason why it should exist rather than not. In other words, we should not
interpret the expression "derived from itself" so as to mean "as from a cause," in
view of the overwhelming fullness of power which can easily be demonstrated
to be in God alone.

What the gentleman does finally grant me is something that hardly allows of
any doubt, but which commonly is hardly ever given serious consideration. It is
of such importance for plucking the whole of philosophy from out of the shadows, that he helps me greatly in my project by confirming it with his authority.

But here he judiciously asks whether I know the infinite clearly and distinctly.
For although I have tried to anticipate this objection, still it occurs so spontaneously to everyone that it is worth responding to it at some length. And so, to
begin with, I will declare here that the infinite *qua* infinite is in no way comprehended; nonetheless it is still understood, insofar as understanding clearly and
distinctly that a thing is such that plainly no limits can be found in it is tantamount to understanding clearly that it is infinite.

And indeed I do distinguish here between "indefinite" and "infinite"; strictly *113*
speaking, I designate only that thing to be "infinite" in which no limits of any
kind are found. In this sense God alone is infinite. However, there are things in
which I discern no limit, but only in a certain respect (such as the extension of
imaginary space, a series of numbers, the divisibility of the parts of a quantity,
and the like). These I call "indefinite" but not "infinite," since such things do not
lack a limit in every respect.

Moreover, I distinguish between the formal meaning of "infinite," or "infinity," and the thing that is infinite. For as far as infinity is concerned, even if we
understand that it is positive in the highest degree, nevertheless we understand it
only in a certain negative fashion, because it depends on our not noticing any
limitation in the thing. But as to the thing itself which is infinite, although our
understanding of the thing is surely positive, still it is not adequate, that is, we do
not comprehend all that is capable of being understood in it. But were we to turn
our eyes toward the sea, even though we neither grasp the whole thing in our
sight nor traverse its great vastness, nevertheless we are said to "see" it. And
were we to view the sea from a distance, so as to take it in all at once, as it were,
with our eyes, we see it only in a confused fashion, just as we have a confused
image of a chiliagon when we take in all of its sides at the same time. But were
we to direct our gaze at close quarters toward some portion of the sea, such a
sight can be very clear and distinct, just as would be the case with imagining a
chiliagon, were our vision restricted to merely one or other of the chiliagon's
sides. By a similar line of reasoning, I grant, as do all the theologians, that God
cannot be grasped by the human intellect, and that he cannot be distinctly known *114*
by those who gaze upon him, as it were, from afar and try mentally to grasp him
whole and all at once. This is the sense in which St. Thomas declared in the text
cited that the knowledge of God is present in us merely "in a certain confused
manner." But those who try to take notice of each of God's perfections one by
one and try not so much to grasp them as to be grasped by them, and to engage
all the powers of their intellect in contemplating them, will surely find that God
is a much fuller and easier subject matter for clear and distinct knowledge than
are any created things.

Nor in that text did St. Thomas deny this, as is obvious from his affirming in
the following article that the existence of God can be demonstrated. However,
wherever I claimed that God could be clearly and distinctly known, I had in mind
only the aforementioned knowledge, which is finite and proportionate to the
humble modality of our mind. Besides, it was not necessary to have a different
understanding of the matter in order to establish the truth of what I have claimed,
as will be readily apparent if one takes note of the fact that I said this in just two
places. The first place was where there was a question of whether there is contained in the idea that we form of God anything real or just the negation of something real, just as perhaps is the case in the idea of cold where there is nothing
more than the negation of heat—a matter about which there can be no doubt. The
second place was where I claimed that existence belongs no less to the nature of
a being that is supremely perfect than having three sides belongs to the nature of

115 a triangle—a fact that can also be understood without an adequate knowledge of God.

Here again he compares one of my arguments with another from St. Thomas, in order to compel me, as it were, to specify just what greater force is to be found in the one argument rather than in the other. Now I seem able to do this without any great degree of vexatiousness, since St. Thomas did not use this argument as his own, nor did he draw the same conclusion as I do; consequently, I am not at variance here on any point with the Angelic Doctor. For his question was whether the proposition "God exists" is self-evident to us, that is, whether it is obvious to everyone. He denies that it is, and rightly so. But the argument he puts to himself can be stated thus: when we understand what is signified by the word "God," we understand it to signify "that than which a greater cannot be signified." But to exist in reality as well as in the intellect is greater than to exist merely in the intellect. Therefore, when we understand what is signified by the word "God," we understand that what is being signified is that God exists in reality as well as in the intellect. There is an obvious flaw in the form of this argument, for the only conclusion he should have drawn is: therefore, when we understand what the word "God" signifies, we understand that God exists in reality as well as in the intellect. But merely being signified by a word does not automatically make what is signified to be true. But my argument went as follows: what we clearly and distinctly understand to belong to the true and immutable nature, or essence, or

116 form of a thing, can truly be affirmed of that thing. But after having investigated with sufficient care what God is, we clearly and distinctly understand that it belongs to his true and immutable nature that he exists. Thus we can at that point rightfully affirm of God that he exists. At least we now have a validly drawn conclusion. Moreover, we cannot deny the major premise, since we have already granted that everything we clearly and distinctly understand is true. We are left with only the minor premise, and here I confess there is no little difficulty. One reason for this is that we are so accustomed to distinguishing existence from essence in the case of all other things, that we do not sufficiently take notice of the extent to which existence belongs more to the essence of God than to the essences of other things. Second, by failing to distinguish what belongs to the true and immutable essence of a thing from what is ascribed to it merely by a construction on the part of the intellect, even if we take sufficient notice of the fact that existence belongs to the essence of God, we do not then conclude that God exists, because we do not know whether God's essence is immutable and true, or whether it is merely an artifact of our own making.

But in order to remove the first part of this difficulty, we must distinguish between possible and necessary existence. We must also take note of the fact that possible existence is contained in the concept or idea of everything that is clearly and distinctly understood, but in no instance is necessary existence so contained, except in the case of the idea of God. For those who pay close attention to the difference between the idea of God and all other ideas will no doubt perceive

117 that, even though we surely understand other things only as existing, it still does not follow from this that they do exist, but only that they can exist, because we do not understand it to be necessary that actual existence be joined with the other properties of these things. But, from the fact that we understand that actual existence is necessarily and always joined with God's other attributes, it readily follows that God exists.

Next, in order to remove the remaining part of this difficulty, we must take notice of the fact that those ideas which do not contain true and immutable natures but natures that are mere constructions devised by the intellect can be divided by the very same intellect, not merely by an act of abstraction but by a clear and distinct operation. As a consequence, what cannot be divided thus by the intellect surely was not devised by the intellect. For example, when I think of a winged horse or an actually existing lion or a triangle inscribed in a square, I easily understand that I could just as well think of a horse without wings or a nonexistent lion or a triangle apart from a square, and so on. As a consequence, these things do not have true and immutable natures. But if I think of a triangle or a square (I leave the lion and the horse out of the discussion here because their natures are not plainly evident to us), then certainly whatever I discern as being contained in the idea of a triangle, such as that its three angles are equal to two right angles, and so on, I will rightfully affirm of the triangle. The same holds for the square with regard to whatever I find in the idea of a square. For although I could understand a triangle while abstracting from the fact that its three angles are equal to two right angles, still I cannot deny this of the triangle by a clear and distinct operation, that is, while correctly understanding what I am saying. Moreover, if I consider a triangle inscribed in a square, not with the purpose of attributing to the square what pertains solely to the triangle or to the triangle what belongs solely to the square, but with the purpose of examining only what arises out of the conjunction of the two together, the nature of this conjunction will be no less true and immutable than that of the square alone or the triangle alone. And thus it will be appropriate to affirm that the area of the square is not less than double the area of the triangle inscribed in it, and to affirm other similar properties that pertain to the nature of this composite figure. *118*

But if I were to think that existence is contained in the idea of a body that is supremely perfect because it is a greater perfection to exist in reality as well as in the intellect than to exist in the intellect alone, I cannot for that reason conclude that this supremely perfect body exists, but only that it can exist. For I am sufficiently cognizant both of the fact that this idea had been devised by my own intellect, which has joined together all bodily perfections, as well as of the fact that existence does not arise from the other bodily perfections, since existence can just as easily be denied or affirmed of them. In fact, in examining the idea of a body, I perceive that there is no power existing in it by means of which a body produces or conserves itself. From this I rightly conclude that necessary existence (which alone is in question here) no more belongs to the nature of a body, supremely perfect though it may be, than it belongs to the nature of a mountain not to have a valley, or to the nature of a triangle to have angles whose sum is greater than two right angles. However, if we now ask not about a body but about a thing that has all the perfections that can exist together and without any regard for the sort of thing it may finally turn out to be, and if we inquire whether existence is to be counted among these perfections, on first blush we surely will be *119* in some doubt. The reason for this is that since our mind, which is finite, is accustomed to ponder these perfections only one by one, it perhaps does not immediately notice how necessary is the conjunction between them. However, were we to examine carefully whether existence belongs to a being which is supremely powerful and what kind of existence it is, we will be able to perceive clearly and distinctly first that at least possible existence belongs to such a being, just as it belongs to all other things of which there is a distinct idea in us, even to those things which are devised through a construction on the part of the intellect. Next, since we cannot think the existence of this being to be possible unless at the same time, taking note of its immense power, we acknowledge that this being can exist by its own power, we here conclude that this being truly exists and has existed from all eternity, for it is very obvious by the light of nature that what can exist by its very own power always exists. And thus we will understand that necessary existence is contained in the idea of a supremely powerful being, not by virtue of a construction on the part of the intellect, but because it belongs to the true and immutable nature of such a being that it exists. And thus, we shall easily perceive that this being which is supremely perfect must have in itself all the other perfections that are contained in the idea of God, such that, by their very nature and without any construction on the part of the intellect, they are all joined together and exist in God.

120   All of these points are readily apparent to one who pays careful attention, and they differ from what I have previously written only in the manner of their explanation, which I have deliberately altered so that I might suit a wide variety of minds. Nor will I here deny that this argument is such that those who do not recall all of what constitutes its proof will easily take it to be a sophism. Thus at the outset I did have considerable doubts about whether I ought to use it, lest perhaps I should provide those who might not grasp the argument with an occasion for disavowing the remaining arguments as well. However, because there are but two ways by which one can prove that God exists (namely, the one through effects and the other through God's essence or nature); and because I explained the former as best I could in the Third Meditation, I did not believe that the latter argument ought to be overlooked later on.

As far as the formal distinction is concerned, which the very learned theologian draws from Duns Scotus, I declare briefly[26] that a formal distinction does not differ from a modal distinction, and that it applies only to incomplete beings, which I have carefully distinguished from complete beings. Moreover, it surely suffices for a formal distinction that one thing be conceived distinctly and separately from another by an act of abstraction on the part of the intellect inadequately conceiving the thing, yet not so distinctly and separately that we understand each one as something existing in its own right and different from every other thing; for this to be the case a real distinction is absolutely required. Thus, for example, the distinction between the motion and the shape of the same body is a formal one. I can understand perfectly well the motion apart from the

---

26. Descartes has a lengthier discussion of the various types of distinctions in *Principles* I, art. 60–2.

shape and the shape apart from the motion and either in abstraction from the body. Nevertheless, I still cannot completely understand the motion apart from the thing in which the motion takes place, or even the shape apart from the thing *121* which has the shape. Moreover, I cannot imagine motion existing in a thing in which there can be no shape, nor a shape existing in a thing which cannot move. In the same way, I cannot understand justice apart from someone who is just, or mercy apart from someone who is merciful. Nor can I imagine that that very same person who is just is incapable of being merciful. But I completely understand what a body is when I think that it merely has extension and shape, is capable of moving, and so on; and I deny that there is anything whatsoever in it that belongs to the nature of the mind. Conversely, I understand that the mind is a complete thing which doubts, understands, wills, and so on, even though I deny that there is anything in it that is contained in the idea of a body. This would be utterly impossible, were there not a real distinction between mind and body.

These, dear gentlemen, are the answers that I have made to the very helpful and intelligent observations of your friend. If I have not yet satisfied him in regard to these observations, I ask that he put me on notice as to what is either lacking or in error. If I might seek this from him through you, I will hold it a great kindness.

Reply to the Second Set of Objections

[. . .] Finally, as to your suggestion that I should put forward my arguments in *155* geometrical fashion so that the reader could perceive them, as it were, in a single intuition,[27] it is worthwhile to indicate here how much I have already followed this suggestion and how much I think it should be followed in the future. I draw a distinction between two things in the geometrical style of writing, namely, the order and the mode [*ratio*] of the demonstration.

Order consists simply in putting forward as first what ought to be known without any help from what comes afterward and then in arranging all the rest in such a way that they are demonstrated solely by means of what preceded them. And I certainly did try to follow this order as carefully as possible in my Meditations. And it was owing to my observance of it that I treated the distinction between the mind and the body not in the Second Meditation but at the end in the Sixth Meditation. And it also explains why I deliberately and knowingly omitted many other things, since they required an explanation of a great many more.

But the mode [*ratio*] of a demonstration is of two sorts: one that proceeds by way of analysis, the other by way of synthesis.

---

27. Marin Mersenne, as the compiler of the *Second Set of Objections*, had stated: "It would be worthwhile if you set out the entire argument in geometrical fashion, starting from a number of definitions, postulates, and axioms. You are highly experienced in employing this method, and it would enable you to fill the mind of each reader so that he could see everything as it were at a single glance [. . .]"

Analysis shows the true way by which a thing has been discovered methodically, and, as it were, "a priori," so that, were the reader willing to follow it and to pay sufficient attention to everything, he will no less perfectly understand a thing and render it his own, than had he himself discovered it. However, analy-

156   sis possesses nothing with which to compel belief in a less attentive or hostile reader, for if he fails to pay attention to the least thing among those that this mode [*ratio*] proposes, the necessity of its conclusions is not apparent; and it often hardly touches at all on many things that nevertheless ought to be carefully noted, since they are obvious to anyone who is sufficiently attentive.

Synthesis, on the other hand, indeed clearly demonstrates its conclusions by an opposite way, where the investigation is conducted, as it were, "a posteriori" (although it is often the case here that this proof is more "a priori" than it is in the analytic mode). And it uses a long series of definitions, postulates, axioms, theorems, and problems, so that if something in what follows is denied, this mode may at once point out that it is contained in what went before. And thus it wrests from the reader his assent, however hostile and obstinate he may be. But this mode is not as satisfactory as the other one nor does it satisfy the minds of those who desire to learn, since it does not teach the way in which the thing was discovered.

It was this mode alone that the ancient geometers normally used in their writings—not that they were utterly ignorant of the other mode, but rather, as I see it, they held it in such high regard that they kept it to themselves alone as a secret.

But in my Meditations I followed analysis exclusively, which is the true and best way to teach. But as to synthesis, which is undoubtedly what you are asking me about here, even though in geometry it is most suitably placed after analysis, nevertheless it cannot be so conveniently applied to these metaphysical matters.

For there is this difference, that the first notions that are presupposed for demonstrating things geometrical are readily admitted by everyone, since they

157   accord with the use of the senses. Thus there is no difficulty there, except in correctly deducing the consequences, which can be done by all sorts of people, even the less attentive, provided only that they remember what went before. And the minute differentiation of propositions was done for the purpose of making them easy to recite and thus can be committed to memory even by the recalcitrant.

But in these metaphysical matters, on the contrary, nothing is more an object of intense effort than causing its first notions to be clearly and distinctly perceived. For although they are by their nature no less known or even more known than those studied by geometers, nevertheless, because many of the prejudices of the senses (with which we have been accustomed since our infancy) are at odds with them, they are perfectly known only by those who are especially attentive and meditative and who withdraw their minds from corporeal things as much as possible. And if these first notions were put forward by themselves, they could easily be denied by those who are eager to engage in conflict.

This was why I wrote "meditations," rather than "disputations," as the philosophers do, or theorems and problems, as the geometers do: namely, so that by this very fact I might attest that the only dealings I would have were with those who, along with myself, did not refuse to consider the matter attentively and to meditate. For the very fact that someone girds himself to attack the truth renders him less suitable for perceiving it, since he is withdrawing himself from considering the arguments that attest to the truth in order to find other arguments that dissuade him of the truth.

But perhaps someone will object here that a person should not seek arguments for the sake of being contentious when he knows that the truth is set before him. But so long as this is in doubt, all the arguments on both sides ought to be assessed in order to know which ones are the more firm. And it would be unfair of me to want my arguments to be admitted as true before they had been scrutinized, while at the same time not allowing the consideration of opposing arguments. *158*

This would certainly be a just criticism, if any of those things in which I desire an attentive and nonhostile reader were such that they could withdraw him from a consideration of any other arguments in which there was the slightest hope of finding more truth than in my arguments. However, the greatest doubt is contained among the things I am proposing; moreover, there is nothing I more strongly urge than that each thing be scrutinized most diligently and that nothing is to be straightforwardly accepted except what has been so clearly and distinctly examined that we cannot but give our assent to it. On the other hand, the only matters from which I desire to divert the minds of my readers are things they have never sufficiently examined and which they derived not on the basis of a firm reason, but from the senses alone. As a consequence, I do not think anyone can believe that he will be in greater danger of error, were he to consider only those things that I propose to him, than were he to withdraw his mind from them and turn it toward other things—things that are opposed to them in some way and that spread darkness—that is, toward the prejudices of the senses.

And thus I am right in desiring especially close attention on the part of my readers; and I have chosen the one style of writing over all the others with which I thought it can most especially be procured, and from which I am convinced that readers will discern a greater profit than they would have thought, since, on the other hand, when the synthetic mode of writing is employed, people are likely to seem to themselves to have learned more than they actually did. But I also think it is fair for me straightforwardly to reject as worthless those criticisms made against me by those who have refused to meditate with me and who cling to their preformed opinions. *159*

But I know how difficult it will be, even for those who pay close attention and earnestly search for the truth, to intuit the entire body of my Meditations and at the same time to discern its individual parts. I think both of these things ought to be done so that the full benefit may be derived from my Meditations. I shall therefore append here a few things in the synthetic style that I hope will prove somewhat helpful to my readers. Nevertheless, I wish they would take note of the fact that I did not intend to cover as much here as is found in my Meditations, otherwise I should then be more loquacious here than in the Meditations themselves; moreover, I will not explain in detail what I do include, partly out of a desire for brevity and partly to prevent anyone who thinks that my remarks here were sufficient from making a very cursory examination of the

Meditations themselves, from which I am convinced that much more benefit is to be discerned.

160   ARGUMENTS PROVING THE EXISTENCE OF GOD AND THE DISTINCTION OF THE
SOUL FROM THE BODY, ARRANGED IN GEOMETRICAL FASHION.

Definitions

I. By the word "thought" I include everything that is in us in such a way that we are immediately aware of it. Thus all the operations of the will, understanding, imagination, and senses are thoughts. But I added "immediately" to exclude those things that follow from these operations, such as voluntary motion, which surely has thought as its principle but nevertheless is not itself a thought.

II. By the word "idea" I understand that form of any thought through the immediate perception of which I am aware of that very same thought. Thus I could not express anything in words and understand what I am saying, without this very fact making it certain that there exists in me an idea of what is being signified by those words. And thus it is not the mere images depicted in the corporeal imagination that I call "ideas." In point of fact, I in no way call these

161   images "ideas," insofar as they are in the corporeal imagination, that is, insofar as they have been depicted in some part of the brain, but only insofar as they inform the mind itself, which is turned toward that part of the brain.

III. By the "objective reality of an idea" I understand the being of the thing represented by an idea, insofar as it exists in the idea. In the same way one can speak of "objective perfection," "objective skill," and so on. For whatever we perceive to exist in the objects of our ideas exists objectively in these very ideas.

IV. The same things are said to exist "formally" in the objects of our ideas when they exist in these objects in just the way we perceive them, and to exist "eminently" in the objects of our ideas when they indeed are not in these objects in the way we perceive them, but have such an amount of perfection that they could fill the role of things existing formally.

V. Everything in which there immediately inheres, as in a subject, or through which there exists, something we perceive (that is, some property, or quality, or attribute whose real idea is in us) is called a "substance." For we have no other idea of substance itself, taken in the strict sense, except that it is a thing in which whatever we perceive or whatever is objectively in one of our ideas exists either formally or eminently, since it is evident by the light of nature that no real attribute can belong to nothing.

VI. That substance in which thought immediately resides is called "mind." However, I am speaking here of the mind rather than of the soul, since the word "soul" is equivocal, and is often used for something corporeal.

VII. That substance which is the immediate subject of local extension and of the accidents that presuppose extension, such as shape, position, movement from

162   place to place, and so on, is called "body." Whether what we call "mind" and what we call "body" are one and the same substance or two different ones, must be examined later on.

VIII. That substance which we understand to be supremely perfect and in which we conceive absolutely nothing that involves any defect or limitation upon its perfection is called "God."

IX. When we say that something is contained in the nature or concept of something, this is the same as saying that it is true of that thing or that it can be affirmed of that thing.

X. Two substances are said to be really distinct from one another when each of them can exist without the other.

Postulates

I ask first that readers take note of how feeble are the reasons why they have up until now put their faith in their senses, and how uncertain are all the judgments that they have constructed upon them; and that they review this within themselves for so long and so often that they finally acquire the habit of no longer placing too much faith in them. For I deem this necessary for perceiving the certainty of things metaphysical.

Second, I ask that readers ponder their own mind and all its attributes. They will discover that they cannot be in doubt about these things, even though they suppose that everything they ever received from the senses is false. And I ask them not to stop pondering this point until they have acquired for themselves the habit of perceiving it clearly and of believing that it is easier to know than anything corporeal.

Third, I ask that readers weigh diligently the self-evident propositions that they find within themselves, such as that the same thing cannot be and not be at the same time, that nothingness cannot be the efficient cause of anything, and the like. And thus readers may exercise the astuteness implanted in them by nature, pure and freed from the senses, but which the objects of sense normally cloud and obscure as much as possible. For by this means the truth of the axioms that follow will easily be known to them.

Fourth, I ask readers to examine the ideas of those natures that contain a combination of many accidents together, such as that the nature of a triangle, the nature of a square, or of some other figure; and likewise the nature of the mind, the nature of the body, and, above all, the nature of God, the supremely perfect being. And I ask them to realize that all that we perceive to be contained in them truly can be affirmed of them. For example, the equality of its three angles to two right angles is contained in the nature of a triangle, and divisibility is contained in the nature of a body, that is, of an extended thing (for we can conceive of no extended thing that is so small that we could not at least divide it in thought). Such being the case, it is true to say of every triangle that its three angles are equal to two right angles, and that every body is divisible.

Fifth, I ask the readers to dwell long and earnestly in the contemplation of the nature of the supremely perfect being; and to consider, among other things, that possible existence is indeed contained in the ideas of all other things, whereas the idea of God contains not merely possible existence, but absolutely necessary existence. For from this fact alone and without any discursive reasoning, they

163

164 will know that God exists. And it will be no less self-evident to them than that
the number 2 is even or that the number 3 is odd, and the like. For there are some
things that are self-evident to some and understood by others only through discursive reasoning.

Sixth, I ask the readers to get into the habit of distinguishing things that are
clearly known from things that are obscure, by carefully reviewing all the examples of clear and distinct perception, and likewise of obscure and confused perception, that I have recounted in my Meditations. For this is something more
easily learned from examples than from rules, and I think that therein I have
either explained or at least to some extent touched upon all the examples pertaining to this subject.

Seventh and finally, when readers perceive that they have never discovered
any falsity in things they clearly perceived, and that, on the other hand, they have
never found truth in things they only obscurely grasped, except by chance, I ask
them to consider that it is utterly irrational to call into doubt things that are
clearly and distinctly perceived by the pure understanding merely on account of
prejudices based on the senses or on account of hypotheses in which something
unknown is contained. For thus they will easily admit the following axioms as
true and indubitable. Nevertheless, many of these could admittedly have been
much better explained and ought to have been put forward as theorems rather
than as axioms, had I wanted to be more precise.

Axioms or Common Notions

165   I. Nothing exists concerning which we could not ask what the cause is of its
existence. For this can be asked of God himself, not that he needs any cause in
order to exist, but because the very immensity of his nature is the cause or the
reason why he needs no cause in order to exist.

II. The present time does not depend on the time immediately preceding it, and
therefore no less a cause is required to preserve a thing than is initially required
to produce it.

III. No thing, and no perfection of a thing actually existing in it, can have nothing, or a nonexisting thing, as the cause of its existence.

IV. Whatever reality or perfection there is in a thing is formally or eminently
in its first and adequate cause.

V. Whence it also follows that the objective reality of our ideas requires a
cause which contains this very same reality, and not merely objectively, but
either formally or eminently. And we should note that the acceptance of this
axiom is so necessary that on it alone depends the knowledge of all things, sensible as well as insensible. For example, how is it we know that the sky exists?
Because we see it? But this vision does not touch the mind except insofar as it is
an idea: an idea, I say, inhering in the mind itself, not an image depicted in the
corporeal imagination. And we are able to judge on account of this idea that the
sky exists only because every idea must have a really existing cause of its objective reality; and this cause we judge to be the sky itself. The same holds for the
rest.

VI. There are several degrees of reality or being; for a substance has more reality than an accident or a mode; and an infinite substance has more reality than a finite substance. Thus there is also more objective reality in the idea of a substance than there is in the idea of an accident; and there is more objective reality *166* in the idea of an infinite substance than there is in the idea of a finite substance.

VII. The will of a thing that thinks is surely borne voluntarily and freely (for this is of the essence of the will), but nonetheless infallibly, toward the good that it clearly knows; and therefore, if it should know of any perfections that it lacks, it will immediately give them to itself, if they are within its power.

VIII. Whatever can make what is greater or more difficult can also make what is less.

IX. It is greater to create or preserve a substance than to create or preserve the attributes or properties of a substance; however, it is not greater to create something than to preserve it, as has already been said.

X. Existence is contained in the idea or concept of everything, because we cannot conceive of something except as existing [*sub ratione existentiae*]. Possible or contingent existence is contained in the concept of a limited thing, whereas necessary and perfect existence is contained in the concept of a supremely perfect being.

Proposition I: The existence of God is known from the mere consideration of his nature.

Demonstration: To say that something is contained in the nature or concept of a thing is the same thing as saying that it is true of that thing (Def. IX). But necessary existence is contained in the concept of God (Ax. X). Therefore it is true *167* to say of God that necessary existence is in him, or that he exists.

And this is the syllogism I already made use of above in reply to the sixth objection;[28] and its conclusion can be self-evident to those who are free of prejudices, as was stated in Postulate V. But since it is not easy to arrive at such astuteness, we will seek the same thing in other ways.

Proposition II: The existence of God is demonstrated *a posteriori* from the mere fact that the idea of God is in us.

Demonstration: The objective reality of any of our ideas requires a cause that contains this same reality not merely objectively but either formally or eminently (Ax. V). However, we have an idea of God (Defs. II and VIII), the objective reality of which is contained in us neither formally nor eminently (Ax. VI), nor could it be contained in anything other than God (Def. VIII). Therefore this idea of God which is in us requires God as its cause, and thus God exists (Ax. III).

Proposition III: The existence of God is also demonstrated from the fact that *168* we ourselves who have the idea of God exist.

Demonstration: Had I the power to preserve myself, so much the more would I also have the power to give myself the perfections I lack (Axs. VIII and IX);

---

28. Descartes's reply to the sixth point raised in the *Second Set of Objections* discusses the criterion of clarity and distinctness and the proof of the existence of God found in Meditation Five. This reply may be found in AT VII, 149–52.

for these are merely attributes of a substance, whereas I am a substance. But I do not have the power to give myself these perfections, otherwise I would already have them (Ax. VII). Therefore I do not have the power to preserve myself.

Next, I cannot exist without my being preserved during the time I exist, either by myself, if indeed I have this power, or by something else which has this power (Axs. I and II). But I do exist, and yet I do not have the power to preserve myself, as has already been proved. Therefore I am being preserved by something else.

Moreover, he who preserves me has within himself either formally or eminently all that is in me (Ax. IV). However, there is in me a perception of many of the perfections I lack, and at the same time there is in me the perception of the idea of God (Defs. II and VIII). Therefore, the perception of these same perfections is also in him who preserves me.

Finally, this same being cannot have a perception of any perfections he lacks or does not have in himself, either formally or eminently (Ax. VIII), for since he has the power to preserve me, as has already been said, so much the more would *169* he have the power to give himself those perfections were he to lack them (Axs. VIII and IX). But he has the perception of all the perfections I lack and that I conceive to be capable of existing in God alone, as has just been proved. Therefore he has these perfections within himself either formally or eminently, and thus he is God.

Corollary: God created the heavens and the earth and all that is in them. Moreover, he can bring about all that we clearly perceive, precisely as we perceive it.

Demonstration: All these things clearly follow from the preceding proposition. For in that proposition I proved the existence of God from the fact that there must exist someone in whom, either formally or eminently, are all the perfections of which there is some idea in us. But there is in us an idea of such great power that the one in whom this power resides, and he alone, created the heavens and the earth and can also bring about all the other things that I understand to be possible. Thus, along with the existence of God, all these things have also been proved about him.

Proposition IV: Mind and body are really distinct.

Demonstration: Whatever we clearly perceive can be brought about by God in precisely the way we perceive it (by the preceding Corollary). But we clearly *170* perceive the mind, that is, a substance that thinks, apart from the body, that is, apart from any extended substance (Post. II); and vice versa, we clearly perceive the body apart from the mind (as everyone readily admits). Therefore, at least by the divine power, the mind can exist without the body, and the body without the mind.

Now certainly, substances that can exist one without the other are really distinct (Def. X). But the mind and the body are substances (Defs. V, VI, and VII) that can exist one without the other (as has just been proved). Therefore the mind and the body are really distinct.

And we should note here that I used divine power as a means of separating mind and body, not because some extraordinary power is required to achieve this separation, but because I had dealt exclusively with God in what preceded, and thus I had nothing else I could use as a means. Nor is it of any importance what power it is that separates two things for us to know that they are really distinct.

Third Set of Objections, by a Famous English Philosopher,[29] *with the Author's Replies*

171

Against Meditation I: Concerning Those Things That Can Be Called into Doubt

Objection I: It is sufficiently obvious from what has been said in this Meditation that there is no κριτήριον [criterion] by which we may distinguish our dreams from the waking state and from true sensation; and for this reason the phantasms we have while awake and using our senses are not accidents inhering in external objects, nor do they prove that such objects do in fact exist. Therefore, if we follow our senses without any other process of reasoning, we will be justified in doubting whether anything exists. Therefore, we acknowledge the truth of this Meditation. But since Plato and other ancient philosophers have discussed this same uncertainty in sensible things, and since it is commonly observed that there is a difficulty in distinguishing waking from dreams, I would have preferred the author, so very distinguished in the realm of new speculations, not to have published these old things.

Reply: The reasons for doubting, which are accepted here as true by the philosopher, were proposed by me as merely probable; and I made use of them not to peddle them as something new, but partly to prepare the minds of readers for the consideration of matters geared to the understanding and for distinguish- *172* ing them from corporeal things, goals for which these arguments seem to me wholly necessary; partly to respond to these same arguments in subsequent Meditations; and partly also to show how firm those truths are that I later propose, given the fact that they cannot be shaken by these metaphysical doubts. And thus I never sought any praise for recounting them again; but I do not think I could have omitted them any more than a medical writer could omit a description of a disease whose method of treatment he is trying to teach.

Against Meditation II: Concerning the Nature of the Human Mind

Objection II: "I am a thing that thinks"; quite true. For from the fact that I think or have a phantasm, whether I am asleep or awake, it can be inferred that I am thinking, for "I think" means the same thing as "I am thinking." From the fact that I am thinking it follows that I am, since that which thinks is not nothing. But when he appends "that is, a mind, or soul, or understanding, or reason," a doubt arises. For it does not seem a valid argument to say: "I am thinking, therefore I am a thought" or "I am understanding, therefore I am an understanding." For in the same way I could just as well say: "I am walking, therefore I am an act of

---

29. That is, Thomas Hobbes.

walking." Thus M. Descartes equates the thing that understands with an act of understanding, which is an act of the thing that understands. Or he at least is equating a thing that understands with the faculty of understanding, which is a power of a thing that understands. Nevertheless, all philosophers draw a distinction between a subject and its faculties and acts, that is, between a subject and its properties and essences; for a being itself is one thing and its essence is another. Therefore it is possible for a thing that thinks to be the subject in which the mind, reason, or understanding inhere, and therefore this subject may be something corporeal. The opposite is assumed and not proved. Nevertheless, this inference is the basis for the conclusion that M. Descartes seems to want to establish.

173

In the same passage he says: "I know that I exist; I ask now who is this 'I' whom I know. Most certainly, in the strict sense, the knowledge of this 'I' does not depend upon things of whose existence I do not yet have knowledge."

Certainly the knowledge of the proposition "I exist" depends on the proposition "I think," as he rightly instructed us. But what is the source of the knowledge of the proposition "I think"? Certainly from the mere fact that we cannot conceive any activity without its subject, for example, leaping without one who leaps, knowing without one who knows, or thinking apart from one who thinks.

And from this it seems to follow that a thing that thinks is something corporeal, for the subjects of all acts seem to be understood only in terms of matter [*sub ratione materiae*], as he later points out in the example of the piece of wax, which, while its color, hardness, shape, and other acts undergo change, is nevertheless understood always to be the same thing, that is, the same matter undergoing a number of changes. However, it is not to be concluded that I think by means of another thought; for although a person can think that he has been thinking (this sort of thinking being merely a case of remembering), nevertheless, it is utterly impossible to think that one thinks, or to know that one knows. For it would involve an infinite series of questions: how do you know that you know that you know that you know?

Therefore, since the knowledge of the proposition "I exist" depends on the knowledge of the proposition "I think," and the knowledge of this latter proposition depends on the fact that we cannot separate thought from the matter that thinks, it seems we should infer that a thing that thinks is material, rather than immaterial.

174

Reply: Where I said "that is, a mind, or soul, or understanding, or reason," and so on, I did not understand by these terms merely the faculties, but the thing endowed with the faculty of thinking, and this is what everyone ordinarily has in mind with regard to the first two terms, and the second two terms are often understood in this sense. And I explained this so explicitly and in so many places that there does not seem to be any room for doubt.

Nor is there a parity here between walking and thinking, since walking is ordinarily taken to refer only to the action itself; whereas thought is sometimes taken to refer to an action, sometimes to refer to a faculty, and sometimes to refer to the thing that has the faculty.

Moreover, I am not asserting that the thing that understands and the act of understanding are identical, nor indeed that the identity of the thing that understands and the faculty of understanding are identical, if "understanding" is taken to refer to a faculty, but only when it is taken for the thing itself that understands. However, I also freely admit that I have used the most abstract terminology possible to signify the thing or substance, which I wanted to divest of all that did not belong to it, just as, contrariwise, the philosopher uses the most concrete terminology possible (namely, "subject," "matter," and "body") to signify a thing that thinks, in order to prevent its being separated from the body.

But I am not concerned that it may seem to someone that the philosopher's way of joining several things together may be more suitable for finding the truth than mine, wherein I distinguish each single thing as much as possible. But let us put aside verbal disputes and talk about the matter at hand.

He says that it is possible for a thing that thinks to be something corporeal, but *175* the contrary is assumed and not proved. I did not at all assume the contrary, nor did I use it in any way as a basis for my argument. Rather, I left it completely undetermined until the Sixth Meditation, where it is proved.

Then he correctly says that we cannot conceive any act without its subject, such as an act of thinking without a thing that thinks, since that which thinks is not nothing. But then he adds, without any reason at all and contrary to the usual manner of speaking and to all logic, that hence it seems to follow that a thing that thinks is something corporeal; for the subjects of all acts are surely understood from the viewpoint of their being a substance [*sub ratione substantiae*] (or even, if you please, from the viewpoint of their being matter [*sub ratione materiae*], i.e., metaphysical matter), but it does not follow from this that it must be understood from the viewpoint of their being bodies [*sub ratione corporum*].

However, logicians and people in general normally say that some substances are spiritual while others are corporeal. And the only thing I proved by means of the example of the piece of wax was that color, hardness, and shape do not belong to the essence [*rationem formalem*] of the wax. For in that passage I was treating neither the essence of the mind nor that of the body.

Nor is it relevant for the philosopher to say here that one thought cannot be the subject of another thought. For who, besides him, has ever imagined that it could be? But, to explain the matter briefly, it is certainly the case that an act of thinking cannot exist without a thing that thinks, nor in general any act or accident without a substance in which it inheres. However, since we do not immediately *176* know this substance itself through itself, but only through its being a subject of certain acts, it is quite in keeping with the demands of reason and custom for us to call by different names those substances that we recognize to be subjects of obviously different acts or accidents, and afterwards to inquire whether these different names signify one and the same thing. But there are certain acts which we call "corporeal," such as size, shape, motion, and all the other properties that cannot be thought of apart from their being extended in space; and the substance in which they inhere we call "body." Nor is it possible to imagine that it is one substance that is the subject of shape and another substance that is the subject of movement from place to place, and so on, since all these acts have in common the one feature of being extended. In addition, there are other acts, which we call "cogitative" (such as understanding, willing, imagining, sensing, and so on), all of which have in common the one feature of thought or perception or consciousness; but the substance in which they inhere we say is "a thing that thinks," or a "mind," or any other thing we choose, provided we do not confuse it with corporeal substance, since cogitative acts have no affinity to corporeal acts, and thought, which is the feature they have in common, is utterly different in kind from extension, which is the feature [*ratio*] the others have in common. But after we have formed two distinct concepts of these two substances, it is easy, from what has been said in the Sixth Meditation, to know whether they are one and the same or different.

177   Objection III: "Which of these things is distinct from my thought? Which of them can be said to be separate from myself?"

Perhaps someone will answer this question thus: I myself who think am distinct from my act of thinking; and, though surely not separated from me, my act of thinking is nevertheless different from me, just as leaping is different from the one who leaps, as has been said before. But if M. Descartes were to show that he who understands and his understanding are one and the same, we shall lapse into the parlance of the schools: the understanding understands, the sight sees, the will wills, and by an exact analogy, the act of walking or at least the faculty of walking will walk. All of this is obscure, untoward, and most unworthy of that astuteness which is typical of M. Descartes.

Reply: I do not deny that I who think am distinct from my act of thinking, as a thing is distinct from a mode. But when I ask "what then is there that is distinct from my act of thinking?", I understand this to refer to the various modes of thinking that are recounted there, and not to my substance. And when I add "what can be said to be separate from myself?", I have in mind simply that all those modes of thinking are within me. I fail to see what occasion for doubt or obscurity can be imagined here.

Objection IV: "It remains then for me to concede that I do not grasp what this piece of wax is through the imagination; rather I conceive[30] it through the mind alone."

178   There is a tremendous difference between imagining (that is, having some idea) and conceiving with the mind (that is, concluding by a process of reasoning that something is or exists). But M. Descartes has not explained to us the basis for their being different. Even the ancient peripatetic philosophers have taught clearly enough that a substance is not perceived by the senses, but is inferred by means of arguments.

---

30. Hobbes here misquotes Descartes (Meditation Two, AT VII, 131). The original has "perceive" (*percipere*), whereas Hobbes has "conceive" (*concipere*).

But what are we to say now, were reasoning perhaps merely the joining together and linking of names or designations by means of the word "is"? It would follow from this that we draw no conclusions whatever by way of argument [*ratione*] about the nature of things. Rather, it is about the designations of things that we draw any conclusions, that is, whether or not we in fact join the names of things in accordance with some convention that we have arbitrarily established regarding the meanings of these terms. If this is the case, as it may well be, then reasoning will depend upon names, names upon imagination, and imagination perhaps, as I see it, upon the motions of the corporeal organs. And thus the mind will be nothing but movements in certain parts of an organic body.

Reply: I have explained here the difference between imagination and a concept of the pure mind when in the example of the piece of wax I enumerated those things in the wax that we entertain in our imagination and those that we conceive with the mind alone. But I also explained elsewhere how one and the same thing, say a pentagon, can be understood by us in one way and imagined by us in another. However, in reasoning there is a joining together not of names but of things signified by these names; and I marvel that the contrary could enter anyone's mind. For who doubts that a Frenchman and a German could come to   *179* precisely the same conclusions about the very same things, even though they conceive very different words? And does not the philosopher bring about his own undoing when he speaks of conventions [*pactis*] that we have arbitrarily established regarding the significations of words? For if he admits that something is being signified by these words, why does he not want our reasonings to be about this something which is signified, rather than about mere words? And certainly by the same license with which he concludes that the mind is a motion he could also conclude that the sky is the earth, or whatever else he pleases.

Against Meditation III: Concerning God

Objection V: "Some of these thoughts are like images of things; to these alone does the word "idea" properly apply, as when I think of a man, or a chimera, or the sky, or an angel, or God."

When I think of a man, I recognize an idea or an image made up of shape and color, concerning which I can doubt whether or not it is the likeness of a man, and likewise, when I think of the sky. When I think of a chimera, I recognize an idea or an image, concerning which I can doubt whether or not it is the likeness of some animal that does not exist but which could exist or which may or may not have existed at some other time.

But a person who is thinking of an angel at times observes in his mind the image of a flame, at other times the image of a beautiful little boy with wings. It seems certain to me that this image bears no resemblance to an angel, and thus is not the idea of an angel. But believing that there are creatures who minister   *180* unto God, who are invisible and immaterial, we ascribe the name "angel" to this thing that we believe in and suppose to exist. Nevertheless, the idea under which I imagine an angel is composed of the ideas of visible things.

It is the same with the sacred name "God": we have neither an image nor an idea of God. And thus we are forbidden to worship God under the form of an image, lest we seem to conceive him who is inconceivable.

It therefore seems there is no idea in us of God. But just as a person born blind who has often been brought close to a fire, and, feeling himself growing warm, recognizes that there is something that is warming him, and, on hearing that this is called "fire," concludes that fire exists, even though he does not know what shape or color it has, and has absolutely no idea or image of fire appearing before his mind; just so, a man who knows that there ought to be some cause of his images or ideas, and some other cause prior to this cause, and so on, is lead finally to an end of this series, namely to the supposition of some eternal cause, which, since it never began to be, cannot have a cause prior to itself, and necessarily concludes that something eternal exists. Nevertheless, he has no idea that he could call the idea of this eternal something; rather he gives a name to this thing he believes in and acknowledges, calling it "God."

Now since it is from this thesis (namely, that we have an idea of God in our soul) that M. Descartes proceeds to prove this theorem (namely, that God—that is, the supremely powerful, wise creator of the world—exists), he ought to have given a better explanation of this idea of God, and he ought thence to have deduced not only the existence of God but also the creation of the world.

181   Reply: Here the philosopher wants the word "idea" to be understood to refer exclusively to images that are of material things and are depicted in the corporeal imagination. Once this thesis has been posited, it is easy for him to prove that there is no proper idea either of an angel or of God. But from time to time throughout the work, and especially in this passage, I point out that I take the word "idea" to refer to whatever is immediately perceived by the mind, so that, when I will or fear something, I number those very acts of willing and fearing among my ideas, since at the same time I perceive that I will and fear. And I used this word because it was common practice for philosophers to use it to signify the forms of perception proper to the divine mind, even though we acknowledge that there is no corporeal imagination in God; moreover, I had no term available to me that was more suitable. However, I think I have given a sufficient explanation of the idea of God to take care of those wishing to pay attention to my meaning; but I could never fully satisfy those preferring to understand my words otherwise than I intend. Finally, what is added here about the creation of the world is utterly irrelevant to the question at hand.

Objection VI: "Again there are other thoughts that take different forms: for example, when I will, or fear, or affirm, or deny, there is always some thing that I grasp as the subject of my thought, yet I embrace in my thought something more than the likeness of that thing. Some of these thoughts are called volitions or affects, while others are called judgments."

182   When someone wills or fears, he surely has an image of the thing he fears or the action he wills; but what more it is that a person who wills or fears embraces in his thought is not explained. Although fear is indeed a thought, I fail to see how it can be anything but the thought of the thing that someone fears. For what is the fear of a charging lion if not the idea of a charging lion combined with the effect that such an idea produces in the heart, which induces in a person who is frightened that animal motion we call "flight"? Now this motion of flight is not thought. It remains therefore that there is no thought in fear except the one that consists in the likeness of the thing feared. The same thing could be said of the will.

Moreover, affirmation and negation are not found without language and designations, so that brute animals can neither affirm nor deny, not even in thought, and therefore they cannot make judgments. Nevertheless, a thought can be similar in both man and beast. For when we affirm that a man is running the thought we have is no different from the one a dog has when it sees its master running. Therefore the only thing affirmation or negation adds to simple thoughts is perhaps the thought that the names of which an affirmation is composed are the names of the same thing in the one who affirms. This is not a matter of grasping in thought something more than the likeness of the thing, but merely the same likeness for a second time.

Reply: It is self-evident that seeing a lion and simultaneously fearing it is different from merely seeing it. Likewise seeing a man running is different from affirming to oneself that one sees him, an act which takes place without using *183* language. And I find nothing here that requires an answer.

Objection VII: "All that remains for me is to ask how I received this idea of God. For I did not draw it from the senses; it never came upon me unexpectedly, as is usually the case with the ideas of sensible things when these things present themselves (or seem to present themselves) to the external sense organs. Nor was it made by me, for I plainly can neither subtract anything from it nor add anything to it. Thus the only option remaining is that this idea is innate in me, just as the idea of myself is innate in me."

If there is no idea of God (and it has not been proved that there is one), this entire inquiry falls apart. Moreover, if it is my body that is in question, then the idea of myself originates in me from sight; if it is my soul that is in question, then there is absolutely no idea of the soul. Rather, we infer by means of reasoning that there is something inside the human body that imparts to it the animal motion by which it senses and is moved. And this thing, whatever it is, we call the "soul," without having an idea of it.

Reply: If there is an idea of God (and it is obvious that there is), this entire objection falls apart. And when he adds that there is no idea of the soul, but rather that the soul is inferred by means of reasoning, this is the same thing as saying that there is no image of it depicted in the corporeal imagination, but that nevertheless there is such a thing as I have called an idea of it.

Objection VIII: "But there is another idea, one derived from astronomical rea- *184* soning, that is, it is elicited from certain notions innate in me. . . ."

It seems there is at any given moment but a single idea of the sun, regardless of whether it is looked at with the eyes or is understood by reasoning that it is many times larger than it appears. For this latter is not an idea of the sun, but an inference by way of arguments that the idea of the sun would be many times larger were it seen at much closer quarters.

But at different times there can be different ideas of the sun: for example, if it is looked at on one occasion with the naked eye and on another occasion through a telescope. But arguments drawn from astronomy do not make the idea of the sun any greater or smaller; rather, they show that an idea of the sun that is drawn from the senses is deceptive.

Reply: Here too what is said not to be an idea of the sun, and yet is described, is precisely what I call an idea.

Objection IX: "Unquestionably, those ideas that display [*exhibent*] substances to me are something more and, if I may say so, contain within themselves more objective reality than those which represent only modes or accidents. Again, the 185 idea that enables me to understand a supreme deity, eternal, infinite, omniscient, omnipotent, and creator of all things other than himself, clearly has more objective reality in it than do those ideas through which finite substances are displayed."

I have frequently remarked above that there is no idea of God or of the soul. I now add that there is no idea of substance, for substance (given that it is matter subject to accidents and changes), is something concluded to solely by a process of reasoning; nevertheless, it is not conceived nor does it display any idea to us. If this is true, how can one say that the ideas that display substances to me are something greater and have more objective reality than those ideas that display accidents to me? Moreover, would M. Descartes please give some thought once again to what he means by "more reality"? Does reality admit of degrees? Or, if he thinks that one thing is greater than another, would he please give some thought to how this could be explained to our understanding with the same level of astuteness required in all demonstrations, and such as he himself has used on other occasions.

Reply: I have frequently noted that I call an idea that very thing which is concluded to by means of reasoning, as well as anything else that is in any way perceived. Moreover, I have sufficiently explained how reality admits of degrees: namely, in precisely the way that a substance is a thing to a greater degree than is a mode. And if there are real qualities or incomplete substances, these are things to a greater degree than are modes, but to a lesser extent than are complete substances. And finally, if there is an infinite and independent substance, it is a thing to a greater degree than is a finite and dependent substance. But all of this is utterly self-evident.

186   Objection X: "Thus there remains only the idea of God. I must consider whether there is anything in this idea that could not have originated from me. I

understand by the word "God" a certain substance that is infinite, independent, supremely intelligent, and supremely powerful, and that created me along with everything else that exists—if anything else exists. Indeed all these are such that, the more carefully I focus my attention on them, the less possible it seems they could have arisen from myself alone. Thus, from what has been said above, I must conclude that God necessarily exists."

On considering the attributes of God in order thence to have an idea of God and to see whether there is anything in it that could not have proceeded from ourselves, I find, unless I am mistaken, that what we think of that corresponds to the word "God" does not originate with us, nor need it originate with anything but external objects. For by the word "God" I understand a "substance," that is, I understand that God exists. But I understand this not through an idea but through a process of reasoning. And this substance I understand to be "infinite": that is, it is something whose boundaries or extremities I cannot conceive or imagine without imagining still more extremities beyond these. From this it follows that what emerges as the correlate of the word "infinite" is not the idea of divine infinity, but that of my own boundaries or limits. This substance I understand to be "independent," that is, I conceive of no cause from which God proceeds. Whence it is manifest that I have no idea corresponding to the word "independent" beyond the memory of my own ideas beginning at various times and their resulting dependencies.

Hence to say that God is "independent" is merely to say that God is among   *187*
the number of those things of whose origin I form no image. In like manner, saying that God is "infinite" is tantamount to our saying that he is among the number of those things whose limits we do not conceive. And thus any idea of God is out of the question, for what sort of idea is it that has neither origin nor boundaries?

God is called "supremely understanding." I ask here: through what idea does M. Descartes understand God's act of understanding?

God is called "supremely powerful." Again, through what idea do we understand power which is of things yet to come, that is, of things that do not exist? Certainly I understand power from the image or memory of past actions, concluding to it thus: something did thus and so; therefore it was able to do it; and therefore, if it exists as the same thing, it will again be able to do thus and so, that is, it has the power to do something. Now these are all ideas that are capable of having arisen from external objects.

God is called "creator of all that exists." I can conjure up for myself some image of creation out of what I have observed, such as a man being born or his growing from something as small as a point to the shape and size he now possesses. No one has any other idea corresponding to the word "creator." However, to prove creation it is not enough to be able to imagine that the world was created. And thus, even if it were demonstrated that something "infinite, independent, supremely powerful, and so on" exists, it still does not follow that a creator exists, unless someone were to believe it is correct to infer from the fact that something exists which we believe to have created all other things that the world has therefore been at some time created by him.

188   Moreover, when he says that the idea of God and of our soul is innate in us, I would like to know if the souls of those in a deep sleep are thinking. If they are not, then during that time they have no ideas. Whence no idea is innate, for what is innate is always present.

Reply: Nothing that we ascribe to God can originate from external objects, as from an exemplar, since nothing in God bears any resemblance to things found in external, that is, corporeal things. However, if we think of something that is unlike these external objects, it obviously does not originate from them but from the cause of that diversity in our thought.

And I ask here how our philosopher deduces [his conception of] God's understanding from external things. But I easily explain the idea I have of God's understanding by saying that by the word "idea" I understand everything that is the form of some perception. For who is there that does not perceive that he understands something? And thus who is there that does not have that form or idea of an act of understanding, and, by indefinitely extending it, does not form an idea of the divine act of understanding? And the same applies to the rest of God's attributes.

But we used the idea of God which is in us to demonstrate God's existence, and such immense power is contained in this idea that we understand that, if in fact God does exist, it would be contradictory for something other than God to exist without having been created by him. And because of these considerations, it plainly follows, from the fact that his existence has been demonstrated, that it has also been demonstrated that the entire world, that is, all the things other than God that exist, have been created by him.

189   Finally, when we assert that some idea is innate in us, we do not have in mind that we always notice it (for in that event no idea would ever be innate), but only that we have in ourselves the power to elicit the idea.

Objection XI: "The whole force of the argument rests on the fact that I recognize that it would be impossible for me to exist, being of such a nature as I am (namely, having in me the idea of God), unless God did in fact exist. God, I say, that same being the idea of whom is in me . . . ."

Since, therefore, it has not been demonstrated that we have an idea of God, and since the Christian religion requires us to believe that God is inconceivable (that is, as I see it, that we have no idea of him), it follows that the existence of God has not been demonstrated, much less the creation.

Reply: When it is asserted that God is inconceivable, this is understood with respect to a concept that adequately comprehends him. But I have repeated *ad nauseam* how it is we have an idea of God. And nothing at all is asserted here that weakens my demonstrations.

Fourth Set of Objections, by Antoine Arnauld, Doctor of Theology

Concerning God

The first proof of the existence of God (the one the author spells out in the   *206*
Third Meditation) has two parts. The first part is that God exists if indeed there
is an idea of God in me. The second part is that I who have such an idea could
be derived only from God.

Regarding the first part, there is one thing that is not proved to me, namely that
when the distinguished gentleman asserted that falsity properly so-called can be
found only in judgments, he nevertheless admits a bit later that ideas can be
false—not formally false mind you, but materially false. This seems to me to be
out of keeping with his first principles.

But I fear I should not be able to explain with enough lucidity my feelings on
a matter that is decidedly obscure. An example will make it clearer. The author
asserts that if cold is but the privation of heat, the idea of cold which represents
it to me as if it were something positive will be materially false.

Moreover, if cold is merely a privation, then there could not be an idea of cold
that represents it to me as something positive, and here the author confuses a
judgment with an idea.

For what is the idea of cold? Coldness itself, insofar as it exists objectively in
the understanding. But if cold is a privation it cannot exist objectively in the
understanding by means of an idea whose objective existence is a positive being.
Thus, if cold is but a privation, there could not be a positive idea of it, and hence
there could never be an idea that is materially false.

This is confirmed by the same argument the distinguished gentleman uses to
prove that the idea of an infinite cannot but be true. For although one could imag-   *207*
ine that such a being does not exist, nevertheless one could not imagine that the
idea of such a being presented nothing real to me.

We can readily say the same thing about every positive idea. For although one
could imagine that cold, which I think is represented by a positive idea, is not
something positive, still one cannot imagine that the positive idea presents to me
nothing real and positive. This is because an idea is not said to be positive in
virtue of the existence it has as a mode of thinking (for on that score all ideas
would be positive), but rather in virtue of the objective existence it contains and
which it presents to our mind. Therefore, though it is possible that this idea is not
the idea of cold, it nevertheless cannot be a false one.

But, you may say, it is false precisely in virtue of its not being the idea of cold.
Actually it is your judgment that is false, were you to judge it to be the idea of
cold. But the idea, in and of itself,[31] is most true. In like manner, the idea of God

---

31. Reading *se* for *te* (AT VII, 207, l. 13).

surely ought not be called false, not even materially, even though someone could transfer it to something that is not God, as idolaters have done.

Finally, what does this idea of cold, which you say is materially false, display to your mind? A privation? Then it is true. A positive being? Then it is not the idea of cold. Again, what is the cause of this positive objective being, which, in your opinion, renders this idea materially false? It is I, you say, insofar as I am derived from nothing. Therefore, the positive objective existence of some idea can be derived from nothing, a conclusion that destroys the principal foundations of the distinguished gentleman.

But let us move on to the second part of the demonstration, where he asks whether I myself who have the idea of an infinite being could be derived from 208 something other than an infinite being, and especially whether I am derived from myself. The distinguished gentleman contends that I could not be derived from myself, in view of the fact that, were I myself to give myself existence, I would also give myself all the perfections an idea of which I observe to be within me. But the theologian replies with the astute observation that "being derived from itself" [*esse a se*] ought to be taken not in a positive sense, but in a negative sense, to the effect that it means the same thing as "not derived from another." "But," he says, "if something is derived from itself (that is to say, not from something else), how do I prove that this thing encompasses all things and that it is infinite? I do not follow you now if you say: 'If it is derived from itself, it would have easily given itself all things.' For neither is it derived from itself as from a cause, nor did it exist prior to itself such that it would chose beforehand what it would later be."

To refute this argument, the distinguished gentleman maintains that "being derived from itself" ought to be taken in a positive rather than a negative sense, even when it applies to God, to the effect that God "stands in the same relationship to himself as an efficient cause does to its effect." This seems to me to be a harsh statement and a false one at that.

Thus, while I am partly in agreement with the distinguished gentleman, I am partly in disagreement with him. For I confess I cannot be derived from myself except in a positive fashion, but I deny that the same may be said of God. In fact, I think it a manifest contradiction that something is derived from itself positively and as it were from a cause. Thus I bring about the same result as our author, but by way of quite another route, and it goes as follows:

For me to be derived from myself, I ought to be derived from myself in a pos-209 itive fashion, and as it were from a cause. Therefore it is impossible for me to be derived from myself.

The major premise of this syllogism is proved by the gentleman's arguments that are drawn from the doctrine that, since the various parts of time can be separated from one another, the fact that I exist now does not entail my existing in the future, unless some cause, as it were, makes me over again at each individual moment.

As to the minor premise, I believe it to be so clear by the light of nature that it is largely a waste of time to try to prove it—a matter of proving the known by means of the less known. Moreover, the author seems to have recognized the truth of this since he has not made bold to disavow it publicly. Please weigh the following statement made in reply to the theologian:[32]

"... I did not say that it is impossible for something to be the efficient cause of itself. For although this is obviously the case when the meaning of "efficient cause" is restricted to those causes which are temporally prior to their effects or are different from them, still it does not seem that such a restriction is appropriate in this inquiry, ... since the light of nature does not stipulate that the nature of an efficient cause requires that it be temporally prior to its effect."

Well done, as far as the first part is concerned. But why has he left out the second part? And why has he not added that the very same light of nature does not stipulate that the essence [*ratio*] of an efficient cause requires that it be different from its effect, unless it is because the very same light of nature did not permit him to assert it?

And since every effect depends upon a cause and thus receives its existence from a cause, is it not patently clear that the same thing cannot depend on itself *210* or receive its existence from itself?

Moreover, every cause is the cause of an effect, and every effect the effect of a cause. Thus there is a reciprocal relationship between cause and effect. But a relationship must occur between two things.

Moreover, it is absurd to conceive of something receiving existence and yet having existence prior to the time we conceive it to have received existence. But this would be the case were we to ascribe the notions of cause and effect to the very same thing in respect to itself. For what is the notion of a cause? It is the giving of existence. And what is the notion of an effect? It is the receiving of existence. But the notion of a cause is prior by nature to that of an effect.

But we cannot conceive of something as a cause [*sub ratione causae*] (as something giving existence), unless we conceive of it as having existence; for no one gives what one does not have. Therefore we would first be conceiving a thing as having existence before conceiving of it as having received it; and yet in the case of whatever receives existence, receiving existence comes before having existence.

This argument can be put differently: no one gives what he does not have; therefore no one can give himself existence, unless he already has it. But if he already has it, why would he give it to himself?

Finally, he claims that it is manifest by the light of nature that creation differs from preservation solely by virtue of a distinction of reason. But it is manifest by the very same light of nature that nothing can create itself. Therefore nothing can preserve itself.

But if we descend from the general thesis to the specific instance [*hypothesim*] of God, the matter will, in my judgment, be even more manifest: God cannot be derived from himself positively, but only negatively, that is, in the sense of not being derived from something else.

And first, it is manifest from the argument put forward by the distinguished *211* gentleman to prove that if a body is derived from itself, then it ought to be

32. Johan de Kater (Johannes Caterus), author of the *First Set of Objections*.

derived from itself in a positive fashion. For, as he says, the parts of time do not depend on one another. Thus, the fact that this body is presumed up until the present time to have been derived from itself (that is, it has no cause) does not suffice to make it exist in the future, unless there is some power in it which, as it were, continuously "remakes" it.

But so far from this argument being relevant to the case of a supremely perfect or infinite being, the opposite could far rather be readily deduced, and for opposite reasons. For contained in the idea of an infinite being is the fact that its duration is also infinite, that is, it is bounded by no limits; and thus it is indivisible, permanent, and possessed of all things all at once [*tota simul*]. Temporal sequence cannot be conceived to be in this idea except erroneously and through the imperfection of our understanding.

Whence it manifestly follows that an infinite being cannot be conceived of as existing even for a moment without at the same time being conceived of as always having existed and as existing in the future for eternity (which is what the author himself teaches in another passage). Hence it is pointless to ask why it would continue to exist.

Further—as is frequently taught by St. Augustine (than whom no one after the time of the sacred authors has ever spoken more nobly and sublimely about God)—in God there is no past or future, but an eternal present. And from this it appears quite evident that it is only with absurdity that one can ask why God continues to exist, since this question obviously involves a temporal sequence of before and after, of past and future, and this ought to be excluded from the notion of an infinite being.

Moreover, God cannot be thought of as being derived from himself positively [*a se positive*], as if he had initially produced himself, for in that case he would have existed before he existed. Rather, God can be thought to be derived from himself solely in virtue of the fact that he really does preserve himself, as the author frequently states.

But preservation is no more consonant with an infinite being than is an initial production. For what, pray, is preservation, except a certain continuous remaking of something? Thus every instance of preservation presupposes an initial production; and for this reason the term "continuation," like the term "preservation," implies a certain potentiality. But an infinite being is the purest actuality, without any potentiality.

Let us conclude then that God can be conceived to be derived from himself [*esse a seipso*] in a positive fashion only by reason of the imperfection of our understanding, which conceives of God after the manner of created things. This will be established even more firmly by means of another argument.

The efficient cause of something is sought only with respect to a thing's existence, not its essence. For example, on seeing a triangle, I may seek the efficient cause that brought about the existence of this triangle, but it would be absurd for me to seek the efficient cause of the fact that the triangle has three angles equal to two right angles. Saying that an efficient cause is the reason for this is not a proper answer to someone making an inquiry; all that can be said is that it is simply the nature of a triangle to have such a property. Thus it is that mathematicians do not demonstrate by way of efficient or final causes, since they do not concern themselves with the existence of their object. But it no less belongs to the essence of an infinite being that it exist, and even, if you will, that it continues in existence, than it is of the essence of a triangle that it have three angles equal to two right angles. Therefore, just as one cannot give an answer by way of efficient causality to the person asking why a triangle has three angles equal to two right angles but must say only that such is the eternal and unchangeable nature of a triangle, just so, to the person asking why God exists or why God continues to exist, the advice should be given that no efficient cause (either inside or outside God), no "quasi-efficient" cause (for I am in disagreement about things not words), is to be sought. Rather, this alone should be claimed as the reason: that such is the nature of a supremely perfect being. *213*

The learned gentleman states that the light of nature dictates that there exists nothing about which it is inappropriate to ask why it exists or to inquire into its efficient cause, or, if it has none, to demand to know why it does not need one. Against this my answer to the person asking why God exists is that one should not reply in terms of an efficient cause. Rather, one should say merely that it is because he is God, that is, an infinite being. And if someone were to ask for the efficient cause of God, we should answer that God needs no efficient cause. And were the inquirer once again to ask why God does not need an efficient cause, we should answer that it is because he is an infinite being, whose existence is his essence; for the only things that need an efficient cause are those in which it is appropriate to distinguish their actual existence from their essence.

Thus is overthrown all that the author adds just after the passages cited: "Thus," he says, "if I thought that nothing could in any way be related to itself the way an efficient cause is related to its effect, it is out of the question that I then conclude that something is the first cause. On the contrary, I would again ask for the cause of that which was being called the 'first cause,'and thus I would never arrive at any first cause of all things."

On the contrary, were I to think we should seek the efficient (or quasi-efficient) cause of any given thing, I would seek a cause of each individual thing that was different from that thing, since it is most evident to me that in no way can *214* something be in the same relation to itself as an efficient cause is to its effect.

The author, in my opinion, should be put on notice so that he can consider these things attentively and diligently, since I certainly know there can scarcely be found a theologian who would not take exception to the statement that God is derived from himself in a positive fashion, and as it were from a cause.

My only remaining concern is whether the author does not commit a vicious circle, when he says that we have no other basis on which to establish that what we clearly and distinctly perceive is true, than that God exists.

But we can be certain that God exists only because we clearly and evidently perceive this fact. Therefore, before we are certain that God exists, we ought to be certain that whatever we clearly and evidently perceive is true.

I add something that had escaped me. What the distinguished gentleman affirms as certain seems to me to be false, namely, that there can be nothing in him, insofar as he is a thing that thinks, of which he is unaware. For this "him, insofar as it is a thing that thinks," he understands to be merely his mind, insofar as it is distinct from his body. But who does not realize that there can be a great many things in the mind, of which the mind is unaware? The mind of an infant in its mother's womb has the power to think, but it is not aware of it. I pass over countless examples similar to this one.

Reply to the Fourth Set of Objections

231   *Reply to the Second Part: Concerning God*

Up to this point I have attempted to refute the distinguished gentleman's arguments and to withstand his attack. From here on, as is the custom for those who struggle with those stronger than themselves, I will not place myself in direct opposition to him; rather, I will dodge his blows.

He brings up only three points in this part; and these can be readily accepted if they are taken in the sense in which he understands them. But I understood what I wrote in a different sense, which also seems to me to be true.

The first point is that certain ideas are materially false. As I understand it, these ideas are such that they present matter for error to the power of judgment. But the gentleman, by considering these ideas taken formally, argues that no falsity is in them.

The second point is that God is derived from himself positively and as it were from a cause. Here I had in mind merely that the reason why God does not need any efficient cause in order to exist is founded on something positive, namely on
232   the very immensity of God, than which there can be nothing more positive. The gentleman proves that God can never be produced or preserved by himself through some positive influence of an efficient cause. I too am in agreement with all of this.

The third and final point is that there can be nothing in our mind of which we are unaware. I understood this with respect to operations, whereas the gentleman, who understands this with respect to powers, denies this.

But let us carefully explain each of these one by one. When the gentleman says that if cold were merely a privation, there could not be an idea [of cold] that represents it as something positive, it is obvious that he is merely dealing with the idea taken formally. For since ideas are themselves forms of a certain sort and are not made up of any matter, whenever we consider them insofar as they represent something, we are taking them not materially but formally. But if we view them not insofar as they represent this or that thing, but merely insofar as they are operations of the understanding, then we could surely say that we are taking them materially. But in that case they would bear absolutely no relationship to the truth or falsity of their objects. Hence it seems to me that we can call these ideas materially false only in the sense I have already described: namely, whether cold be something positive or a privation, I do not on that account have a different idea of it; rather, it remains the same in me as the one I have always had. And I say that this idea provides me with matter for error if it is true that cold is a privation and does not have as much reality as heat, because, in considering either of the ideas of heat or cold just as I received them both from the senses, I cannot observe any more reality being shown me by the one idea than by the other. *233*

And it is obviously not the case that I have confused judgment with an idea, for I have said that material falsity is to be found in the latter, whereas only formal falsity can exist in the former.

However, when the distinguished gentleman says that the idea of cold is coldness itself insofar as it exists objectively in the understanding, I think a distinction is in order. For it often happens in the case of obscure and confused ideas (and those of heat and cold should be numbered among them) that they are referred to something other than that of which they really are ideas. Thus, were cold merely a privation, the idea of cold would not be coldness itself as it exists objectively in the understanding, but something else which is wrongly taken for that privation: namely, a certain sensation having no existence outside the understanding.

But the same analysis does not hold in the case of the idea of God, or at least when the idea is clear and distinct, since it cannot be said to be referred to something with which it is not in conformity. But as to confused ideas of gods which are concocted by idolaters, I fail to see why they too cannot be called materially false, insofar as these ideas provide matter for their false judgments. Nevertheless, surely those ideas that offer the faculty of judgment little or no occasion for error are presumably less worthy of being called materially false than do those that offer it considerable occasion for error; however, it is easy to exemplify the fact that some ideas offer a greater occasion for error than others. For this occasion does not exist in confused ideas formed at the whim of the mind *234* (such as the ideas of false gods) to the extent that it does in ideas that come to us confused from the senses (such as the ideas of heat and cold), if, as I said, it is in fact true that they display nothing real. But the greatest occasion of all for error is in ideas that arise from the sensitive appetite. For example, does not the idea of thirst in the man with dropsy in fact offer him matter for error when it provides him an occasion for judging that drinking something will do him good, when in fact it will do him harm?

But the distinguished gentleman asks what it is that is shown to me by this idea of cold, which I have said to be materially false. He says: if it shows a privation, then it is true; if it shows a positive being, then it is not the idea of cold. Quite true. However, the sole reason for my calling this idea materially false is that, since it is obscure and confused, I could not determine whether or not what it shows me is something positive outside my sensation. Thus I have an occasion for judging that it is something positive, although perhaps it is merely a privation.

Hence one should not ask what the cause is of this positive objective being that causes this idea to be materially false, since I am not claiming that this materially false idea is caused by some positive being, but rather that it is caused solely by the obscurity that nevertheless does have something positive as its subject, namely the sensation itself.

And surely this positive being is in me insofar as I am a true thing; but the obscurity, which alone provides me an occasion for judging that this idea of the sensation of cold represents something external to me which is called "cold," does not have a real cause, but arises solely from the fact that my nature is not perfect in every respect.

My basic principles are in no way weakened by this objection. However, since I never spent very much time reading the books of the philosophers, it might have been a cause for worry that I did not sufficiently take note of their manner of speaking when I asserted that ideas that provide the power of judgment with matter for error are materially false, had it not been for the fact that I found the word "materially" used in the same sense as my own in the first author that came into my hands: namely in Francisco Suárez's *Metaphysical Disputations*, Disp. IX, sect. 2, no. 4.

But let us move on to the most significant items about which the distinguished gentleman registers his disapproval. However, in my opinion, these things seem least deserving of disapproval: namely, in the passage where I said that it is fitting for us to think that in a sense God stands in the same relationship to himself as an efficient cause does to its effect. For in that very passage I denied what the distinguished gentleman says is a harsh saying, and a false one at that: namely, that God is the efficient cause of himself. For in asserting that "in a certain sense, God stands in the same relationship to himself as an efficient cause," I did not take the two relationships to be identical. And in saying by way of preface that "it is wholly fitting for us to think . . . ," I meant that my sole explanation for these things is the imperfection of the human understanding. However, I asserted this throughout the rest of the passage; for right at the very beginning, where I said that there exists nothing about which it is inappropriate to inquire into its efficient cause, I added "or, if it does not have one, to demand why it does not need one." These words are a sufficient indication that I believed there exists something that needs no efficient cause. But what, besides God, can be of this sort? And a short time later I said that "in God there is such great and inexhaustible power, that he never needed the help of anything in order to exist. Moreover, God does not now need a cause in order to be preserved; thus, in a manner of speaking, God is the cause of himself." Here the expression "cause of himself" can in no way be understood to mean an efficient cause; rather, it is merely a matter of the inexhaustible power of God being the cause or the reason why he needs no cause. And since this inexhaustible power or immensity of essence is incomparably positive, I said that the cause or the reason why God does not need a cause is a positive one. This could not be said of anything finite, even if it is supremely perfect in its own kind. But if a finite thing were said to be derived from itself, this could only be understood in a negative sense, since no reason derived from its positive nature could be put forward, on the basis of which we might understand that it does not need an efficient cause.

And in like manner, in all the other passages in which I compared the formal cause or reason derived from God's essence (on account of which God does not need a cause, either in order to exist or to be preserved) with the efficient cause (without which finite things cannot come into existence), I always did this in such a way that the difference between the formal cause and the efficient cause may come to be known from my very own words. Nowhere have I said that God preserves himself by means of some positive influence, as is the case with created things preserved by him; on the contrary, I merely said that the immensity of power or essence, on account of which he needs no one to preserve him, is something positive.   *237*

And thus I can readily agree with everything the distinguished gentleman puts forward to prove that God is not the efficient cause of himself and that he preserves himself neither by means of any positive influence nor by means of a continuous reproduction of himself. This is the only thing that is achieved from his arguments. However, as I hope is the case, even he will not deny that this immensity of the power, on account of which God does not need a cause in order to exist, is in God something positive, and that nothing similarly positive can be understood in anything else on account of which it would not require an efficient cause in order to exist. This is all I meant when I said that, with the exception of God alone, nothing can be understood to be derived from itself unless this is understood in a negative sense. Nor was there any need for me to assume any more than this in order to resolve the difficulty that had been put forward.

However, since the distinguished gentleman warns me here with such seriousness that "there can scarcely be found a theologian who would not take exception to the proposition that God is derived from himself in a positive fashion, and as it were from a cause," I will explain a bit more carefully why this way of speaking seems to me to be extremely helpful and even necessary in treating this question, and also why it seems to me to be quite removed from suspicion of being likely to cause someone to take offense.

I am aware that theologians of the Latin Church do not use the word *causa* ["cause"] in speaking of divine matters, when they are discussing the procession of persons in the Most Holy Trinity. And whereas theologians of the Greek Church use the words αἴτιον ["cause"] and ἀρχὴν ["principle"] interchangeably, theologians of the Latin Church prefer to use only the word *principium* ["principle"], taking it in its most general sense, lest from their manner of speaking they provide anyone an occasion on this basis for judging the Son to be less than the   *238* Father. But where no such danger of error is possible, and the discussion concerns not God considered as triune but only as one, I fail to see why the word "cause" should be shunned to such a degree, especially when we arrive at a point where it seems quite helpful and almost necessary to use it.

However, there can be no greater use for this term than if it aids in demonstrating the existence of God, and no greater necessity for it than if the existence of God manifestly could not be proved without it.

But I think it is obvious to everyone that a consideration of efficient causes is the primary and principal, not to say the only means of proving the existence of God. However, we cannot pursue this proof with care unless we give our mind the freedom to inquire about the efficient causes of all things, including even God himself, for by what right would we thence exclude God before we have proved that he exists? We must therefore ask with respect to every single thing whether it is derived from itself or from something else. And the existence of God can indeed be inferred by this means, even if we do not provide an explicit account of how one is to understand that "something is derived from itself." For those who follow exclusively the lead of the light of nature immediately at this juncture form a certain concept common to both efficient and formal cause alike, i.e., what is derived from something else [*est ab alio*] is derived from it as it were from an efficient cause; but whatever is derived from itself [*est a se*] is derived as it were from a formal cause, that is, because it has an essence of such a type that it does not need an efficient cause.For this reason I did not explain this doctrine in my Meditations; rather I assumed it to be self-evident.

239

But when those who are accustomed to judging that nothing can be the efficient cause of itself and to distinguishing carefully an efficient cause from a formal cause see the question being raised as to whether something is derived from itself, it easily happens that, while thinking that this expression refers only to an efficient cause properly so-called, they do not think the expression "derived from itself" should be understood to mean "as from a cause," but only negatively as meaning "without a cause," with the result that there arises something concerning which we must not ask why it exists. Were this rendering of the expression "derived from itself" to be accepted, there could not be an argument [*ratio*] from effects to prove the existence of God, as the author of the First Set of Objections has shown. Therefore this rendering is in no way to be accepted.

However, to give an apt reply to this, I think it is necessary to point out that there is a middle ground between an efficient cause properly so-called and no cause at all: namely the positive essence of a thing, to which we can extend the concept of an efficient cause in the same way we are accustomed in geometry to extend the concept of an exceedingly long arc to the concept of a straight line, or the concept of a rectilinear polygon with an indefinite number of sides to the concept of a circle. And I fail to see how this can be explained any better than by saying that in this query the meaning of "efficient cause" should not be restricted to those causes which are temporally prior to their effects or are different from them. For, first, the question would be pointless, since everyone knows that the same thing cannot exist prior to itself or be different from itself. Second, we could remove one of these two conditions from its concept and yet the notion of an efficient cause would remain intact.

240

For the fact that an efficient cause need not be temporally prior is evident from the fact that it has the defining characteristic [*rationem*] of a cause only during the time it is producing an effect, as has been said.

But from the fact that the other condition as well cannot be set aside, one ought to infer only that it is not an efficient cause taken in the strict sense, and I grant this. However, one ought not infer that it is in no sense a positive cause which can be compared by way of analogy to an efficient cause; and this is all that is called for in my argument. For by the very same light of nature by which I perceive that I would have given myself all the perfections of which there is an idea in me (if indeed I had given myself existence), I also perceive that nothing can give itself existence in that restricted sense in which the term "efficient cause" is typically used, namely in such a way that the same thing, insofar as it gives itself existence, is different from itself, insofar as it receives existence, since being the same thing and not being the same thing (that is, being different from itself), are contradictory.

And thus, when the question arises whether something can give itself existence, one must understand this to be equivalent to asking whether the nature or essence of anything is such that it needs no efficient cause in order to exist.

And when one adds that if there were such a thing, it would give itself all the perfections of which there is some idea in it, if indeed it does not have them, the meaning of this is that this thing cannot fail to have in actuality all the perfec- *241* tions that it knows. The reason for this is that we perceive by the light of nature that a thing whose essence is so immense that it does not need an efficient cause in order to exist also does not need an efficient cause in order to possess all the perfections that it knows, and that its own proper essence gives it in an eminent fashion all that we can think an efficient cause is capable of giving to any other things.

And the words "if it does not yet have them, it will give them to itself," are helpful only in explaining the matter, since we perceive by the same light of nature that this thing cannot now have the power and the will to give itself anything new, but that its essence is such that it possesses from eternity all that we can now think it would give itself, if it did not already possess it.

Nevertheless, all these modes of speaking, which are taken from the analogy of an efficient cause, are particularly necessary in order to direct the light of nature in such a way that we pay particular attention to them. This takes place in precisely the same way in which Archimedes, by comparing the sphere and other curvilinear figures with rectilinear figures, demonstrated various properties of the sphere and other curvilinear figures that otherwise could hardly have been understood. And just as no one raises objections regarding proofs of this sort, even if during the course of them one is required to consider a sphere to be similar to a polyhedron, I likewise think I cannot be blamed here for using the analogy of an efficient cause in order to explain those things that pertain to a formal cause, that is, to the very essence of God.

And there is no possible danger of error in this matter, since that one single aspect which is a property of an efficient cause, and which cannot be extended to *242* a formal cause, contains a manifest contradiction, and thus is incapable of being believed by anyone, namely that something is different from itself or that it simultaneously is and is not the same thing.

Moreover, one should note that we have ascribed to God the dignity inherent in being a cause in such a way that no indignity inherent in being an effect would follow thence in him. For just as theologians, in saying that the Father is the *principium* ["principle"] of the Son, do not on that account grant that the Son came from a principle; just so, although I have granted that God can in a certain sense be called the cause of himself, nevertheless nowhere have I in the same way called him an effect of himself. For it is customary to use the word "effect" primarily in relation to an efficient cause, and is regarded as less noble than its efficient cause, although it is often more noble than other causes.

However, when I here take the entire essence of a thing for its formal cause, I am merely following in the footsteps of Aristotle, for in his *Posterior Analytics*, Book II, chapter 11, having passed over the material cause, he calls the αἰταν ["cause"] the τὸ τί ἦν εἶναι ["the what it was to be"] or, as philosophers writing in Latin traditionally render it, the *causa formalis* ["formal cause"], and he extends this to all the essences of all things, since at this point he is dealing not with the causes of a physical composite (any more than I am here), but more generally with the causes from which some knowledge could be sought.

But it was hardly possible for me to discuss this matter without ascribing the term "cause" to God. This can be shown from the fact that, when the distinguished gentleman attempted to do the same thing I did by a different route, he nevertheless was completely unsuccessful, at least as I see it. For after using a number of words he shows that God is not the efficient cause of himself, since the defining characteristic [*ratio*] of "efficient cause" requires it to be different from its effect. Then he shows that God is not derived from himself in a positive sense, where one understands the word "positive" to mean the positive influence of a cause. Next he shows that God does not truly preserve himself, if by "preservation" one means the continuous production of a thing. All of this I readily grant. At length he tries to prove that God cannot be said to be the efficient cause of himself because, he says, the efficient cause of a thing is sought only with respect to the thing's existence, but not at all with respect to its essence. But existing is no less of the essence of an infinite being than having three angles equal to two right angles is of the essence of a triangle. Thus, if one is asked why God exists, one should no more answer by way of an efficient cause than one should do if asked why the three angles of a triangle are equal to two right angles. This syllogism can easily be turned against the distinguished gentleman in the following way: even if an efficient cause is not sought with respect to essence, still it can be sought with respect to existence; but in God essence and existence are not distinguished; therefore one can seek an efficient cause of God.

But in order to reconcile these two positions, someone who seeks to know why God exists should be told that one surely ought not respond in terms of an efficient cause in the strict sense, but only in terms of the very essence or formal cause of the thing. And precisely because in God existence is not distinguished from essence, the formal cause is strikingly analogous to an efficient cause, and thus can be called a "quasi-efficient cause."

Finally, he adds that the reply to be made to someone who is seeking the efficient cause of God is that he has no need of one; and to someone quizzing us further as to why God does not need one, the reply should be that this is because God is an infinite being whose existence is his essence. For the only those things that need an efficient cause are those in which actual existence can be distinguished from essence. On the basis of these considerations he says he overturns what I had said, namely that were I to think that nothing could somehow be related to itself the same way that an efficient cause is related to an effect, I would never, in inquiring into the causes of things, arrive at any first cause of all things. Nevertheless, it appears to me that my position has not been overturned nor has it been shaken or weakened. Moreover, on this depends the principal force not just of my argument but of absolutely all the arguments that can be put forward to prove the existence of God from effects. Yet virtually every theologian holds that no proof can be put forward unless it is from effects.

And thus, when he disallows the analogy of an efficient cause being ascribed to God's relationship to himself, far from making the argument for God's existence transparent, he instead prevents readers from understanding it, especially at the end where he concludes that, were he to think that an efficient or quasi-efficient cause were to be sought for anything, he would be seeking a cause of that thing which is different from it. For how would those who do not yet know God inquire into the efficient cause of other things so as in this way to arrive at a knowledge of God, unless they thought that one could seek the efficient cause of anything whatever? And finally, how would they make an end of their search for God as the first cause, if they thought that for any given thing one must look   *245* for a cause that is different from it?

The distinguished gentleman certainly appears to be doing the very same thing here that he would do, were he to follow Archimedes (who spoke of the properties that he had demonstrated of a sphere by means of an analogy with rectilinear figures) and were to say: "If I thought that a sphere could not be taken for a rectilinear or quasi-rectilinear figure having an infinite number of sides, I would attach no force to this demonstration, since strictly speaking the argument holds not for a sphere as a curvilinear figure, but merely for a sphere as a rectilinear figure having an infinite number of sides." It is, I say, as if the distinguished gentleman, while not wanting to characterize the sphere thus, and nevertheless desirous of retaining Archimedes' demonstration, were to say: "if I thought that the conclusion Archimedes drew there was supposed to be understood with respect to a rectilinear figure having an infinite number of sides, I would not admit this conclusion with respect to the sphere, since I am both certain and convinced that a sphere is in no way a rectilinear figure." Obviously in making these remarks he would not be doing the same thing as Archimedes had done; on the contrary, he would definitely prevent himself and others from correctly understanding Archimedes' demonstration.

I have pursued these matters here at somewhat greater length than perhaps the subject required, in order to show that it is a matter of greatest importance to take care lest there be found in my writings the least thing that theologians may justly find objectionable.

Finally, as to the fact that I did not commit a vicious circle when I said that it is manifest to us that the things we clearly and distinctly perceive are true only because God exists; and that it is manifest to us that God exists only because we   *246* perceive this fact clearly, I have already given a sufficient explanation in the Reply to the Second Set of Objections, sections 3 and 4, where I drew a distinction between what we are actually perceiving clearly and what we recall having clearly perceived sometime earlier. For first of all it is manifest to us that God exists, since we are attending to the arguments that prove this; but later on, it is enough for us to recall our having clearly perceived something in order to be certain that it is true. This would not suffice, unless we knew that God exists and does not deceive us.

Now as to the doctrine that there can be nothing in the mind, insofar as it is a thing that thinks, of which it is not aware, this appears to me self-evident, because we understand that nothing is in the mind, so viewed, that is not a thought or is not dependent upon thought. For otherwise it would not belong to the mind insofar as it is a thing that thinks. Nor can there exist in us any thought of which we are not aware at the very same moment it is in us. For this reason I have no doubt that the mind begins to think immediately upon its being infused into the body of an infant, and at the same time is aware of its thought, even if later on it does not recall what it was thinking of, because the images [*species*] of these thoughts do not inhere in the memory.

However, it should be noted that although we surely are always actually aware of the acts or operations of our mind, but this is not always the case with regard to faculties or powers, except potentially. In other words, when we prepare our-

247   selves to use some faculty, if this faculty is in the mind, we are immediately and actually aware of it. And therefore we can deny that it is in the mind if we are unable to become aware of it.

412   ## Sixth Set of Objections

After a very careful and thorough reading of your *Meditations* and the replies you made to the objections that have so far been raised, we find there still remain some concerns which you would do well to remove.

413   The first concern is that from the fact that we think it does not seem entirely certain that we exist. For in order for you to be certain that you think, you ought to it is to think, or what thought is, or again what your existence is. And since you do not yet know what these things are, how can you know that you think or that you exist? Therefore, when you say "I think" and when you add "therefore I am," you really do not know what you are saying. In fact, you are utterly ignorant of what you are saying or thinking, since this seems to require you to know that you know what you are saying, and this in turn requires you to be cognizant of the fact that you know that you know what you are saying, and so on *ad infinitum*. Thus it is evident that you cannot know whether you exist or even whether you think.

However, turning to the second concern, when you say that you think and that you exist, someone might argue that you are mistaken, that you are not thinking but are merely being moved, and that you are merely a corporeal motion, since no one has as yet been able to grasp that argument of yours whereby you think you have demonstrated that what you call thought cannot be a corporeal motion. Have you therefore used your method of analysis to dissect all the motions of your subtle matter in such a way that you are certain that you could show us, who pay very close attention and who are, we think, rather intelligent people, that it is self-contradictory for our thoughts to be dispersed among those corporeal motions?

The third concern is quite similar. Several church fathers, along with the Platonists, believed that angels are corporeal (and thus the Lateran Council[33] concluded that angels can be represented pictorially). They believed precisely the same thing regarding the rational soul, with some church fathers actually of the opinion that the soul is transmitted to one by one's parents; nevertheless they declared that both angels and the human soul think. Thus they seem to have believed that this could take place through corporeal motions, or even that angels were themselves corporeal motions; and in no way did they distinguish thought   *414* from these motions. This point can be confirmed by the thoughts of apes, dogs, and other animals. For dogs bark while sleeping as if they were chasing after hares or robbers. And when they are awake they know they are running, just as when they are asleep they know they are barking, even though we do not acknowledge, as you do, that there is something in them that is distinct from their bodies. But if you deny that a dog knows that it runs or thinks, leaving aside the fact that you assert this without proof, the dog itself might perhaps form a similar opinion about us, namely that we do not know whether we are running or thinking while we run or think. For you do not see the dog's internal mode of operating, any more than the dog observes yours; and there are great men who today ascribe the power of reasoning to brute animals, or who in previous times have done so. So foreign is it to us to believe that all of the functions of these animals can be adequately explained by means of the science of mechanics (that is, without reference to sense, life, and soul), that we are willing to risk everything in order to prove that this position is both impossible[34] and worthy of ridicule. And finally there are plenty of people who will say that man himself has neither sense nor intellect, and that he can do everything by means of mechanical devices and without any mind, given the fact that an ape, a dog, and an elephant can perform all their activities in this way. For if the paltry reasoning power of brute animals differs from the reasoning power of men, it differs merely in degree, and does not form the basis for an essential difference.

The fourth concern is with regard to the knowledge possessed by an atheist. When the atheist declares "if equals are subtracted from equals the remainders will be equal" or "the three angles of a rectilinear triangle are equal to two right angles," and a thousand similar examples, he claims that his knowledge is certain and even, according to your rule, most evident. For he cannot think of these

---

33. There have been five Lateran Councils; most likely the council being referred to here is the Fourth Lateran Council (1215). This council issued a summary of orthodox doctrines entitled *Firmiter,* directed against the Albigensians, among others. This summary affirmed that all beings, both spiritual and corporeal, i.e., those angelic and earthly, were created by God and that the creation of human beings was subsequent to that of angels. There is no suggestion whatever in this summary that angels are material; in fact, *Firmiter* very clearly assumes a distinction between spiritual creatures and corporeal creatures. Nor, for that matter, is there any discussion of the iconography of angels.

34. For some reason the authors of the *Sixth Set of Objections* used the Greek *adunaton* rather than one of the obvious Latin terms. Perhaps this was in imitation of Aristotle, who used this term throughout his works to characterize the views of opponents.

415 statements without believing them to be most certain. The atheist contends that this is so true that, even if God did not exist and were not possible, as he believes, he would be no less certain of these truths than were God really to exist. And he denies that any grounds for doubting can be brought forward to him which would at all distress him or cause him to be in doubt. What then do you bring forward? That God, if he exists, can deceive him? But he will deny that he can be deceived in these matters even if God exerts the full thrust of his omnipotence to this purpose.

From this there arises a fifth concern which is rooted in that deception which you wholly deny of God. A great many theologians believe that the damned, both angels and men, are continually being deceived by the idea placed in them by God of a fire that torments them, so that they give the firmest credence and believe they see most clearly and perceive that they really are being tormented by fire, even though there is no fire. This being the case, is it not possible that God can deceive us with similar ideas and find continual amusement at our expense by sending species or ideas into our souls? Thus we think we see clearly and perceive with each of our senses things that nevertheless are not outside us, so that neither the heavens nor the earth exist, nor do we have arms, feet, eyes, and so on. God could surely do this without injustice or wickedness, since he is the supreme lord of all things, and has absolute power in the management of his possessions, especially since this contributes to checking men's pride and punishing them for their sins, whether this be because of original sin or because of some other causes which are hidden from us. These points seem definitely to be confirmed in those passages in Scripture which show us that we can know nothing. For example, the passage in Paul, I Cor. 8:2: "If anyone," he says, "thinks

416 he knows anything, he has not yet known as he ought to know." And in the passage in Ecclesiastes 8:17: "I understood that of all the works of God man can find no reason for the things that happen under the sun; and the more someone labors to seek it out the less he will find; even if a wise man were to say that he knows, he will not be able to find it." However, the entire book makes it apparent that the wise man speaks as he does on account of carefully thought out reasons and not impetuously or thoughtlessly, especially when a question is raised regarding the mind, which you contend is immortal. For Ecclesiastes 3:19 declares that "the death of a man is the same as the death of beasts." But lest you reply that this is to be understood only in respect to the body, the author of Ecclesiastes adds that "man has no preeminence over a beast." And speaking of this very spirit of man he denies that there is anyone who knows whether it goes upward (that is, whether it is immortal) or goes downward with the spirits of animals (that is, whether it perishes). Nor is it appropriate for you to maintain that this is being uttered in the persona of an unbeliever; were that the case, the writer ought to have warned us about this and to have refuted what he had alleged. Nor again is it appropriate for you to deny that you should reply to these things on the grounds that Scripture is a matter for theologians. For since you are a Christian, it is fitting for you to be prepared to reply to all those who raise an objection against the faith, but especially against those views you desire to maintain, and to do as satisfactory a job as you possibly can.

The sixth concern arises from the indifference of judgment or freedom, which you refuse to ascribe to the perfection of the will but only to its imperfection, so that indifference is eliminated whenever the mind clearly perceives what is to be believed or done or left undone. Do you not see that by maintaining these positions you are destroying God's freedom, since you are removing from his will *417* that indifference as to whether he will establish this world rather than some other world or no world at all, even though it is a matter of faith that from all eternity God was indifferent as to whether he should establish one world or countless worlds or even no worlds at all? But who doubts that God has always seen with the clearest intuition all that is to be done or left undone? The clearest vision and perception of things does not therefore eliminate the indifference of choice. And if indifference cannot be compatible with human freedom, neither will it be compatible with divine freedom, since the essences of things are, like numbers, indivisible and immutable. Thus indifference is included no less in the divine freedom of choice than in human freedom of choice.

The seventh concern deals with the surface on which, or by means of which, you say all sensations take place. For we do not understand how it could happen that it is neither a part of the bodies which are sensed nor a part of the air and the vapors, given that you deny that it is any part or even the outer surface of these things. Nor, for that matter, do we grasp your claim that there are no real accidents which pertain to some body or substance and which could exist by divine power without any subject, and which really do exist in the Sacrament of the Altar. Nevertheless, there is no reason for our professors to be perturbed by your views until they see whether you are going to prove them in your treatise on physics, which you give us cause to anticipate and which they scarcely believe will put these views forward so clearly that they can or must be embraced, with earlier teachings being rejected.

The eighth concern arises from your reply to the *Fifth Set of Objections*. How can the truths of geometry or metaphysics, such as the ones you call to mind, be immutable and eternal, and yet not be independent of God?[35] For what type of *418* cause is it according to which these truths depend upon God? Could God have brought it about that there never was such a thing as the nature of a triangle? And how, pray tell, could God bring it about from all eternity that it was not true that twice 4 is 8 or that a triangle does not have three angles? Therefore either these truths depend solely on an intellect that is thinking of them or on existing things, or else they are independent, since it seems God could not have brought it about that any of these essences or truths were not from all eternity.

Finally, the ninth concern is especially troubling to us. You claim that one should not place any trust in the operations of the senses and that the certainty of the intellect is far greater than that of the senses. For how can the intellect enjoy any certainty unless it has previously acquired it from properly disposed senses? Moreover, how can the intellect correct an error on the part of one of the senses unless some other sense first corrects the error? On account of refraction, a stick

35. See AT VII, 380.

submerged in water appears bent, even though it is straight. What is going to correct this error? The intellect? Hardly. It is the sense of touch. And the same determination must obtain in the other instances. Thus if you employ all the senses when they are in good working order and are always presenting the same data, you will achieve the greatest certainty of which man is naturally capable. But this certainty will often elude you if you place your trust in the operation of the mind, which is often mistaken in matters about which it believed doubt to be impossible.

These are the main concerns that give us pause. Please also append to these a certain procedure, along with certain identifying characteristics, that would render us most certain that when we understand so completely one thing apart from another, it is certain that the one is so distinct from the other that they could subsist separately, at least by the power of God. In other words, how can we with
419   certainty know clearly and distinctly that this distinction made by the intellect does not arise exclusively from the intellect itself, but proceeds from things themselves? For when we contemplate the immensity of God without thinking about his justice, or when we contemplate his existence without thinking about the Son or the Holy Spirit, do we not completely perceive this existence, or God as existing, apart from these persons—which some unbeliever could deny, just as you deny that mind or thought pertains to the body? Thus just as one argues poorly when one concludes that the Son and the Holy Spirit are essentially distinct from God the Father or can be separated from him, so too no one will grant you that thought or the human mind are distinct from the body, even though you conceive the one apart from the other and utterly deny the one of the other, and even though you do not think that this takes place through some act of abstraction on the part of your mind. Surely, if you handle these concerns in a satisfactory manner, then, as far as we are concerned, absolutely nothing else remains which would displease our theologians.

Appendix

A few questions raised by others are appended here, so that you might reply to these together with the immediately preceding ones, since they address the same argument. Certain very learned and insightful people wished to have the following three points explained more carefully:

1) How do I know with certainty that I have a clear idea of my soul?

2) How do I know with certainty that this idea is completely different from anything else?

420   3) How do I know with certainty that this idea contains absolutely nothing corporeal?[36]

Reply to the Sixth Set of Objections

1. It is indeed true that no one can be certain that he thinks or that he exists unless he knows what thought is and what existence is. This is not to say that it requires

---

36. The *Sixth Set of Objections* continues with a letter from "Various Philosophers and Geometers to Descartes."

a knowledge which is reflective or which is acquired through demonstration, much less a knowledge of reflective knowledge, through which one knows that one knows, and again knows that one knows that one knows, and so on *ad infinitum*. This sort of knowledge can never be had about anything. Rather, it is quite sufficient that one knows it by that inner knowledge which always precedes reflective knowledge. This inner knowledge, in the case of thought and existence, is innate in all men in such a way that we could not really be without it, even if perhaps we are overwhelmed by preconceived opinions and are attentive more to words than to their meanings, and thus could imagine that we do not have such knowledge. Thus when someone notices that he is thinking and that it follows from this that he exists, even though perhaps he had never before sought to know what thought is or what existence is, still he cannot fail to have a sufficient knowledge of each of these, so that on this score he is satisfied.

2. Nor too is it possible, when someone notices that he thinks and understands what it is to be moved, that he would believe himself to be mistaken and that he is not thinking but only being moved. For since the idea or notion he has of thought is plainly different from that of corporeal motion, it is necessary   *423* for him to understand the one to be different from the other. However, on account of his habit of ascribing to one and the same subject many different properties among which no connection is known, it could happen that he doubts or even that he affirms that he is one and the same thing which thinks and which moves from place to place. And one should note that there are two ways in which things of which we have different ideas can be taken to be one and the same thing: namely, either by a unity and identity of nature or merely by a unity of composition. Thus, for example, we surely do not have the same idea of figure and motion, just as we do not have the same idea of the act of understanding and the act of willing, nor of bones and flesh, nor of thought and an extended thing. But nevertheless we clearly perceive that the very same substance which is able to take on a shape is also capable of being moved, and thus that what has a shape and what is capable of being moved are one and the same thing by virtue of a unity of nature. Likewise, a thing that understands and a thing that wills are also one and the same by virtue of a unity of nature. However we are not perceiving the same aspect about a thing which we consider under the form of bone and which we consider under the form of flesh. For this reason we cannot take them to be one and the same thing by virtue of a unity of nature, but only by virtue of a unity of composition, that is, insofar as it is one and the same animal which has bones and flesh. But the question before us now is whether we perceive that a thing that thinks and an extended thing are one and the same by virtue of a unity of nature? In other words, do we find between thought and extension the same sort of affinity or connection that we observe between shape and motion or between the act of understanding and the act of willing? Or rather, are they said to be one and the same   *424* merely by virtue of a unity of composition, insofar as they both are found in the same man, just as bones and flesh are found in the same animal? I accept the latter view, since I observe a distinction or difference in every respect between the nature of an extended thing and that of a thing that thinks, which is no less than the difference I observe between bones and flesh.

However, you say in addition that no one has as yet been able to grasp my demonstration. Lest this conflict, which involves an appeal to authority, be detrimental to the truth, I am forced to reply that while not very many people have as yet examined the demonstration, still there are several who affirm that they understand it. And just as a lone witness who has sailed to America and declares that he has seen the Antipodes[37] warrants greater credence than a thousand others who deny them on the grounds that they have no acquaintance with them; so likewise, in the case of those who appropriately examine the weightiness of arguments, greater authority attaches to the one person who says he correctly understands some demonstration than to the thousand others who, without providing any proof, claim that this very same demonstration cannot be understood by anyone. For although they themselves do not understand it, this is no impediment to others being able to understand it. Indeed, by drawing this conclusion on the grounds they do, they show they do not reason with sufficient care and thus do not warrant having very much faith placed in them.

Finally, there is the question of whether I have used my method of analysis to dissect all the motions of my subtle matter in such a way that I am certain that I could show people who pay very close attention and who are, to their way of thinking, rather intelligent, that it is self-contradictory for our thoughts to be dis-

425   persed among corporeal motions. This, as I interpret it, is to say that thoughts and corporeal motions are one and the same. My answer to this is that it is indeed most certain to me, but I do not promise that others will be persuaded of it, however attentive and astute they may think they are, at least not so long as they turn their attention not to things purely intelligible but only to things imaginable, as those people appear to have done who imagined that the distinction between thought and motion is to be understood by way of a dissection of some subtle matter. For this distinction is to be understood solely from the fact that the notion of a thing that thinks and that of an extended or mobile thing are utterly different and independent of one another, and that it is self-contradictory for these things, which are clearly understood by us to be different and independent, not to be able to be established separately, at least by God. Thus, however often we find them in one and the same subject (as, for example, thought and corporeal motion in the same man), we should on that account believe that there they are one and the same not by virtue of a unity of nature, but only by virtue of a unity of composition.

3. What is asserted here regarding the Platonists and their followers has already been rejected by the entire Catholic Church and commonly by all the philosophers. Now the Lateran Council did indeed conclude that angels could be depicted pictorially, nevertheless it did not on that account grant that angels are corporeal. And even if they really were believed to be corporeal, their minds certainly cannot be understood to be any more inseparable from angelic bodies than men's minds are from human bodies. And surely, were we here to entertain the notion that a human soul is transmitted to one by one's parents, we could not

---

37. Located approximately 350 miles southeast of New Zealand, the Antipodes Islands were not discovered until early in the 19th century.

therefore conclude that it was corporeal, but only that it proceeds from the parents' soul, just as the body arises from the parents' body. As far as dogs and apes 426 are concerned, even if I were to grant that there is thought in them, it would not in any way follow from this that the human mind is not distinct from the body, but rather that in other animals too their minds are distinct from their bodies. This was the position espoused by these very same Platonists, whose authority was just now being praised. In this they were following the Pythagoreans, as is evident from their belief in metempsychosis. However, not only have I declared that there is no thought whatever in brute animals, as is here being assumed by my critics, I also proved it by means of the strongest of arguments, arguments that to date have not been refuted by anyone. But actually those who claim that dogs while awake know they are running and even while asleep that they are barking (as if these people were well acquainted with the animal's hearts) assert this but do not prove it. For even if they add that they do not believe that the operations of beasts can be explained by means of the science of mechanics without reference to sense, life, and soul (this I take to mean "without reference to thought," for I have not denied that there is in brute animals something commonly called "life," or a corporeal soul, or an organic sense), to the extent that these people are "willing to risk everything proving that this position is both impossible and worthy of ridicule," still, this should not be taken to be a proof. And the same can be said with regard to any other assertion, however true it may be. In fact, people do not usually take risks unless their arguments lack probative force. And since at one time great men mocked claims about the existence of the Antipodes in nearly the same way, I believe we should not immediately take to be false what others mock.

Finally there is the added remark: "there are plenty of people who will say that man himself has neither sense nor intellect, and that he can do everything by means of mechanical devices and without any mind, given the fact that an ape, a 427 dog, and an elephant can perform all their operations in this way. . . ." Yet surely this argument fails to prove anything except perhaps that certain men conceive everything so confusedly and adhere so tenaciously to prematurely formed beliefs (which they understand in merely a verbal fashion) that, rather than change them, they deny regarding themselves what they cannot help always experiencing within themselves. For surely we cannot avoid always experiencing within ourselves that we think. It may be shown that brute animals can perform all their operations without any thought, but one should not on that account conclude that therefore one also does not think. The only exception would be someone who has persuaded himself beforehand that he functions in no way different from brute animals and who, for the sole reason that he ascribes thought to animals, so stolidly adheres to the statement that "men and brute animals function in the same way," that, on being shown that brute animals do not think, he prefers to rid himself of that thought of his, of which he cannot fail to be aware, rather than change his opinion that he functions in the same way as brute animals. Nevertheless, I am not easily convinced that there are many men of this sort. But indeed if it be granted that thought is not distinct from corporeal motion, there are many more to be found who contend with much better reason that it is the same thing that is in brute animals and in us, since they observe all the corporeal motions in animals that they find in us. And they add that a difference that is merely a matter of degree does not alter the essence, even though they think perhaps there is less reasoning power in beasts than there is in us; nevertheless, they quite properly infer that the minds of animals are manifestly in precisely the same species as our own minds.

428   4. As to the knowledge possessed by an atheist, it is easy to demonstrate that it is not immutable and certain. For, as I have already asserted, the less powerful the author imputes the author of his being to be, the greater will be the occasion he will have for questioning whether perhaps he is of so imperfect a nature that he is deceived even in things that seem to him most evident. And he will never be able to free himself of this doubt unless he first recognizes that he has been created by a true God who cannot deceive.

5. The statement that it is self-contradictory for men to be deceived by God is clearly demonstrated from the fact that the form of deception is non-being, toward which a supreme being cannot tend. And on this point all theologians are in agreement and on it depends all the certainty of the Christian faith. For why should we believe in things revealed by God if we thought that sometimes we are deceived by him? And although theologians commonly affirm that the damned are tormented by the fire of hell, still they do not on that account believe that the damned are "being deceived by a false idea that God has implanted in them of a tormenting fire," but rather that the damned are truly being tormented by a fire, for "just as the incorporeal spirit of a living man is naturally confined in a body, so too after death it can easily be confined in corporeal fire through divine power, and so on." See the Master, *IV Sent.,* Dist. 44.[38]

However, as to the Scripture passages, I do not think it is my place to answer questions about them, except when they appear to be in opposition to some opinion that is unique to me. For when the Scriptures are brought to bear against beliefs that are common among all Christians, such as are those which are here *429* being attacked, namely, that something can be known and that human souls are not like those of animals, I should I be fearful of the charge of arrogance if I did not prefer to be satisfied with the replies that have already been discovered by others, rather than think up new ones. For I have never involved myself in theological studies except insofar as they contributed to my private instruction, nor do I experience within me sufficient divine grace to believe myself called to these sacred studies. And thus I proclaim that I will not make any replies in the future regarding objections such as these. However, I will not yet adhere to this change in policy, lest perhaps I provide people an occasion for believing that I am silent because I could not provide a sufficiently appropriate explanation for the passages cited. [. . .][39]

---

38. Peter Lombard (c. 1100–1160) acquired the title "Master of the Sentences" in virtue of his *Four Books of Sentences,* which he compiled between 1148 and 1151. This systematically organized collection of quotations from church fathers and later theologians became a standard theological text for nearly 500 years.

39. Descartes continues with explanations of the biblical passages.

6. As for freedom of the will, the account to be given in the case of God is vastly different from the one to be given in our own case. For it is self-contradictory for the will of God not to have been indifferent from all eternity to everything that has happened or ever will happen, since it is impossible to imagine the idea of anything good or true, anything to be believed or to be done or to be left undone being in the divine intellect prior to his will having determined itself to bring these things about such as they are. Nor am I speaking here of temporal priority; rather, there is not even a priority of order or of nature or of a distinction of reason reasoned,[40] as they say, as if this idea of the good impelled God to choose one thing rather than another. Thus, for example, God did not will to create the world in time because he saw that it would be better this way than were he to have created it from all eternity. Nor did he will that the three angles of a triangle should be equal to two right angles because he knew that it could not be otherwise, and so on. On the contrary, it is because he willed to create the world in time that it is better than were he to have created it from all eternity. And the fact that it is true and inalterable that the three angles of a triangle should necessarily equal two right angles is owing to the fact that God willed it to be so; and the same for the other cases. Nor is there any problem in the fact that it could be said that the merits of the saints are the cause of their gaining eternal life, for their merits are not a cause in the sense that they determine God to will something, but merely in the sense that they are the cause of an effect of which God has from all eternity willed their merits to be the cause. And thus God's supreme indifference is the supreme proof of his omnipotence. But as for man, since he finds that the nature of every good and every truth is already determined by God and that his will could not be directed toward something else, it is evident that he embraces the good and the true the more willingly, and hence also the more freely, according as he sees it more clearly; and that he is never indifferent except when he does not know which alternative is better or truer, or certainly when he does not see it so plainly that he cannot be in doubt regarding it. And thus there is a vast difference between the indifference that pertains to human freedom and the indifference that pertains to divine freedom. Nor is it of any relevance here that the essences of things are said to be indivisible. For first of all, no essence can pertain univocally to God and to a creature. And second, indifference does not pertain to the essence of human freedom, since not only are we free when ignorance of what is right renders us indifferent, but we are also free (and especially so), when a clear perception impels us to pursue something.

7. I conceive of the surface by which I think our senses are affected no differently than all mathematicians and philosophers normally conceive it, or at least ought to conceive it. They distinguish it from the body and suppose that it lacks any depth. However, the word "surface" is taken in two senses by mathematicians. In one sense, they use it to refer to a body to whose length and breadth alone they

40. This is a term used by some medieval writers to designate mental distinctions, or "distinctions of reason," for which there is no foundation or basis in reality; rather, such a distinction arises exclusively through reflective activity on the part of the intellect. See Francisco Suárez, *Metaphysical Disputations*, Disp. VII, 1, sec. 4–5.

direct their attention and which is viewed without reference to its having any depth, although they are not denying that it does have some or other depth. In the second sense, they use it merely to refer to a mode of a body, that is, when all its depth is denied. And for this reason, in order to avoid ambiguity, I asserted that I was speaking of that surface which is merely a mode and hence cannot be a part of a body; for a body is a substance, and a mode cannot be a part of a substance. But I did not deny that the surface is the outer limit of a body; on the contrary, it can just as appropriately be called the outer limit of the contained body as much as of the body that contains, in the sense in which those bodies are said to be con-
434   tiguous whose outer limits are touching one another. For surely, when two bodies touch one another, each one's outer limit is one and the same;[41] and this extremity is a part of neither body, but is the same mode of each body and can remain if these bodies are removed, provided only that other bodies having precisely the same size and shape replace them. In fact, that sort of place which Aristotelians call the "surface of a surrounding body"[42] cannot be understood to be a surface in any other sense except in the one in which it is not a substance but a mode. For the position of a tower is not changed even if the air surrounding the tower is changed or even if some other body is substituted in its place; thus the surface, which is here taken to be the place, is a part of neither the surrounding air nor the tower.

However, in order to reject[43] the reality of accidents, it does not appear to me necessary to demand additional proofs over and above those I have already treated. For first, since every sensation takes place through touch, nothing but the surface of bodies can be sensed. But if there are real accidents, they ought to be something different from that surface, which is merely a mode. Therefore, if they exist they cannot be sensed. But has anyone ever believed they existed if he did not think they are sensed? Second, it is altogether contradictory that there should be real accidents, since anything real can exist separately from any other subject. But whatever can exist thus separated is a substance, not an accident. Nor is there
435   relevance to the claim that real accidents can be separated from their subjects not naturally but only through divine power, for "taking place naturally" merely means "taking place through the ordinary power of God," which in no way differs from God's extraordinary power and whose impact on the world is no different. Thus if everything that can exist naturally without a subject is a substance, then whatever can exist without a subject—even if through God's power, however extraordinary it may be—must also be called a substance. Indeed I do admit that one substance can inhere[44] in another substance; but when this happens it is not the substance itself that has the form of an accident, but merely the mode of

---

41. Aristotle, *Physics,* Book IV, chapter 4, 211a34.

42. Aristotle, *Physics,* Book IV, chapter 4, 212a6–6a.

43. Literally, to "drive off the stage by clapping." A literal, but more contemporary translation might be to "hiss off the stage." Descartes's use of such a scornful term does little to conceal his utter contempt for the medieval Aristotelian doctrine of accidents—or for Aristotelianism generally.

44. *Accidere.*

its inherence. For example, when clothing[45] inheres in a man, it is not the clothing itself but merely the man's state of being clothed that is an accident. But since the chief reason which moved philosophers to posit real accidents was that they thought that perceptions of the senses could not be explained without them. I promised that in my writings in physics I would describe this in minute detail, addressing each of the senses one by one. This is not to say that I wanted any of my views to be taken on faith; rather I thought that right-thinking people would easily surmise what I could achieve regarding the other senses, given what I have already explained in the *Dioptrics* in regard to sight.

8. It is evident to anyone who takes note of the immensity of God that there can be absolutely nothing that does not depend on him. This is true not merely for everything that subsists, but for all order, every law, and every rational basis for what is true and good. For otherwise, as was said a short while ago, God would plainly not have been indifferent to creating the things he created. For if some rational basis for what is good were to have existed prior to God's preordaining of things, this would have determined him to what was best to do. On the contrary, however, because God has determined himself toward those things that ought now to be made, they are for that reason, as Genesis has it, "very good."[46] *436* In other words, the reason for their goodness depends on the fact that God willed to make them so. Nor is it necessary to inquire in regard to the types of cause it is by which this goodness, or the other truths—both mathematical as well as metaphysical—depend upon God. For since those who enumerated the types of causes perhaps did not pay attention to this type of causing, it is hardly any wonder that they gave no name to it. In fact, however, they did give a name to it: it could be called an "efficient cause," and for the same reason that a king is the one who puts a law "into effect," even though the law is not itself something existing physically, but is merely a "moral being," as they say. Nor too is it necessary to ask how God could have been able to bring it about from all eternity that it not be true that twice 4 is 8, and so on. For I admit that this cannot be understood by us. On the other hand, however, I rightly understand that there can be nothing in any class of being which does not depend upon God, and that it would have been easy for God to establish certain things such that we men would not understand that these things could be otherwise than they are. Thus it would be illogical to doubt something we correctly understand because of something we neither understand nor observe any reason why we should understand it. Hence we should not think that eternal truths depend upon the human intellect or upon other existing things. Rather they depend on God alone, who, as supreme legislator, has established them from all eternity.

---

45. *Habitus* is the state of being surrounded by a noncausal, nonmeasuring environment. It is one of the ten predicaments or predicate categories of medieval Aristotelian logic. The standard medieval example of a *habitus* is the state of being clothed. See Thomas Aquinas, *Commentary on Aristotle's Metaphysics,* Book V, lesson 9, sec. 892; Book XI, lesson 12, sec. 2377.

46. Genesis 1:31.

9. For us to observe correctly what sort of certainty belongs to sense, we must distinguish three levels, as it were, within it. To the first pertains only that by which the corporeal organ is immediately affected by external objects. And this
437   can only be the motion of the particles of the organ in question and the change in configuration and position resulting from that motion. The second level includes everything that immediately results in the mind from its being united to the corporeal organ which is thus affected. And such are the perceptions of sorrow, tickling, thirst, hunger, colors, sound, taste, smell, heat, cold, and the like, which arise from the union and, as it were, the intermingling of mind and body, as was asserted in the Sixth Meditation. Finally, the third level includes all those judgments we have been accustomed to make from our youth regarding things outside us, on the occasion of motions in the corporeal organs.

For example, when I see a stick, one should not think that some "intentional species" wing their way from the stick to the eye, but merely that rays of light reflected from the stick excite certain motions in the optic nerve and, by this means, in the brain, as I have explained at sufficient length in the *Dioptrics*. And it is in this motion of the brain, which we have in common with brute animals, that the first level of sensing consists. But from this there follows the second level of sensing which extends only to the perception of color or light reflected from the stick. It arises from the fact that the mind is so intimately conjoined with the brain that it is affected by the motions which take place in it; and nothing else is to be assigned to sense, if we wish to distinguish it carefully from the intellect. For it is on the basis of this sensation of color by which I am affected that I judge a stick existing outside me has color, and it is on the basis of the extension of this color, its boundaries and relation of its position to the parts of my brain, that I draw conclusions regarding the stick's size, shape, and distance. And this is the case even though people commonly attribute these two activities to sense, and
438   were I therefore here to assign them to the third level of sensing, still it is manifest that it depends upon the intellect alone. And I have demonstrated in the *Dioptrics* that size, distance, and shape can be perceived only by reasoning from one of these aspects to another. But the difference lies solely in the fact that when we make judgments now for the first time on account of some new observation we attribute them to the intellect. But as to those judgments we made from our earliest years—made in precisely the same way as the ones we make now—concerning things which affected our senses, or even things to which we concluded by means of a process of reasoning, we assigned them to sense. And we made this assignment because habit makes us reason and judge very quickly, or rather we recall judgments we had for a long time been making regarding similar things, and thus we fail to distinguish these operations from a simple perception of sense.

Thus it is evident that when we declare that the certainty of the intellect is far greater than that of the senses, we mean merely that the judgments we make as adults as a result of new observations are more certain than those we formed in early childhood without any reflection at all. No doubt this is true. For it is obvious that it is not a question here of the first and second levels of sensing, since there cannot be any falsity in it. Hence when it is asserted that a stick in water appears broken on account of refraction, this is the same as saying that how it appears to us is the basis on which a child would judge it to be broken and even the basis on which we make the same judgment in accordance with the precon- ceived opinions with which we have become accustomed from our youth. But I cannot grant what is added here, namely, that this error is corrected by touch and not by the intellect. The reason is that, even though it is through touch that we judge the stick to be straight (this judgment taking place in the same way as that to which we have been accustomed from infancy and which therefore is called "sense"), nevertheless this does not suffice to correct an error of sight. On the contrary, in addition we need to have some power of reasoning to teach us that in this matter we ought to give more credence to a judgment based on touch than to a judgment elicited from sight. Since this power of reasoning has not been in us from our infancy, it must be ascribed not to sense but to the intellect alone. And therefore in this very case it is the intellect alone that corrects an error of sense; and no instance can ever be brought forward in which error results from our trusting the operation of the mind more than sense.

439

10. Since the difficulties that remain are put forward more as doubts than as objections, I am not so arrogant that I would dare to reply that I will provide a satisfactory account for those difficulties concerning which to this day I see men of great intelligence and learning have doubts. Still, so that I might perform to my capacity and that I not fail in my cause, I will candidly state how it happened that I completely freed myself from these same doubts. For thus I will be delighted if perhaps these same things be used by others; but if not, at least I will not be aware of any rashness on my part.

When I first made a real distinction between the human mind and the body on the basis of arguments displayed in these *Meditations* and inferred that the mind is more known than the body, and so on, I surely was compelled to give my assent because I observed nothing in them which was incoherent or which was not deduced from evident principles according to the rules of logic. But I confess I was not for that reason fully convinced; and the same thing happened to me that happens to astronomers who, after having been won over by arguments that the sun is several times larger than the earth, still cannot bring themselves to judge that the sun is not smaller than the earth when they are actually turning their eyes toward it. But I advanced further and passed over to a consideration of physical things by placing my trust in the same basic principles. I did this first by attend- ing to the ideas or notions of anything at all that I found within myself. I dili- gently distinguished them one from the other so that all my judgments would be congruent with them. As a result, I observed that absolutely nothing belongs to the concept of a body except that it is something which has length, breadth, and depth, and that it is capable of various shapes and motions. I also found that these shapes and motions are merely modes which no power could cause to exist apart from a body. But colors, smells, tastes, and the like are merely certain sensations existing in my thought, differing no less from bodies than does pain from the shape or motion of the weapon that is inflicting the pain. Finally, I observed that heaviness, hardness, the power of heating, attracting, and purging, and all the

440

other qualities we experience in bodies, consist exclusively in motion or the privation of motion and the configuration and arrangement of their parts.

441   Since these opinions differ considerably from those which I had previously held regarding physical things, I then began to consider the reasons why I had previously believed otherwise. And I observed that the chief reason was that, beginning from infancy, I had made various judgments regarding physical things, insofar as they aided in the preservation of the life I was entering, and I later retained the same opinions I had previously conceived. And since at that age the mind used the corporeal organs less properly and was very firmly attached to them, it did not do any thinking apart from them and perceived things only in a confused fashion. And although it was conscious of its own nature and possessed within itself an idea of thought as well as an idea of extension, nevertheless, since it understood nothing without also at the same time imagining something, it took them both to be one and the same, referring to the body all the notions it had of things that are related to the intellect. And since I never freed myself later in life from these preconceived opinions, I did not know anything at all with enough distinctness and I assumed that everything was corporeal, even though I assumed that the ideas or concepts of these very things which I took to be corporeal were often such that they referred to minds rather than to bodies.

For I conceived of heaviness, for example, as if it were a certain real quality which is present in solid bodies. Although I called it a "quality," referring it to the bodies in which it inhered, nevertheless, by adding that it was "real," I actually thought it was a substance. In the same way, clothing, taken in itself, is a sub-

442 stance, even though when referred to the man who is clothed it is a quality. And again, the mind, even though it is really a substance, can nevertheless still be called a quality of the body to which it is joined. And although I imagined that heaviness is diffused throughout the entire body that is heavy, still I did not ascribe to it that very same extension which constitutes the nature of a body. For the true extension of a body is such that it excludes any mutual penetrability of its parts. However, I thought there was as much heaviness in a ten-foot-long piece of wood as there was in a one-foot-long bar of gold or some other metal. In fact I judged that all the heaviness could be contracted to a mathematical point. Indeed, I also saw that heaviness, while remaining coextensive with the body which is heavy, could exert its entire force in any part of the body. For if the body were suspended by a rope, it could pull on the rope with all its force just as if this heaviness were only in the part touching the rope and were not diffused throughout the remaining parts—regardless of the part to which the rope might be attached. And it is in precisely this way that surely I now understand the mind to be coextensive with the body, the whole of the mind in the whole body, and the whole mind in every one of its parts. But it appears that the belief that this idea of heaviness was drawn from the one I had of the mind is chiefly attributable to the fact that I believed that heaviness carried bodies toward the center of the earth as if it contained within itself some knowledge. For this certainly could not take place without knowledge, nor could any knowledge occur unless it be in a mind. Nevertheless, I also used to attribute a few other properties to heaviness which cannot be understood to be attributable in the same way to a mind: for example, that it is divisible, measurable, and so on.

But after I had taken sufficient note of these things, I carefully distinguished *443* the idea of the mind from the ideas of the body and corporeal motion, and I came to realize that all the other ideas of real qualities or substantial forms which I had formerly possessed had been put together or fabricated by me from those previously mentioned ideas. Thus I easily freed myself from all the doubts that have been proposed here. For first of all, I had no doubt about whether I possessed a clear idea of my mind, inasmuch as I had an intimate awareness of it. Nor did I have any doubt about whether this idea was utterly different from the ideas of other things and about whether it contained anything corporeal. For although I had sought true ideas of these other things as well, and I seemed to know all of them in a general sort of way, still I utterly failed to find anything in them that was not completely different from the idea of the mind. And I saw that there is a far greater distinction between things such as mind and body, which appeared distinct even though I thought attentively about both of them, than there is between things which are such that when we think of both of them we do not see that one of these can exist apart from the other—despite the fact that we can understand one while not thinking about the other. Thus the immensity of God can readily be understood even if no attention is given to his justice; but if attention is given to both, it is utterly self-contradictory for us to think that God is immense but not just. Moreover, the existence of God can also be rightly understood, even if one were ignorant of the persons of the Holy Trinity, inasmuch as they can be perceived only by a mind illumined by faith. But when they have been perceived, I deny that a real distinction can be understood to obtain among *444* them by reason of the divine essence, although it may be allowed by reason of their relations to one another.

And finally I was not fearful about my being obsessed about my method of analysis or about having made an error when, because I saw that there are certain bodies that do not think, or rather because I clearly understood that certain bodies can exist without thought, I preferred to argue that thought does not belong to the nature of the body, rather than conclude that thought is a mode of the body on the grounds that there are certain other bodies—human bodies, for example—which do think. For I have never really seen or perceived that human bodies think, but merely that it was the same men who possess both thought and a body. And I observed that this occurs as a result of combining a thing that thinks with a something corporeal, because, in examining by itself a thing that thinks, I observed nothing in it that belonged to the body, just as I observed no thought in corporeal nature, when I considered it by itself. On the contrary, however, in examining all the modes of body and mind, I observed absolutely nothing whose concept did not depend on the concept of the thing of which it was a mode. Because we often see two things joined together, one should not conclude that they are one and the same. But because we sometimes observe one of them apart from the other, it is quite appropriate to draw the inference that they are different. Nor should the power of God deter us from drawing this inference, since

445

it is no less contradictory in its very concept that what we clearly perceive to be two different things should become one and the same, intrinsically and not through a combination, than that things which are in no way distinct should be separated. And thus, if God were to bestow upon certain bodies the power of thinking (as in fact he has done in the case of human bodies), he can decouple this very power from them, and thus it is no less really distinct from them.

Nor do I marvel at the fact that at one time, before I had freed myself from the preconceived opinions of the senses, it surely was the case that I perceived rightly that 2 and 3 make 5, and that when equals are subtracted from equals the remainders are equal, and many similar examples, since nevertheless I did not believe that the soul of a man is distinct from his body. For it is easy for me to observe that it did not happen that while I was still just a young child I would make a false judgment regarding those propositions which everyone equally admits, for at that time they were not yet of any use to me; nor do children learn to count 2 and 3 before they are capable of judging whether they make 5, and so on. On the contrary, however, from my infancy I had conceived of mind and body as one single thing, for my observation that I was composed of mind and body was confused. And it occurs in nearly every instance of imperfect knowledge that many things are grasped simultaneously as if they were one thing, but which later on must be distinguished by means of a more careful scrutiny.[47]

---

47. Descartes ends the *Reply to the Sixth Set of Objections* by answering the letter from "Various Philosophers and Geometers."

VI

CORRESPONDENCE (1641–1644)

To Mersenne, Idea Defined and Discussed (July 1641)

If I am not mistaken, the person who had written you the Latin letter you showed III, 391 me[1] is not yet able to take sides in the judgments we should make about things. He expresses himself too well when he explains his own thoughts to make it credible that he has not understood those of others. Instead, I am convinced that, being prejudiced in his opinions, he has trouble favoring anything opposed to his judgments. Thus I foresee that this will not be the last dispute we shall have together. On the contrary, I imagine that this first letter is like a challenge he is presenting to me, to see how I shall receive it, and whether, after I have opened the field to all comers, I shall not pretend to measure my weapons against his, *392* and to test my strength against his. I assure you that I should take a special pleasure in having to deal with clever people like him, if, judging by what he has shown me, he did not also seem too deeply committed. But I very much fear that in his case all my work would be useless, and that, whatever pains I take to satisfy him, and to withdraw him from the unfortunate commitment I see him involved in, he will not plunge yet further forward in searching for ways to contradict me.

Is it credible that, as he says, he could not understand what I mean by the idea of God, by the idea of the soul, and by the ideas of nonsensible things, since I do not mean anything else by them than what he must necessarily have understood himself when he wrote you that he did not understand my meaning at all? For he does not say that he has conceived of nothing under the name of God, of the soul, and of nonsensible things. He says only that he does not know what is to be understood by their ideas. But if he conceived of something by these names, as it cannot be doubted that he did, he knew at the same time what was to be understood by their ideas, since what is to be understood is nothing else but the very same thing he has conceived of. For I do not simply call by the name of "idea" the images that are depicted in the imagination. On the contrary, I do not in the least call them by that name, insofar as they belong to the corporeal imagination. But in general, I call "idea" everything in our mind, when we conceive of some- *393* thing, by whatever fashion we conceive of it.

But I understand that he is not among those who believe it impossible to conceive of something when they cannot imagine it, as if there were in us only that one single way of thinking and of conceiving. He recognized well that I was not of that opinion; and he also showed sufficiently that he did not think it either, since he himself said that God cannot be conceived of by the imagination. But if

---

Selections on pp. 207–21 translated by Marjorie Grene and Roger Ariew.

1. The correspondent is unknown.

it is not through the imagination that he is conceived of, either we are conceiving of nothing when we speak of God (which would show an appalling blindness), or we conceive of him in some other way. But in whatever way we conceive of him, we have the idea of him, since we could not express anything by our words, when we understand what we are saying, without its being certain from that very fact that we have within ourselves the idea of the thing signified by our words.

Thus, if he wants to take the word "idea" in the way in which I said explicitly that I was taking it, without lingering over the equivocation of those who restrict it to the mere images of material things formed in the imagination, it will be easy to recognize that by the idea of God I understand nothing but what all men have the habit of understanding when they speak of him, and what he must necessarily have understood himself. Otherwise, how could he have said that God is infinite and incomprehensible, and that he cannot be represented by our imagination? And how could he affirm that those attributes, and an infinity of others that express his greatness for us, are suitable for him, if he did not have the idea of him? Thus we must continue to agree that we have the idea of God, and that we cannot fail to know what that idea is, or what is to be understood by it. For without that idea we would not know anything at all about God. And it would be no use to say, for example, that *God exists,* and that some attribute or perfection belongs to him. That would be to say nothing, since it would bring no meaning to our minds. And that would be the most impious and impertinent thing in the world.

In the case of the soul, the matter is even clearer. For, since it is, as I have demonstrated, nothing but a thing that thinks, it is impossible that we could ever think of anything if we did not have at the same time the idea of our soul, as of a thing capable of thinking of everything that we think. It is true that a thing of this nature could not be imagined, that is, could not be represented by a corporeal image. But we must not be surprised at this. For our imagination is capable only of representing to itself things that fall under the senses; and since our soul has neither color, nor odor, nor taste, nor anything of all that belongs to the body, it is not possible for the soul to imagine it or to form an image of it. But it is not for all that any less conceivable. On the contrary, since it is through the soul that we conceive of all things, it is also more conceivable on its own than all the other things together.

After that, I am obliged to tell you that your friend has in no way grasped my meaning, when, to mark the distinction that obtains between the ideas in the imagination and those in the mind, he says that the former are expressed by names and the later by propositions. For whether they are expressed by names or by propositions, that is not what makes them belong to the mind or to the imagination. Both can be expressed in both those ways. But it is the manner of conceiving of them that makes the difference between them, in such a way that all we conceive of without an image is an idea of pure mind, and all we conceive of with an image is an idea of the imagination. And as the limits of our imagination are very short and very narrow, while our mind has hardly any limits, there are few things, even corporeal things, we can imagine, although we are capable of conceiving of them. And even the whole science we might perhaps believe to be most subject to our imagination, because it considers only magnitudes, shapes, and motions, is in no way founded on the fantasms of the imagination, but only on the clear and distinct notions of our mind. Those who have studied these matters at all deeply know this well enough.

But by what inference could he draw, as he has done, from my writings to the effect that the idea of God must be expressed by the proposition "God exists," the conclusion that the principal argument I use to prove his existence is nothing but a case of begging the question? He must see very well indeed, to be able to   *396* see what I never had the intention of saying, and what would never have occurred to me before I had seen his letter. I drew the proof of the existence of God from the idea that I find in myself of a supremely perfect being, and that is the ordinary notion that we have of him. And it is true that the simple consideration of such a being leads so easily to the knowledge of his existence, that it is almost the same thing to conceive of God, and to conceive that he exists. But this does not prevent the idea we have of God, or of a supremely perfect being, from being very different from the proposition "God exists." And it does not prevent us from being able to use the first as means or antecedent for proving the second.

In the same way, it is certain that after we have come to know the nature of our mind, by the steps through which I came to that knowledge, and have come to know by this means that the mind is a spiritual substance, since I see that only those attributes that belong to spiritual substances are appropriate for it, it was not necessary to be a great philosopher to conclude, as I have done, that it is therefore not corporeal. But without doubt it needs a very open intelligence, and one built differently than that usual among men, to see that the one does not follow from the other, and to find some flaw in this reasoning. That is what I beg him to make me see, and what I expect to learn from him, when he takes the trouble to instruct me about it. As for me, I shall not withhold my small elucidations, if he needs them, and if he is willing to proceed with me in good faith.   *397*

To Gibieuf,[2] Ideas and Abstraction (January 19, 1642)

I have long known and predicted that my thoughts would not be to the taste of the   *III, 473* multitude, and that where the plurality of voices took place, those thoughts would be easily condemned. Nor did I desire the approbation of private individuals, since I would be sorry if they did anything for my sake that could be disagreeable in the eyes of their colleagues, and also because it is customary to obtain that approbation so easily for all the books that are no more heretical than mine, that   *474* I thought the reason people would think I did not have it would not be disadvantageous for me. But that has not prevented me from offering my *Meditations* to your faculty, in order to let the faculty examine them more carefully, and if those

---

2. Guillaume Gibieuf (c. 1591–1650) was an Oratorian priest, author of a treatise on free will, *De libertate Dei et hominis*.

of so celebrated a body found no good reasons to reprove me for them, that can assure me of the truths that they contain.

As to the principle by which it seems to me I know that the idea I have of something *is not made inadequate by me through an abstraction of the intellect,* I draw that only from my own thought or consciousness. For, being assured that I cannot have any knowledge of what is outside me, except through the intermediary of the ideas that I have had of it within myself, I take care not to relate my judgments immediately to things and to attribute to them nothing positive that I do not first perceive in the ideas of them. But I also believe that what I find in these ideas is necessarily in the things themselves. Thus, to know that my idea is in no way rendered incomplete, or *inadequate,* by some abstraction of my mind, I examine only whether I have in any way derived it, not from something outside me more complete, but from some other idea I have within me
475   more ample and more complete—and have done this by an *abstraction of the intellect,* that is, by turning my thought away from one part of what is comprised in that more ample idea, in order to apply it better to the other part and to make me that much more attentive. Thus, when I consider a shape without thinking of the substance or the extension of which it is the shape, I am making a mental abstraction. I can easily recognize this abstraction afterward by considering whether I have in any way derived the idea I have from the shape alone, apart from some other more ample idea I also had within me, to which it was joined in such a way that, although we can think of the one without paying any attention to the other, we are nevertheless unable to deny the one of the other when we think of both ideas together. For I see clearly that the idea of a shape is so joined to the idea of extension and that of substance, since it is impossible that I conceive of a shape while denying that it has an extension, or of an extension while denying that it is the extension of some substance. But the idea of a substance that is extended and has a shape is complete, since I can conceive of it all alone, and deny of it all the other things of which I have ideas. But it is, in my view, entirely clear that the idea I have of a substance that thinks is complete in this way, and that I have no other idea prior to it in my mind, and joined to it
476   in such a way that I cannot easily conceive of them both while denying one of the other. But if there were anything of that sort in me, I would necessarily have to know it. It will perhaps be said that the difficulty still remains, because, although I conceive of the soul and the body as two substances such that I can conceive one without the other, even when I deny one of the other, I am nevertheless not always sure that they are such as I conceive of them. But we must return to the rule mentioned above, namely, that we cannot have any knowledge of things, except through the ideas that we conceive of them, and that consequently we should make no judgments except in conformity with those ideas, and we ought even to think that everything that conflicts with those ideas is absolutely impossible and implies a contradiction. Thus, we have no reason to be assured that there is no mountain without a valley, except that we see that the ideas of them can never be complete when we consider the one without the
477   other, even though we could, by abstraction, have the idea of a mountain or of a place that slopes upward, without considering that we could also descend the

same slope downward. Thus we can say that it implies a contradiction to say there are atoms, or parts of matter that have extension and yet are indivisible, since we cannot have the idea of an extended thing without also having the idea of a half of it, or a third of it, nor consequently without conceiving of it as divisible into two or three. For, from this alone, that I consider the two halves of a part of matter, however small it may be, as two complete substances, *the ideas of which are not made inadequate by me through an abstraction of the intellect,* I conclude with certainty that they are really divisible. And if someone said to me that, although I cannot so conceive of them, I do not know, for all that, whether God has not joined them together by a bond so tight that they are entirely inseparable, and so I have no reason to deny it: I should reply that, by whatever bond he can have joined them, I am certain that he can also disjoin them, so that, speaking absolutely, I have reason to call them divisible, since he   *478* has given me the power to conceive of them as such. And I say the same of the soul and of the body, and generally of all the things of which we have diverse and complete ideas. That is, I say that it implies a contradiction that they are inseparable. But I do not for all that deny that there may be in the soul or in the body a number of properties of which I have no idea. I deny only that there are any that conflict with the ideas I have of them, and among others, with the idea I have of their distinction. For otherwise God would be a deceiver, and we would have no rule by which to assure ourselves of the truth.

The reason I believe the soul is always thinking is the same that makes me think the light is always shining, even though there are no eyes to see it; that heat is always hot, though no one is being warmed by it; that body, or extended substance, always has extension; and, in general, that what constitutes the nature of a thing is always in it, while it exists. Thus it would be easier for me to believe that the soul ceased to exist, when it is said that it stops thinking, than to conceive of it as existing without thought. And I see no difficulty here, unless it is considered unnecessary to believe that it is thinking when no memory of this is   *479* retained afterward. But if we take into account the fact that we have a thousand thoughts every night, and even when awake we have a thousand thoughts in an hour, of which no trace whatsoever remains in the memory, and which seem to us no more useful that those we may have had before birth, it will be much less difficult to be persuaded of my view than to judge that a substance whose nature is to think can exist and nevertheless not think at all.

I do not see any difficulty in understanding that the faculties of imagination and sensing belong to the soul, since these are species of thoughts, and nevertheless that they belong to the soul insofar as it is joined to the body, since these are the kinds of thoughts without which we can conceive of the soul in all its purity.

As to the case of animals, we do indeed observe in them movements like those that follow from our imaginations and sensations, but are not for all that imaginations or sensations. And on the contrary, since these same movements can also be made without imagination, we have arguments proving that they do take place in this way in animals, as I hope to show clearly by describing in detail all the architecture of their members and the causes of their movements.

480   But I fear that I have already bored you with the length of this letter. I shall
count myself very happy if you continue the honor of your good will and the
favor of your protection.

To Buitendijck,[3] Possibility of Doubting God's Existence (1643)

IV, 62   In the letters you did me the honor of writing to me, I find three questions which
clearly show the care and sincerity with which you seek learning, so that nothing
could make me happier than to reply to you.

The first question is whether it is ever permissible to doubt about God—that
63   is, whether it is naturally permissible to doubt God's existence. Here, in the matter of doubting, I think we should distinguish between what pertains to the intellect and what pertains to the will. For as to the intellect, since it is not a faculty
of choice, we should not ask whether anything is permissible for it, but only
whether it is possible. And it is certain that there are very many people whose
intellect can doubt God's existence. And in this number are all those who are
unable to give an evident proof of his existence, even though they are possessed
of the true faith. For faith belongs to the will, and, leaving that to one side, a person who has faith can inquire by means of natural reason whether there is a God,
and thus doubt God. As to the will, we must also distinguish between doubt as
an end and doubt as a means. For if someone takes as his aim to doubt about God
in order to persist in this doubt, he is sinning gravely, since he wishes to remain
in doubt on a topic of such importance. But if someone proposes to himself doubt
as a means to pursuing a clearer knowledge of truth, he is doing something altogether pious and worthy, since no one can wish the end without also wishing the
means. And in the Holy Scripture itself men are often urged to seek the knowledge of God through natural reason. Nor does he sin who, for the same purpose,
temporarily puts out of his mind all the knowledge he can have of God. For we
do not need indefinitely to be thinking that God exists. Otherwise it would neither be permissible to sleep, nor to do anything else, since every time we do
something else, we put aside for that time all the knowledge we can have of the
divinity.

The second question is, whether it is ever permissible to assume something
64   false in matters that concern God. Here we must distinguish between the true
God, clearly known, and false gods. For indeed once God is clearly known, it is
not only not permissible, it is even impossible for the human mind to attribute
anything false to him, as I have explained in my *Meditations,* pp. 152, 159, 262,
and elsewhere.[4] But it is true that something false can be hypothetically attributed to false gods, that is, either evil spirits or idols or other such gods invented
by the error of the human mind (for even in Holy Scripture they are called gods),
or even to the true God when he is known only in a confused way. But such attri-
bution can be good or evil insofar as the end for which the hypothesis is made is

---

3. Buitendijck seems to have been one of the curators of the College of Dordrecht.
4. AT VII, 138, 144, and 233.

good or evil. For what is thus imagined and attributed hypothetically is not thereby affirmed by the will as true, but only proposed for examination to the intellect. And so it does not include the basis for good or evil, or, if it does include it, it does so only in dependence on the end for which the hypothesis was made. Therefore, a person who invents a deceiving God (or even the true God, but not yet clearly enough known to himself or to others, for whose sake he is setting up his hypothesis) and who is not misusing this fiction for a bad purpose, in order to persuade others of something false concerning the divine power, but only in order better to illuminate his intellect, so that he may come to a better knowledge of God or show him more clearly to others, such a man, I say, is not really sinning, but acting so that good may come. For there is no malice in this; he is rather doing something absolutely good, and he cannot be reproached for this, except by slander.

The third question is about motion, which you believe I assign to animals in place of a soul. But I do not recall ever having written that motion constitutes the soul of animals. I have not announced my view on this subject. However, since, by the word *soul* we usually mean a substance, and since I hold that motion is a mode of bodies (and I do not admit various kinds of motions, but only local motion, which is common to all bodies, whether animate or inanimate), I do not wish to say that motion is the soul of animals, but rather with Holy Scripture (Deuteronomy chap. 12, verse 23) that blood is their soul. For blood is a fluid body in very rapid motion, the subtler part of which is called spirit, and which, flowing continually from the arteries through the brain into the nerves, moves the whole machine of the body.

65

To Elisabeth,[5] **Primitive Notions (May 21 and June 28, 1643)**

The favor with which Your Highness has honored me in sending her command-ments in writing is greater than I had ever dared to hope. It comforts my unwor-thiness better than what I would have hoped for with passion, which would have been to receive them by word of mouth, if I had been permitted to pay homage to you and to offer you my very humble services when I was last at the Hague. For I would have had too many marvels to admire at the same time; and seeing superhuman discourse issue from a body such as painters give to angels, I would have been overwhelmed in the same way as those must be, I should think, who, coming from earth, are just entering into heaven. That would have made me less able to reply to Your Highness, who doubtless already noticed this weakness in me, when I had the honor of speaking to her earlier. And your kindness wished to comfort me by leaving me the traces of your thoughts on paper, where, reread-ing them several times, and becoming accustomed to considering them, I am really less overcome, but even more full of admiration, observing that they not

III, 663

664

---

5. Princess Elisabeth of Bohemia (1618–1680) became one of Descartes's principal cor-respondents in the 1640s. Descartes dedicated both the *Principles* and *Passions of the Soul* to her.

only appear ingenious at first sight, but so much the more judicious and solid, the more they are examined.

And I can say with truth that the question Your Highness proposes seems to me to be the question that can most justifiably be asked of me in view of the writings I have published. For there are two things in the human soul on which depends all the knowledge we can have of its nature: one of them, that it thinks, the other that, being united to a body, it can act and suffer with the body. I have 665   said hardly anything about the latter, and have taken pains only to make the former well understood. That was because my chief aim was to prove the distinction that exists between the soul and the body. For this purpose the former alone was of use, and the other would have been harmful. But since Your Highness sees so clearly that it is impossible to hide anything from her, I shall here try to explain the way in which I conceive of the union of the soul with the body, and how it has the force to move the body.

First, I consider that there are in us certain primitive notions, which are, as it were, originals under whose aegis we form all the rest of our knowledge. And there are only a very few such notions. For after the most general—of being, of number, of duration, etc., which belong to everything we can conceive of—we have, for the body in particular, only the notion of extension, from which those of shape and motion follow. And for the mind alone, we have only the notion of thought, in which are included the perceptions of the intellect and the inclinations of the will. Finally, for the soul and the body together, we have only that of their union, on which depends the notion of the force that the soul has to move the body and the body to act on the soul, causing its sensations and its passions.

I also consider that all of human science consists only in distinguishing these notions well, and in attributing each of them only to the things to which they 666   belong. For when we wish to explain some difficulty by means of a notion that does not belong to it, we cannot fail to go wrong. In the same way, too, we go wrong when we try to explain one of these notions by another. For, since they are primitive, each of them cannot be understood except through itself. And, as the use of our senses has made the notions of extension, of shapes, and of motions more familiar to us than the others, the chief cause of our errors consists in the fact that we ordinarily want to use these notions to explain things to which they do not belong—as when we want to use the imagination to conceive of the nature of the soul, or when we want to conceive of the way in which the soul moves the body through the way in which one body is moved by another body.

In the *Meditations,* which Your Highness condescended to read, I tried to give a conception of the notions that belong to the soul alone, distinguishing them from those that belong to the body alone. That is why the next thing I have to explain is how to conceive of those things that belong to the union of the soul with the body, leaving aside those that belong to body alone or to mind alone. It seems to me that what I have written at the end of my *Reply to the Sixth Set of Objections* can serve this purpose. For we cannot look for these simple notions anywhere except in our soul, which by its nature contains them all in itself, but which does 667   not always sufficiently distinguish them from one another, or does not attribute them to the objects to which they should be attributed.

Thus, I believe that up to now we have often confused the notion of the force with which the soul acts on the body with the force by which one body acts on another. And we have attributed both of them, not to the soul, since we do not yet know it, but to the different qualities of bodies, such as weight, and heat, and others that we imagined were real, that is, having an existence distinct from that of the body, and consequently being substances, even though we called them qualities. And to conceive of them we sometimes used notions that are in us in order to know the body, and sometimes those that are there in order to know the soul, according to whether what we attributed to them was material or immaterial. For example, in supposing that weight is a real quality, of which we have no other knowledge except that it has the power to move the body in which it is contained toward the center of the earth, we have no trouble conceiving of how it moves this body, or how it is joined to it. And we do not consider at all that this is done through the real contact of one surface by another. For we experience in ourselves that we have a particular notion for conceiving of that. And I believe that we misuse that notion when we apply it to weight—which is nothing really distinguished from body, as I hope to show in my physics[6]—but is given to us for conceiving of the way in which the soul moves the body.   *668*

I would be showing that I do not know well enough the incomparable mind of Your Highness if I used more words to explain myself, and would be too presumptuous if I dared to think that my reply must satisfy her entirely. But I shall try to avoid the one and the other, adding no more here, except that, if I am capable of writing or saying something that can please her, I shall always count it a great honor to take up my pen, or to go to the Hague in this connection, and that there is nothing in the world that is dearer to me than to try to obey her commandments. But I cannot here conform to the observation of the Hippocratic oath she enjoined on me, since she has not communicated to me anything that does not deserve to be seen and admired by all. On this subject I can only say that, prizing infinitely the letter I have received from you, I shall treat it as misers do their treasures. The more they prize them, the more they hide them, and begrudging the sight of them to the rest of the world, they place their greatest happiness in looking at them. So I will be glad to enjoy in solitude the benefit of looking at your letter.

* * *

[. . .] But I judged that it was these meditations, rather than thoughts demand-   *III, 693* ing less attention, that caused Your Highness to find obscurity in the notion we have of the union of soul and body, since it does not seem that the human mind is capable of conceiving very distinctly of both the distinction between the soul and body and their union at the same time. For that, one would need to conceive of them as a single thing and also to conceive of them as two—which is self-contradictory. I assumed that Your Highness still had very much present in her mind the arguments proving the distinction between the soul and the body; and I did

---

6. See *Principles* IV, art. 20–7.

694   not want to ask her to put them aside in order to represent to herself the notion
of the union everybody always experiences in himself without philosophizing—
namely, that he is a single person who has both a body and thought of such a
nature that the thought can move the body and can sense the accidents that happen to it. Accordingly, in my previous letter I made use of the comparison of
weight and other qualities we commonly imagine to be united to some bodies, as
thought is united to ours. And I did not worry over the fact that this comparison
is lame, given that these qualities are not real, as we imagine them to be. This
was because I believed that Your Highness was already entirely persuaded that
the soul is a substance distinct from the body.

But, since Your Highness remarks that it is easier to attribute matter and extension to the soul than to attribute to it the capacity for moving a body and being
moved by it without having any matter, I ask her to attribute freely this matter
and this extension to the soul; for that is nothing else than to conceive of the soul
as united to the body. And after having formed a proper conception of this, and
having experienced it in herself, it will be easy for her to consider that the matter she has attributed to this thought is not thought itself, and that the extension
of this matter is of a different nature from the extension of this thought, in that
the former has a determinate place, such that it excludes all other bodily exten-
695   sion, and this is not the case with the latter. And thus, Your Highness will easily
be able to return to the knowledge of the distinction between soul and body, in
spite of having conceived of their union.

Finally, I think that it is very necessary to have properly understood the principles of metaphysics once in a lifetime, because they are what gives us the
knowledge of God and of our soul. I also think that it would be very harmful to
occupy one's understanding frequently in meditating on them, because this
would impede it from performing the functions of the imagination and the
senses. The best thing for a person is to be content in keeping in memory and in
belief the conclusions he has once derived, and then to use the rest of his time for
the study of thoughts in which the understanding acts in concert with the imagination and the senses. [. . .]

To Mesland,[7] **On Freedom (May 2, 1644)**

IV, 111   I know that it is very difficult to enter into the thoughts of another, and experience has taught me how difficult my thoughts seem to others. This means that I
have been much obliged by the trouble you have taken to examine them. I can
only have a very high opinion of you when I see that you possess these thoughts
in such a way that they are now more yours than mine. Moreover, the difficulties
it has pleased you to propose to me are rather in the subject matter and in the
deficiency of my expression than in any deficiency of your intelligence. For you

---

7. Denis Mesland (1616–1672) was a Jesuit professor at La Flèche. He was sent out as a
missionary to the New World in 1645 and remained there until his death.

have provided the solution to the chief difficulties. But I will not refrain from stating here my views on all of them.

I admit that with respect to physical or moral causes, which are particular and limited, we often find that those that produce some effect cannot produce others that seem smaller. Thus a man, who can produce another man, cannot produce an ant. And a king, who can make a whole people obey him, sometimes cannot obtain obedience from a horse. But when it is a question of a universal and indeterminate cause, it seems to me that it is a very evident common notion that *what can do more, can do less* and that *the whole is greater than its part.* Correctly understood, this notion extends as well to all the particular causes, both moral and physical. For it would be more for a man to be able to produce both men and *112* ants than only to be able to produce men, and it would be a greater power for a king to command even horses than only to command his people. Thus it is claimed that the music of Orpheus can move even beasts, in order to attribute to him even more power.

It matters little whether my second demonstration, founded on our own existence, is considered different from the first, or only as an explanation of the first. But just as it is an effect of God to have created me, so it is also an effect of God to have placed in me the idea of him. And there is no effect coming from him through which we cannot demonstrate his existence. However, it seems to me that all those demonstrations based on effects come down to one, and also that they are not complete if those effects are not evident to us. (That is why I preferred to consider my own existence rather than that of the heavens and the earth, of which I am not so certain.) Nor are they complete if we do not join to them the idea we have of God. For my soul being finite, I cannot know that the order of causes is not infinite except insofar as I have within me that idea of the first cause. And even though a first cause is admitted, I cannot say that it is God, unless I truly have the idea of God. I have suggested this in my *Reply to the First Set of Objections,*[8] but in a few words, in order not to show contempt for the arguments of others, who commonly admit that *there is no progression to infinity.* As for me, I do not admit it. On the contrary, I believe that *there is such a progression in the division of the parts of matter,* as will be apparent in my treatise *113* on philosophy, which is just being published.[9]

I do not in the least know that I have determined that God always does what he knows to be the most perfect, and it does not seem to me that a finite mind can judge that. But I have tried to shed light on the proposed difficulty concerning the cause of errors, on the assumption that God made the world entirely perfect—since, assuming the contrary, that difficulty disappears entirely.

I am much obliged to you for informing me of the passages in St. Augustine that can help in authorizing my opinions. Some other friends of mine have already done something similar.[10] And I take great satisfaction in the fact that my thoughts agree with those of so sainted and excellent a person. But I am not at

8. AT VII, 106.

9. A reference to the *Principles;* see *Principles* II, art. 20.

10. See the letter *To Colvius* of November 14, 1640.

all of the habit of thought of those who desire that their opinions appear new. On the contrary, I accommodate mine to those of others insofar as truth allows me to do so.

I make no more distinction between the soul and its ideas than between a piece of wax and the various shapes it can receive. And since it is not strictly an action, but a passion in the wax that it receives different shapes, it seems to me that it is also a passion in the soul to receive such and such an idea, and that it is only the soul's volitions that are actions. And it seems to me that ideas are placed in the soul, partly by the objects that touch the senses, partly by the impression in the brain, partly also by dispositions that have preceded in the soul itself, and by the motions of its will. In the same way the wax receives its shapes partly from other bodies that exert pressure on it, partly from shapes or other qualities that are already in it, such as the fact that it is more or less heavy or soft, etc., and partly also from its motion when, after it has been agitated, it has itself the power to continue to move itself.

As for the difficulty we have in learning the sciences, and in representing clearly to ourselves the ideas that are naturally known to us, it comes from the false prejudices of our childhood and from other causes of our errors, which I have tried to explain at sufficient length in the writing that I have in press.[11]

As to memory, I believe that the memory of material things depends on the traces that remain in the brain after some image has been imprinted there; and the memory of intellectual things depends on certain other traces that remain in thought itself. But the latter are of a different kind from the former, and I could not explain them by any example taken from corporeal things, which would require a very different example. On the other hand, the traces in the brain make it fit to move the soul in the same way it had moved it before, and thus to make it remember something, just as the folds that are made in a piece of paper or in a cloth make it more fit to be folded again as it had been previously than if it had never been folded.

The moral error that takes place when we believe something false with good reason—for example, because an upright man has said it to us—contains no privation, when we affirm it only to regulate the actions of our life, in a matter of which we cannot morally know better. And thus it is not strictly an error. But it would be one if we affirmed it as a truth of physics, since the testimony of an upright man does not suffice for that.

As to free will, I have not seen what the Reverend Father Petau[12] has written about it. But as you explain your opinion on this subject, it does not seem that mine is very far distant from it. For first I ask you to observe that I have not said that man is indifferent except where he lacks knowledge. But I have indeed said that he is the more indifferent, the fewer arguments he knows that can push him to choose one side rather than the other—something, it seems to me, that can be denied by no one. And I agree with you when you say that our judgment can be suspended; but I have tried to explain the means by which it can be suspended.

---

11. Another reference to the *Principles;* see *Principles* I, art. 71–4.
12. Denis Petau (1583–1652), a French Jesuit who had written a treatise on free will.

For it seems to me certain that *from a great light in the intellect there follows a* 116 *great inclination in the will,* so that, when we see very clearly that a thing is right for us, it is very difficult, and even, I believe, impossible to stop the course of our desire while we stay with the same thought. But since the nature of the soul is to be hardly attentive for a moment to a single thing, as soon as our attention is diverted from the arguments that led us to know that this choice was right for us, and we retain in our memory only the fact that it seemed to us desirable, we can represent to our mind some other argument that can make us doubtful of it, and thus make us suspend our judgment, and even form a contrary judgment. Thus, since you do not place freedom precisely in indifference, but in a real and positive power of self-determination, there is no difference between our opinions except in name. For I do claim that this power is in the will. But, since I do not see that it is of another kind when it is accompanied by indifference, which you say is an imperfection, than when it is not so accompanied, and since there is nothing in the intellect but light, like that in the intellect of the blessed who are confirmed in grace, in general I call free whatever is voluntary, while you want to restrict that name to the power of self-determination, which is accompanied by indifference. But in what concerns words, I want nothing so much as to follow usage and example.

As for animals without reason, it is evident that they are not free, since they 117 do not have that positive power of self-determination. But freedom in them is a pure negation, that of not being forced or constrained.

Nothing has prevented me from speaking of the freedom that we have to follow good or evil, except that I wished to avoid theological controversies as far as I could, and to hold myself within the bounds of natural philosophy. But I admit to you that wherever there is occasion to sin, there is indifference. And I do not believe that to do ill it is necessary to see clearly that what we are doing is bad. It is enough to see it confusedly, or only to remember that we formerly judged that it was so, without in any way seeing it, that is, without paying attention to the arguments that prove it. For, if we are seeing it clearly, it would be impossible to sin during the time in which we were seeing it in that way. That is why it is said that *every sin is ignorant.* And we do not stop deserving, even though, seeing very clearly what must be done, we do it infallibly, and without any indifference, as Jesus Christ did in this life. For, since man cannot always pay perfect attention to the things that he ought to do, it is a good action to do so, and by this means to bring it about that our will follows so strongly the light of our intellect that it cannot be in the least indifferent. As for the rest, I did not say that grace wholly prevented indifference, but only that it makes us lean more to one side than to the other, and thus that it lessens indifference, but does not 118 lessen freedom. From this, it seems to me, it follows that freedom does not consist in indifference.

As to the difficulty of conceiving how it was both free and indifferent for God to bring it about that it was not true that the three sides of a triangle were equal to two right angles, or in general that contradictories cannot both be true, it is easy to remove this difficulty by considering that the power of God can have no limits. Then we can also consider that our mind is finite and created with such a

nature that it can conceive as possible the things that God willed to be truly possible, but not created in such a way that it can also conceive as possible things that he could have willed possible, but which nevertheless he willed to make impossible. For the first consideration makes us recognize that God cannot have been determined to make it true that contradictories cannot both be true, and that, consequently, he could have done the contrary. But the other assures us that, although this is true, we should not try to comprehend it, since our nature is not capable of such comprehension. And further, if God willed to make some truths necessary, that is not to say that he willed this of necessity. For it is one thing to
119 will that they be necessary, and another to will this of necessity, or to be necessitated to will it. I readily admit that there are contradictions so evident that we cannot represent them to our minds without our judging them to be entirely impossible, like the one that you propose: *that God could have brought it about that creatures would not be dependent upon him.* But to recognize the immensity of his power, we should never in any way represent to ourselves or conceive of any preference or priority between his intellect and his will. For the idea we have of God teaches us that there is in him only one action, wholly simple and wholly pure. The words of St. Augustine express this very well: *"Because you see them, they are,* etc.,"[13] since in God *seeing* and *willing* are simply one thing.

I distinguish lines from surfaces and points from lines, as one mode distinguished from another mode. But I distinguish bodies from surfaces, from lines, and from points that modify them, as between a substance and its modes. And there is no doubt that some mode appearing in the bread remains in the holy sacrament, seeing that its external shape, which is a mode, remains there. As for the extension of Jesus Christ in the holy sacrament, I have not at all explained it, since I was not obliged to, and I abstain as far as is possible for me from questions of theology—especially since the Council of Trent has said that he is present *"with that form of existence which we can scarcely express in words."* These words I have purposely inserted at the close of my *Reply to the Fourth Set of*
120 *Objections,* to excuse me from giving an explanation. But I dare to say that, if men were more accustomed than they are to my way of philosophizing, it would be possible to make them understand a way of explaining that mystery which would shut the mouth of the enemies of our religion, and which they could not contradict.[14]

There is a great difference between *abstraction* and *exclusion.* If I simply said that the idea I have of my soul does not represent it to me as dependent on the body, and identified with it, that would be only an abstraction of which I could form only a negative argument, and that would lead to a poor conclusion. But I say that this idea represents it to me as a substance that can exist even though everything that pertains to the body is excluded from it. From this I form a positive argument, and conclude that it can exist without the body. And that exclu-

---

13. Augustine, *Confessions,* book XIII, chap. 31.
14. For this explanation, see the *Letter to Mesland* of February 9, 1645, AT IV, 162–72.

sion of extension is seen very clearly in the nature of the soul from the fact that we cannot conceive of half a thing that thinks, as you have very aptly observed.

I would not ask you to take the trouble of sending me what it has pleased you to write about my *Meditations,* since I hope to go to France soon, where I shall, if I can, have the honor of seeing you.

VII

PRINCIPLES OF PHILOSOPHY (1644–1647)

Author's Letter to the Translator of the Book, Which May Serve Here as Preface

IXb, 1   Sir,[1]

The version of my *Principles* you have taken the trouble to make so polished and well finished causes me to hope that the work may be read by more persons in French than in Latin, and that it will be better understood. My only apprehension is that the title may repel some people who have not been nourished upon letters, or else who have a bad opinion of philosophy because what they have been taught has not satisfied them; and this makes me think that it would be a good thing to add a preface to expound the subject matter of the book, the design I had in writing it, and the use to be derived from it. But although it would be appropriate for me to write this preface because I ought to know these things bet-

2   ter than anyone else, I can promise nothing on my own account but a summary of the principal points which seem to me should be treated in it; and I leave it to your discretion to communicate to the public whatever you deem desirable.

I should have desired first of all to explain in it what philosophy is, beginning with the most ordinary matters, such as that this word philosophy signifies the study of wisdom, and that by wisdom we understand not only prudence in affairs, but also a perfect knowledge of all things that man can know, both for the conduct of his life and for the conservation of his health and the invention of all the arts. In order for this knowledge to serve these ends, it is essential that it should be derived from first causes; thus, to study to acquire it (what is properly termed philosophizing), we must begin with the investigation of these first causes, that is, the Principles. It is also necessary that these Principles should have two conditions attached to them. First of all, they should be so clear and evident that the mind of man cannot doubt their truth when it attentively applies itself to consider them. Second, it is on them that the knowledge of other things depends, so that the Principles can be known without these last, but the other things cannot reciprocally be known without the Principles. We must accordingly try to deduce from

---

Selections on pp. 222–72 translated by Elizabeth S. Haldane and G. R. T. Ross and substantially revised by Marjorie Grene and Roger Ariew.

1. The translator to whom the letter is addressed is the Abbé Claude Picot (c. 1601–1668). Again, the letter was added to the 1647 French edition of the *Principles*. Descartes lived with Picot during various trips to Paris and even traveled with him on a visit to La Flèche. As a result, he had access to Picot's translation from 1644 to 1647 and took the opportunity to suggest both minor changes and major revisions. This translation is primarily from the Latin edition; significant additions from the French edition are indicated within angle brackets.

these Principles the knowledge of the things that depend on them, so that there will be nothing in the whole series of the deductions made from them that is not perfectly manifest. It is really only God alone who has perfect wisdom, that is to say, who has a complete knowledge of the truth of all things; but it may be said   *3* that men have more or less wisdom according as they have more or less knowledge of the most important truths. And I think that there is nothing in this regarding which all the learned do not concur.

I should in the next place have caused the utility of this philosophy to be considered and shown that, since it extends over everything the human mind can know, we are entitled to hold that it alone distinguishes us from savages and barbarians, and that the civilization and refinement of each nation is proportionate to the superiority of its philosophy. In this way a state can have no greater good than the possession of true philosophy. And, in addition, it would have been pointed out that, for every person in particular, it is not only useful to live with those who apply themselves to this study, but that it is incomparably better to set about it oneself—just as it is doubtless much better to avail oneself of one's own eyes for the direction of one's steps, and by the same means to enjoy the beauty of color and light, than to close one's eyes and trust to the guidance of another. But this last is still better than to hold them closed and not have any but oneself to act as guide. Strictly speaking, living without philosophy is precisely to have one's eyes closed without ever trying to open them; and the pleasure of seeing all the things that sight reveals is in no way comparable to the satisfaction given by the knowledge of those things opened up to us by philosophy. And finally, this study is more necessary for the regulation of our manners and for our conduct in life than is the use of our eyes in the guidance of our steps. The brute beasts, who   *4* only have their bodies to preserve, devote their constant attention to the search for the sources of their nourishment; but men, whose principal part is the mind, ought to make their principal care the search after wisdom, which is its true source of nutriment. And I am likewise able to assure myself that there are many who would not fail to make the search if they had any hope of success in so doing, and knew to what an extent they were capable of it. There does not exist a soul so ignoble, so firmly attached to the objects of the senses, that it does not sometimes turn away from these to aspire after some other greater good, even though it is frequently ignorant as to what that good consists in. Those most favored by fortune, who have abundance of health, honor, and riches, are no more exempt from this desire than others; on the contrary, I am persuaded that it is those very people who yearn most ardently after another good more perfect and supreme than all those they possess already. And this sovereign good, considered by natural reason without the light of faith, is none other than the knowledge of the truth through its first causes, that is, the wisdom whose study is philosophy. And because all these things are absolutely true, it would not be difficult to persuade people of them, if they were well argued and expressed.

But since we are prevented from believing these doctrines by experience—which shows us that those who profess to be philosophers are frequently less wise and reasonable than others who have never applied themselves to the study—I should have explained succinctly here in what all the knowledge we   *5* now possess consists, and to what degrees of wisdom we have attained. The first of these contains only notions which of themselves are so clear that they may be acquired without any meditation. The second includes all of what the experience of the senses shows us. The third, what the conversation of other men teaches us. And for the fourth we may add to this the reading, not of all books, but especially of those written by persons who are capable of giving us good instruction, for this is a species of conversation held with their authors. And it seems to me that all the wisdom we usually possess is acquired by these four means only; for I do not place divine revelation in the same rank, because it does not lead us by degrees, but raises us at a stroke to an infallible belief. From all time there have been great men who have tried to find a fifth road by which to arrive at wisdom, one incomparably more elevated and assured than these other four. That road is to seek out the first causes and the true principles from which reasons may be deduced for all that we are capable of knowing; and those who have made this their special work have been called philosophers. At the same time I do not know that up to the present day there have been any in whose case this plan has succeeded. The first and principal ones whose writings we possess are Plato and Aristotle, between whom the only difference is that the former, following the steps of his master Socrates, ingenuously confessed that he had never yet been able to discover anything for certain, and was content to set down the things that seemed to him to be probable, adopting certain principles whereby he tried to account for other things for this end. Aristotle, on the other hand, had less candor; and although he had been Plato's disciple for twenty years, and possessed no other principles than his master's, he entirely changed the method of stating them, and proposed them as true and certain, although there was no appearance of his having ever held them to be such. But these two men had great minds and acquired much wisdom by the four methods mentioned before, and this gave them great authority, so that those who succeeded them were more bent on following their opinions than in forming better ones of their own. The main dispute between their disciples was as to whether everything should be doubted, or whether there were some things that were certain. And this carried them, both on the one side and on the other, into extravagant errors; for certain of those who argued for doubt, extended it even to the actions of life, so that they omitted to exercise ordinary prudence in its conduct; and those who supported the doctrine of certainty, supposing it to depend on the senses, trusted to them entirely. This was carried to such a point that it is said that Epicurus ventured to affirm, contrary to all the reasonings of the astronomers, that the sun is no larger than it appears. A fault that may be observed in most disputes is that since the truth is a mean between the two opinions that are maintained, each disputant removes himself so much the farther from it, the greater his desire to contradict. But the error of those who tended too much to the side of doubt was not followed for long, and that of the others has been in some degree corrected by the recognition of the fact that in many instances the senses deceive us. At the same time I do not know that this error has been entirely removed by showing that certainty is not in the senses, but only in the understanding, when it has evident perceptions; and that while we only possess the knowledge acquired by the first four degrees of wisdom, we should not doubt those things that appear to be true in what concerns the conduct of life, while yet we should not hold them to be so certain that we may not change our minds regarding them when obliged to do so by some evident reason. Because of not having known this truth—or else, if there are those who have known it, because of neglecting it—the greater part of those in recent centuries who aspired to be philosophers have blindly followed Aristotle. Thus they have frequently corrupted the sense of his writings, attributing various opinions to him that he would not recognize as his, if he were to return to this world. Those who have not followed him (among whom many of the best minds are to be found) have yet been imbued with his teaching in their youth, for it forms the sole teaching in the Schools; and these minds were so much occupied with this, that they were incapable of attaining to a knowledge of true Principles. And although I respect them all and would never wish to make myself disliked by denouncing them, I can give a proof of my assertion, which I do not think any one of them will deny, which is that they have all taken for granted some particular principle they have not perfectly understood. For example, I have known none of them who did not presuppose weight in terrestrial bodies, but although experiment proves to us very clearly that the bodies we call heavy descend towards the center of the earth, we do not for all that know the nature of what is called gravity, that is, the cause or principle that makes bodies descend in this way, and we must derive it from elsewhere. The same may be said of the void and atoms, of heat and cold, of dryness and humidity, of salt, sulfur, mercury, and all other similar things which some have adopted as their principles. And none of the conclusions deduced from a nonevident principle can be evident, even though they are deduced from them in an evident and valid manner. From this it follows that none of the reasonings they based on such principles could give them any certain knowledge of anything, nor in consequence bring them one step further in the search after wisdom. And if they have discovered any truth this has only come to pass by means of some of the four methods above mentioned. All the same, I do not desire in any way to detract from the honor to which each of them may aspire; I am only obliged to say for the consolation of those who have never studied that, just as in traveling, when we turn our backs on the place we desire to go to, the longer and more quickly we walk, the further we recede from our destination, so that though we are afterwards put back on the right road, we cannot arrive at our destination as soon as if we had not walked before in the wrong direction; so when our principles are bad, the more we cultivate them and the more carefully we apply ourselves to derive various consequences from them, thinking that we are philosophizing very well, the further we are moving from the knowledge of the truth and from wisdom. From this we must conclude that those who up to now have learned least about what has been called philosophy are the most capable of apprehending the truth.

After having made these matters very clear, I should have desired to set forth the reasons that serve to prove that the true principles by which we may arrive at that highest point of wisdom in which the sovereign good of the life of man consists are those I have put forward in this book. And only two are sufficient for this: the first that the principles must be very clear, and the second that we may deduce all other things from them; for only these two conditions are required for true principles. And I can easily prove that they are very clear, first of all by the manner in which I have found them, that is, by rejecting all those propositions in respect to which I could find the slightest occasion for doubt; for it is certain that those which could not be rejected in this way when application was made to their consideration are the most evident and clear of all that the human mind can know. Thus, in considering that he who would doubt all things cannot yet doubt

10   that he exists while he doubts, and that what reasons thus, in being unable to doubt of itself and yet doubting all else, is not what we call our body, but what we call our soul or thought, I have taken the being or existence of this thought as the first principle from which I have very clearly deduced the following: namely, that there is a God who is the author of all that is in the world, or who, being the source of all truth, has not created in us an understanding liable to be deceived in the judgments it forms on matters of which it has a very clear and distinct perception. These comprise all the principles I make use of respecting immaterial or metaphysical things, from which I very clearly deduce those of corporeal or physical things, that is, that there are bodies extended in length, breadth, and depth, which have various shapes and move in various ways. These, in sum, are all the principles from which I deduce the truth of other things. The other reason that proves the clarity of these principles is that they have been known from all time and even received as true and indubitable by all men, with the sole exception of the existence of God, which has been placed in doubt by some people because they have ascribed too much to the perceptions of the senses, and because God can neither be seen nor touched. But although all the truths I place in my Principles have been known from all time and by everyone, nevertheless there has never yet been anyone, as far as I know, who has recognized them as the principles of philosophy, that is to say, as principles from which may be

11   derived a knowledge of all things that are in the world; that is why it here remains to me to prove that they are such. And it appears to me that I cannot do better than cause this to be established by experience, that is to say, by inviting my readers to read this book. For although I have not treated of everything, and although this is impossible, I consider that I have so explained all those matters with which I have had occasion to deal, that those who read them with attention will have reason to persuade themselves that there is no need to seek other principles than those I have brought forward in order to arrive at all the most exalted knowledge of which the human mind is capable. And this will more especially be the case if, after having read my works, they take the trouble to consider how many diverse questions are explained there, and if, perusing also the works of others, they observe how few are the probable reasons that can be given to explain the same questions by principles differing from mine. And in order that they may undertake this with greater ease, I should have been able to say to them that those who are imbued with my opinions have much less trouble in understanding the works of others and in recognizing their true value than those who are not so imbued; and this is diametrically opposite to what I have just said of those who have begun with the ancient philosophy, that is, that the more they have studied it the less they are capable of properly understanding the truth.

I should also have here added a word of advice as regards the method of reading this book, which is that I should desire it first to be run through in its entirety like a novel, without forcing one's attention unduly upon it or stopping at diffi-   *12* culties that may be met with, so that a general knowledge may be arrived at of the matters of which I have treated; and after that, if it is found that the reader wants them to be examined more carefully and has the curiosity to inquire about their causes, it may be read a second time in order to notice the sequence of my reasoning. But the reader must not immediately cast it aside, if he cannot follow the argument adequately throughout or understand the whole of its bearing. It is only necessary to mark with a pen the places where a difficulty is found, and to continue to read without interruption to the end. Then if the book is taken up for a third time, I venture to say that the reader will discover the solution of the greater part of the difficulties which have formerly been marked, and that if certain ones still remain, their solution will be discovered on a further rereading.

I have noticed on examining the nature of many different minds that there are almost none of them so dull or slow of understanding that they are incapable of sound opinions, and even of attaining all the highest sciences, if they were trained in the right way. And this may also be proved by reason. For, since the principles are clear and nothing must be deduced from them except by very evident reasoning, we all have sufficient intelligence to understand the conclusions that depend on them. But in addition to the drawbacks of prejudice from which no one is entirely exempt (although it is those who have studied bad science the most who are most harmed), it almost always happens that those of moderate   *13* intelligence neglect to study because they do not consider themselves capable of doing so, and that the others who are more eager hasten on too quickly. And from this it comes that they often accept principles that are not really evident, and from them derive consequences that are uncertain. That is why I want to assure those who too greatly disparage their powers that there is nothing in my writings they are not capable of understanding completely if they take the trouble to examine them; while I also warn the others that even the most superior minds will require much time and attention to understand all the matters I intended to include in them.

Following on this, and in order to make very clear the end I have had in view in publishing them, I would like to explain here what seems to me to be the order that should be followed in our self-instruction. To begin with, a man who as yet has merely the common and imperfect knowledge that may be acquired by the four methods before mentioned, should above all try to form for himself a code of morals sufficient to regulate the actions of his life, because this does not permit any delay, and we ought above all other things to endeavor to live well. After that he should likewise study logic—not the logic of the Schools, because properly speaking it is only a dialectic that teaches how to make the things we know understood by others, or even to repeat, without forming any judgment on them, many words respecting those we do not know, thus corrupting rather than increasing good sense—but the logic that teaches us how best to direct our rea-   *14* son in order to discover those truths of which we are ignorant. And since this is very dependent on custom, it is good for him to practice the rules for a long time on easy and simple questions such as those of mathematics. Then, when he has acquired a certain skill in discovering the truth in these questions, he should begin seriously to apply himself to the true philosophy, the first part of which is metaphysics, containing the principles of knowledge, among which is the explanation of the principal attributes of God, the immateriality of our souls, and all the clear and simple notions that are in us. The second is physics, in which, after having found the true principles of material things, we examine generally how the whole universe is composed, and then in particular what is the nature of this earth and of all the bodies most commonly found around it, like air, water, and fire, magnetic ore, and other minerals. It is then necessary to inquire individually into the nature of plants, animals, and above all of man, so that we may afterwards be able to discover the other sciences useful to man. Thus philosophy as a whole is like a tree whose roots are metaphysics, whose trunk is physics, and whose branches, which issue from this trunk, are all the other sciences. These reduce themselves to three principal ones, namely, medicine, mechanics, and morals—by morals I mean the highest and most perfect moral science which, presupposing a complete knowledge of the other sciences, is the ultimate degree of wisdom.

15   But just as it is not from the roots or the trunk of trees that one gathers the fruit, but only from the extremities of their branches, so the main use of philosophy is dependent on those of its parts that we cannot learn until the end. Although, however, I am ignorant of almost all of these, the zeal I have always shown in trying to render service to the public caused me to print ten or twelve years ago certain essays on things I appeared to have learned. The first part of these essays was a *Discourse on the Method of Rightly Conducting One's Reason and Seeking Truth in the Sciences,* in which I summarized the principal rules of logic and of an imperfect system of morals which may be followed provisionally while we still know none better. The other parts were three treatises: the first *Dioptrics;* the second *Meteors,* and the last *Geometry.* In the *Dioptrics* I intended to show that we could make sufficient progress in philosophy to attain by its means a knowledge of those arts useful to life, because the invention of the telescope, which I there explained, is one of the most difficult ever attempted. In the treatise on *Meteors* I endeavored to make clear the difference between the philosophy I cultivate and that taught in the Schools, where the same subject is usually treated. Finally in the *Geometry* I professed to show that I had found certain matters of which men were previously ignorant, and thus to afford occasion for believing

16   that many more may yet be discovered, in order by this means to incite all men to the search after truth. From this time onwards, foreseeing the difficulty which would be felt by many in understanding the foundations of metaphysics, I tried to explain the principal points in a book of *Meditations* which is not very large, but whose volume has been increased, and whose matter has been much illuminated, by the objections many very learned persons have sent me in regard to them, and by the replies I have made to them. Then, finally, when it appeared to me that these preceding treatises had sufficiently prepared the mind of readers to accept the *Principles of Philosophy,* I likewise published them, and I divided the book containing them into four parts, the first of which contains the principles of knowledge, which is what may be called First Philosophy or Metaphysics. That is why it is better to read beforehand the Meditations which I have written on the same subject, in order that it may be properly understood. The other three parts contain what is most general in physics, that is, an explanation of the first laws or principles of nature, the manner in which the heavens, fixed stars, planets, comets, and generally all the universe are composed. Then the nature of this earth, and of air, water, fire, and magnetic ore is dealt with more particularly, for these are the bodies that may most commonly be found everywhere around it, as also all the qualities observed in these bodies, such as light, heat, weight, and the like. By this means I believe myself to have begun to explain the whole of philosophy in order, without having omitted anything that ought to precede the last *17* things of which I have written. But in order to carry this plan to a conclusion, I should afterwards in the same way explain in further detail the nature of each of the other bodies on the earth, that is, minerals, plants, animals, and above all man, then finally treat exactly of medicine, morals, and mechanics. All this I should have to do in order to give to mankind a complete body of philosophy; I do not feel myself to be so old, I do not so much despair of my strength, and I do not find myself so far removed from a knowledge of what remains that I should not venture to endeavor to achieve this design, if I had the means of making all the experiments I would need in order to support and justify my reasoning. But seeing that great expense is requisite for this end, to which the resources of an individual like myself could not attain if he were not given assistance by the public, and not seeing that I can expect that aid, I conceive it to be henceforth my duty to content myself with studying for my own private instruction, trusting that posterity will excuse me if I fail henceforth to work on its behalf.

In order, however, to show in how far I believe myself to have already been of service to my fellowmen, I will here state what are the fruits I believe may be gathered from my Principles. The first is the satisfaction we must derive from discovering in them certain truths of which we have been ignorant up to now; for although frequently the truth does not so much affect our imagination as do falsity and pretense, because it seems less wonderful and more simple, yet the satisfaction it brings is always more lasting and solid. The second fruit is that, in *18* studying these Principles, we will little by little accustom ourselves to judge better of all things with which we come in contact, and thus to become wiser. In this regard they will have an effect contrary to that of the ordinary philosophy, for it may easily be observed in those who are known as pedants that it renders them less capable of reasoning than they would have been had they never learned it at all. The third fruit is that the truths they contain, being perfectly clear and certain, will remove all subjects of dispute, and thus dispose men's minds to gentleness and concord. On the other hand, the controversies of the Schools, by insensibly making those who learn them more argumentative and opinionated, are possibly the chief causes of the heresies and dissensions that now plague the world. The last and principal fruit of my Principles is that by cultivating them we may discover many truths that I have not expounded, and thus, passing little by little from one to the other, acquire in time a perfect knowledge of the whole of philosophy and attain to the highest degree of wisdom. For we see in all the arts that, although they are rude and imperfect at first, yet because they contain something true whose effect is revealed by experience, they come little by little to perfection through practice. So, when we have true principles in philosophy, we cannot fail by following them to meet occasionally with other truths; and there is no way in which we can better prove the falsity of those of Aristotle than by pointing out that no progress has been attained by their means in all the centuries in which they have been followed.

19

    I know very well that there are minds that make such haste and use so little circumspection in what they do that, even with quite solid foundations, they cannot build anything firm and secure; and because it is commonly such men who are most ready to write books, they may in a short time spoil all that I have done, and if their writings are accepted as mine, or as representing my opinions, they may introduce uncertainty and doubt into my mode of philosophizing from which I have carefully tried to banish them. I have lately had experience about this in connection with one of them who might have been expected to have followed me most closely, and of whom I had even written "that I was so assured of his intelligence that I did not believe him to have any opinion I should not gladly have avowed as my own";[2] for a year ago he published a book entitled *Fundamenta Physicae,* in which, although he had apparently said nothing regarding physics and medicine that he had not derived from my writings—from those published as well as from another still imperfect regarding the nature of animals that fell into his hands—yet because he had transcribed badly, changed the order, and denied certain truths of metaphysics upon which the whole of physics ought to rest, I am obliged entirely to disavow his work, and here to beg readers never to attribute to me any opinion unless they find it expressly stated in my works, and never to accept anything as true in my writings or elsewhere, unless they see it to be very clearly deduced from true Principles.

20

    I well know likewise that many centuries may pass until all the truths that may be deduced from these principles are so deduced, because the greater part of those that remain to be discovered depend on certain particular experiments which will never be brought about by chance, but which should be investigated with care and expenditure by very intelligent men, and because it will be unlikely that the same people who have the capacity for availing themselves of them will have the means of contriving them, and also because the majority of the best minds have formed such a bad conception of philosophy as a whole, owing to the defects they have observed in what has been in vogue until now, that they will not be able to discover a better. But finally, if the difference observable between these principles and those of all other men, and the great array of truths which may be deduced from them, causes them to perceive how important it is to continue in the search after these truths, and to observe to what a degree of wisdom, to what perfection of life, to what happiness they may lead us, I am convinced that no one will be found who will not attempt to occupy himself with so profitable a study, or at least will not favor and endeavor to assist with all his might

---

2. The reference is to Henricus Regius. Descartes's comments refer to his *Letter to Voetius,* AT VIIIb, 3–194, specifically to p. 163.

those who employ themselves in this way with success. I trust that posterity may behold this success.

Part I. The Principles of Human Knowledge

1. For a person inquiring into the truth, it is necessary once in his life to doubt all things, as far as this is possible.   VIIIa, 5

Since we were once children and made judgments concerning things presented to our senses while we did not yet have the entire use of our reason, many judgments thus precipitately formed prevent us from arriving at the knowledge of the truth. It seems that there is no way we can deliver ourselves from these, unless we undertake once in our lives to doubt all things in which the slightest trace of uncertainty can be found.

2. We ought to consider as false all things we can doubt.

It will even be useful to reject as false all things in which we can imagine the least doubt, so that we may discover with greater clarity those which are absolutely true and easiest to know.

3. We should not in the meantime use this doubt for the conduct of our life.

But in the meantime it is to be observed that we should use this doubt only when we are engaged in contemplating truth. For, as regards the conduct of our life, we are frequently required to follow merely probable opinions, because the opportunities for action would in most cases pass away before we could free ourselves from our doubts. And when, as frequently happens with two courses of action, we do not perceive the probability of the one more than the other, we must yet select one of them.

4. Why we can doubt sensible things.

But because we desire to apply ourselves only to the search after truth, we will first doubt whether sensible things or things we have imagined really exist. First,   6
we know that our senses have deceived us before, and it is prudent not to trust too much in what has even once deceived us. Second, we continually seem to feel or imagine innumerable things in sleep which have no existence. To those who thus resolve to doubt all, there is apparently no mark by which they can distinguish with certainty being asleep from being awake.

5. Why we can likewise doubt mathematical demonstrations.

We will also doubt all the other things which have formerly seemed to us quite certain, even mathematical demonstrations and those principles we formerly thought quite self-evident. One reason is that those who have fallen into error in reasoning on such matters have held what we see to be false as perfectly certain and self-evident, but a yet more important reason is that we have been told that God who created us can do all that he wishes. For we are still ignorant of whether he may not have wished to create us in such a way that we will always be deceived, even in the things we believe ourselves to know best—since this does not seem less possible than our being occasionally deceived, which experience tells us is the case. And if we think that an omnipotent God is not the author of our being, and that we subsist of ourselves, or through some others, yet the less perfect we suppose the author to be, the more reason we have to believe that we are not so perfect that we cannot be continually deceived.

6. We have free will, which allows us to withhold assent from dubious things, and thus prevents our falling into error.

But whoever turns out to have created us, and even if he should prove to be all-powerful and deceitful, we still experience a freedom through which we may abstain from accepting as true and indisputable those things of which we do not have certain knowledge, and thus prevent ourselves from ever being deceived.

7. We cannot doubt our existence without existing while we doubt; and this is the first thing that we can know when we philosophize in an orderly way.

While we thus reject everything we can possibly doubt, and feign that it is false, it is easy to suppose that there is no God, no heaven, no bodies, and that we have no hands, no feet, indeed no body; but we cannot in the same way conceive that we who doubt these things are not; for there is a contradiction in conceiving that what thinks does not, at the same time as it thinks, exist. And hence this conclusion I think, therefore I am, is the first and most certain that occurs to one who philosophizes in an orderly way.

8. This furnishes us with the distinction between the soul and the body, or between what thinks and what is corporeal.

This, then, is the best way to discover the nature of mind and the distinction between it and the body. For, in considering what we are, we who suppose that all things apart from ourselves <and outside our thought> are false, observe very clearly that there is no extension, shape, local motion, or anything attributable to body, which pertains to our nature, but only thought alone; and consequently this notion of our thought precedes that of all corporeal things and is the most certain, since we still doubt whether there are any other things in the world, while we already perceive that we think.

9. What thought is.

By the word thought I understand everything we are conscious of as operating in us. And that is why not only understanding, willing, imagining, but also feeling, are here the same thing as thinking. For if I say I see, or I walk, therefore I am, and if by seeing and walking I mean the action of my eyes or my legs, which is the work of my body, my conclusion is not absolutely certain; this is because, as often happens in sleep, I think I see or I walk, although I never open my eyes or move from my place, and the same thing perhaps might occur if I had no body at all. But if I mean only to talk of my sensation, or my consciously seeming to see or to walk, it becomes quite true, because my assertion now refers only to my mind, which alone is concerned with my feeling or thinking that I see and I walk.   *8*

10. Things perfectly simple and clear of themselves are obscured by the logical definitions <of the Schools>, and should not be counted among the things capable of being acquired by study, <but are inborn in us>.

I do not here explain various other terms I already use or will afterwards use, because they seem to me sufficiently self-evident. And I have often noticed that philosophers err in trying to explain things that are perfectly simple and self-evident by logically constructed definitions; as a result, they render them more obscure. When I stated that this proposition *I think, therefore I am* is the first and most certain that presents itself to those who philosophize in an orderly fashion, I did not for all that deny that we must first know *what thought, existence, and certainty are*, and that *in order to think we must exist*, and such like; but because these are such simple notions that of themselves give us no knowledge of anything that exists, I did not think them worthy of being enumerated.

11. How our mind is better known than our body.

But in order to understand how the knowledge we have of our mind not only precedes that of our body, but is also more evident, it must be observed that it is well known by the natural light <in our souls>, that no qualities or properties belong to nothingness; and that where some are perceived there must necessarily be some thing or substance on which they depend. And the same light shows us that we know a thing or substance so much the better, the more properties we observe in it. And we certainly observe many more properties in our mind than in any other thing, inasmuch as there is nothing that excites us to knowledge of whatever kind which does not even much more certainly compel us to knowledge of our mind. To take an example, if I persuade myself that there is an earth because I touch or see it, by that very same fact, and by a yet stronger reason, I should be persuaded that my mind exists, because it may be that I think I touch   *9* the earth even though there is possibly no earth existing at all, but it is not possible that I who form this judgment, and my mind which judges thus, should be nonexistent, and so in other cases. <We can conclude the same of all the other things that enter our minds, namely, that we who think of them exist, even though the things themselves may be false or have no existence.>

12. The reason why this is not equally known to everyone.

Those who did not philosophize in an orderly way have held other opinions on this subject because they never distinguished their mind from their body with sufficient care. For although they had no difficulty in believing that they themselves existed and that they were more certain of this than of any other thing, they did not observe that by "themselves" they ought merely to understand their minds <when metaphysical certainty was in question>; on the contrary, since they understood by it their bodies, which they saw with their eyes, touched with their hands, and to which they wrongly attributed the power of sense-perception, they were not able to perceive the nature of the mind.

13. In what sense the knowledge of all other things depends on the knowledge of God.

But when the mind, which thus knows itself but still doubts all other things, looks around in order to try to extend its knowledge further, it first finds in itself the ideas of many things, and while it contemplates these simply and neither affirms nor denies that there is anything outside itself similar to these ideas, it is beyond any danger of falling into error. The mind likewise discovers certain common notions out of which it frames various demonstrations which absolutely convince us of their truth if we pay attention to them. For example, the mind has within itself the ideas of number and figure; it also has such common notions as "if equals are added to equals, the result is equal." From these it is easy to demonstrate that the three angles of a triangle are equal to two right angles, etc. Now the mind perceives these and similar things as true as long as it attends to the premises from which they are derived. But since it cannot always devote this attention to them <when it remembers the conclusion and does not attend to the order of its deduction>, and conceives that it may have been created of such a nature that it has been deceived even in what is most evident, it sees clearly that it has great cause to doubt the truth of such conclusions and to realize that it can have no certain knowledge until it has come to know the author of its origin.

14. The existence of God may be rightly demonstrated from the fact that necessary existence is included in the conception we have of him.

The mind afterwards considers the various ideas it has and discovers there the idea of a being who is omniscient, omnipotent, and absolutely perfect—by far the most important idea; it recognizes in it not merely possible and contingent existence, as in all the other ideas it has of things it clearly perceives, but absolutely necessary and eternal existence. And just as it perceives that it is necessarily contained in the idea of a triangle that it should have three angles that are equal to two right angles, it is absolutely persuaded that the triangle has three angles equal to two right angles. In the same way from the fact that it perceives that necessary and eternal existence is contained in the idea it has of an absolutely perfect being, it has clearly to conclude that this absolutely perfect being exists.

15. Necessary existence is not similarly included in the notion we have of other things, but merely contingent existence.

The mind will be the better assured of the truth of this conclusion if it observes that it does not have the idea of any other thing in which existence is necessarily contained. And from this it realizes that the idea of an absolutely perfect being is not framed in it by means of itself, nor does it represent a chimera, but that it is a true and immutable nature, which cannot but exist, since existence is necessarily contained in it.

16. Prejudice prevents many from knowing clearly the necessity for the existence of God.

Our mind would have no trouble in persuading itself of this truth if it were wholly free from prejudice to begin with; but inasmuch as we are accustomed to distinguish essence from existence in all other things, and as we can at will imagine many ideas of things which neither are nor have been, it may easily occur that *11* when we do not steadily contemplate this absolutely perfect being, we will doubt whether the idea we form of him is not one of those we frame at pleasure, or one of those which do not include existence in their essence.

17. The greater the objective perfection in our ideas, the greater its cause.

Further, when we reflect on the various ideas that are in us, it is easy to perceive that there is not much difference between them when they are considered only as modes of thinking, but they are widely different in another way, since the one represents one thing, and the other another; and their cause must be more perfect as what they represent of their objects is more perfect. For this is just the same as in the case of someone said to have the idea of a machine in the construction of which there is much skill displayed; we have reason to ask how he obtained the idea, that is, whether he saw somewhere a similar machine made by another, or had a thorough knowledge of the science of mechanics, or his force of mind was so great that he was able to invent the machine on his own without having seen anything similar anywhere else. For the whole of the ingenuity involved in the idea which is possessed by this man objectively, as in a picture, must exist in its first and principal cause, whatever that may be, not only objectively or representatively, but also formally or eminently.

18. From this we may demonstrate that there is a God.

So, because we find within ourselves the idea of a God, or a supremely perfect being, we are able to investigate the cause that produces this idea in us; but after having considered the immensity of the perfection it possesses, we are constrained to admit that we can consider it only as emanating from an all-perfect being, that is, from a God who truly exists. For it is not only made manifest by the natural light that nothing can be the cause of anything whatever, and that the more perfect cannot proceed from the less perfect so as to be thus produced as *12* by its efficient and total cause, but also that it is impossible for us to have any idea of anything whatever, if there is not within us, or outside us, an original that contains all the perfections belonging to the idea. But as we do not in any way possess all those absolute perfections of which we have the idea, we must conclude that they reside in some other nature different from ours—that is, in God;

or at least that they were once in him, and it follows from this most manifestly that they are there still.

19. Although we do not comprehend the whole nature of God, there is yet nothing we know so clearly as his perfections.

This is quite certain and manifest to those who have accustomed themselves to contemplate God and to turn their attention to his infinite perfections. For, though we do not comprehend them because the nature of the infinite is such that we, being finite, cannot comprehend them, yet we conceive them more clearly and distinctly than any material thing, because, being simpler and not being limited by anything that may obscure them, they occupy our mind more fully.

20. We are not the cause of ourselves, but are caused by God, and consequently there is a God.

But since everyone does not notice this, and because, when we have a notion of some machine in which there is much skill displayed, we know sufficiently well the manner in which we have acquired this idea, and because we cannot even recollect when the idea we have of a God has been communicated to us by God, since it has always been present in us, we must yet inquire who then is the author of our being, given that we have in us the idea of the infinite perfections of God. For the light of nature makes it very clear that whoever knows something more perfect than himself cannot be the author of his being, because then he would have given himself all the perfections of which he has the idea; and consequently he could not subsist by any other than by him who possesses all these perfections in himself, that is, by God.

13 21. The mere duration of our life suffices to prove the existence of God.

We cannot doubt the truth of this demonstration as long as we observe the nature of time or the duration of things; for this is of such a kind that its parts do not depend one upon the other, and never coexist; and from the fact that we now exist, it does not follow that we will exist a moment from now, if some cause—the same that first produced us—does not continue to produce us, that is to say, to conserve us. And we can easily recognize that there is no strength in us whereby we may conserve ourselves, but that he who has so much power that he can conserve us out of himself must by so much the greater reason conserve himself, or rather not require to be conserved by any other, for, in short, he is God.

22. In recognizing the existence of God in the manner here explained, we also recognize all his attributes, insofar as they may be known by the natural power of mind.

There is a great advantage in proving the existence of God in this way by his idea: we recognize at the same time what he is, insofar as the weakness of our nature permits. For when we reflect on the idea of him implanted in us, we perceive that he is eternal, omniscient, omnipotent, the source of all goodness and truth, creator of all things, and finally that he has in himself everything in which we can clearly recognize some infinite perfection not limited by any imperfection.

23. God is not corporeal and does not perceive by means of the senses as we do, nor is he the originator of sin.

There are many things in the world which are in some respects imperfect or limited, although we notice in them certain perfections; it is accordingly not possible that any of these belong to God. Thus because the nature of bodies includes divisibility along with local extension, and divisibility indicates imperfection, it is certain that God is not body. And although it is of some advantage for us to have senses, yet because all sensation involves being acted upon and that indicates dependence on something else, we conclude that God does not have senses, but that he understands and wills—not indeed as we do, by operations which are in some way distinct from one another, but by a single identical and very simple action by which he understands and wills and effects everything. When I say everything, I mean all *things;* for he does not will the evil of sin because that evil is not a thing.

24. In passing from the knowledge that God exists to the knowledge of his creatures, we must remember that our understanding is finite and the power of God infinite.

Since God alone is the true cause of all that is or can be, we will doubtless follow the best method of philosophizing, if, from the knowledge we have of his nature, we pass to an explanation of the things he has created, <and if we try to deduce it from the notions that exist naturally in our minds,> for in this way we will obtain a perfect science, that is, knowledge of the effects through their causes. But in order that we may undertake this task with most security from error, we must remember that God, the creator of all things, is infinite and that we are altogether finite.

25. We must believe all that God has revealed, even though it may surpass our capacities.

Thus if God reveals to us or to others certain things concerning himself that surpass the natural reach of our minds, such as the mysteries of the incarnation and the Trinity, we will have no difficulty in believing them, although we may not clearly understand them. For we should not think it strange that in the immensity of his nature, as also in the objects of his creation, there are many things beyond the range of our comprehension.

26. We must not try to dispute about the infinite, but just consider that everything in which we find no limits is indefinite, such as the extension of the world, the divisibility of its parts, the number of the stars, etc.

We will thus never hamper ourselves with disputes about the infinite, since it would be absurd that we who are finite should undertake to determine anything

regarding it, and by this means in trying to comprehend it, regard it, so to speak,
15 as finite. That is why we do not care to reply to those who ask whether half of an
infinite line is infinite, and whether an infinite number is even or odd, and so on,
because it is only those who imagine their mind to be infinite who appear to find
it necessary to investigate such questions. As for us, while we regard things in
which, in a certain sense, we observe no limits, we shall not for all that state that
they are infinite, but merely hold them to be indefinite. Thus because we cannot
imagine an extension so great that we cannot at the same time conceive that there
may be one yet greater, we shall say that the magnitude of possible things is
indefinite. And because we cannot divide a body into parts which are so small
that each part cannot be divided into others yet smaller, we shall consider that its
quantity may be divided into parts whose number is indefinite. And because we
cannot imagine so many stars that it is impossible for God to create more, we
shall suppose their number to be indefinite, and so in other cases.

27. The difference between the indefinite and the infinite.

We call these things indefinite rather than infinite in order to reserve for God
alone the name of infinite, first because in him alone we observe no limitation
whatever, and because we are quite certain that he can have none; second,
because, in regard to other things, we do not in the same way positively understand them to be in every respect unlimited, but merely negatively admit that
their limits, if they exist, cannot be discovered by us.

28. We must not inquire into the final, but only into the efficient causes of created things.

Finally we will not seek for the reason of natural things from the end which
God or nature has set before him in their creation <and we will entirely banish
the search for final causes from our philosophy>. For we should not take so much
upon ourselves as to believe that God could take us into his counsels. But regard-
16 ing him as the efficient cause of all things, we shall merely try to discover by the
light of nature he has placed in us, applied to those attributes of which he has
been willing we should have some knowledge, what must be concluded regarding the effects that we perceive by the senses. But we must keep in mind what
has been said, that we must trust this natural light only so long as nothing contrary to it is revealed by God himself.

29. God is not the cause of our errors.

The first of God's attributes that comes into consideration here is that he is
supremely true and the source of all light, so that it is completely contradictory
that he should deceive us, that is to say, that he should be properly and positively
the cause of the errors to which we know from experience we are subject. For
although among men the capacity to deceive would seem to be a mark of subtlety of mind, yet the will to deceive proceeds only from malice, or fear, or weakness, and consequently it cannot be attributed to God.

30. As a result, all that we perceive clearly is true, and this delivers us from the doubts put forward above.

It follows from this that the light of nature, or the faculty of knowledge God has given us, can never disclose to us any object that is not true, inasmuch as the natural light encompasses it, that is, inasmuch as it perceives it clearly and distinctly. For we would have had reason to think God a deceiver if the faculty he had given us was so perverted that <when using it properly> we would mistake the false for the true. This should deliver us from the supreme doubt that encompassed us when we did not know whether our nature had been such that we had been deceived in things that seemed most clear. It should also protect us against all the other reasons already mentioned which we had for doubting. The truths of mathematics should now be above suspicion, for they are most manifest. And if we perceive anything by our senses, either waking or sleeping, if it is clear and distinct, and if we separate it from what is obscure and confused, we will easily assure ourselves of what is the truth. There is no need to say more on this particular subject here, since I have treated of it fully in the *Meditations on Metaphysics,* and what I intend to say later will serve to explain it more accurately. *17*

31. Our errors are but negations with respect to God, while with respect to ourselves they are privations or defects.

But as it happens that, although God is not a deceiver, we so frequently fall into error, if we desire to investigate the origin and cause of our errors in order to guard against them, we must take care to observe that they do not depend so much on our intellect as on our will, and that they are not such as to require the actual concurrence of God in order that they may be produced. In this way, so far as he is concerned, they are but negations, while with respect to us they are defects or privations.

32. There are but two modes of thought in us, the perception of the intellect and the action of the will.

For all the modes of thinking that we observe in ourselves may be related to two general modes: perception, or the operation of the intellect, and volition, or the operation of the will. Thus sense-perception, imagining, and conceiving purely intelligible things are just different methods of perceiving; but desiring, holding in aversion, affirming, denying, doubting: all these are different modes of willing.

33. We deceive ourselves only when we form judgments about anything inadequately perceived.

When we perceive anything, we are in no danger of misapprehending it as long as we do not judge of it in any way; and even when we judge of it we should not fall into error, provided that we do not give our assent to what we do not perceive clearly and distinctly. What usually misleads us is that we very frequently form a *18* judgment although we do not have an accurate perception of what we judge.

34. Not only the intellect, but also the will is requisite for judgment.

I admit that we can judge of nothing unless our intellect intervenes, because there is no reason to suppose we can judge of what we do not perceive in any way; but the will is also essential if we are to give our assent to what we have in some manner perceived. Nor, in order to form any judgment whatever, is it necessary that we should have a perfect and entire perception of a thing; for we often give our assent to things of which we have never had any but a very obscure and confused knowledge.

35. The will is more extended than the intellect and our errors proceed from this cause.

Further, the perception of the intellect extends only to the few objects presented to it, and is always very limited. The will, on the other hand, may in some sense be called infinite, because we perceive nothing that may be the object of some other will, even of the immeasurable will of God, to which our will cannot also extend, so that we easily extend it beyond what we clearly perceive. And when we do this, it is no wonder if it happens that we err.

36. Our errors cannot be imputed to God.

And although God has not given us an omniscient intellect, we must not for that reason believe that he is the author of our errors. For all created intellect is finite, and it is of the nature of finite intellect not to extend to all things.

37. The principal perfection of man is to have the power of acting freely or through the will, and this is what makes him deserving of either praise or blame.

That the will should extend widely is in accordance with its nature, and it is the greatest perfection in man to be able to act by its means, that is, freely, and by so doing we are in a peculiar way masters of our actions and thereby merit praise or blame. For we do not praise automata, although they respond exactly to the movements they were designed to produce, since their actions are performed necessarily. We praise the workman who has made them because he has formed them with accuracy and has done so freely and not of necessity. And for the same reason, when we choose what is true, much more credit is due to us when the choice is made freely, than when it is made of necessity.

38. Our errors are defects in the way we act, but not in our nature; the faults of subordinates may often be attributed to other masters, but never to God.

It is very true that whenever we err there is some fault in the way we act, or in the manner we use our freedom, but for all that there is no defect in our nature, because our nature is the same whether we judge rightly or wrongly. And even though God could have given us so great an intellect that we should never have fallen into error, we have no right to demand this of him. For although among men, if someone had the power of preventing an impending evil and yet did not do so, we would judge him to be its cause; God is not to be regarded as responsible for our errors, even though he could have brought it about that we should not. For the power some men possess over others has been instituted for the purpose of their hindering evil from being done by others, while the power held over the universe by God is altogether absolute and free. This is why we should be grateful for the good things he has granted us and not complain that he does not bestow from his bounty all that we know he might have dispensed.

39. The freedom of the will is self-evident.

It is so evident that we are possessed of a free will that can give or withhold its assent, that this may be counted as one of the first and most common notions found innately in us. We have already a very clear proof of this, for at the same time as we tried to doubt all things and even supposed that he who created us   20
employed his unlimited powers in deceiving us in every way, we perceived in ourselves a liberty such that we were able to abstain from believing what was not perfectly certain and indubitable. But that of which we could not doubt at such a time is as self-evident and clear as anything we can ever know.

40. We likewise know certainly that everything is preordained by God.

But because what we have already learned about God proves to us that his power is so immense that it would be a crime for us to think ourselves ever capable of doing anything he had not already preordained, we should soon be involved in great difficulties if we undertook to make his preordinations harmonize with the freedom of our will, and if we tried to comprehend them both at one time.

41. How the freedom of the will may be reconciled with divine preordination.

Instead of this, we will have no trouble at all if we recollect that our mind is finite, and that the power of God is infinite—the power whereby he has not only known from all eternity what is or what can be, but also willed and preordained it. In this way we may have intelligence enough to come clearly and distinctly to know that this power is in God, but not enough to comprehend how he leaves the free action of man indeterminate; and, on the other hand, we are so conscious of the liberty and indifference which are in us, that there is nothing that we comprehend more clearly and perfectly. For it would be absurd to doubt what we inwardly experience and perceive as existing within ourselves just because we do not comprehend a matter which from its nature we know to be incomprehensible.

42. How, although we do not will to err, we nevertheless err by our will.

But inasmuch as we know that all our errors depend on our will, and as no one wants to go wrong, we may wonder that we err at all. However, we must observe   21
that there is a great difference between willing to go wrong and willing to give one's assent to opinions in which error is sometimes found. For although there is

no one who expressly wants to err, there is hardly anyone who is not willing to give his assent to things in which unsuspected error is to be found. And it even frequently happens that it is the very desire to know the truth that causes those who are not fully aware of the order in which it should be sought for, to pass judgment on things of which they have no real knowledge and so to fall into error.

43. We cannot err if we give our assent only to what we clearly and distinctly perceive.

But it is certain that we will never take the false for the true if we give our assent only to what we perceive clearly and distinctly. Since God is no deceiver, the faculty of knowledge he has given us cannot incline toward the false, nor can the faculty of assenting, as long as we do not extend it beyond those things we clearly perceive. And even if this could not be rationally demonstrated, we are by nature so disposed to give our assent to what we clearly perceive that we cannot possibly doubt its truth.

44. We will always judge badly when we assent to what we do not clearly perceive, although our judgment may be true; it is frequently our memory that deceives us by leading us to believe that certain things had been satisfactorily established by us.

It is also certain that whenever we give our assent to some argument we do not exactly understand, we either go wrong or, if we arrive at the truth, it is only by chance, and thus we cannot be certain that we are not in error. It is true that it rarely happens that we assent to things we notice we have not perceived, because the light of nature teaches us that we must not make judgments of anything we do not know. But we frequently err when we presume we have perceived certain things; and once they are committed to memory, we give them our assent as if we had fully perceived them, whereas we never perceived them at all.

45. What a clear and distinct perception is.

22 There are even a number of people who throughout all their lives perceive nothing so correctly as to be capable of judging of it properly. For the knowledge upon which a certain and indubitable judgment can be formed should be not only clear but also distinct. I call a perception clear when it is present and apparent to an attentive mind, in the same way as we say that we see objects clearly when, being present to the regarding eye, they operate upon it with sufficient strength. But I call a perception distinct when it is clear and so different from all other objects that it contains within itself nothing but what is clear.

46. It is shown from the example of pain that a perception may be clear without being distinct, but it cannot be distinct unless it is clear.

When, for instance, a severe pain is felt, the perception of this pain may be very clear, and yet not always distinct, because people usually confuse the perception with the obscure judgment they form about its nature, assuming as they do that something exists in the affected part similar to the sensation of pain, even though it is only the sensation they perceive clearly. In this way perception may be clear without being distinct, and cannot be distinct without also being clear.

47. In order to remove the prejudices of our youth, it must be considered what is clear in each of our simple notions.

Indeed, in our early years our mind was so immersed in the body that it perceived nothing distinctly, although it perceived much sufficiently clearly; and because even then it formed many judgments, numerous prejudices were contracted from which the majority of us can hardly ever hope to become free. But in order that we may now free ourselves from them I will here enumerate all those simple notions that constitute our thoughts, and distinguish whatever is clear in each of them from what is obscure, or likely to cause us to err.

48. All the objects of our perceptions are to be considered either as things or the affections of things, or else as eternal truths; the enumeration of things.

I distinguish all the objects of our knowledge into either things or the affections of things, or eternal truths having no existence outside our thought. Of the *23* things we consider as real, the most general are *substance, duration, order, number,* and other similar matters which extend to all classes of things. I do not, however, observe more than two ultimate classes of things: intellectual or thinking things, pertaining to the mind or to thinking substance, and material things, pertaining to extended substance or to body. Perception, volition, and every mode of perception and willing pertain to thinking substance; while to extended substance pertain magnitude or extension in length, breadth and depth, shape, motion, situation, divisibility into parts themselves divisible, and the like. Besides these, there are, however, certain things we experience in ourselves that should be attributed neither to mind nor body alone, but to the close and intimate union of body and mind, as I shall later on explain in the proper place. Such are the appetites of hunger, thirst, etc., and also the emotions or passions of the mind which do not depend on thought alone, as the emotions of anger, joy, sadness, love, etc.; and, finally all the sensations such as pain, pleasure, light and color, sounds, odors, tastes, heat, hardness, and all other tactile qualities.

49. Eternal truths cannot be thus enumerated, and this is not needed.

What I have enumerated up to now are regarded either as the qualities of things or their modes. <We must now talk of what we know as eternal truths.> When we apprehend that it is impossible that anything can come from nothing, the proposition "nothing comes from nothing" is not to be considered as an existing thing, or the mode of a thing, but as a certain eternal truth which has its seat in our mind and is a common notion or axiom. The following are of the same nature: "it is *24* impossible that the same thing be and not be at the same time," "what has been done cannot be undone," "he who thinks must exist while he thinks," and very many other propositions which it would not be easy to enumerate completely. But <this is not necessary since> we cannot fail to recognize them when the occasion presents itself, provided we have no prejudices to blind us.

50. These eternal truths are clearly perceived, but not by all, because of prejudice.

As regards the common notions, indeed, there is no doubt that they may be clearly and distinctly perceived, for otherwise they would not deserve to bear this name; but it is also true that there are some which, in regard to all men, do not deserve the name equally with others, because they are not equally perceived by all. Not, however, that I believe the faculty of knowledge to extend further with some men than with others; it is rather that these common opinions are opposed to the prejudices of some who are thereby prevented from easily perceiving them, although they are perfectly manifest to those who are free from these prejudices.

51. What substance is: a name we cannot attribute in the same sense to God and to his creatures.

With respect to those matters we consider as being things or modes of things, it is necessary that we should examine them here one by one. By substance, we can understand nothing else than a thing which so exists that it needs no other thing in order to exist. And in fact only one substance can be understood which clearly needs nothing else, namely, God. We perceive that all other things can exist only by the help of God's concurrence. That is why the word substance does not pertain *univocally* to God and to other things, as they say in the Schools, that is, there is no meaning that can be distinctly understood as common to God and to his creatures.

52. It may be attributed univocally to soul and to body; how we know substance.

Created substances, however, whether corporeal or thinking, may be under-
25   stood under this common concept; for they are things that need only the con-
currence of God in order to exist. But yet substance cannot be first discovered merely from the fact that it is an existing thing, for that fact alone is not observed by us. We may, however, easily discover it by means of any one of its attributes, because it is a common notion that nothing is possessed of no attributes, properties, or qualities. For this reason, when we perceive any attribute, we can conclude that some existing thing or substance to which it may be attributed is necessarily present.

53. Each substance has a principal attribute: the attribute of the mind is thought, while that of body is extension.

But although any one attribute is sufficient to give us a knowledge of substance, there is always one principal property of substance which constitutes its nature and essence, and to which all other properties are referred. Thus extension in length, breadth, and depth constitutes the nature of corporeal substance; and thought constitutes the nature of thinking substance. For all else that may be attributed to body presupposes extension, and is but a mode of an extended thing; as everything that we find in mind is but so many diverse forms of thinking. Thus, for example, shape is unintelligible except in an extended thing, and motion likewise in an extended space; so imagination, feeling, and will are unintelligible except in a thinking thing. But, on the other hand, we can understand extension without shape or action, and thinking without imagination or sensation, and so on with the rest; as is quite clear to anyone who attends to the matter.

54. How we may have clear and distinct notions of thinking substance, of corporeal substance, and of God.

We may thus easily have two clear and distinct notions or ideas, the one of created thinking substance, the other of corporeal substance, provided we carefully separate all the attributes of thought from those of extension. We can also have a clear and distinct idea of an uncreated and independent thinking substance, that is, of God, provided that we do not suppose that this idea represents to us all things in God, and that we do not mingle anything fictitious with it, but simply attend to what is evidently contained in the idea, and which we are aware pertains to the nature of an absolutely perfect being. For no one can deny that such an idea of God is in us, unless he <groundlessly> asserts that the mind of man cannot have any knowledge of God.

26

55. How we can also have a distinct understanding of duration, order, and number.

We will likewise have a very distinct understanding of *duration, order,* and *number,* if, in place of mingling with the idea that we have of them what properly speaking pertains to the conception of substance, we merely consider that the duration of each thing is a mode under which we will consider this thing insofar as it continues to exist; and if in the same way we think that order and number are not really different from the things that are ordered and numbered, but that they are only the modes under which we consider these things.

56. What are modes, qualities, and attributes.

And, indeed, when we here speak of a *mode* we mean nothing more than what elsewhere is termed *attribute* or *quality.* But when we consider substance as modified or diversified, we use the word *mode*; and when from the disposition or variation it can be named as of such and such a kind, we use the word *quality* <to designate the different modes which cause it to be so termed>; and finally when we more generally consider that these modes or qualities are in substance we term them *attributes.* And because any variation is incomprehensible in God, we cannot ascribe to him modes or qualities, but simply attributes. And even in created things what always remains unmodified, like existence and duration in the existing and enduring thing, should not be called a quality or mode, but an attribute.

57. Some attributes pertain to things and others to thought; what duration and time are.

27   Some of the attributes or modes are in things themselves and others are only in our thought. Thus time, for example, which we distinguish from duration taken in its general sense and which we describe as the measure of movement, is only a mode of thinking; for we do not indeed understand the duration of things which are moved as different from that of the things which are not moved, as is evident from the fact that if two bodies are moved for the space of an hour, the one quickly, the other slowly, we do not count the time longer in one case than in the other, although there is much more movement in one of the two bodies than in the other. But in order to measure the duration of all things, we usually compare their duration with the duration of the greatest and most regular motions, which are those that create years and days, and these we call time. Hence this adds nothing to duration, taken in general, but a mode of thought.

58. Number and all universals are simply modes of thought.

Similarly, number, when considered abstractly or generally and not in created things, is but a mode of thinking; and the same is true of everything called universals <in the Schools>.

59. How universals arise and the five common ones: genus, species, difference, property, and accident.

Universals arise solely from the fact that we avail ourselves of one and the same idea in order to think of all individual things that have a certain similitude. When we understand under the same name all the objects represented by this idea, that name is universal. For example, when we see two stones, and without thinking further of their nature than that there are two, we form in ourselves an idea of a certain number we call the number two; and when afterwards we see two birds or two trees, and we observe without further thinking about their nature that there are two of them, we again take up the same idea we had before. This idea is universal; and we give to this number the universal name two. In the same
28   way when we consider a three-sided figure we form a certain idea we call the idea of a triangle, and afterwards we make use of it as a universal in representing to ourselves all the figures having three sides. But when we notice more particularly that some three-sided figures have a right angle and others do not, we form the universal idea of a right triangle, which, being related to the preceding as to a more general, may be termed a *species;* and the right angle is the universal *difference* by which right triangles are distinguished from all others. If we further observe that the square of the hypotenuse is equal to the squares of the two other sides, and that this *property* belongs only to this species of triangle, we may

term it a <universal> property of the species. Finally, if we suppose that some of the triangles are moved and others are not moved, we should take that to be a universal *accident* of the same; and thus we commonly enumerate the five universals: *genus, species, difference, property,* and *accident.*

60. Of distinctions, and first of real distinction.

But as to the number in things themselves, this proceeds from the distinction between them, and distinction is of three sorts, namely, *real, modal*, and of *reason*. A *real distinction* is properly speaking found between two or more substances; and we can conclude that two substances are really distinct one from the other from the sole fact that we can clearly and distinctly understand the one without the other. For in accordance with the knowledge we have of God, we are certain that he can accomplish what we distinctly understand. That is why from the fact that we now have, for example, the idea of an extended or corporeal substance, although we do not yet know certainly whether such a thing exists at all, we can conclude that it may exist; and if it does exist, any one part of it which we can demarcate in our thought must be distinct from every other part of the same substance. Similarly, because each one of us understands that he thinks, and that in thinking he can shut off from himself every other substance, either thinking or extended, we may conclude that each of us, similarly regarded, is really distinct from every other thinking substance and from every corporeal substance. And even if we suppose that God had united a body to a soul so closely that it was impossible to bring them together more closely, and made a single thing out of the two, they would yet remain really distinct one from the other notwithstanding the union; because however closely God connected them he could not set aside the power he possessed of separating them, or conserving one of them apart from the other, and those things God can separate, or conceive in separation, are really distinct.

29

61. Of modal distinction.

There are two sorts of modal distinctions, namely, one between the mode properly speaking and the substance of which it is the mode, and another between two modes of the same substance. The former we recognize by the fact that we can clearly understand substance without the mode that we say differs from it, while conversely we cannot understand this mode without the substance. There is, for example, a modal distinction between shape or motion and the corporeal substance in which both exist; there is also a distinction between affirming or recollecting and the mind. As to the other kind of distinction, its characteristic is that we are able to recognize one mode without the other and *vice versa*, but we cannot know either the one or the other without recognizing that both subsist in one common substance. If, for example, a stone is moved and is square, we can understand the square figure without knowing that it is moved, and conversely, that it is moved without knowing that it is square; but we cannot understand this motion and shape without the substance of the stone. As for the distinction whereby the mode of one substance is different from another substance, or from

30

the mode of another substance, as the motion of one body is different from another body or from mind, or else as motion is different from duration, it appears to me that we should call it real rather than modal, because we cannot clearly understand these modes apart from the substances of which they are the modes and which are really distinct.

62. Of the distinction of reason.

Finally the distinction of reason is between substance and some one of its attributes without which it is not possible that we should have a distinct knowledge of it, or between two such attributes of the same substance. This distinction is made manifest from the fact that we cannot have a clear and distinct idea of such a substance if we exclude from it such an attribute; or we cannot have a clear idea of one of the two attributes if we separate it from the other. For example, because there is no substance that does not cease to exist when it ceases to endure, duration is only distinct from substance by thought; all the modes of thinking we consider as though they exist in the objects differ only in thought both from the objects of which they are the thought and from each other in a common object. I recollect having elsewhere conflated this sort of distinction with modal distinction (near the end of the *Reply to the First Set of Objections* to the *Meditations on First Philosophy*),[3] but then it was not necessary to treat accurately of these distinctions, and it was sufficient for my purpose at the time simply to distinguish them both from the real.

63. How we may distinctly know thought and extension, inasmuch as the one constitutes the nature of mind and the other that of body.

We may likewise consider thought and extension as constituting the natures of intelligent substance and corporeal substance; and then they must not be considered otherwise than as the very substances that think and are extended, that is, as mind and body; for we know them in this way very clearly and distinctly. It is moreover easier to know a substance that thinks, or an extended substance, than substance alone, without regarding whether it thinks or is extended. For we experience some difficulty in abstracting the notions that we have of substance from those of thought or extension, for in truth they do not differ except in thought, and our conception is more distinct not because it includes fewer properties, but because we distinguish accurately what it does include from all other notions.

31

64. How we may also distinctly know them as modes of substance.

We may likewise consider thought and extension as modes of substance—that is, insofar as we consider that one and the same mind may have many different thoughts, and that one body, retaining the same size, may be extended in many different ways (sometimes it may be greater in length and less in breadth or depth, and sometimes on the contrary greater in breadth and less in length). We

---

3. AT VII, 120–1.

then distinguish them modally from substance, and they may be understood not less clearly and distinctly, provided that we do not think of them as substances or things separate from others, but simply as modes of things. Because when we regard them as in the substances of which they are the modes, we distinguish them from these substances, and take them for what they actually are; while, on the contrary, if we wish to consider them apart from the substances in which they are, that will have the effect of our taking them as self-subsisting things and thus confounding the ideas of mode and substance.

65. How we may likewise know their modes.   *32*

Similarly, we shall best apprehend the diverse modes of thought such as understanding, imagining, recollecting, willing, etc., and the diverse modes of extension, or those pertaining to extension, such as all shapes, the situation of parts, and their movements, provided that we consider them simply as modes of the things in which they are; and as for motion we shall best understand it, if we inquire only about locomotion, without taking into account the force that produces it, which I shall nevertheless endeavor to set forth in its proper place.

66. We also have a clear knowledge of our sensations, emotions, and appetites, although we frequently err in the judgments we form of them.

There remain our sensations, emotions, and appetites, as to which we may likewise have a clear knowledge, if we take care to include in the judgments we form of them only that which we know to be precisely contained in our perception of them, and of which we are intimately conscious. But it is most difficult to observe this condition, in regard to our senses at least, because there is no one who has not judged from our youth on that all things we were accustomed to sense existed somehow outside our thoughts, and that they were entirely similar to our sensations, that is, to the conception we had of them. Thus, when, for example, we saw a certain color, we thought we saw something that existed outside of us and clearly resembled the idea of color we were then experiencing in ourselves, and from the habit of judging in this way we seemed to see this so clearly and distinctly that we held it to be certain and indubitable.

67. We frequently make mistakes even in judging pain.

The same is true in regard to all our other sensations, even pleasure and pain. For although we do not believe that these things exist outside of us, we do not usually regard them as solely in our mind or our perception, but as being in our hands, feet, or some other part of our body. But there is no reason we should be *33* required to believe that the pain, for example, that we feel as it were in our foot is anything outside our mind, any more than the light we think we see in the sun is in the sun <as it is in us>; for both these are prejudices of our youth, as will appear clearly in what follows.

68. How we can distinguish in such matters what we know clearly from that in which we can err.

Further, in order that we may here distinguish what is clear from what is obscure, we must note that pain, color, and other things of the sort are clearly and distinctly perceived when considered simply as sensations or thoughts. But when they are judged to be things existing outside of our mind, we can in no way understand what sort of things they are. And when anyone says that he sees color in a body or feels pain in one of his limbs, it is the same as if he told us that he saw or felt something there, but was absolutely ignorant of its nature, or else that he did not know what he was seeing or feeling. For although, perhaps, when he examines his thoughts with less attention, he easily persuades himself that he has some knowledge of it, because he supposes that there is something resembling the sensation of color or pain he is experiencing, yet if he investigates what is represented to him by this sensation of color or pain, appearing as they do to exist in a colored body or painful part, he will find that he is really ignorant of it.

69. We know size, shape, etc., quite differently from color and pain, etc.

This will be more especially evident if we consider the fact that size in a body which is seen, or shape or motion (local motion at least—for philosophers, by imagining other sorts of motion than this, have rendered its nature less intelligible to themselves), or situation, or duration, or number, and the like, which we
34 clearly perceive in all bodies, as has been already described, are known by us in an entirely different way from that in which color is known in the same body, or pain, odor, taste, or any of the properties which, as previously mentioned, should be attributed to the senses. For although in observing a body we are not less certain of its existence from the color we perceive in its regard than from the shape that bounds it, we nevertheless know that property in it which causes us to call it shaped with much greater clarity than we know what causes us to say that it is colored.

70. We can judge of sensible things in two ways, in one of which we avoid error, while in the other we fall into error.

It is thus evident that when we say we perceive colors in objects, it is the same as though we said that we perceive something in the objects whose nature we do not know, but which produces a very clear and vivid sensation in us that we call the sensation of color. But there is a great deal of difference in our manner of judging: as long as we judge that there is something in objects of which we have no knowledge (that is in things, such as they are, from which sensation comes to us), we avoid error; indeed, we actually guard against it, for we are less likely to judge rashly of a thing we have been forewarned we do not know. But when we think we perceive a certain color in objects although we have no real knowledge of what it is we are calling a color, and we can find no intelligible resemblance between the color we suppose to be in objects and what we experience in our senses, yet, because we do not observe this or remark in these objects certain other qualities like size, shape, number, etc., that we clearly know are or may be in objects, as our senses or understanding show us, it is easy to allow ourselves to fall into the error of holding that what we call color in objects is something *35* entirely resembling the color we perceive, and then supposing that we have a clear perception of what we do not perceive at all.

71. The principal cause of error is found in the prejudices of childhood.

It is here that the first and principal cause of our errors is to be found. For in the first years of life the mind was so closely tied to the body that it applied itself to nothing but those thoughts by which it was aware of things affecting the body; it did not yet refer these to anything existing outside itself, but merely felt pain when the body was hurt, or experienced pleasure when the body received some good, or else if the body was so <slightly> affected that it did not experience any great good or evil, it encountered different sensations, namely, those we call the senses of taste, smell, sound, heat, cold, light, colors, and the like, which in truth represent nothing to us outside of our mind, but vary in accordance with the diversity of the parts and modes in which the body is affected. The mind at the same time also perceived sizes, shapes, motions, and the like, which were exhibited to it, not as sensations, but as things or the modes of things existing, or at least capable of existing, outside thought, although it did not yet observe the distinction between the two. And afterwards when the machine of the body, so constituted by nature that it can by its own inherent power turn here and there, by turning fortuitously this way and the other, pursued what was useful and avoided what was harmful, the mind which was closely tied to it, reflecting on the things it pursued or avoided, remarked first of all that they existed outside itself, and attributed to them not only sizes, shapes, motions, and other such properties it perceived as things or modes of things, but also tastes, smells, and the like, the sensations of which it perceived that these *36* things caused in it. And as all other things were only considered insofar as they were useful for the body in which it was immersed, the mind judged that there was more or less reality in each body, as the impressions made on the body were more or less strong. Hence the belief arose that there was much more substance or corporeal reality in rocks or metals than in air or water, because the sensations of hardness and weight were much more strongly felt. And thus it was that air was only regarded as anything when it was agitated by some wind, and we experienced it to be either hot or cold. And because the stars did not give more light than tiny lighted candles, the mind did not hold them to be larger than such flames. Moreover, because it did not as yet remark that the earth turned on its own axis, and that its surface was curved like a sphere, it was more ready to apprehend that it was immobile and that its surface was flat. And we have in this way been imbued with a thousand other such prejudices from infancy, which in later youth we quite forgot we had accepted without sufficient examination, admitting them as though they were utterly true and certain, and as if they had been known by means of our senses or implanted in us by nature.

72. The second cause of our errors is that we cannot forget these prejudices.

Although in coming to years of maturity, when the mind, being no longer wholly subject to the body, does not refer everything to it, but also inquires into the truth of things as they are in themselves, we find that many of the judgments we had formed are false, yet it is not easy to eradicate false judgments from our memory, and as long as they remain there they may be the cause of many errors. Thus, for example, since from our earliest years we imagined stars to be minute bodies, we have great difficulty in imagining anything different from this first conception, although astronomical reason tells us that they are among the largest bodies—so greatly does prejudiced opinion affect our beliefs.

37

73. The third cause is that we grow tired when we apply our attention to objects not present to the senses; we are therefore in the habit of judging these, not from present perceptions, but from preconceived opinions.

Further, our mind cannot pause to consider any one thing with attention without difficulty and fatigue, and it applies itself with the greatest difficulty to those objects present neither to the senses nor to the imagination. This may be due to the nature of the mind, because of its union with the body, or because in the first years of our life we are so much occupied with feeling and imagining that we have acquired a greater facility and habit for thinking in this way than in any other. As a result, people's understanding of substance is limited to what is imaginable and corporeal and even sensible. For they do not know that the only things imaginable are those that exist in extension, motion, and shape, while there are many others that are intelligible; and they persuade themselves that there is nothing that can subsist but body, and finally, that there is no body that is not sensible. And since in truth we do not perceive any object as it is in itself by sense alone, as will be clearly shown later on, it comes to pass that most men perceive nothing except in a confused way, throughout their whole life.

74. The fourth cause is that we attach our concepts to words that do not accurately correspond to reality.

And finally, because we attach all our concepts to the words used to express them, and as we commit to memory our thought in connection with these words, and as we more easily recall to memory words than things, we can scarcely conceive of anything so distinctly as to be able to separate what we conceive completely from the words chosen to express it. In this way most men apply their attention to words rather than things, and this is the cause of their frequently giving their assent to terms they do not understand, either because they believe that they formerly understood them, or because they think that those who informed them understood their signification correctly. And although this is not the place in which to treat particularly of this matter, inasmuch as I have not yet dealt with the nature of the human body, nor even shown that any body exists at all, still it appears to me that what I have already said may serve to enable us to distinguish those of our concepts that are clear and distinct from those in which there is obscurity and confusion.

38

75. A summary of what has to be observed in order to philosophize correctly.

That is why, if we desire to philosophize seriously, and apply ourselves to the search for all the truths we are capable of knowing, we must in the first place rid ourselves of our prejudices, and take the greatest care to set aside all the opinions we formerly accepted, until, on applying to them further examination, we discover them to be true. We should afterwards hold an orderly review of the notions we have within us, and judge to be true those and only those which present themselves to our apprehension as clear and distinct. In this way we will know, first of all that we exist, insofar as our nature is to think, and at the same time that there is a God on whom we depend; and after having considered his attributes we shall be in a position to inquire into the truth of all other things, since God is their cause. In addition to the notions we have of God and of our thoughts, we shall likewise find within us a knowledge of many propositions that are eternally true, such as nothing comes from nothing, etc. We shall also find there the idea of a corporeal or extended nature which may be moved, divided, etc., and also of the sensations that affect us, such as those of pain, color, taste, etc., although we do not as yet know the cause of our being so affected. And comparing <what we now know by examining those things in their order> with our former confused knowledge, we shall acquire the habit of forming clear and distinct concepts of all we can know. And in these few precepts it appears to me *39* that the main principles of human knowledge are contained.

76. We ought to prefer divine authority to our perceptions, but, excluding this, we should not assent to anything we do not clearly perceive.

Above all, we should impress on our memory as an infallible rule that what God has revealed to us is incomparably more certain than anything else, and that we ought to submit to divine authority rather than to our own judgment even though the light of reason may seem to us to suggest something opposite with the utmost clearness and evidence. But in things in regard to which divine authority reveals nothing to us, it would be unworthy of a philosopher to accept anything as true that he has not ascertained to be such, and to trust more to the senses, that is, to judgments formed without consideration in childhood, than to the reasoning of maturity.

Part II. The Principles of Material Things

1. The reasons for our having a certain knowledge of the existence of *40*
material things.

Although we are all persuaded that material things exist, yet because we have doubted this before and have placed it in the rank of the prejudices of our childhood, it is now necessary that we should inquire into the arguments by which we may accept this with certainty. To begin with we feel that without doubt all our sensations proceed from something different from our mind. For it is not in our power to have one sensation rather than another, since each one is clearly dependent on the thing affecting our senses. It is true that we may

inquire whether this thing is God or something different from God. But inasmuch as we sense, or rather are stimulated by sense to have a clear and distinct perception of matter extended in length, breadth, and depth, the various parts of which have various shapes and motions, and give rise to the sensations we have of colors, smells, pains, etc., if God immediately and of himself presented
41   to our mind the idea of this extended matter, or merely permitted it to be caused in us by something lacking extension, shape, or motion, there would be nothing to prevent him from being regarded as a deceiver. For we clearly apprehend this matter as different from God, or ourselves, or our mind, and appear to see very clearly that the idea of it is due to things outside ourselves to which it is wholly similar. But God cannot deceive us, because deception is repugnant to his nature, as has been explained. And therefore we must conclude that there is something extended in length, breadth, and depth, and possessing all those properties we clearly perceive to pertain to extended things. And this extended thing is called by us either body or matter.

2. How we likewise know that the human body is closely united to the mind.

It may be concluded also that a certain body is more closely united to our mind than any other, from the fact that pain and other of our sensations occur without our foreseeing them; the mind is aware that these do not arise from itself alone, nor pertain to it insofar as it is a thinking thing, but only insofar as it is united to another thing, extended and mobile, which is called the human body. But this is not the place to explain this matter further.

3. Sensory perceptions do not teach us what is really in things, but merely what is useful or harmful to man's composite nature.

It will be sufficient for us to observe that sensory perceptions are related simply to the intimate union of body and mind, and that while by their means we are made aware of what in external bodies can profit or hurt this union, they do not present them to us as they are in themselves unless occasionally and accidentally.
42   Thus, <after this observation> we will without difficulty set aside all the prejudices of the senses and in this regard rely upon our intellect alone, by reflecting carefully on the ideas implanted in it by nature.

4. The nature of body does not consist in weight, hardness, color, and so on, but in extension alone.

In this way we shall perceive that the nature of matter, or body in its universal aspect, does not consist in its being hard, or heavy, or colored, or affecting our senses in some other way, but solely in its being something extended in length, breadth, and depth. For as regards hardness, we do not know anything of it by sense, except that the portions of the hard bodies resist the motion of our hands when they come in contact with them; but if, whenever we moved our hands in some direction, all the bodies in that part retreated with the same speed as our hands approached them, we should never feel hardness; and yet we have no reason to believe that the bodies receding in this way would on this account lose what makes them bodies. It follows that the nature of body does not consist in hardness. The same reason shows us that weight, color, and all the other qualities of the kind perceived in corporeal matter may be taken from it while it remains intact; thus it follows that the nature of body depends on none of these.

5. This truth about the nature of body is obscured by prejudices regarding rarefaction and the void.

There still remain two reasons for doubting whether the true nature of body consists solely in extension. The first is the prevalent opinion that most bodies are capable of being rarefied and condensed, so that when rarefied they have greater extension than when condensed; indeed, the subtlety of these people goes so far as to distinguish the substance of a body from its quantity, its quantity from its extension. The second reason is that if we understand there to be nothing in a place but extension in length, breadth, and depth, we are not in the habit of saying that there is a body there, but only space and further empty space, which most people persuade themselves is a mere negation.

6. In what way rarefaction occurs.

But as regards rarefaction and condensation, whoever will examine his own thoughts and refuse to admit anything he does not clearly perceive will not allow that there is anything in these processes but a change of shape—that is to say, rare bodies are those between whose parts there are many gaps filled with other bodies; and those are called dense bodies, on the other hand, whose parts, by approaching one another, either render these distances less than they were, or remove them altogether, in which case the body is rendered so dense that it cannot be denser. And yet it does not possess less extension than when the parts occupied a greater space, owing to their being further removed from one another. For the extension of the pores or the gaps which a body's parts do not occupy <when it is rarefied> should not be attributed to the body but to the other bodies occupying these gaps. Just as when we see a sponge filled with water or some other liquid, we do not suppose that for this reason each part of the sponge is more extended than when it is compressed and dry, but only that its pores are wider, and that it is therefore distributed over a larger space.

7. Rarefaction cannot be intelligibly explained in any other way.

I am indeed unable to say why this rarefaction of bodies has been explained by some as the result of augmentation of quantity rather than by the example of the sponge. For although when air and water are rarefied we do not see any pores made larger, nor any new body added to fill them, it is yet less consonant with reason to suppose something unintelligible in order to give a merely verbal explanation of how bodies are rarefied, than to conclude in consequence of that rarefaction that there are pores or gaps that become greater, and are filled with some new body, although we do not perceive this new body with the senses. For there is no reason that requires us to believe we should perceive by our senses all the bodies around us. And we see that it is very easy to explain rarefaction in this manner, though not in any other. And finally it would be undoubtedly contradictory to suppose that any body should be increased by a new quantity or new extension without the addition to it of a new extended substance, that is, a new body. This is because it is impossible to conceive any addition of extension or quantity without the addition of a substance having quantity or extension, as will be shown more clearly below.

8. Quantity and number differ only in thought from what has quantity and is numbered.

Quantity differs from extended substance, or number from what is numbered, not in reality, but only in our conception. Thus, to take an example, we may consider the whole nature of corporeal substance comprised within a space of ten feet, although we do not attend to this measure of ten feet, because it is clear that the thing conceived is the same in any one part of that space as in the whole. And vice versa, we can think of the number ten also as a continuous quantity of ten feet without attending to any particular determinate substance, because the conception of the number of ten is plainly the same, whether considered in reference to the measure of ten feet, or to any other ten; and we cannot conceive a continuous quantity
45   of ten feet without thinking of some extended substance of which it is the quantity, but yet we can conceive it without thinking of that determinate substance. In reality, however, it is impossible that even the least part of such quantity or extension can be taken away without taking away likewise an equal amount of substance; on the other hand, not the least part of the substance can be removed without our diminishing its quantity and extension by the same amount.

9. Corporeal substance, when distinguished from its quantity, is confusedly conceived as something incorporeal.

Although, however, some express themselves otherwise on this subject, I cannot think that they regard it otherwise than as I have just said; for when they distinguish substance from extension or quantity, either they mean nothing by the word substance, or they merely form in their minds a confused idea of incorporeal substance which they falsely attribute to corporeal substance, and leave to extension, which they nevertheless call an accident, that true idea of this corporeal substance; thus it is easy to see that their words are not in harmony with their thoughts.

10. What space or internal place is.

Space or internal place and the corporeal substance contained in it do not differ other than in the way they are conceived of by us. For, in truth, the same extension in length, breadth, and depth, which constitutes space, constitutes body; and the difference between them consists only in the fact that we consider extension as particular in body and think of it as changing whenever body changes; in space, on the contrary, we attribute to extension a generic unity, so that after having removed from a certain space the body that occupied it, we do not suppose that we have also removed the extension of that space, because it appears to us that the same extension remains so long as it is of the same size and shape, and preserves the same position in relation to certain other bodies, by which we determine this space.

11. In what sense it may be said that space is not different from corporeal   *46*
substance.

And it will be easy for us to recognize that the same extension constituting the nature of body likewise constitutes the nature of space; the two do not differ, except as the nature of the genus or species differs from the nature of the individual. Suppose that, in order to discern the idea we have of any body, such as a stone, we reject from it all that is not essential to the nature of body. In the first place, then, we may reject hardness, because if the stone were liquefied or reduced to powder, it would no longer possess hardness, and yet it would not cease to be a body; let us in the next place reject color, because we have often seen stones so transparent that they had no color; again we reject weight, because we see that fire, although very light, is yet body; and finally we may reject cold, heat, and all the other qualities of the kind either because they are not thought of as in the stone, or else because with the change of their qualities the stone is not for that reason considered to have lost its nature as body. After examination we will find that there is nothing remaining in the idea of body except that it is extended in length, breadth, and depth; and this is comprised in our idea of space, not only of what is full of body, but also of what is called a void.

12. How space is different from body in our mode of conceiving it.

There is, however, some difference in our mode of conceiving them; for if we remove a stone from the space or place where it was, we think that the extension of this stone has also been removed from it, because we consider it to be singular and inseparable from the stone itself. But at the same time we suppose that the same extension of place occupied by the stone remains, though the place it formerly occupied has been taken up with wood, water, air, and any other bodies, or even has been supposed to be empty, because we now consider extension in general, and it appears to us that the same is common to stones, wood, water,   *47*
air, and all other bodies, and even to a void if there is such a thing, provided that it is of the same magnitude and shape as before, and preserves the same position in regard to the external bodies that determine this space.

13. What external place is.

The words place and space signify nothing different from the body said to be in a place, and merely designate its size, shape, and position as regards other bodies. For it is necessary in order to determine this position to observe certain others we consider to be immovable; and according as we regard different bodies we may find that the same thing at the same time changes its place, and does not change it. For example, if we consider a man seated at the stern of a vessel when it is carried out to sea, he may be said to be in one place if we regard the parts of the vessel with which he preserves the same position; and yet he will be found continually to change his position, if regard is paid to the neighboring shores in relation to which he is constantly receding from one, and approaching another. And further, if we suppose that the earth moves, and that it takes precisely the same path from west to east as the vessel does from east to west, it will again appear to us that he who is seated at the stern does not change his position, because that place is determined by certain immovable points we imagine to be in the heavens. But if at length we are persuaded that there are no points in the universe that are really immovable, as will presently be shown to be probable, we shall conclude that there is nothing that has a permanent place except insofar as it is fixed by our thought.

14. The difference between place and space.

48   However, the terms place and space are different, because place indicates position more expressly than size or shape, while, on the contrary, we more often think of the latter when we speak of space. For we frequently say that a thing has succeeded to the place of another, although it does not possess exactly either its size or its shape; but we do not for all that mean that it occupies the same space as the other; and when the position is changed, we say that the place also is changed, although the same size and shape exist as before. And so if we say that a thing is in a particular place, we simply mean that it is situated in a certain manner in reference to certain other things; and when we add that it occupies a certain space or place, we likewise mean that it is of a definite size or shape <so as exactly to fill the space>.

15. How external place is rightly taken to be the surface of the surrounding body.

And thus we never distinguish space from extension in length, breadth, and depth; but we sometimes consider place as internal to the thing placed, and sometimes as external to it. Internal place is indeed in no way distinguished from space; but we sometimes regard external place as the surface immediately surrounding the thing placed in it. And it is to be observed that by surface we do not here mean any portion of the surrounding body, but merely the extremity between the surrounding body and that surrounded, which is but a mode; or we mean the common surface, a surface that is not a part of one body rather than of the other and is always considered the same, as long as it retains the same size and shape. For although all the surrounding body with its surface is changed, we should not imagine that the body which was surrounded by it had for all that changed its place, if it meanwhile preserved the same position in regard to other bodies that are regarded as immovable. Thus if we suppose that a ship is carried along in one direction by the current of a stream, and is impelled by a contrary wind in another direction in an equal degree, so that its position is not changed with regard to the banks, we are ready to admit that it remains in the same place although we see that the whole surrounding surface is in a state of change. *49*

16. It is contrary to reason to say that there is a void or space in which there is absolutely nothing.

As regards a void in the philosophic sense of the word, that is, a space in which there is no substance, it is evident that such a thing cannot exist, because the extension of space or internal place is not different from that of body. For, from the mere fact that a body is extended in length, breadth, or depth, we have reason to conclude that it is a substance; because it is absolutely inconceivable that nothing should possess extension, we ought to conclude also that the same is true of the space which is supposed to be void—namely, that since there is extension in it, there is necessarily also substance.

17. A void, in the ordinary sense, does not exclude all body.

And when we take this word void in its ordinary sense, we do not mean a place or space in which there is absolutely nothing, but only a place in which there are none of those things we expected to find there. Thus because a pitcher is made to hold water, we say that it is empty when it contains nothing but air. Or if there are no fish in a fishpond, we say that there is nothing in it, even though it is full of water. Similarly we say a vessel is empty when, in place of the merchandise it was designed to carry, it is loaded only with sand so that it may resist the impetuous violence of the wind. Finally we say in the same way that a space is empty when it contains nothing sensible, even though it contains created matter and self-existent substance; for we do not normally consider things except those detected by our senses. And if, in place of keeping in mind what we should understand by these words—void and nothing—we afterwards suppose that in the space termed void there is not only nothing sensible, but nothing at all, we will fall into the same error as if, because a pitcher is usually termed empty when it contains nothing but air, we were therefore to judge that the air contained in it is not a substantive thing. *50*

18. How the prejudice concerning the absolute void is to be corrected.

We have almost all lapsed into this error from the beginning of our lives, for, seeing that there is no necessary connection between the vessel and the body it contains, we thought that God at least could remove all the body contained in the vessel without its being necessary that any other body should take its place. But to correct this error, it is necessary to remark that while there is no connection between the vessel and that particular body it contains, there is an absolutely necessary one between the concave shape of the vessel and the extension considered generally that must be contained in this cavity; so that it is not more contradictory to conceive a mountain without a valley than such a cavity without the extension it contains, or this extension without the substance which is extended, because nothing, as has already been frequently remarked, cannot have extension. And therefore, if it is asked what would happen if God removed all the body contained in a vessel without permitting its place to be occupied by another body, we shall answer that the sides of the vessel will thus come into immediate contact with one another. For two bodies must touch when there is nothing between them, because it is manifestly contradictory for these two bodies to be apart from one another, or that there should be a distance between them, and yet that this distance should be nothing; for distance is a mode of extension, and without extended substance it cannot therefore exist.

19. This confirms what was said of rarefaction.

51   After we have thus remarked that the nature of corporeal substance consists only in its being an extended thing, or that its extension is not different from what has been attributed to space, however empty, it is easy to discover that it is impossible that any one of these parts should in any way occupy more space at one time than another, and thus that it may be rarefied other than in the manner explained above; or again it is easy to perceive that there cannot be more matter or corporeal substance in a vessel when it is filled with gold or lead, or any other body that is heavy and hard, than when it only contains air and appears to be empty; for the quantity of the parts of matter does not depend on their weight or hardness, but only on the extension which is always equal in the same vessel.

20. From this the impossibility of atoms may be demonstrated.

We also know that there cannot be any atoms or parts of matter which are by their own nature indivisible <as some philosophers have imagined>. For however small the parts are supposed to be, yet because they are necessarily extended we are always able in thought to divide any one of them into two or more parts; and thus we know that they are divisible. For there is nothing we can divide in thought which we do not hence recognize to be divisible; and therefore if we judge it to be indivisible, our judgment would be contrary to the knowledge we have of the matter. And even should we suppose that God had reduced some portion of matter to a smallness so extreme that it could not be divided into smaller parts, it would not for all that be properly called indivisible. For though God had rendered the particle so small that it was beyond the power of any creature to divide it, he could not deprive himself of his power of division, because it is absolutely impossible that he should lessen his own omnipotence, as was said

52   before. And therefore, absolutely speaking, it will remain divisible <to the smallest extended particle>, because it is such from its nature.

21. The extension of the world is likewise indefinite.

We likewise recognize that this world, or the totality of corporeal substance, is extended without limit, because wherever we imagine a limit we are not only still able to imagine beyond that limit spaces indefinitely extended, but we perceive these to be in reality such as we imagine them, that is to say that they contain in them corporeal substance indefinitely extended. For, as has been already shown very fully, the idea of extension we perceive in any space whatever is exactly the same as the idea of corporeal substance.

22. Thus the matter of the heavens and of the earth is one and the same, and there cannot be a plurality of worlds.

It is thus not difficult to infer from all this, that the earth and heavens are forged of the same matter, and that even if there were an infinite number of worlds, they would all be formed of this matter; from this it follows that there cannot be a plurality of worlds, because we clearly understand that the matter whose nature consists in its being an extended substance already occupies all the imaginable spaces where these other worlds could be, and we cannot find in ourselves the idea of any other matter.

23. All the variety in matter, or all the diversity of its forms, depends on motion.

There is therefore but one matter in the whole universe, and we know this by the simple fact of its being extended. All the properties we clearly perceive in it may be reduced to this one: that it is divisible and thus mobile according to its parts, and hence capable of being affected in all the ways we perceive as arising from the motion of its parts. For its division by thought alone makes no difference to it; but all the variation in matter, or diversity in its forms, depends on motion. This the philosophers have doubtless observed, inasmuch as they have said that nature was the principle of motion and rest, and by nature they understood that by which all corporeal things become such as they are experienced to be. *53*

24. What motion is in common parlance.

But motion (that is, local motion, for I can conceive no other kind, and do not think that we ought to conceive any other in nature), in the vulgar sense, is nothing more than *the action by which any body passes from one place to another.* And just as we have remarked above that the same thing may be said to change and not to change its place at the same time, we can say that it moves and does not move at the same time. For a man who is seated in a ship setting sail thinks he is moving when he looks at the shore he has left and considers as fixed, but not if he regards the vessel he is on, because he does not change his position in reference to its parts. Likewise, because we are accustomed to think that there is no motion without action and that in rest there is cessation of action, the person thus seated may more properly be said to be at rest than in motion, since he does not feel any action in himself.

25. What motion is, properly speaking.

Not looking to popular usage, but to the truth of the matter, let us consider what should be understood by motion according to the truth of the thing; we may say, in order to attribute a determinate nature to it, that it is the transference of one part of matter or one body from the vicinity of those bodies that are in immediate contact with it, and which are regarded as at rest, into the vicinity of oth-
54   ers. By one body or by one part of matter I understand everything transported together, although it may be composed of many parts which in themselves have other motions. And I say that it is the transference and not either the force or the action that transfers, in order to show that the motion is always in the mobile thing, not in the mover; for these two do not seem to me to be accurately enough distinguished. Further, I understand that it is a mode of the mobile thing and not a substance, just as shape is a mode of the shaped thing, and rest of that which is at rest. [. . .]

Part III. The Visible World

80 ### 1. We cannot think too highly of the works of God.

Having now determined certain principles of material things which were derived, not from the prejudices of the senses, but from the light of reason, so that we cannot doubt of their truth, we should examine whether we can explain all the phenomena of nature from these alone. And we shall begin with those that are the most general, and on which the others depend, such as the general structure of the visible world. But in order that we may philosophize correctly in this matter, two things are to be observed. The first is that we must always keep before our minds the infinite power and goodness of God, and not fear to fall into error by imagining his works to be too great, too beautiful, and too perfect, but that, on the contrary, we must take care lest, if we suppose any limits to exist in them of which we have no certain knowledge, we may seem to be insufficiently sensible of the greatness and power of the Creator.

2. We ought to beware lest we presume too much in supposing ourselves to understand the ends God set before himself in creating the world.

The second is that we ought to beware lest we think too highly of ourselves. This we should appear to do if we supposed the universe to have certain limits not presented to our knowledge without at the same time being assured of it by divine revelation, which would be making our knowledge extend beyond what
81 God has made; but this would be even more so if we persuaded ourselves that all

things were created by God only for us, or even if we were to suppose that by the powers of our mind we could understand the ends he set before himself in creating the universe.

3. In what sense it can be said that all things were created for man.

For although it may be a pious thought, as far as morals are concerned, to believe that God has created all things for us to the extent that it incites us to a greater gratitude and affection toward him, and although it is true in some respect, because there is nothing created from which we cannot derive some use, even if it is only the exercise of our minds in considering it and being incited to worship God by its means, it is yet not at all probable that all things have been created for us in such a manner that God has had no other end in creating them. And it seems to me that such a supposition would be certainly ridiculous and inept in reference to questions of physics, for we cannot doubt that an infinity of things exist, or did exist, though now they have ceased to exist, which have never been beheld or comprehended by man and which have never been of any use to him. [. . .]

Part IV. The Earth

188. What is to be borrowed from treatises on animals and man to complete the knowledge of material things. 315

I would add no more to this Fourth Part of the *Principles of Philosophy*, if (as I previously intended) I was going to write two others, namely a Fifth and a Sixth Part, the fifth on living things, that is on animals and plants, and the sixth on man. But because I am not yet completely clear about all of the matters I would like to treat in these two last parts, and do not know whether I am likely to have sufficient leisure <or be able to make the necessary experiments> to complete them, I shall here add a little about the objects of the senses in order not to delay these earlier parts too long or to allow anything to be missing which I should have reserved for the others. For up to this point I have described the earth and all the visible world as if it were simply a machine in which there was nothing to consider but the shape and motion of its parts, and yet our senses cause other things to be presented to us, such as colors, smells, sounds, and other such things; if I did not speak of them, it might be thought that I had omitted the main part of the explanation of the things in nature.

189. What sensation is and how it operates.

It must be realized that although the human soul informs the whole body, it has its principal seat in the brain, and it is there that it not only understands and imagines, but also senses. It does this by means of the nerves that stretch like filaments

from the brain to all the other members, with which they are so connected that we
316 can hardly touch any part of the human body without causing the extremities of
some of the nerves spread over it to be moved; and this motion passes to the other
extremities of those nerves collected in the brain around the seat of the soul, as I
have explained fully enough in Discourse Four of the *Dioptrics.*[4] But the motions,
that are thus excited in the brain by the nerves, affect the soul or mind, which is
intimately connected with the brain, in diverse ways according to the variety of
the motions themselves. And the various states of our mind, or thoughts that
immediately arise from these motions, are called sensory perceptions, or, in common language, sensations.

**190. The different kinds of sensation; first of the internal, that is, the
passions or emotions of the mind and of the natural appetites.**

The varieties of these sensations depend first on the difference in the nerves
themselves, and then on the differences of the motions occurring in the individual nerves. However, we do not have so many individual senses as individual
nerves; it is enough merely to distinguish seven different main kinds, two of
which belong to the internal senses, and five to the external. The nerves extending to the stomach, esophagus, throat, and the other internal parts serving the satisfaction of our natural wants, constitute one of our internal senses, called the
natural appetite. The minute nerves extending to the heart and the neighborhood
of the heart operate on the other internal sense embracing all the emotions of the
mind or passions, and emotions such as joy, sadness, love, hate, and the like. For,
to take an example, when the blood is pure and well tempered, so that it dilates
in the heart more readily and strongly than usual, this so enlarges and moves the
little nerves scattered around the openings, that there is, as a result, a correspon-
317 ding motion in the brain affecting the mind with a certain natural sense of cheer-
fulness; and as often as these same nerves are moved in the same way, even
although it is from other causes, they excite in us this same feeling. Thus the
imagination of the attainment of some good does not contain in itself the feeling
of joy, but it causes the animal spirits to pass from the brain to the muscles in
which these nerves are embedded; and thus dilating the openings of the heart, it
causes these small nerves to move in a manner that necessarily produces the sensation of joy. When we are given news, the mind first judges of it, and if it is
good it rejoices with an intellectual joy independent of any bodily disturbance—
which the Stoics did not deny to their wise man <although they wished to regard
him as free from all passion>. But as soon as this spiritual joy proceeds to the
imagination, the spirits flow from the brain to the muscles about the heart and
these excite a motion in the small nerves by which another motion is excited in
the brain giving the soul the feeling of animal joy. In the same way when the
blood is so thick that it flows sluggishly into the ventricles of the heart, and is not
there sufficiently dilated, it excites in the same nerves a motion quite different
from the preceding, which, communicated to the brain, gives a sensation of sadness to the mind, although it is itself perhaps ignorant of the cause of the sadness.

4. AT VI, 109–14.

And the other causes <which move these little nerves in the same way> may likewise give the same sensation to the soul. But the other movements of the same small nerves produce other emotions, such as those of love, hate, fear, anger, etc. insofar as they are merely emotions or passions of the mind, that is, insofar as they are confused thoughts which the mind does not have from itself alone, but because it is intimately united to the body, receiving its impressions therefrom. For there is the greatest difference between these and the distinct thoughts we have of what ought to be loved, chosen, or shunned <although they are often found together>. The natural appetites such as hunger, thirst, etc., are likewise feelings excited in the mind by means of the nerves of the stomach, throat, etc., *318* and are entirely different from the will which we have to eat, drink, etc. <and to do all that we think proper for the conservation of the body>; but because this will or appetition nearly always accompanies them, they are called appetites.

191. The external senses, and first the sense of touch.

As regards the external senses, everyone acknowledges five, because there are five different kinds of objects that stimulate the nerves which are their organs, and because there is the same number of kinds of confused thoughts excited in the soul by these motions in the nerves. In the first place there are nerves terminating in the skin all over the body. The skin serves as a medium by which the nerves can come into contact with any material body whatever, and be moved by these bodies, in one way by their hardness, in another by their gravity, in another by their heat, in another by their humidity, etc.; and these nerves excite as many different sensations in the mind as there are different modes by which they are moved, or their ordinary motion is prevented, and from this a corresponding number of tactile qualities derive their names. In addition, when these nerves are moved a little more vehemently than usual, and yet in such a way that our body is in no way injured, this causes a sense of gratification which is naturally agreeable to the mind, inasmuch as it gives evidence of the powers of the body to which it is closely joined. But if this action <is strong enough to> cause our body to be hurt in some way, that gives us a sensation of pain and in this way we see why bodily pleasure and pain, though absolutely contrary sensations, are almost similar in the objects causing them.

192. Taste.

Then the other nerves spread over the tongue and the neighboring parts are variously moved by the particles of the bodies which are separate from one another and float in the saliva in the mouth, and thus cause the various tastes to be felt according to the variety of their own shapes.

193. Smell.

Third, two nerves or appendages to the brain (for they do not go beyond the skull), are moved by the corporeal particles separated and floating in the air—not *319* indeed by any particles whatsoever, but only by those which, when drawn into the nostrils, are subtle and lively enough to enter the pores of the bones, so-called spongy, and thus reach the nerves. And from the various motions of these particles, the various sensations of smell arise.

194. Hearing.

Fourthly, two other nerves hidden in the internal cavities of the ears receive the tremors and vibrations of all the surrounding air, for the air agitating the small membranes of the tympanum at the same time disturbs a chain of little bones which are attached to it, and to which these nerves adhere, and from the variety of these movements the sensations of different sounds arise.

195. Sight.

Finally, the extremities of the optic nerves, making up the coating in the eyes called the retina, are not moved by the air, nor by any other material object, but only by the globules of the second element, from which we derive the sensation of light and colors, as I have already sufficiently explained in the *Dioptrics* and *Meteors*.[5]

196. The soul does not feel except insofar as it is in the brain.

It is however easily proved that the soul feels those things affecting the body not insofar as it is in each member of the body, but only insofar as it is in the brain <where the nerves by their movements convey to it the various actions of the external objects touching the parts of the body in which they are embedded>. For, in the first place, there are many illnesses which, although they affect the brain alone, yet either disorder or altogether take away from us the use of our senses; just like sleep itself, which affects the brain alone, and yet every day during a great part of the time takes from us our sensory faculties, which are afterwards restored to us on awakening. Secondly, from the fact that although the brain is healthy <as are the members in which the organs of the external senses are to be found>, if the paths by which the nerves pass from the external parts to the brain are obstructed, that sensation is lost in these members. And finally, we sometimes feel pain as if it were in certain of our members, and yet its cause is not in these members where it is felt, but in others through which pass the nerves extending to the brain from the parts where the pain is felt. And I could prove this by innumerable experiments; however, here one will suffice. When a girl suffering from a serious infection of the hand was seen by a surgeon, the custom was followed to bandage her eyes lest she would be upset by seeing the dressing. After some days, as gangrene set in, her arm had to be cut off from the elbow and several linen cloths tied together were substituted in place of the amputated limb, so that she was quite unaware of what had been done; meanwhile, however, she had various pains, sometimes in one of the fingers of the hand that had been cut off, and sometimes in another. This could clearly happen only because the nerves

320

---

5. *Dioptrics,* Discourse 6, AT VI, 130–47; *Meteors,* Discourses 8–10, AT VI, 325–66.

which previously had been carried all the way from the brain to the hand, and afterwards terminated in the arm near the elbow, were affected there in the same way as it was their function to be stimulated for the purpose of impressing the sensation of pain in this and that finger on the mind residing in the brain. <And this shows clearly that pain in the hand is not felt by the mind insofar as it is in the hand, but as it is in the brain.>

197. Mind is of such a nature that from the motion of the body alone various sensations can be excited in it.

It can also be proved that our mind is of such a nature that motions in the body are alone sufficient to cause it to have all sorts of thoughts with no likeness to any of the motions that give rise to them; and especially that there may be excited in it those confused thoughts called feelings or sensations. For we see that words, whether uttered by the voice or merely written, excite in our minds all sorts of thoughts and emotions. On the same paper, with a pen and ink, by moving the point of the pen ever so little over the paper in a certain way, we can form letters   *321* that bring to the minds of our readers thoughts of battles, tempests, or furies, and the emotions of indignation and sadness; while if the pen is moved in another, hardly different way, thoughts may be given of quite a different kind, namely, those of tranquillity, peace, pleasantness, and the quite opposite emotions of love and joy. Someone will perhaps reply that writing and speech do not immediately excite any emotions in the mind, or images of things different from the letters and sounds, but as it were various acts of the understanding; and from these the mind, making them the occasions, then constructs for itself the images of various things. But what will we say of the sensations of pain and pleasure? If a sword moved toward our body cuts it, from this alone pain results which is certainly no less different from the local motion of the sword or of the part of the body that is cut, than are color or sound or smell or taste. And therefore, as we see clearly that the sensation of pain is easily excited in us merely from the local motion of our body in contact with another body, we may conclude that our mind is of such a nature that certain local motions can excite in it all the other sensations.

198. There is nothing known of external objects by the senses but their shape, size, or motion.

In addition, we observe no difference in the nerves that may cause us to judge that some convey one thing rather than another to the brain from the organs of the external sense, nor again that anything is conveyed there except the local motion of the nerves themselves. And we see that this local motion excites in us not only the sensations of pleasure or pain, but also those of sound and light. For if we receive a blow in the eye hard enough for the vibration to reach the retina, we see   *322* myriads of sparks which are still not outside our eye; and when we place our finger on our ear, we hear a murmuring sound whose cause cannot be attributed to anything but the agitation of the air trapped within it. Finally we can likewise frequently observe that heat and other sensible qualities, inasmuch as they are in objects, and also the forms of purely material things, such as those of fire, are produced in them by the motions of certain other bodies, and that these again also produce other motions in other bodies. And we can very well conceive how the motion of one body can be caused by that of another, and diversified by the size, shape, and motion of its parts, but we can in no way understand how these same things (namely, size, shape, and motion) can produce something entirely different in nature from themselves, like those substantial forms and real qualities many suppose to exist in bodies; nor likewise can we understand how these forms or qualities have the power to produce motion in other bodies. But since we know that our soul is of such a nature that the various motions of body suffice to produce in it all the various sensations it has, and as we see by experience that some of the sensations are really caused by such motions, though we do not find anything but these motions to pass through the organs of the external senses to the brain, we may conclude that we in no way likewise apprehend that in external objects like light, color, smell, taste, sound, heat, cold, and the other tactile qual-

323   ities, or what are called their substantial forms, there is anything but the various dispositions of these objects which have the power of moving our nerves in various ways.

199. There is no phenomenon in nature that has not been dealt with in this treatise.

And thus by a simple enumeration it may be deduced that there is no phenomenon in nature whose treatment has been omitted in this treatise. For there is nothing that can be counted as a phenomenon of nature, except what is apprehended by the senses. And with the exception of motion, size, and shape, which are to be found in every body, we perceive nothing outside us by means of our senses, but light, color, smell, taste, sound, and tactile qualities; and I have just proved that these are nothing more, as far as is known to us, than certain dispositions of objects consisting of size, shape, and motion <so that there is nothing in all the visible world, insofar as it is merely visible or sensible, but the things I have explained there>.

200. There are no principles in this treatise not accepted by all men; this philosophy is not new, but is the most ancient and most common of all.

But I also want it to be noted that although I have tried here to give an explanation of the whole nature of material things, I have nevertheless made use of no principle that has not been approved by Aristotle and by all the other philosophers of every age; so that this philosophy, instead of being new, is the most ancient and common of all. For I have only considered the shape, motion, and size of each body, and examined what must follow from their mutual interaction according to the laws of mechanics, confirmed as they are by certain and daily experience. But no one ever doubted that bodies move and have various sizes and shapes, according to the difference of which their motions also vary, and that from mutual collision those that are larger are divided into many smaller, and thus change their shape. We have experience of this not only by a single sense, but by several, for example, by touch, sight, and hearing; we also distinctly imagine and understand this. This cannot be said of other things that come under our senses, such as colors, sounds, and the like, which are perceived not by means of several senses, but by single ones; for their images are always confused in our minds, and we do not know what they are. *324*

201. *Certain sensible bodies are composed of imperceptible particles.*

I consider that in each body there are many particles that cannot be perceived by our senses, and this perhaps will not be approved by those who take their senses as a measure of the things they can know. <But it seems to me to be doing great wrong to human reason if we do not consider that knowledge goes beyond what we see>; for no one can doubt that there are bodies so small that they cannot be perceived by any of our senses, if only we consider what is added each moment to those bodies increasing little by little, and what is removed from those diminishing in the same fashion. We see a tree grow day by day, and it is impossible to understand how it becomes larger than it was before, except by conceiving that some body is added to it. But who has ever observed by means of the senses the small bodies added each day to the plant that grows? Those at least who hold quantity to be indefinitely divisible should acknowledge that the particles may become so small as to be absolutely imperceptible. And indeed it should not be wondered at that we are unable to perceive very minute bodies, for the nerves, which must be set in motion by objects in order to produce a sensation, are not very minute, but are like small cords consisting of a quantity of yet smaller fibers, and thus they cannot be moved by very minute bodies. Nor do I think that anyone who uses his reason will deny that we do much better to understand what takes place in small bodies, whose minuteness prevents us from perceiving them, by what we see occurring in those that we do perceive <and thus explain everything in nature, as I have tried to do in this treatise>. This is preferable to explaining certain things by inventing all sorts of novelties with no relation to those that are perceived <such as prime matter, substantial forms, and all the whole range of qualities which many are in the habit of assuming, any one of which is more difficult to understand than all the things they are supposed to explain>. *325*

202. *The philosophy of Democritus is no less different from ours than from the commonly accepted one <of Aristotle and others>.*

But Democritus also imagined that there were certain corpuscles that had various shapes, sizes, and motions, from whose conglomeration and interaction all sensible bodies arose; and nevertheless by common consent his philosophy is universally rejected. To this I reply that it was never rejected by anyone because he considered particles smaller than those that can be perceived by the senses in bodies and attributed to them various sizes, shapes, and motions, for no one can doubt that there are in reality many such particles, as has already been shown. But this philosophy was rejected, in the first place because it presupposed certain indivisible corpuscles—a hypothesis I also completely reject; in the second place it was rejected because Democritus imagined a void around them, which I demonstrate to be an impossibility; in the third place because he attributed to them gravity, the existence of which I deny in any body insofar as it is considered by itself, because it depends on the relation of position and motion that bodies bear to one another; and finally because he had not explained in detail how all things arose from the interaction of the corpuscles alone, or, if he explained it in regard to certain cases, his explanations were not consistent. If we may judge from those of his opinions that have been preserved, this at least is the verdict we must give on his philosophy. I leave it to others to judge as to whether what I have written in philosophy has been sufficiently coherent <and whether it is fertile enough in yielding conclusions for us. As for the consideration of shape, size, and motion, this has been admitted by Aristotle and all other philosophers, as well as by Democritus, and as I reject all of Democritus'suppositions, with this one exception, while I reject practically all that has been supposed by the others, it is clear that this method of philosophizing has no more affinity with that of Democritus than with any of the other particular sects.>

203. How we may arrive at a knowledge of the shapes, <sizes>, and motions of the imperceptible particles of bodies.

But since I assign determinate shapes, sizes, and motions to the imperceptible particles of bodies, as if I had seen them, but admit that they do not fall under the senses, someone will perhaps ask how I have come to my knowledge of them. To this I reply that I first considered generally the simplest and best understood principles implanted in our mind by nature, and examined the principal differences that could be found between the sizes, shapes, and positions of bodies imperceptible on account of their smallness alone, and what observable effects could be produced by the various ways in which they impinge on one another. And finally, when I found like effects in the bodies perceived by our senses, I considered that they might have been produced from a similar interaction of such bodies, especially as no other way of explaining them could be suggested. And for this end the example of certain artifacts was of use to me, for I can see no difference between these and natural bodies, except that the effects of machines depend for the most part on the operation of certain <tubes, springs, or other> instruments, which, since men necessarily make them, must always be large enough to be capable of being easily perceived by the senses. The effects of natural causes, on the other hand, almost always depend on certain organs minute enough to escape our senses. And it is certain that there are no rules in mechanics that do not hold good in physics, of which mechanics forms a part or species <so that all that is artificial is also natural>; for it is not less natural for a clock, made of the proper number of wheels, to indicate the hours, than for a tree which has sprung from this or that seed, to produce a particular fruit. Accordingly, just as those who apply themselves to the consideration of automata, when they know the use of a certain machine and see some of its parts, easily infer from these the manner in which others they have not seen are made, so from considering the sensible effects and parts of natural bodies, I have tried to discover the nature of the imperceptible causes and particles contained in them.

204. With regard to the things our senses do not perceive, it is sufficient   *327*
to explain their possible natures, though perhaps they are not what we
describe them to be <and this is all that Aristotle has tried to do>.

But here it may be said that although I have shown how all natural things can be formed, we have no right to conclude on this account that they were produced by these causes. For just as there may be two clocks made by the same crafts-man, which although they indicate the time equally well and are externally in all respects alike, yet in no way resemble one another in the composition of their wheels, so doubtless there are many different ways in which all things we see could be formed by the great artificer <without its being possible for the mind of man to be aware which of these means he has chosen to use>. This I most freely admit; and I believe that I have done all that is required of me if the causes I have assigned are such that they correspond to all the phenomena manifested by nature <without inquiring whether it is by their means or by others that they are produced>. And it will be sufficient for the needs of life to know such causes, for medicine and mechanics, and in general all these arts that can be developed with the use of physics, have for their end only perceptible effects that are accordingly to be counted among the phenomena of nature. And in case it is supposed that Aristotle did, or desired to do, more than this, it must be remembered that he expressly says in the first book of the *Meteorology,* in the beginning of the sev-enth chapter, that with regard to things not manifest to the senses, he considers that he supplies sufficient explanations and demonstrations of them, if he merely shows that they may be such as he explains them to be.

205. Nevertheless there is a moral certainty that everything is such as it has
been shown to be.

But nevertheless, that I may not injure the truth, we must consider <two kinds of certainty and> first of all what has moral certainty; that is, a certainty that suf-fices for the conduct of life, though if we regard the absolute power of God, what is morally certain may be uncertain. <So those who have never visited Rome do not doubt its being a city in Italy, although it may very well be that everyone who has told them this has deceived them.> If, for instance, anyone wishing to read a letter written in Latin but encoded so that the characters are not placed in their proper order, takes it into his head to read B wherever he finds A and C where he   *328* finds B, thus substituting for each letter the one following it in the alphabet, and if in this way he finds that there are certain Latin words composed of these, he will not doubt that the true meaning of the writing is contained in these words. It is true that he discovers this by conjecture, and it is possible that the writer did not arrange the letters in this order of succession, but in some other, and thus con-cealed another meaning in it; this is so unlikely to occur, <especially when the

coded message contains many words,> that it may seem incredible. But they who observe how many things regarding the magnet, fire, and the fabric of the whole world are here deduced from a very small number of principles, even if they thought that I took up these principles at random and without good grounds, may still acknowledge that it could hardly happen that so much would be coherent if they were false.

206. We possess even more than a moral certainty.

And further there are some, even among natural things, that we regard to be absolutely, and more than morally, certain. This certainty is founded on the metaphysical ground that as God is supremely good and cannot err, the faculty he has given us of distinguishing truth from falsehood, cannot lead us into error so long as we use it properly and thereby perceive something distinctly by means of it. Of this nature are mathematical demonstrations, the knowledge that material things exist, and the evidence of all clear reasoning that is carried on about them. Among these truths it seems to me there should be counted those conclusions which have been arrived at in this treatise, if people consider that they are derived in a continual series from the first and simplest principles of human knowledge. And this is especially so, if it is sufficiently understood that we can *329* perceive no external objects unless some local motion is excited by them in our nerves, and that such motion cannot be excited by the fixed stars, owing to their immense distance from us, unless a motion is also produced in them, and in the whole intervening heavens; once this is accepted, all the other phenomena, at least the more general things I have advanced about the world and earth, cannot be understood except in the way I have explained them.

207. Nevertheless all my opinions are submitted to the authority of the church.

At the same time, recalling my insignificance, I affirm nothing, but submit all these things to the authority of the Catholic Church, and to the judgment of those wiser than myself; and I wish no one to believe anything I have written, unless he is personally persuaded by the force and evidence of reason.

VIII

LATE WORKS AND CORRESPONDENCE (1645 ON)

To Mesland, On Freedom (February 9, 1645)

As to free will, I agree entirely with what the Reverend Father has written. And *IV, 173* to explain my opinion still more clearly, I desire first of all that it be observed that *indifference* seems to me, strictly speaking, to denote that state in which the will finds itself, when it is not carried by the knowledge of what is true or what is good to follow one side rather than the other. And it is in this sense that I was taking it when I said that the lowest degree of freedom consisted in allowing ourselves to be determined to things to which we are wholly indifferent. But perhaps there are others who mean by this word *indifference* that positive faculty we have of determining one or the other of two contraries, that is, of pursuing or fleeing, of affirming or denying a particular thing. I did not deny that this positive faculty is in the will. Indeed, I think it is there, not only whenever it is not at all carried by the weight of any argument to one side rather than to another, but even when this faculty is involved in all the other actions of the will, so that it is never determined without using that faculty. Thus, even when a very evident argument carries us to something, even though, *morally* speaking, it is difficult for us to do the contrary, nevertheless, speaking *absolutely,* we can do it. For we are always free to prevent ourselves from pursuing a good clearly known to us or from admitting an evident truth, provided only that we think it a good to witness in this way the freedom of our will.

Further, it must be observed that freedom can be considered in the actions of the will either before they are accomplished or at the very moment when they are being accomplished.

Now considered in the actions of the will before they have been accomplished, freedom implies indifference understood in the second sense, but not in the first. When we oppose our own judgment to orders received from others, we tell ourselves that we are freer when we do what no one else has ordered us to *174* do, and when we follow our own judgment, than when we do what is forbidden to us. However, we cannot speak in the same way when we oppose our own judgment and our own items of knowledge, and say that we are freer to do those things that seem to us neither good nor evil, or in which we see as many arguments for good as for evil, than we are to do those things in which we see much more good than evil.

In fact, greater freedom consists either in a greater facility of self-determination or in a greater use of that positive power we have to follow the worse while

---

Selections on pp. 281–92 and 297–323 translated by Elizabeth S. Haldane and G.R.T. Ross and substantially revised by Marjorie Grene and Roger Ariew. All other selections in this section translated by Marjorie Grene and Roger Ariew.

seeing the better. If we follow the side where we see more good, we determine ourselves more easily. But if we follow the opposite side, we make more use of our positive power. And thus we can always act more freely in the things in which we see more good than evil, than in the things we call *adiaphora* or indifferent. In this sense also we can say that the things we are ordered to do by others and which we would otherwise not do ourselves, we do less freely than we do those we have not been ordered to do. For the judgment that they are difficult to do is opposed to the judgment that it is good to do what one is ordered to do, and the more these two judgments move us equally, the more they confer on us indifference taken in the first sense.

On the other hand, considered in the actions of the will while they are being accomplished, freedom does not imply any indifference, whether we take it in the first or the second sense, since what is done cannot remain undone, given that one does it. But freedom consists only in the facility of execution, and thus free, spontaneous, and voluntary are all one and the same thing. It is in this sense that I wrote that I was carried so much the more freely toward something, the more I was impelled toward it by arguments, for it is certain that our will then moves with more facility and impetus.

175

To Clerselier,[1] Concerning Principles (June or July 1646)

IV, 443 The hope I had of soon being in Paris is the reason why I am less concerned about writing to those whom I hope to have the honor of seeing there. Thus it is already some time since I received what you took the trouble of writing to me. But I thought you would not be too worried about having a reply to the question

444 you put to me about the problem of what should be taken as the first principle, since you yourself have already replied to it better than I could have done.

I add simply that the word "principle" can be taken in various senses. It is one thing to seek for a common notion so clear and so general that it can serve as principle for proving the existence of all beings, or *entities,* that are yet to be known, and another to search for a being whose existence is better known to us than that of any other, so that it can serve as principle for our knowledge of them.

In the first sense, it can be said that *"it is impossible for the same thing to be and not to be at the same time"* is a principle. It can serve, in general, not strictly to make known the existence of anything, but only to bring it about that, when we know it, we confirm its truth by such reasoning: it is impossible that what is, is not; and I know that a certain thing is; hence I know that it is impossible for it not to be. This has very little importance and does not make us any wiser.

In the other sense, the first principle is that our soul exists, since there is nothing whose existence is better known to us.

I also add that it is not a condition we ought to require of a first principle, that it be such that all other propositions can be reduced to or demonstrated from it.

---

1. Claude Clerselier (1614–1684) was a French government official and the first editor of Descartes's works and correspondence.

It is enough that it can be used to find several of them, and that there is no other on which this one depends, or which can be more easily discovered. For it is pos- *445* sible that there is nowhere in the world any principle to which alone all things can be reduced. And the way in which other propositions are reduced to this one: *it is impossible for the same thing to be and not be at the same time,* is superfluous and useless. On the other hand it is highly useful in assuring ourselves of the existence of God, and then of the existence of all created things, to start by the consideration of our own existence. [. . .]

*To the Marquis of Newcastle,*² About Animals (November 23, 1646)

[. . .] I wholly subscribe to Your Excellency's judgment about the chemists. I *IV, 569* believe they use words in an uncommon sense only to make it appear that they *570* know what they do not know. I also believe that what they say about the revival of flowers by their salt is only a fiction without foundation, and that their extracts have qualities other than those of the plants from which they are taken. We can experience this very clearly, given the fact that wine, vinegar, and brandy, which are three different extracts made from the same grapes, have such different tastes and qualities. Indeed, in my opinion, their salt, sulfur, and mercury differ from one another no more than do the four elements of the philosophers, or than water differs from ice, foam, or snow. For I think that all bodies are made of one and the same matter, and that there is nothing that makes any difference between them, except that the small parts of the matter that make up some shapes as distinct from others are arranged differently from those that make up the others. That is what I hope Your Excellency will find well explained at sufficient length in my *Principles of Philosophy,* which will soon be published in French. [. . .]

As for the intelligence or the thought that Montaigne³ and some others attrib- *573* ute to beasts, I cannot agree with them. Not that I am disturbed by the statement that men have an absolute empire over all the other animals; for I declare there are some stronger than us, and I believe there can be some which have a natural cunning capable of deceiving the subtlest men. But I consider that they imitate or surpass us only in such of our actions as are not controlled by our thought. For it often happens that we walk and that we eat without in any way thinking of what we are doing. And it is in this way, without using our reason, that we repel the things that hurt us and parry the blows aimed at us. In the same way, even if we expressly willed not to place our hands before our head when we happen to fall, we could not prevent ourselves from doing it. I also believe that, like the

---

2. William Cavendish (1592–1676) was a literary author and horseman, the husband of Margaret Cavendish, philosopher, and the brother of Charles Cavendish, lover of mathematics and patron of Thomas Hobbes.

3. Michel de Montaigne (1533–1592) was a reviver of Pyrrhonian skepticism and the author of the *Essays.*

beasts, we would [be able to] walk[4] without having learned to, if we had no thought. And they say that those who walk in their sleep sometimes swim across streams in which they would drown if awake. As for the movements of our passions, although they are accompanied by thought in us, since we have the faculty of thinking, it is nevertheless very evident that they do not depend on it, since they often arise in spite of ourselves. And consequently they can exist in animals, and even be more violent than they are in men, without our having to conclude from this that animals have thoughts.

574

In fact, there are none of our external actions that could assure those who examine them that our body is not simply a machine that moves itself, but contains a soul that has thoughts, were it not for words or other signs made in reference to topics that present themselves without relation to any passion. I say words or other signs, since the deaf use signs in the same way we use our voice. And I say that these signs must have reference to exclude the talk of parrots, but not that of madmen, which does not stop referring to the topics that occur, although it does not follow reason. And I add that words or signs must not be related to any passion, to exclude not only cries of joy and sorrow and the like, but also to exclude everything that can be taught by artifice to animals. For if you teach a magpie to say hello to its mistress when it sees her come in, it can be done only by making the utterance of this word become the motion of one of its passions. For instance, this will be a motion of the hope it has of eating, if it has habitually been given a tidbit when it says the word. And all the other things as well that people make dogs, horses, and monkeys do, are only movements of their fear, their hope, or their joy, in such a way that they can perform them without any thought. But it is, in my view, most remarkable that speech, thus defined, is fit for man alone. For even though Montaigne and Charron[5] have said that there is more difference between man and man than between man and beast, there has nevertheless never been found any beast so perfect that it used some sign to make other animals understand something that had no relation at all to its passions. And there is no man so imperfect that he does not do this—so that those who are deaf and dumb invent special signs by which they express their thoughts. This seems to me a very strong argument to prove that what brings it about that beasts do not speak as we do is that they have no thought, and not that they lack the organs for it. And it cannot be said that we speak to one another but that we do not understand them. For, as dogs and some other animals express their passions to us, they would surely express their thoughts as well, if they had any.

575

I know well that beasts do many things better than we do, but I am not surprised at that. For that very fact serves to prove that they act naturally and by springs, like a clock, which tells the time better than our judgment can tell us. And there is no doubt that when the swallows come in the spring, they act in this like clocks. All that honeybees do is of the same nature, as well as the order

---

4. Reading *marcherions* for *mangerions*.

5. Pierre Charron (1541–1603) was a follower of Montaigne. A selection of his main work, *De la Sagesse* (1601, 1604), can be found in Ariew, Cottingham, and Sorell, pp. 51–67.

maintained by cranes in flying, and that of monkeys in fighting, if it is true that they observe an order. Moreover, the instinct to bury their dead is not stranger   *576* than that of dogs and cats, which scratch the earth to bury their excrement, although they hardly ever do bury it—which shows that they do it only by instinct, and without thinking about it. The most one can say is that although animals do not act in any way that assures us they think, since the organs of their bodies are not very different from ours, it can be conjectured that there is some thought attached to those organs, such as we experience in ours, although theirs is much less perfect. To this I have nothing to reply, except that, if they thought as we do, they would have an immortal soul as we do. But that is not probable, since there is no reason to believe this of some animals without believing it of all of them, and there are some too imperfect for us to be able to believe this of them, like the oysters, sponges, etc.

To Chanut, On Nicholas Cusa and the Infinite (June 6, 1647)[6]

As I was passing through here on my way to France, I learned from M. Brasset[7]   *V, 50* that he had sent your letters to Egmond, and although my trip was urgent, I decided to wait for them. But since they were received at my lodgings three hours after I had left, they were sent on to me at once. I found in them great proofs of your friendship and your tact. I was frightened, in reading the first pages, to learn that M. du Rier had spoken to the queen about one of my letters, and that she had asked to see it. Afterward, I was reassured when I came to the place where you write that she heard it read with some satisfaction. I do not know whether I was more filled with admiration that she had so easily understood   *51* things that the most learned consider very obscure, or with joy that my letters had not displeased her. But my admiration was redoubled when I saw the force and the weight of the objections that Her Majesty had noted concerning the size I attributed to the universe. And I wished that your letter had found me in my usual quarters, since I could better collect my mind there than in the room of an inn, and so I could have disentangled myself a bit better from such a difficult and judiciously posed question. However, I do not claim that this gives me an excuse; and, providing I am allowed to think that it is to you alone that I am writing, so that veneration and respect do not confuse my imagination too much, I will force myself to put down here all I can say on this topic.

---

6. Hector-Pierre Chanut (1601–1662) was a French diplomat and brother-in-law of Clerselier. He was appointed French ambassador to Sweden in 1649 and persuaded Descartes to accept Queen Christina's invitation to her court. Queen Christina is, of course, the queen referred to in the letter; du Rier was her physician. Nicholas Cusa (1401–1464) was a theologian who became cardinal (1446). His views on the infinity of the world can be found in *De docta ignorantia,* II, chap. 1, and *Idiota de mente,* chap. 2 and 3. Notwithstanding what Descartes asserts about him, Cusa's views on the infinite are remarkably like Descartes's.

7. The place Descartes refers to is The Hague; Brasset was French chargé d'affaires there.

In the first place, I remember that Cardinal Cusa and several other scholars have assumed the world to be infinite, without ever having been censured by the Church on this subject. On the contrary, it is thought to be honoring God to con-ceive of his works as very great. And my opinion is less difficult to accept than theirs, since I do not say that the world is *infinite,* but only *indefinite.* There is a remarkable enough difference between these two. For to say that something is infinite, we have to have some argument that makes us know it as such, and we can have that only in the case of God. But to say that it is indefinite, it is suffi-cient to have no argument by which the world can be proved to have limits. Thus it seems to me that we cannot prove, or even conceive, that there are limits in the matter of which the world is composed. For in examining the nature of that mat-ter, I find that it does not consist of anything except that it has extension in length, breadth, and depth, in such a way that everything that has these three dimensions is a part of that matter. And there cannot be any entirely empty space, that is, any space that does not contain any matter, since we cannot conceive of a space such that we do not conceive of these three dimensions in it, and hence of matter. But, in assuming the world to be finite, we already imagine beyond it some spaces that have their three dimensions, and thus are not purely imaginary, as the philosophers call them, but contain in themselves matter—matter which, not being able to be anywhere but in the world, makes it plain to see that the world extends beyond the limits we wished to attribute to it. Thus, having no argument to prove, and not even being able to conceive, that the world has lim-its, I call it *indefinite.* But for all that I cannot deny that it may perhaps have some limits known by God, although they are incomprehensible to me: this is why I do not say absolutely that it is *infinite.*

When its extension is considered in this way, if it is compared with its dura-tion, it seems to me that it only gives us occasion to think that there is no time imaginable before the creation of the world in which God could not have created it, if he had wished to. I do not think that we have any grounds for concluding that he did in fact create it an indefinitely long time ago, since the actual or true existence that the world has had for 5,000 or 6,000 years is not necessarily con-nected with the possible or imaginary existence that it could have had before that, in the way that the actual existence of the spaces one conceives of around a globe (that is, taking the world as *finite*) is connected with the actual existence of that same globe. Further, if from the indefinite extension of the world we could infer the eternity of its duration with regard to time past, we could still better infer the eternity of the duration it would have in the future. For faith teaches us that, although the earth and the heavens will perish, that is, will change their appear-ance, nevertheless the world, that is, the matter of which they are composed, will never perish. This is apparent from the fact that faith promises an eternal life to our bodies after the resurrection, and consequently also to the world in which they will exist. But from that infinite duration that the world will have in the future, it cannot be inferred that it has always been from all eternity, since all the moments of duration are independent of one another.

As for the prerogatives that religion accords to man, and which seem difficult to believe in if the extension of the universe is supposed to be indefinite, they deserve some explanation. For even though we can say that all created things are made for us insofar as we can derive some advantage from them, still I do not know that we are obliged to believe that man is the goal of the creation. Yet it is said that *all things are made for his (that is, for God's) sake,* that it is God   *54* alone who is the final as well as the efficient cause of the universe. And as far as creatures are concerned, insofar as they are reciprocally of use to one another, each one can claim this advantage, that all those of use to it are made for its sake. It is true that the six days of creation are described in Genesis in such a way that man seems to be its principal subject. But we can say that since this story of Genesis was written for man, it is chiefly things that concern him that the Holy Ghost wanted to specify and that he did not speak there of anything except as they related to man. And because preachers, taking care to urge us to the love of God, are accustomed to represent to us the various uses we can derive from other creatures, and say that God made them for us, and do not make us consider the other ends for which it could also be said that he made them, because that is irrelevant to their topic, we are much inclined to believe that they were made only for us. But the preachers go further. For they say that every man in particular is indebted to Jesus Christ for all the blood he shed on the cross, just as if he had died only for a single person. In this they do indeed speak the truth; but, as that does not prevent his having redeemed by that same blood a very great number of other men, so I do not see that the mystery of the incarnation, and all the other advantages that God has given to man, prevent his   *55* having given an infinity of other great goods to an infinity of other creatures. And although I do not at all on that account infer that there are intelligent creatures in the stars or elsewhere, I do not see, either, that there is any argument by which it could be proved that there are none. But I always leave undecided questions of that sort, rather than denying or affirming anything about them. It seems to me that no other difficulty remains, except for our having believed for a long time that we have great advantages over other creatures. This makes it appear that we are losing all our advantages when we alter our opinion. But I distinguish between those of our goods that can be lessened through others' possessing similar goods, and those that cannot be so lessened. Thus a man who had a thousand *pistoles* would be very rich, if there were no other people in the world who had as much, and the same person would be poor if everyone else had more. And in this way all the praiseworthy qualities give more glory to those who have them when they occur in fewer people. That is why it is customary to envy the glory and riches of another. But virtue, knowledge, health, and in general all the other goods, considered in themselves, not in relation to honor, are no less in us if they are also found in many others. That is why we have no reason to be angry that they exist in many others. But the goods that can exist in all the intelligent creatures of an indefinitely large world are of this number.   *56* They do not lessen those we possess. On the contrary, when we love God, and through him join ourselves willingly to all the things he has created, the more we conceive of them as greater, nobler, more perfect, the more we also esteem ourselves, since we are part of a more finished whole, and the more we have reason to praise God because of the immensity of his works. When Holy Scripture speaks in various places of the innumerable multitude of angels, it completely confirms this opinion. For we judge that the least of angels are incomparably more perfect than men. And the astronomers who, when they measure the size of the stars, find them much larger than the earth, also confirm this. For if, from the indefinite extension of the world, we infer that it must have inhabitants elsewhere than on earth, we can infer this also from the extension that all the astronomers attribute to it—since there is no one of them who does not judge that the earth is smaller in comparison to the whole of the heavens than a grain of sand is in comparison to a mountain.

I now pass to our question concerning the causes that often incline us to love one person rather than another, before we know his merit. And about this I note two things, one of which is in the mind and the other in the body. But as for the one only in the mind, it presupposes so many things concerning the nature of our souls, that I should not dare to undertake to deduce them in a letter. I will speak only of that of the body. It consists in the disposition of the parts of our brain, whether that disposition has been placed there by the objects of the senses, of from some other cause. For the objects that touch our senses move some parts of our brain through the mediation of the nerves, and there make, as it were, some folds, which are unfolded when the object stops acting. But the part where they were made afterward remains apt to be folded again in the same way by any object that somehow resembles the former object, even it does not resemble it in everything. For example, when I was a child, I loved a girl of my age who had a slight squint. By this means the impression made by sight in my brain when I looked at her cross-eyes, became so closely linked to what aroused in me the passion of love, that for a long time afterward, when I saw people with a squint, I felt more inclined to love them than others, just because they had that deficiency. Nevertheless, I did not know that was the reason. On the contrary, after I had reflected on it, and had recognized that this was a deficiency, I was no longer moved by it. Thus, when we are moved to love someone without knowing the reason, we may believe that this is because he has some similarity to something in another object we have previously loved, without our knowing what it was. And although it is usually a perfection rather than a defect that thus attracts us to love, still, since it can sometimes be a defect, as in the example I mentioned, a wise man must not give in entirely to this passion before he has considered the merit of the person for whom we feel ourselves moved. But since we cannot love equally all those in whom we find equal merit, I believe we are obliged to esteem them equally. And since the chief good of life is to have affection for some, we are right to prefer those to whom our secret inclinations join us, provided that we also observe some merit in them. Further, when our secret inclinations have their cause in the mind, and not in the body, I believe they should always be followed. And the chief mark that makes them known is that those that come from the mind are reciprocal, which does not happen often to the others.

Notes Directed Against a Certain Program Published in Belgium at the End of the Year 1647 Under This Title: An Explanation of the Human Mind or Rational Soul: In Which It Is Shown What It Is and What It May Be (1648)

VIIIb

A few days ago I received two pamphlets attacking me,[8] one openly and *341* directly, the other covertly and indirectly. The first does not trouble me much. Indeed, I am indebted to the author for the very fact that with all his inordinate labor he has succeeded in collecting nothing but groundless quibbles and slanders that no one could believe. Thus, he has shown clearly that he could find nothing in my writings to which he could reasonably take exception and has confirmed their truth better than he would have done by praising them; and moreover he has effected this at the expense of his own reputation. The other pamphlet troubles me more, though I am not mentioned openly in the discussion and it is published without the name of its author or printer; for it contains opin- *342* ions I judge most pernicious and false and is issued in the name of a Program which may be affixed to church doors and exposed to the view of any chance reader. It is said, moreover, that it was printed in another form, under the name of a certain individual whose doctrine is believed by many to be identical with my own. As a result, I am forced to expose his errors, so that they may not be attributed to me by those who happen to come across these papers and who have not read any of my writings.

The following is the *Program* in its latest form:

AN EXPLANATION of the Human Mind or Rational Soul: in which it is shown what it is, and what it may be.

1. *The human mind is that by which acts of thought are first accomplished by man; it consists of the faculty of thinking, or internal principle, alone.*

2. *As far as the nature of things are concerned, they seem to allow that the mind may be either a substance, or a mode of a corporeal substance; or, if we follow some other philosophers who state that extension and thought are attributes inherent in certain substances, as in subjects, then, since these attributes are not mutually opposed but different, there is no* *343* *reason why mind should not be an attribute coexisting in the same subject with extension, though the one attribute is not included in the concept of the other. Whatever we can conceive of can exist. But mind can be conceived of, so that it can be any one of the aforesaid, for none of them involves a contradiction. Therefore it may be any one of these things.*

3. *Hence those who assert that we conceive of the human mind clearly and distinctly, as though it were necessarily and really distinct from the body, are in error.*

---

8. The first was *Consideratio theologica*, by Jacobus Revius, and the second the anonymous *Programma*, by Regius, reproduced by Descartes in these *Notes*.

4. *The fact that mind is in truth nothing other than a substance, or an entity really distinct from body, in actuality separable from it, and capable of existing apart and independently, is revealed to us in the Holy Scriptures in many places. And thus what, in the view of some, through the study of nature some may find doubtful, what is already placed beyond all doubt for us by the divine revelation in the Scriptures.*

5. *Nor is it any objection that we can have doubts about the existence of the body, but cannot have doubts about the existence of the mind. For this only proves that, as long as we can have doubt about the existence of the body, we cannot say that mind is a mode of body.*

344 6. *Although the human mind is a substance really distinct from body, nevertheless, as long as it is in the body, it is organic in all its actions. And therefore as there are diverse dispositions of the body, so there are correspondingly diverse processes of the mind.*

7. *Since mind is of a different nature from body and from the disposition of body, and cannot arise from this disposition, it is incorruptible.*

8. *Since in our conception of it, the mind has no parts or any extension, it is useless to speculate whether it exists as a whole in the whole or as a whole in each individual part.*

9. *The mind can be affected in equal degree by imaginary and real things; hence, the study of nature leaves us doubtful whether any bodies are really perceived by us. But even this doubt is removed by divine revelation in the Scriptures, whereby it is beyond all doubt that God created heaven and earth, and all that is in them, and even now conserves them.*

10. *The bond that keeps body and soul in union is the law of the immutability of nature whereby every individual thing persists in the state in which it is, until it is thrown out of that state by some other thing.*

11. *As mind is a substance and is produced in the process of generation, the most accurate opinion seems to be that of those who hold that the rational soul is brought into existence by God, at generation, by an immediate act of creation.*

345

12. *The mind has no need of innate ideas, or notions, or axioms, but of itself the faculty of thinking suffices for performing its own acts.*

13. *Therefore all common notions, engraved on the mind, owe their origin to the observation of things or to tradition.*

14. *In fact the very idea of God implanted in the mind is the outcome of divine revelation, or tradition, or the observation of things.*

15. *Our concept of God, or the idea of God that exists in our mind, is not a strong enough argument to prove the existence of God, since it is not the case that all things of which we have concepts exist; and this idea, as conceived of by us, and imperfectly, does not, more than the concept of any other thing, transcend our proper powers of thought.*

16. *The thought of the mind is twofold: intellect and will.*

17. *Intellect is perception and judgment.*

18. *Perception is sense, memory, and imagination.*   *346*

19. *All sensation is the perception of some corporeal motion, which requires no intentional species, and it is effected, not in the external sense organs, but in the brain alone.*

20. *The will is free, and inclines indifferently to opposites in nature, as our self-consciousness bears us witness.*

21. *Will is self-determining, and is to be termed blind no more than vision is to be termed deaf.*

"No one more easily attains a great reputation for piety than the superstitious and the hypocritical."

An examination of the *Program*.

Notes to the Title.

I observe that in the title we are promised not just bare assertions regarding the rational soul, but an explanation of it, so that we must believe that in this pro-   *347* gram are contained all, or at least the principal arguments, which the author had, not only for proving his propositions, but also for unfolding them, and that no other arguments are to be expected from him. I approve of his calling the rational soul "the human mind," for thus he avoids the ambiguity of the word "soul" and in this point he follows me.

Notes to the Individual Articles.

In the first article he seems to aim with imperfect success at a definition of the rational soul, for he omits the genus (that is, that it is a substance, or a mode, or something else) and he expounds only the *differentia,* which he has borrowed from me, for no one before me, so far as I know, has asserted that the rational soul consists in one thing alone, namely the faculty of thinking or the internal principle by means of which we think.

In the second article he begins to speculate about its genus and says that "the nature of things seems to allow that the human mind may be either a substance or a mode of a corporeal substance."

This assertion involves a contradiction, no less than if he had said, "the nature of things allows that a mountain can exist with or without a valley." For a distinction must be drawn between things which from their nature can change—like the facts that I am at present either writing or not writing, that one man is prudent, another imprudent—and things which never change, such as are all the things that pertain to the essence of anything, as is generally acknowledged by philosophers. Of course there is no doubt that it can be said of contingent things   *348* that the nature of things permits these things to be either one way or another: for example, that I am at present either writing or not writing. But when the point at issue is the essence of something, it is manifestly foolish and contradictory to say that the nature of things allows that it may be in some other state except in the

one in which it really is. And it is no more of the nature of a mountain to be without a valley than it is of the nature of the human mind to be what it is, namely, a
substance, if it is a substance, or, indeed, a mode of a corporeal substance, if in
truth it is such a mode. Of this our author endeavors at this point to convince us,
and to prove it he throws in these words, "or if we are to follow some other
philosophers, etc.," while by "other philosophers" he obviously means me, for I
was the first to consider thought the principal attribute of incorporeal substance,
and extension the principal attribute of corporeal substance. But I did not say that
these attributes were in these substances as in subjects distinct from them. Here
we must take care not to understand the word "attribute" to mean simply "mode."
Whenever we see a quality assigned to anything by nature, whether it is a mode
susceptible to change, or the absolutely immutable essence of that thing, we call
that quality its attribute. Thus there are many attributes in God, but no modes.
Thus, too, one of the attributes of any substance is that it exists *per se*. The extension of any body can, within itself, admit various modes, for if a body is spheri-
cal, that is one mode of its extension, and another if it is square; but extension
itself, which is the subject of these modes, is not in itself a mode of corporeal
substance, but an attribute, which constitutes the essence and nature of material
substance. Thus, finally, there are various modes of thought, for affirmation is a
different mode of thought from negation, and so on; but thought itself, being the
internal principle from which these modes arise, and in which they are inherent,
is not conceived of as a mode, but as an attribute which constitutes the nature of
a substance. Whether this substance is corporeal or incorporeal is the question at
present before us.

349

He adds that "these attributes are not mutually opposed, but different." Again
there is a contradiction in these words, for when the question concerns attributes
that constitute the essence of substances, there can be no greater opposition
between them than the fact that they are different. Once it is admitted that "this
is different from that," it is equivalent to saying that "this is not that"; but to be
and not to be are contraries. "Since these attributes are not mutually opposed,"
he says, "but different, there is no reason why mind should not be an attribute
coexisting in the same subject with extension, though the one attribute is not
included in the concept of the other." In these words there is an obvious fallacy,
for he comes to a conclusion with regard to every possible attribute, which can
be valid only in the case of modes properly so called; and yet he nowhere proves
that the mind, or internal principle of thought, is such a mode. On the contrary,
from his own words in article five, I shall soon demonstrate that this is not so. Of
the other attributes that constitute the natures of things, it cannot be said that
those which are different, and of which neither is contained in the concept of the
other, are coexistent in one and the same subject, for this is equivalent to saying
that one and the same subject has two different natures, and this involves a contradiction, at least so long as the subject in question is simple and not composite—as in the present case.

350

Three points are to be noted here, a sufficient grasp of which would have prevented this writer from falling into such obvious errors.

First, it belongs to the theory of modes that, although we can easily understand a substance apart from a mode, we cannot, conversely, clearly understand a mode unless at the same time we conceive of the substance of which it is a mode (as I have explained in *Principles* I, art. 61), and all philosophers are agreed on this point. That our author, however, has paid no respect to this rule, is manifest from his fifth article. In that passage he admits that "we can have doubts about the existence of the body, but cannot have doubts about the existence of the mind." Hence it follows that the mind can be understood by us apart from the body, and thus is not a mode of the body.

The second point I would note here is the difference between simple and composite entities. A composite entity is one which is found to have two or more attributes, any one of which can be understood distinctly apart from the other, for it is from the fact that one can be thus conceived of distinctly without the other that each of these constituent elements is known to be, not a mode of the other, but a thing, or the attribute of a thing which can exist without the other. A simple entity is one in which such attributes are not found. Hence it is clear that this *351* subject in which we understand only extension and the various modes of extension is a simple entity. So, too, is a subject in which we understand only thought and the various modes of thought. But that in which we observe both extension and thought is a composite entity—namely, a man, an entity consisting of soul and body. Our author seems to assume that man is simply a body, of which the man's mind is but a mode.

Finally, we must note here that there is frequently a principal substance in subjects composed of several substances. This we consider in such a way as to treat any of the remaining substances that we connect with it as nothing more than a mode. Thus a man who is dressed may be considered as composed of man and clothes, but being dressed, with respect to the man, is only a mode, although clothes are substances. In the same way our author might, in the case of man, who is composed of soul and body, consider body the principal element, in relation to which having a soul, or being capable of thought, is nothing other than a mode. But it is foolish to infer from this that the soul itself, or that in virtue of which the body thinks, is not a substance different from the body.

He endeavors to confirm his opinion by means of the following syllogism: "Whatever we can conceive of can exist. But the mind can be conceived as one of the aforesaid (namely, a substance or a mode of a corporeal substance); for none of those things involves a contradiction. Therefore, etc." Here it must be noted that although the rule, "whatever we can conceive of can exist," is mine, and true, as long as the question concerns a clear and distinct concept, in which *352* the possibility of the thing to be realized is contained (because God can bring about everything we clearly perceive to be possible), nevertheless we must not make rash use of this rule. A man might easily imagine that he rightly understood something which in reality he did not understand, being utterly blinded by some sort of prejudice. This is the case of our author when he maintains that there is no contradiction involved in the statement that one and the same thing possesses either of two natures that are utterly incompatible—namely, that it is a substance or a mode. If he had merely said that he perceived no reasons for believing the human mind to be an incorporeal substance rather than a mode of a corporeal substance, his ignorance might have been excused. If he had said that no reasons could be found by human intelligence to prove either alternative, his arrogance would certainly have been reprehensible, but his statement would have contained no contradiction. But when he says that the "nature of things allows that the same thing may be a substance or a mode," his words are altogether self-contradictory and betray the irrationality of his mind.

In the third article he makes known his judgment concerning me. For it was I who wrote that "the human mind can be clearly and distinctly perceived as a substance different from corporeal substance." Our author, however, though he relies on no other arguments than the self-contradictory ones he has unfolded in the preceding article, proclaims that I am in error. Of that I take no account. Nor do I examine the words "of necessity" or "in actuality," which contain a certain ambiguity; for they are not of great moment.

353   I also decline to examine the statements regarding Holy Scripture in the fourth article, lest I should appear to assume the right of investigating another man's religion. This much I shall say: Here we must distinguish between three types of questions. Certain things are believed through faith alone—such are the mystery of the Incarnation, the Trinity, and the like. Others, however, though they have a certain bearing on faith, can nevertheless be investigated by natural reason; the existence of God and the distinction between the human soul and the body are generally ranked among these by orthodox theologians. Finally, there are others which do not in any way belong to the sphere of faith, but only to the sphere of human reason, such as the question of the squaring of the circle or of making gold by the art of alchemy. And even as those men abuse the words of Holy Scripture, who, from a distorted interpretation they give them, presume to answer these last questions, so do those others diminish its authority who undertake to solve the first type of question by arguments sought from philosophy alone. Nevertheless all theologians contend that these questions should be shown to be in no way incompatible with the light of nature, and to this end they direct their principal studies. As for questions of the second class, not only do they deem them in no way incompatible with the light of nature, but they even encourage philosophers to solve these questions to the best of their abilities by means of theories grounded in human reason. But never have I seen anyone who would affirm that the laws of nature allow that anything should be otherwise than the Holy Scriptures teach, unless he wished to show indirectly that he had no faith in the Scriptures. For as we were born men before we became Christians, it is beyond belief that any man should seriously embrace opinions he thinks contrary to that right reason that constitutes a man, in order that he may cling to the faith through which he is a Christian.

354   But perhaps our author does not imply this, for his words are: "Through the study of nature some may find doubtful what is already placed beyond all doubt for us by the divine revelation in the Scriptures." I find a twofold contradiction in these words. In the first place, he assumes the doctrine that the essence of one and the same thing, which must be assumed always to remain the same (because,

if it is supposed to become different, it will be by this very fact a different thing, to be indicated by a different name), is nevertheless doubtful, as far as the study of nature goes, and accordingly changeable. The second contradiction is in the word "some," because, as nature is the same for all men, a thing that can be doubtful only to "some" is not by nature doubtful.

The fifth article is to be related to the second rather than to the fourth, for in it the author is concerned not with divine revelation, but with the nature of mind—the question as to whether it is a substance or a mode. To prove the defensibility of the view that mind is nothing other than a mode, he attempts to refute an objection taken from my writings. I wrote that we could not doubt that our mind exists, because, from the very fact that we doubt, it follows that our mind exists, but that meantime we might doubt whether any bodies exist; from this I deduced and demonstrated that mind is clearly perceived by us as an existing thing, or substance, even supposing we have no concept whatever of the body and deny that any bodies exist—and, accordingly, that the concept of mind does not involve any concept of body. He thinks he can explode this argument by saying that "it only proves that, as long as we can have doubt about the existence of the body, we cannot say that mind is a mode of body." Here he shows that he is *355* utterly ignorant of what it is that philosophers term a "mode"; for the nature of a mode consists in this, that it can by no means be understood unless the concept of the thing of which it is a mode is involved in its own concept—as I have explained above. Our author, however, admits that mind can sometimes be cognized apart from the body, namely, when there are doubts about the existence of the body; from this it assuredly follows that mind cannot be said to be a mode of body. And what is sometimes true about the essence or nature of a thing is always true. Nevertheless he affirms that the nature of things allows that mind may be only a mode of the body. These two statements are manifestly irreconcilable.

In the sixth article I fail to apprehend his meaning. Certainly I remember hearing in the Schools that the soul is the act of the organic body, but until this day I never heard the soul itself called "organic." For this reason I beg our author's indulgence, to the end that, as I have nothing certain to base my remarks on at this point, I may expound my conjectures, not as though they were true to fact, but simply as conjectures. I seem to observe two irreconcilable statements. One of these is to the effect that the human mind is a substance really distinct from the body. This the author openly states, but, as far as he can, provides no argument on the point, and contends that it can be proved only by the authority of the Holy Scripture. The other statement is that that same human mind, in all its activities, is organic or instrumental, that is to say, that it does not act of itself, but is used by the body just as it uses its limbs and other corporeal modes, and so he *356* affirms in effect, if not in so many words, that the mind is nothing other than a mode of the body, as though he had drawn up his whole artillery of argument to prove this point and this alone. These two statements are so manifestly contraries that I do not think the author wished them both, at one and the same time, to find credence with readers, but deliberately coupled them together, so that he might in some way give satisfaction to the more simple minded, and to his friends the theologians, by his citation of Scriptural authority, and that, in the meantime, his more keen-witted readers might realize that, when he said "mind is distinct from body," he was speaking ironically, and that he was entirely of the opinion that mind is nothing but a mode.

In the seventh article again, and in the eighth, he seems to be speaking merely ironically. And he retains the same Socratic figure of speech in the latter part of article nine. But in the first part he appends a reason to his assertion, and thus, it would seem, he is to be taken seriously in this passage. He teaches that, as far as nature shows, it is doubtful whether any bodies are really perceived by us, and submits as his reason the statement that "the mind can be affected in equal degree by imaginary and real things." If this theory is to be received as true, it must be supposed that we have no use of the faculty called the intellect, but only of that faculty usually called the "common sense" whereby images of things are received, whether they are imaginary or real, so that they affect the mind—a faculty which philosophers commonly admit animals also possess. But surely those who have an intellect, and are not fashioned like the horse or mule, even although
357   they are affected not only by images of real things but also by those occurring in the brain from other causes (as happens in sleep), can distinguish the one kind of image from the other with the utmost clarity by the light of reason. The method by which this happens, surely and infallibly, I have explained in my writings so accurately that I am convinced that no one who has read through them, and is capable of understanding them, can be a skeptic.

In the tenth and eleventh articles it is still possible to suspect him of irony. If the soul is believed to be a substance, it is foolish and ridiculous to say "the bond that keeps body and soul in union is the law of the immutability of nature whereby every individual thing persists in the state in which it is." For it is just as true of disunited things as of united things that they persist in the same state as long as nothing changes that state. This is not at present the point at issue. The question is: how does it happen that the mind is united with the body and not separated from it? But if soul is supposed to be a mode of body, it is rightly said that no bond of union need to be sought other than the fact that it persists in the state in which it is, since modes have no other state than that they inhere in the things of which they are modes.

In article twelve he appears to dissent from me only in words, for when he says that the mind has no need of innate ideas, or notions, or axioms, and at the same time allows it the faculty of thinking (to be considered natural or innate), he makes an affirmation in effect identical with mine, but denies it in words. For I never wrote or concluded that the mind required innate ideas which were in some way
358   different from its faculty of thinking; but when I observed the existence in me of certain thoughts which proceeded, not from external objects or from the determination of my will, but solely from the faculty of thinking within me, then, in order that I might distinguish the ideas or notions (which are the forms of these thoughts) from other thoughts adventitious or factitious, I termed the former "innate." In the same sense we say that in some families generosity is innate, in others certain diseases like gout or stones, not that on this account the babies of these families suffer from these diseases in their mother's womb, but that they are born with a certain disposition or propensity for contracting them.

The conclusion he deduces in article thirteen from the preceding article is indeed extraordinary. For this reason, he says (that is, because the mind has no need of innate ideas, but the faculty of thinking is sufficient of itself), "all common notions engraved on the mind owe their origin to the observation of things or to tradition"—as though the faculty of thinking could of itself execute nothing, nor perceive nor think anything except what it received from observation or tradition, that is, from the senses. This is so far from being true, that, on the contrary, any man who rightly observes the limitations of the senses, and what precisely it is that can penetrate through this medium to our faculty of thinking, must admit that no ideas of things, in the form in which we envisage them by thought, are presented to us by the senses. So much so that in our ideas there is nothing that was not innate in the mind, or faculty of thinking, except only these circumstances that point to experience—the fact, for instance, that we judge that this or that idea, which we now have present to our thought, is to be referred to a certain external thing, not that these external things transmitted the ideas themselves   *359* to our minds through the organs of sense, but because they transmitted something which gave the mind occasion, by means of an innate faculty, to form these ideas at this time rather than at another. For nothing reaches our mind from external objects through the sense organs beyond certain corporeal motions, as our author himself asserts, in article nineteen, taking the doctrine from my *Principles;* but even these motions, and the figures arising from them, are not conceived of by us exactly as they occur in the sense organs, as I have explained at great length in my *Dioptrics.*[9] Hence it follows that the ideas of the motions and figures are themselves innate in us. So much the more must the ideas of pain, color, sound, and the like be innate, so that our mind may, on the occasion of certain corporeal motions, represent these ideas to itself, for they have no likeness to the corporeal motions. Could anything be imagined more absurd than that all common notions inherent in our mind should arise from these motions, and should be incapable of existing without them? I should like our author to instruct me as to what corporeal motion it is which can form in our mind any common notion, for example, the notion that "things equal to the same thing are equal to one another," or any other he pleases; for all these motions are particular, but common notions are universal having no affinity with the motions and no relation to them.

He goes on to affirm, in article fourteen, that even the idea of God in us is the   *360* outcome, not of our faculty of thinking, in which it is innate, but of divine revelation, tradition, or observation. We shall more easily realize the error of this assertion if we reflect that anything can be said to be the outcome of another, either because this other is its proximate and primary cause, without which it could not exist, or only because it is a remote and accidental cause, which, certainly, gives the primary cause occasion to produce its effect at one time rather than at another. Thus all workmen are the primary and proximate causes of their work, but those who give them orders, or promise them a reward, so that they may perform these works, are accidental and remote causes, because they probably would not have performed the tasks without being asked. There is no doubt

---

9. *Dioptrics,* Discourses 1 and 6.

that tradition or observation is a remote cause, inviting us to give attention to the idea we can have of God, and to present it vividly to our thought. But no one can maintain that this is the proximate and efficient cause, except the man who thinks that we can understand nothing about God, except his being called "God," or the corporeal forms used by painters to represent God to us in pictures. For observation, if it takes place through the medium of sight, can of its own proper power present nothing to the mind beyond pictures, and pictures consisting only of a permutation of corporeal motions, as our author himself tells us. If it takes place through the medium of hearing, it presents nothing beyond words and sounds; if through the other senses, it has nothing in it which can have reference to God. And surely it is manifest to every man that sight, of itself and by its proper function, presents nothing beyond pictures, and hearing nothing beyond voices or sounds, so that all these things that we think of, beyond these voices or pictures,

361   as being symbolized by them, are presented to us by means of ideas which come from no other source than our faculty of thinking, and are accordingly, together with that faculty, innate in us, that is, always existing in us potentially; for existence in any faculty is not actual but merely potential existence, since the very word "faculty" designates nothing more or less than a potentiality. But no one can affirm that we can understand nothing beyond a name or a bodily effigy with regard to God, unless he openly professes himself to be an atheist, and moreover destitute of all intellect.

     After expounding his opinion concerning God, our author, in article fifteen, tries to refute all the arguments I used to prove God's existence. At this point it occurs to one to marvel at the man's self-confidence, in that he imagines that he can so easily and in so few words overturn all that I have built up by dint of long and concentrated meditation, and to the explanation of which I have devoted a whole book. But all the arguments I have adduced in this matter can be reduced to two. In the first place I have shown that we have a notion or idea of God such that, when we sufficiently attend to it and ponder the matter in the manner I have expounded, we realize from this contemplation alone that it is not possible that God does not exist, since existence—not merely possible or contingent as in the ideas of all other things, but altogether necessary and actual—is contained in this concept. It is not only I who take this argument for a certain and evident demonstration; many others do so also, including some pre-eminent in learning and

362   intelligence who have carefully investigated the matter. The author of the *Program* tries to refute this argument in this fashion: "Our concept of God, or the idea of God that exists in our mind, is not a strong enough argument to prove the existence of God, since it is not the case that all things of which we have concepts exist." By these words he shows that he has read my writings, but has in no way had either the capacity or the will to understand them. For the point of my argument is not the idea in general, but its peculiar property, a property evident in the highest degree in the idea we have of God, and which can be found in the concept of no other thing, namely, the necessity of existence, which is required as that crown of the perfections without which we cannot understand God. The other argument I used to prove the existence of God I deduced from my clear proof of the fact that we should not have had the faculty of conceiving all the per-

fections we recognize in God, had it not been true that God exists, and that we were created by Him. Our author thinks he has more than exploded this argument by saying that the idea we have of God does not, any more than the concept of any other thing, transcend our proper powers of thinking. If by these words he only means that the concept we have of God without the aid of supernatural grace is no less natural than all the concepts we have of other things, he agrees with me; but on that basis nothing can be concluded against me. If, however, he thinks that that concept does not involve more objective perfections than all the others taken together, he is obviously wrong. I myself, on the other hand, have founded *363* my argument entirely on this superabundance of perfections, in which our concept of God transcends other concepts.

In the six remaining articles there is nothing worthy of note except the fact that, when he wishes to distinguish the properties of the soul, he speaks of them confusedly and inappropriately. I have said that these are all to be subordinated to two principal properties, one of which is the perception of the intellect, the other the determination of the will. These two our friend calls "intellect" and "will." Then he subdivides what he calls "intellect" into "perception" and "judgment." In this point he differs from me, for when I saw that to constitute the form of the judgment over and above perception, which is required as a basis for judgment, there must be affirmation and negation, and that it is frequently open to us to withhold our assent, even if we perceive a thing, I referred the act of judging, which consists in nothing but assent—that is, affirmation or negation—not to the perception of the intellect, but to the determination of the will. Thereafter he enumerates among the forms of perception nothing but sense, memory, and imagination; we may gather from this that he admits no pure intellection (that is, an intellection not dealing with any corporeal images), and, accordingly, that he himself believes that we have no knowledge of God, or of the human mind, or of other incorporeal things. Of this I can imagine but one cause, namely, that the *364* thoughts he has concerning these things are so confused that he never observes in himself a pure thought, different from any corporeal image.

Finally, in closing, he adds these words, taken from some portion of my writings: "No one more easily attains a great reputation for piety than the superstitious and the hypocritical." I fail to see what he means by these words, unless perhaps he ascribes to hypocrisy the use he has made of irony in many places, but I do not think that by that means he can attain a great reputation for piety.

For the rest, I am forced to admit here that I am covered with shame to think that in the past I praised this author as a man of most penetrative intelligence, and wrote somewhere or other that "I did not think he taught any doctrines which I should be unwilling to acknowledge as my own."[10] But in truth when I wrote these words I had not yet seen any specimen of his work in which he was not a faithful copyist, except only on one occasion in one little phrase which brought such ill results to him that I hoped he would make no further venture along that

---

10. Cf. the Preface to the *Principles,* AT IX, 19, referring to the *Letter to Voetius,* AT VIIIb, 163.

line;[11] and, as I saw him in other matters embrace with a great show of zeal the opinions that I considered nearest the truth, I attributed this to his intelligence and insight. But now a manifold experience compels me to conclude that he is swayed not so much by love of truth as by love of novelty. As he holds all he has learned from others to be old-fashioned and obsolete, thinking nothing sufficiently novel except what he has hammered out of his own brain, and, at the same time, is so unhappy in his inventions, that I have never noted a single word in his writings (excluding what he transcribed from others), which I did not condemn as containing some error, I must therefore warn all those who are convinced that he is a champion of my opinions, that of these opinions—I speak, not only of those on metaphysics, on which he openly opposes me, but also of those on physics, for he treats this subject somewhere in his writings—there is none that he does not state badly and distortedly. Hence it causes me more indignation that such a doctor should handle my writings and undertake to interpret, or in other words, to falsify them, than that other men should attack them with the utmost bitterness. [. . .]

365

To More,[12] **Replies to Objections (February 5, 1649)**

V, 268 [. . .] 1. You ask me why, to define the body, I say that it is an extended substance, rather than a sensible, tangible, or impenetrable substance. But the state of affairs warns you, that if you say "sensible substance," you are making a definition based on the relation to our senses. In this way you explain only one of its properties, not its whole essence, which, since it can exist even though no men exist, certainly cannot depend on our senses. Nor, further, do I see why you say that it is absolutely necessary that all matter be sensible. On the contrary, there is no matter that is not clearly insensible if it is divided into parts much smaller than the particles of our nerves, and if its individual parts are in sufficiently rapid motion.

As to that argument of mine you call "perverse and almost sophistical," I used it only to refute the opinion of those who, like you, believe every body to be sensible, an opinion which, in my judgment, it clearly and demonstratively refutes. For a body can retain its corporeal nature even though to sense it is neither soft nor hard, nor cold, nor hot, nor has, indeed, any sensible quality whatsoever.

In order to fall into the error you seem to want to attribute to me by your comparison of the wax that, although it can be neither square nor round, cannot, however, have no shape at all, I would have to conclude from the fact that according

---

11. This is a reference to Regius's thesis that man is an *ens per accidens* (a being by accident), which precipitated many of the problems at the University of Utrecht. See Descartes's *Letters to Regius,* AT III, 460–2 and 491–510.

12. Henry More (1614–1687) was a leading member of a Group of Platonists based at Christ's College, Cambridge. He attempted to combine neo-platonism with the new philosophy of Descartes and Galileo. However, he became increasingly more critical toward Cartesian philosophy in his later years.

to my principles all sensible qualities consist in the fact that the particles of a   *269*
body move or are at rest in certain ways—from this I would have to conclude, I
say, that none of its particles are in motion or at rest. Such a thing never entered
my mind. Thus body is not well defined as sensible substance.

Now let us see if it can more aptly be said that body is impenetrable or tangible substance in the sense in which you have explained it.

But, again, tangibility and impenetrability in body are something like risibil-
ity in man, a property of the fourth mode, according to the common laws of logic,
not a true and essential *differentia,* which I claim consists in extension. Hence,
just as man is not defined as an animal who can laugh, but as a rational animal,
so body is not to be defined through impenetrability, but through extension. This
is confirmed by the fact that tangibility and impenetrability have a relation to
parts and presuppose the concept of division and termination. Yet we can conceive of a continuous body of indeterminate or indefinite size, in which nothing
is considered except extension.

But, you say, "God or an angel or any other self-subsistent thing is extended,
and so your definition is broader than what it defines." Indeed, I am not accustomed to disputing about words, and so, if from the fact that God is everywhere,
someone wants to say that he is in some way extended, let him do so. But I deny
that true extension, as it is usually understood by everyone, is found either in God
or in angels or in our mind, or, in short, in any substance that is not a body. For   *270*
by an extended being people usually understand something imaginable—
whether it is a real being or being of reason I leave to one side. In this being we
can distinguish by the imagination various parts of determinate magnitude and
shape, no one of which is the same as the others, and we can also transfer in the
imagination some of these parts into the place of others, but two cannot be imagined to be in one and the same place at the same time. But nothing of this kind
can be said of God or of our mind. For they are not imaginable, but only intelligible. Nor can they be distinguished into parts, especially not into parts that have
determinate sizes and shapes. Hence we easily imagine that both the human mind
and God and at the same time a number of angels can be in one and the same
place. So it clearly follows that no incorporeal substances are, strictly speaking,
extended. I understand them to be powers or forces of some sort, which, although
they act on extended things, are not themselves extended—just as fire is in red
hot iron, even though the fire is not iron. That nevertheless some people confuse
the notion of substance with that of an extended thing comes from their mistaken
preconceived opinion that nothing can exist or be intelligible unless it is also
imaginable. And in truth nothing falls under the imagination that is not somehow
extended. Yet, to be sure, just as we may say that health belongs only to man,
although by analogy medicine and temperate air and many other things can be
called healthy, so I call extended only that which is imaginable, as having parts
beyond parts of determinate size and shape, although other things can indeed be
called extended by analogy.

2. To move to your second difficulty: if we examine what that extended being   *271*
is that I have described, we plainly find that it is the same as space, which most
people think is sometimes full, sometimes empty, sometimes real, sometimes

imaginary. For in a space, even if imaginary and empty, everyone easily imagines various parts of determinate size and shape, but they can in no way conceive two parts penetrating one another at the same time in one and the same place, since it implies a contradiction that this could happen without some part of space being removed. But since I consider that such real properties cannot exist except in a real body, I dare to assert that there can be no genuinely empty space and that every extended being is a true body. Nor am I troubled by the fact that I differ in this from the great men Epicurus, Democritus, and Lucretius. For I saw that they had not followed any firm argument, but the false preconception with which we have all been imbued from the earliest age. Since, as I warned in *Principles* II, art. 3, our senses do not always show us external bodies just as they really are, but only insofar as they relate to us and can help or harm us, nevertheless we all judged, when we were children, that there is nothing in the world except what is shown us by our senses, and that all the spaces in which we sense nothing are empty. Now since this prejudice was never in any way rejected by Epicurus, Democritus, and Lucretius, I do not need to follow their authority.

272   But I am astonished that a man otherwise so perspicacious, when he sees that he cannot deny that there is some substance in all space, since all the properties of extension are truly found in it, prefers to say that divine extension fills the space in which there are no bodies, rather than to say that no space at all can be wholly without body. For, as I said earlier, this supposed extension of God can in no way be the subject of the true properties we distinctly perceive in all space. For God is neither imaginable nor distinguishable into parts that are measurable and have shape.

    However, you readily admit that no vacuum can occur naturally. You are concerned about the divine power, which you think can remove all that is in any container, and at the same time keep the sides from meeting. I, indeed, since I know that my intellect is finite, and that God's power is infinite, set no limit to this; but I consider only what can be and cannot be perceived by me, and I take great care that my judgment should agree with my perception. Hence I boldly assert that God can do everything that I perceive to be possible; but I am not so bold as to deny, on the contrary, that it is possible for him to do what conflicts with my conception, but I only say that it involves a contradiction. Therefore, since I see that it conflicts with my conception that all body should be removed from the container and an extension remain in it, which I conceive no differently than I previously conceived the body contained in it, I say that it implies a contradiction that such an extension should remain there after the body has been removed, and therefore I say that the sides of the container must collapse. This is entirely con-

273 sonant with my other opinions: for I say elsewhere that there is no motion at all that is not in a sense circular.[13] From this it follows that it cannot be distinctly understood that God removes some body from the container unless it is at the same time understood that some other body, or the sides of the container, move into its place by circular motion.

---

13. *Principles* II, art. 33.

3. In the same way I also say that it implies a contradiction that there should be atoms which we conceive as both extended and indivisible, although God could have made them such that no creature could divide them, we certainly cannot understand him to have deprived himself of the power of dividing them.[14] Nor is your comparison valid that things that have been done cannot be undone. For we do not take it as a sign of incapacity when someone cannot do what we do not understand to be possible, but only when he cannot do one of those things that we distinctly perceive as possible. Now we certainly perceive it to be possible that the atom be divided, since we suppose it to be extended; and therefore, if we judge that it cannot be divided by God, we judge that God cannot do something that we nevertheless perceive as possible. But we do not in the same way perceive it to be possible that what is done can be undone; on the contrary, we perceive that it plainly cannot be done; and hence that it is no defect in God that he cannot do this. However, the same argument does not hold about the divisibility of matter. For even if I cannot enumerate all the parts into which it is divisible, and say for that reason that their number is indefinite, still I cannot assert that their division cannot be completed by God, since I know that God can do *274* many more things than I can encompass with this thought. Moreover, I agreed in *Principles* II, art. 34, that this indefinite division of certain parts of matter can in fact happen.

4. It is in my view not a matter of affected modesty, but of necessary caution, when I say that some things are indefinite rather than infinite. For it is only God whom I understand positively to be infinite. Of other things, such as the extension of the world, the number of parts into which matter is divisible, and similar things, I profess that I do not know whether they are absolutely infinite. I know only that I know of no end in them, and therefore with respect to me I call them indefinite.

And although our mind is not the measure of things or of the truth, it certainly ought to be the measure of those that we affirm or deny. For what is more absurd or more unconsidered than to want to make a judgment about those things the perception of which we admit our mind cannot achieve?

Moreover, I am surprised that you seem to want to do this, since you say "if extension is infinite only in relation to us, then it will in fact be finite." But further, you also imagine some divine extension that goes further than the extension of bodies, and you suppose that God has parts beyond parts, and is divisible, and you even attribute to him all the essence of a corporeal thing.

But to remove all your scruples, when I say that the extension of matter is indefinite, I believe this suffices to prevent anyone from trying to invent a space beyond it into which the particles of my vortices can escape. For, in my opinion, *275* wherever such a place is conceived of, there is some matter, since, when I say that matter is indefinitely extended, I am saying that it extends further than anything that can be conceived of by man.

But nevertheless I consider that there is the greatest difference between the amplitude of the extension of that body and the amplitude of the divine substance or essence—I do not say divine extension, because strictly speaking there is none. Therefore I call the latter simply infinite, but the former indefinite.

---

14. *Principles* II, art. 20.

For the rest, I do not admit what you so generously concede, that my other opinions could stand, even if what I have written about the extension of matter were refuted. For it is one of the principal and, in my view, the most certain foundations of my physics, and I confess that no arguments satisfy me in physics itself, unless they involve that necessity that you call logical or contradictory, provided only that you except those things that can be known only by experience, such as the fact that there is only one sun around this earth, or one moon, and so on. Since in other things you are not hostile to my meaning, I hope you will easily assent to this, too, if you only consider that it is a prejudice of many to consider that an extended being in which there is nothing moving our senses is not truly corporeal substance, but only empty space, and that there is not body that is not sensible, and no substance that does not fall under the imagination and is therefore extended.

276   5. But the greatest of the prejudices of which we have been persuaded since childhood is that living brutes think.

No other reason moves us to believe this, except that we see that a number of beasts'members do not differ much from ours in external shape and motion, and that we believe there is just one principle of motion in us, namely, the soul, that both gives movement and thinks; so we do not doubt that some such soul is to be found in them.

However, after I had realized that there are two different principles of motion—one, indeed, plainly mechanical and corporeal, depending only on the force of the spirits and the arrangement of the organs, can be called the corporeal soul, and the other incorporeal, that is, the mind, or that soul I defined as thinking substance—I inquired carefully whether the movement of animals arose from these two principles, or from one only. When I saw clearly that they could all arise from that principle alone which is corporeal and mechanical, I held it to be certain and demonstrated that we could in no way prove that there is any thinking soul in brutes. Nor do I hesitate because of the acuteness and sagacity of dogs and foxes, or all the others things that are done by brutes for the sake of food, sex, or fear. For I claim that I can easily explain all these things simply through the arrangement of their organs.

Still, although I hold it as demonstrated that it cannot be proved that there is any thought in brutes, at the same time I do not think it can be proved that there
277 is none, since the human mind cannot penetrate their hearts. But when I examine what is more probable in this matter, I see no argument in favor of animals having thoughts except this one: that, since they have eyes, ears, tongue, and other sense organs like us, it is probable that they feel as we do; and since thought is included in our manner of sensing, similar thought is also to be attributed to them. This argument, since it is very obvious, has taken hold of the minds of all men from their earliest age. However, there are other arguments, much more numerous and more powerful, though not so obvious to all, that plainly urge the opposite. To mention one: it is less probable that worms, midges, and caterpillars have immortal souls than that they move like machines.

This is so, first, because it is certain that in the bodies of animals, as in ours also, there are bones, nerves, muscles, blood, and animal spirits, and the other organs so disposed that they can produce all the movements we observe in brutes by themselves, and without any thought. This is clear in convulsions, since, with the mind unwilling, the machinery of the body often moves itself more violently and in more different ways than it could be moved with the help of the will.

Further, since art imitates nature, and men can fabricate various automata, with which there is motion without any thought, it seems reasonable to agree that nature too can produce automata, made with more consummate art, namely, all the brutes. This is more likely since we find no argument to show that where *278* there is an arrangement of organs such as we see in animals, there is any reason to add thought. And at the same time it is more worthy of admiration that some mind is found in every human body, than that none should be in any brutes.

But of all the arguments that can persuade us that beasts are destitute of thought, the chief, in my view, is as follows. Granted that in a single species some are more perfect than others, no differently than among men—as can be seen in horses and dogs, some of whom learn much more quickly than others what they are taught. Granted also that they all easily communicate to us by voice or other bodily movements their natural impulses, like anger, fear, hunger, and the like. Nevertheless it has never been observed that any brute beast arrived at such perfection that it could use true speech, that is, that it indicated by words or signs something that can be ascribed to thought alone, and not to a natural impulse. For speech is the only certain sign of thought concealed in the body, and all men, even the stupidest and most insane, make use of it, but not any brute. Therefore this can be taken to be the true *differentia* between man and brutes.

For the sake of brevity, I omit here other reasons for denying thought to brutes. It should be noted, however, that I am speaking of thought, not of life or sense. For I deny life to no animal, since I hold that life consists solely in the heat of the body. Nor do I deny sense either, insofar as it depends on a corporeal organ. And thus my opinion is not so cruel to beasts as it is kind to men—at least to those *279* who are not subject to the Pythagorean superstition—since it absolves them of the suspicion of crime when they eat and kill animals. [. . .]

The Passions of the Soul (1649)

Part I. Of the passions in general and incidentally of the whole   *XI, 327*
nature of man.

1. Whatever is a passion with respect to a given subject is always an action in some other respect.

The defectiveness of the sciences we have received from the ancients is nowhere more apparent than in what they have written on the passions. For, although this is a matter that has always been much investigated, and although it would not appear to be one of the most difficult, since, as everyone has experience of the passions in himself, there is no need to borrow any observation from elsewhere to discover their nature, nevertheless what the ancients taught about

328   them is so slight, and for the most part so far from credible, that I cannot entertain any hope of approaching the truth except by shunning the paths they followed. That is why I shall be obliged to write here just as though I were treating a matter that no one had ever touched on before me. And, to begin with, I consider that whatever occurs or recurs the philosophers generally call a passion with respect to the subject to which it occurs, and an action in respect to the subject that causes it to occur. Thus although the agent and the patient are often very different, the action and the passion are still the same thing, with two different names in view of the two different subjects to which it may be ascribed.

2. To understand the passions of the soul, the functions of the soul must be distinguished from those of the body.

Next I consider that we do not observe the existence of any subject that acts more immediately upon our soul than the body to which it is attached, and that we must consequently believe that what is a passion in the soul is usually an action in the body. Thus there is no better means of arriving at a knowledge of our passions than examining the difference between the soul and the body, in order to know to which of the two we should attribute each one of the functions within us.

329   **3. What rule we must follow to bring about this result.**

As to this, we shall not find much difficulty if we realize that all that we experience as being in us, and that we see can exist in wholly inanimate bodies, must be attributed to our bodies alone. On the other hand, all that is in us which we cannot in any way conceive as possibly pertaining to a body must be attributed to our soul.

4. The heat and movement of the limbs proceed from the body, and thoughts from the soul.

Thus, since we cannot conceive of the body as thinking in any way, we have reason to believe that all kinds of thought that exist in us belong to the soul. And because we do not doubt that there are inanimate bodies that can move in as many as, or in more different, ways than ours, and have as much heat or more— experience shows us this in a flame, which has much more heat and motion on its own than any of our limbs—we must believe that all the heat and all the movements within us pertain only to the body, inasmuch as they do not at all depend on thought.

330   **5. It is an error to believe that the soul supplies motion and heat to the body.**

In this way we shall avoid a very considerable error into which many have fallen, so much so that I believe this is the primary cause that has prevented our being able to explain satisfactorily as yet the passions and other things belonging to the soul. It consists in observing that all dead bodies are deprived of heat and consequently of movement, and in imagining that the absence of soul was what was causing these movements and this heat to stop. Thus, without any justification it was believed that our natural heat and all the movements of our body depend on the soul—while in fact we ought, on the contrary, to believe that the soul quits us in death only because this heat ceases and the organs serving to move the body decay.

6. What difference there is between a living and a dead body.

In order, then, to avoid this error, let us consider that death never comes to pass through the fault of the soul, but only because one of the principal parts of the body decays; and let us judge that the body of a living man differs from that of a dead man just as does a watch or other automaton (that is, a machine that moves   *331* by itself) when it is wound up and contains in itself the corporeal principle of those movements for which it is designed, along with all that is required for its action, differs from the same watch or other machine when it is broken and the principle of its movement ceases to act.

7. A brief explanation of the parts of the body and of some of its functions.

In order to make this more intelligible, I shall here explain in a few words the way in which the bodily machine is composed. There is no one who does not already know that there are in us a heart, a brain, a stomach, nerves, arteries, veins, and things of that kind. We also know that the food we eat descends into the stomach and bowels, where its sap, passing into the liver and into all the veins, mingles with and thereby increases the quantity of blood that they contain. Those who have heard even a minimum about medicine also know how the heart is composed, and how all the blood in the veins can easily flow from the vena cava into its right side and from there pass into the lungs by the vessel we call the arterial vein, and then return from the lung into the left side of the heart, by the vessel called the venal artery, and finally pass from there into the great artery, whose branches spread throughout the body. Likewise, all those whom the   *332* authority of the ancients had not entirely blinded, and who were willing to open their eyes and investigate the opinion of Harvey on the circulation of the blood, do not doubt that all the veins and arteries of the body are like streams through which the blood flows unceasingly with great swiftness, taking its course from the right cavity of the heart through the arterial vein, whose branches are spread over the whole of the lung, and joined to that of the venous artery, by which it passes from the lung into the left side of the heart. From these, again, it goes into the great artery, whose branches, spread throughout all the rest of the body, are united to the branches of the vein which once more carry the same blood into the right cavity of the heart. Thus these two cavities are like sluices through each of which all the blood passes in the course of each circuit it makes in the body. We further know that all the movements of the limbs depend on the muscles, and that these muscles are opposed to one another in such a way that when one contracts it draws toward itself the part of the body to which it is attached. And at the same time this causes the opposing muscle to relax. Then if at another time the latter contracts, it causes the former to relax and draws back to itself the part to which they are attached. Finally, we know that all these movements of the muscles, as well as the senses, all depend on the nerves, which are, as it were, small filaments or little tubes proceeding from the brain, which, like the brain, contain a certain very subtle air or wind called the animal spirits.

333   **8. What the principle of these functions is.**

But it is not usually known in what way these animal spirits and these nerves contribute to our movements and to the senses, nor what the corporeal principle is that causes them to act. That is why, although I have already made some mention of these matters in my other writings,[15] I shall not omit here to say briefly that so long as we live there is a continual heat in our heart—a kind of fire that the blood maintains there—and that this fire is the corporeal principle of all the movements of our limbs.

9. How the movement of the heart takes place.

Its first effect is to dilate the blood with which the cavities of the heart are filled. That is why this blood, needing to occupy a larger space, passes forcefully from the right cavity into the arterial vein, and from the left into the great artery. Then when this dilation stops, new blood immediately enters from the vena cava into the right cavity of the heart and from the venous artery into the left. For there are little membranes at the entrances of these four vessels, so disposed that they do not allow the blood to enter the heart except through the last two, nor to leave except through the two others. The new blood that has entered the heart is then immediately rarefied there, in the same way as the blood that preceded it. And that is precisely what constitutes the pulse, or beating, of the heart and arteries, so that this beating is repeated as often as new blood enters the heart. It is also just this that gives the blood its motion, and causes it to flow unceasingly and very rapidly in all the arteries and veins. By this means it carries the heat it acquires in the heart to all the parts of the body and supplies them with nourishment.

334

10. How the animal spirits are produced in the brain.

But what is most important here is that all the liveliest and subtlest parts of the blood that heat has rarefied in the heart enter continuously in large quantities into the cavities of the brain. And the reason they go there rather than elsewhere is that all the blood that issues from the heart through the great artery takes its course in a straight line toward that place, and, not being able to enter it in its entirety, because there are only very narrow passages there, only those of its parts that are the most agitated and the subtlest pass through, while the rest spread

---

15. *Discourse on Method*, AT VI, 46–55.

abroad into all the other portions of the body. But these very subtle parts of the blood form the animal spirits, and for this end they have no need to undergo any *335* other alteration in the brain, except to be separated from the other less subtle portions of the blood. For what I am here calling spirits are nothing but bodies, and their one peculiarity is that they are bodies of extreme minuteness and that they move very quickly, like the particles of flame issuing from a torch. Thus it is that they never remain at rest in any place, and just as some of them enter into the cavities of the brain, others issue forth through the pores in its substance, which conduct them into the nerves, and from there into the muscles, by means of which they move the body in all the different ways in which it can be moved.

11. How the movements of the muscles take place.

For the only cause of all the movements of the limbs is that certain muscles contract, and that those opposing them relax, as has already been said. And the only cause of one muscle's contracting rather than that opposing it is that some additional amount of animal spirits, however little, comes to it rather than to the other. Not that the spirits proceeding from the brain suffice in themselves to move these muscles; but they determine the other spirits already in these two muscles to leave one of them *en bloc* and to enter into the other. By this means the one they leave becomes longer and more relaxed, and the one they enter, *336* being rapidly distended by them, contracts, and pulls the limb to which it is attached. This is easy to conceive, provided we know that there are very few animal spirits continually proceeding from the brain to each muscle, and that there are always a quantity of others in rapid motion enclosed in the same muscle, sometimes moving just by turning in the same place—that is, when they do not find any passage open to let them out—and sometimes by flowing into the opposing muscle. Since there are little openings in each of these muscles through which the spirits can flow from one to the other, so arranged that when the spirits that come from the brain to one of them have more force—however little—than those that go to the other, they open all the passages through which the spirits of the other muscle can pass into this one, and at the same time they close all those by which the spirits in this one can pass into the other. By this means all the spirits formerly contained in these two muscles very quickly collect in one of them and thus distend and shorten it, while the other one becomes extended and relaxed.

12. How external objects act on the sense organs.

We have still to know the causes that prevent the spirits from always flowing into the muscles in the same way—and bring it about that some spirits sometimes *337* flow into certain muscles rather than others. For in addition to the action of the soul, which in us (as I shall say below) is truly one of these causes, there are two others of which I must take note, that depend only on the body. The first consists of the diversity of the movements excited by their objects in the organs of sense. This I have already explained fully in the *Dioptrics*,[16] but so that those who see

---

16. *Dioptrics*, Discourse 4.

this work may not have to read others, I shall here repeat that there are three things to consider in the nerves: namely, first, their marrow or interior substance, which extends in the form of little filaments from the brain, from which it originates, to the extremity of the other limbs to which these filaments are attached; secondly, the membranes surrounding them, which, being coterminous with those that cover the brain, form small tubes in which these filaments are enclosed; and finally, the animal spirits, which are carried by these same tubes from the brain to the muscles, and are the reason why these filaments remain perfectly free and extended there, so that the least thing that moves the part of the body to which the extremity of any one of them is attached, causes by that same means the part of the brain from which it proceeds to move—just as when you pull one end of a cord, the other end is made to move.

338 **13. This action of external objects may lead the spirits in different ways into the muscles.**

I also explained in the *Dioptrics* how all the objects of sight communicate themselves to us only through the fact that, by the interposition of transparent bodies between them and us, they move locally the little filaments of the optic nerves at the back of our eyes, and then the parts of the brain from which these parts proceed.[17] The objects move them, I say, in as many different ways as the differences they cause us to see in things. By this I mean, not immediately the movements occurring in the eye, but those occurring in the brain, which represent these objects to the soul. As an example of this, it is easy to conceive how sounds, smells, tastes, heat, pain, hunger, thirst, and generally speaking all the objects of our other external senses as well as of our internal appetites also excite in our nerves some movement that passes through them to the brain. And in addition to the fact that these different movements cause our soul to have different sensations, they can also cause the spirits, apart from the soul, to take their course toward certain muscles rather than toward others, and thus to move our limbs. I shall demonstrate this here only by an example.
339 If someone quickly thrusts his hand against our eyes as if to strike us, even though we know him to be our friend, that he only does it in jest, and that he will take great care not to hurt us, we still have trouble preventing ourselves from closing our eyes. And this shows that it is not by the intervention of the soul that our eyes close, seeing that it happens against our will, which is the soul's only, or at least its principal, activity. Rather, it is because the machine of our body is so formed that the motion of the hand toward our eyes excites another motion in our brain, which conducts the animal spirits into the muscles, causing the eyelids to close.

14. Differences among the spirits can also make them take different courses.

The other cause that serves to conduct the animal spirits differently into the muscles is the unequal agitation of these spirits and the difference in their parts. For when some of their parts are coarser and more agitated than others, they pass further forward in a straight line into the cavities and pores of the brain and by

---

17. *Dioptrics*, Discourse 6.

this means are conducted into other muscles than those they would enter if they had less force.

15. The causes of their diversity.

This inequality may proceed from the different materials of which they are composed, as we see in the case of those who have drunk a lot of wine. The vapors of this wine, entering quickly into the blood, rise from the heart to the brain, where they are converted into animal spirits stronger and more abundant than those ordinarily there, which are thus capable of moving the body in many strange ways. This inequality of spirits may also proceed from different dispositions of the heart, liver, stomach, spleen, and all the other parts that contribute to their production. For we must here notice chiefly certain little nerves inserted at the base of the heart, which serve to enlarge and to narrow the entrances of its cavities, so that the blood, dilating there more or less forcibly, produces spirits disposed in various ways. We must also notice that although the blood entering the heart arrives there from all the other parts of the body, it often happens that it is more forcibly driven from some parts than from others because the nerves and muscles leading to these particular parts press or agitate it to a greater extent, and that, according to the diversity of the parts from which most of it comes, it dilates variously in the heart and then produces spirits with different qualities. Thus, for example, the part that comes from the lower part of the liver, where the spleen is located, dilates differently in the heart *341* from the blood coming from the veins of the arms or legs, and this, finally, quite differently from the juice of food when, newly issued from the stomach and bowels, it passes directly through the liver to the heart.

16. How all the limbs may be moved by the objects of the senses and by the animal spirits without the aid of the soul.

Finally, we must observe that the machine of our body is so composed that all the changes undergone by the movement of the spirits may cause them to open certain pores in the brain more than others, and reciprocally that when one of the pores is opened more or less than others by the action of the nerves employed by the senses—to however small a degree it may be—this changes something in the movement of the spirits and causes them to be conducted into the muscles that serve to move the body in the way it is usually moved when such an action takes place. In this way all the movements that we make without a contribution of our will, as frequently happens when we breathe, walk, eat, and in fact perform all those actions common to us and the brutes: all these movements depend only on the conformation of our limbs and on the course that the spirits, excited by the *342* heat of the heart, follow naturally in the brain, nerves, and muscles—just as the movements of a watch are performed simply by the strength of the springs and the form of the wheels.

17. What the functions of the soul are.

After we have thus considered all the functions pertaining to the body alone, it is easy to recognize that there is nothing in us that we ought to attribute to our soul except our thoughts, which are mainly of two sorts, the one being the actions of the soul, and the other its passions. Those I call its actions are all our volitions, since we find by experience that these proceed directly from our soul, and appear to depend on it alone. On the other hand, we may usually term our passions all those kinds of perceptions or of knowledge that are found in us, since it is often not our soul that makes them what they are, and since the soul often receives them from the things represented by them.

18. Of the will.

343   Our volitions, again, are of two sorts. One set consists of those actions of the soul that terminate in the soul itself, as when we will to love God, or, generally speaking, apply our thoughts to some object that is not material. The others are actions that terminate in our body, as when, from the simple fact that we will to take a walk, it follows that our legs move and that we walk.

19. Of perception.

Our perceptions are also of two sorts, and one group has the soul as cause and the other the body. Those that have the soul as cause are the perceptions of our acts of will, and of all the imaginations or other thoughts that depend on them. For it is certain that we cannot will anything without by the same means perceiving that we will it. And although in regard to our soul it is an action to want something, we may say that it is also one of our passions to perceive that we will it. Yet because this perception and this will are really one and the same thing, the more noble always supplies the denomination, and so we are not in the habit of calling it a passion, but only an action.

344   **20. Of the imaginations and other thoughts formed by the soul.**

When our soul applies itself to imagine something that does not exist, as when it represents to itself an enchanted palace or a chimera, and also when it applies itself to consider something that is only intelligible and not imaginable—for example, to consider its own nature—the perceptions it has of these things depend principally on the act of will that causes it to perceive them. That is why we usually consider these as actions rather than passions.

21. Of the imaginations that have the body only as cause.

Among the perceptions caused by the body, the largest part depend on the nerves, but there are also some that do not depend on them, and that we call imaginations, as we do those I have just spoken of, from which, however, they differ inasmuch as our will has no part in forming them. And this means that they cannot be placed in the number of the actions of the soul. They proceed only from the fact that when the spirits are agitated in different ways and meet with traces of different preceding impressions that have been effected in the brain,
345   they happen to take their course through certain pores rather than through others. Such are the illusions of our dreams, and also the daydreams we often have when

awake, and when our thought wanders aimlessly without applying itself to anything of its own accord. But although some of these imaginations are passions of
the soul, taking this word in its more correct and exact meaning, and since they
may all be thus termed if we take it in a more general sense, yet because they do
not have a cause of so notable and determinate a description as the perceptions
the soul receives by the mediation of the nerves, and because they appear to be
only a shadow and a picture, before we can distinguish them very well, we must
consider the difference prevailing among these others.

22. Of the difference that exists among the other perceptions.

All the other perceptions I have not yet explained come to the soul by the mediation of the nerves, and there is this difference between them, that we relate them
in the one case to external objects that strike our senses, in the other to our soul.

23. Of the perceptions that we relate to external objects.   *346*

Those we relate to things outside ourselves, namely, to the objects of our
senses, are caused, at least when our opinion is not false, by those objects, which,
causing certain movements in the organs of the external senses, also, through the
mediation of the nerves, excite certain movements in the brain, which cause the
soul to perceive them. Thus when we see the light of a torch and hear the sound
of a bell, this light and this sound are two different actions, which, simply by fact
that they excite two different movements in certain of our nerves, and by their
means in the brain, give the soul two different sensations, which we relate in such
a way to the subjects that we suppose to be their cause, that we think we see the
torch itself and hear the bell, and not that we perceive only the movements that
proceed from them.

24. Of the perceptions that we relate to our body.

The perceptions we relate to our body or to some of its parts are those that we
have of hunger, thirst, and other natural appetites, to which we may unite pain,
heat, and the other affections that we feel as if in our own limbs, and not as in   *347*
external objects. We may thus perceive at the same time, and by the mediation of
the same nerves, the cold of our hand and the heat of the flame to which it is
approaching, or, on the other hand, the heat of the hand and the cold of the air to
which it is exposed, without there being any difference between the actions that
cause us to feel the heat or the cold in our hand, and those that make us perceive
what is outside us, except that from the fact of one of those actions following the
other, we judge that the first is already in us, and that what follows is not yet in
us, but is in the object that causes it.

25. Of the perceptions we relate to our soul.

The perceptions we relate solely to the soul are those whose effects we feel as
though they were in the soul itself, and as for which we do not usually know any
proximate cause to which we could relate them. Such are the feelings of joy,

anger, and other such sensations, which are sometimes excited in us by the objects that move our nerves and sometimes also by other causes. But although all our perceptions, both those that we relate to external objects and those that we relate to the different affections of our body, are truly passions in respect to our 348 soul, when we use this word in its most general sense, yet we are in the habit of restricting it to refer only to those that are related to the soul itself, and it is only the latter that I have undertaken to explain under the name of the passions of the soul.

26. The imaginations which depend on the fortuitous movements of the spirits may be just as truly passions as the perceptions that depend on the nerves.

It remains for us to observe here that all the same things that the soul perceives by the mediation of the nerves may also be represented by the fortuitous course of the animal spirits, without there being any difference except that the impressions coming into the brain through the nerves are usually more lively or definite than those excited there by the spirits. That is why I said in Article 21 that the latter resemble the shadow or picture of the former. It should also be observed that it sometimes happens that this picture is so similar to the thing it represents that we may be mistaken about the perceptions that relate to external objects, or at least those that relate to certain parts of our body, but that we cannot be thus deceived about the passions, inasmuch as they are so close to, and so entirely within, our soul, that it is impossible for it to feel them without their being actually such as it feels them to be. Thus often when we are asleep, or sometimes 349 even when we are awake, we imagine certain things so forcibly, that we think we see them before us, or feel them in our body, although they do not exist at all; but although we may be asleep or dreaming, we cannot feel sad or moved by any other passion, without its being very true that the soul actually has this passion within it.

27. The definition of the passions of the soul.

After having considered how the passions of the soul differ from all its other thoughts, it seems to me that we may define them generally as the sensations or excitations of the soul which we relate especially to it, and which are caused, maintained, and fortified by some movement of the spirits.

28. Explanation of the first part of this definition.

We may call the passions perceptions when we make use of this word generally to signify all the thoughts that are not actions or volitions of the soul, but not when the term is used only to signify evident knowledge. For experience shows us that those who are the most agitated by their passions are not those who know 350 them best, and that they are among the number of perceptions which the close alliance existing between soul and body renders confused and obscure. We may also call them sensations, because they are received into the soul in the same way as are the objects of our external senses, and are not differently known by it. But we can better call them excitations of the soul, not only because that name can be attributed to all the changes that occur in it—that is, to all the different thoughts it may have, but particularly because, of all the kinds of thoughts it can have, there are no others that so powerfully agitate and excite it as those passions.

29. Explanation of the second part.

I add that they relate particularly to the soul, in order to distinguish them from the other sensations that are related, some to external objects, as are scents, sounds, and colors, others to our body, like hunger, thirst, and pain. I also add that they are caused, maintained, and strengthened by some movement of the spirits, in order to distinguish them from our volitions, which we may call excitations of the soul that relate to it, but which are caused by itself; and also in order to explain their ultimate and most proximate cause, which plainly distinguishes them from other sensations.

30. The soul is united conjointly to all the parts of the body.   *351*

But in order to understand all these things more perfectly, it is necessary to know that the soul is really joined to the whole body, and that, strictly speaking, we cannot say that it exists in any one of its parts to the exclusion of the others, because it is one and somehow indivisible, owing to the disposition of its organs, which are so related to one another, that when any one of them is removed, this makes the whole body defective; and because it is of a nature that has no relation to extension, nor to dimensions, nor to other properties of the matter of which the body is composed, but only to the whole conglomerate of its organs. This is clear from the fact that we could not in any way conceive of the half or the third of a soul, or of the space it occupies, and because it does not become smaller owing to the amputation of some parts of the body, but separates itself entirely when the assemblage of its organs is dissolved.

31. There is a small gland in the brain in which the soul exercises its functions more particularly than in the other parts.

It is also necessary to know that although the soul is joined to the whole body, nevertheless there is in the body a certain part in which the soul exercises its   *352* functions more particularly than in all the others. And it is usually believed that this part is the brain, or possibly the heart—the brain, because it is with it that the organs of sense are connected, and the heart, because it is in it that we apparently feel the passions. But after examining the matter with care, it seems to me I have plainly recognized that the part of the body in which the soul exercises its functions immediately is in no way the heart, nor the whole of the brain, but merely the most inward of its parts, namely, a certain very small gland situated in the middle of its substance and so suspended above the duct through which the animal spirits of its anterior cavities communicate with those of the posterior, that the slightest movements taking place in it may alter very greatly the course of the spirits, and, reciprocally, that the smallest changes occurring in the course of the spirits can do much to change the movements of this gland.

32. How we know that this gland is the principal seat of the soul.

353

The reason that persuades me that apart from this gland the soul cannot have any other location in all the body is this: I consider the fact that the other parts of the brain are all double, just as we also have two eyes, two hands, two ears; and finally all the organs of our external senses are double; and inasmuch as we have but one solitary and simple thought of one particular thing at one and the same moment, it must necessarily be the case that there must be somewhere a place where the two images coming to us from the two eyes, or where the two other impressions proceeding through the double organs of the other senses, can unite before arriving in the soul, so that they may not represent to it two objects instead of one. And it is easy to conceive that these images or other impressions might unite in this gland by the mediation of the spirits that fill the cavities of the brain. But there is no other place in the body where they can be thus united unless they are so in this gland.

33. The seat of the passions is not in the heart.

354

As to the opinion of those who think that the soul receives its passions in the heart, it is in no way to be considered, for it is founded only on the fact that the passions cause us to feel some change taking place there. And it is easy to observe that this change is not felt in the heart except through the medium of a small nerve that descends toward it from the brain, just as pain is felt in the foot by means of the nerves of the foot, and the stars are perceived as in the heavens by means of their light and of the optic nerves. Thus it is no more necessary that our soul should exercise its functions immediately in the heart, in order to feel its passions there, than it is necessary for the soul to be in the heavens in order to see the stars there.

34. How the soul and the body act on one another.

Let us then conceive here that the soul has its principal seat in the little gland that exists in the middle of the brain, from which it radiates forth through all the remainder of the body through the mediation of the spirits, nerves, and even the blood, which, participating in the impressions of the spirits, can carry them through the arteries into all the limbs. And recollecting what has been said above about the machine of our body, that is, that the little filaments of our nerves are so distributed in all its parts, that, on the occasion of the different movements excited there by sensible objects, they open the pores of the brain in different ways. And this causes the spirits contained in these cavities to enter in different ways into the muscles, by means of which they can move the muscles in all the different ways in which they are capable of being moved. And all the other causes that can move the spirits in different ways are sufficient to conduct them to different muscles. Let us here add that the small gland that is the principal seat

of the soul is so suspended between the cavities containing the spirits that it can   *355*
be moved by them in as many different ways as there are sensible differences in
the objects. But it can also be moved in different ways by the soul, which is of
such a nature that it receives in itself as many different impressions—that is, that
it has as many different perceptions—as there are different movements in this
gland. Reciprocally, likewise, the machine of the body is so formed that, from the
simple fact that this gland is differently moved by the soul, or by such another
cause, whatever it may be, it thrusts the spirits surrounding it toward the pores of
the brain, which conducts them through the nerves into the muscles, by which
means it causes them to move the limbs.

**35. Example of the way in which the impressions of objects unite in the
gland that is in the middle of the brain.**

   Thus, for example, if we see some animal approaching us, the light reflected
from its body depicts two images of it, one in each of our eyes, by means of the
optic nerves. Then these two images form two others in the interior surface of the
brain that faces its cavities. From there, by means of the spirits with which the
cavities are filled, these images so radiate toward the little gland surrounded by
these spirits, that the movement forming each point of one of the images tends
toward the same point of the gland toward which the movement forming the   *356*
point of the other image is directed—a point which represents the same part of
this animal. By this means the two images in the brain form only one on the
gland, which, acting immediately upon the soul, causes it to see the shape of this
animal.

36. Example of the way in which the passions are excited in the soul.

   And besides that, if this figure is very strange and frightful—that is, if it has a
close relationship with the things that have formerly been harmful to the body—
this excites in the soul the passion of anxiety and then that of courage, or else that
of fear and consternation, according to the particular temperament of the body or
strength of the soul, and according as we have already been secured by defense
or by flight against the harmful things to which the present impression is related.
For in some men it disposes the brain in such a way that the spirits reflected from
the image thus formed in the gland proceed from there to take their places partly
in the nerves that serve to turn the back and dispose the legs for flight, and partly
in those that so increase or diminish the openings of the heart, or at least which
so agitate the other parts from which the blood is sent to it, that this blood, being
there rarefied in a different way from usual, sends to the brain spirits adapted to
maintain and strengthen the passion of fear, i.e., adapted to hold open or to
reopen the pores of the brain that conduct them into the same nerves. For from   *357*
the fact alone that these spirits enter these pores, they excite a particular movement in this gland, which is instituted by nature to cause the soul to be sensible
of this passion. And because these pores are related principally to the little nerves

that serve to contract or enlarge the openings of the heart, this causes the soul to feel the passion chiefly as if it were in the heart.

37. How it seems that they are all caused by some movement of the spirits.

The same thing occurs in all the other passions, namely, they are caused chiefly by the spirits contained in the cavities of the brain, inasmuch as they take their course toward the nerves that serve to enlarge or contract the openings of the heart, or to drive the blood in the other parts to it in various ways, or, in whatever fashion it may be, to maintain the same passion. We may clearly understand from this why I have specified in my definition of the passions above, that they are caused by some particular movement of the spirits.

358 ### 38. Example of the movements of the body that accompany the passions and do not depend on the soul.

For the rest, in the same way as the course taken by the spirits toward the nerves of the heart suffices to give the movement to the gland by which fear is placed in the soul, so, too, by the simple fact that at the same time certain spirits proceed toward the nerves which serve to move the legs so that they flee, they cause another movement in the same gland, by means of which the soul feels and is aware of that flight, which in this way may be excited in the body by the disposition of the organs alone, and without the soul's contributing to it.

39. How one and the same cause may excite different passions in different men.

The same impression which the presence of a terrifying object makes on the gland, and which causes fear in certain men, may excite in others courage and confidence. The reason for this is that not all brains are constituted in the same way, and that the same movement of the gland which in some excites fear, in others causes the spirits to enter the pores of the brain that conduct them partly into
359 the nerves serving to move the hands for the purpose of self-defense, and partly into those that agitate and drive the blood toward the heart in the manner requisite to produce the spirits proper for the continuance of defense, and to retain the desire for it.

40. The principal effect of the passions.

For it is necessary to observe that the principal effect of all the passions in men is that they incite and dispose their soul to want those things for which they prepare their body, so that the feeling of fear incites it to wish to take flight, that of courage to wish to fight, and so on.

41. What the power of the soul is in regard to the body.

But the will is so free in its nature that it can never be constrained, and of the two sorts of thoughts I have distinguished in the soul—of which the first are its actions, that is, its volitions, and the other its passions, taking this word in its most general significance, which comprises all kinds of perceptions—the former are absolutely in its power, and can be changed only indirectly by the body, while on the other hand the latter depend absolutely on the actions that govern and direct them, and they can be altered only indirectly by the soul, except when it is itself their cause. And the whole action of the soul consists in this, that solely because it wills something, it causes the little gland to which it is closely united to move in the way requisite to produce the effect that relates to this volition. *360*

42. How we find in our memory the things we wish to remember.

Thus when the soul wishes to recollect something, this volition causes the gland, by inclining successively to different sides, to thrust the spirits toward different parts of the brain until they come across that part where the traces left there by the object we wish to recollect are found. For these traces are none other than the fact that the pores of the brain, by which the spirits have formerly followed their course because of the presence of this object, have by that means acquired a greater facility than the others for being once more opened by the spirits coming toward them in the same way. Thus these spirits, in coming into contact with these pores, enter into them more easily than into the others, by which means they excite a special movement in the gland which represents the same object to the soul, and causes it to know that this is what it wished to remember.

43. How the soul can imagine, be attentive, and move the body.

361

Thus when we wish to imagine something we have never seen, this volition has the power of causing the gland to move in the manner requisite to drive the spirits toward those pores of the brain by the opening of which this particular thing may be represented. Thus when we wish to apply our attention for some time to the consideration of one particular object, this volition holds the gland for the time being to the same side. Thus, finally, when we want to walk or to move our body in some special way, this volition causes the gland to thrust the spirits toward the muscles that serve to bring about this result.

44. Each volition is naturally united to some movement of the gland; but that, through effort or habit, it may be united to others.

At the same time it is not always the wish to excite in us some movement or bring about some result that is able so to excite the gland, for this changes according as nature or habit have united each movement of the gland differently to each particular thought. Thus, for example, if we wish to adjust our eyes to look at an object very far away, this volition causes the pupils to enlarge; and if *362* we wish to set them to look at an object very nearby, this volition causes them to contract. But if we think only of enlarging the pupil of the eye, we may indeed have the volition, but still we cannot enlarge it, because nature has joined the movement of the gland that serves to thrust forth the spirits toward the optic nerve in the manner requisite for enlarging or diminishing the pupil, not with the wish to enlarge or diminish it, but with that of looking at objects that are far away or nearby. And when in speaking we think only of the sense of what we want to say, that causes us to move the tongue and lips much more quickly and much better than if we thought of moving them in all the many ways requisite to utter the same words, inasmuch as the habit we acquired in learning to speak has caused us to join the action of the soul—which can move the tongue and lips through the mediation of the gland—with the meaning of the words that follow those movements, rather than with the movements themselves.

45. What the power of the soul is in regard to the passions.

Our passions as well cannot be directly excited or removed by the action of our will, but they can be so indirectly through the representation of things that are usually united to the passions we want to have and are contrary to those we want to reject. Thus, in order to incite courage in ourselves and remove fear, it is not sufficient to have the will to do so, but we must also apply ourselves to consider the reasons, the objects, or the examples that persuade us that the peril is not great; that there is always more safety in defense than in flight; that we should have the glory and the joy of having vanquished, while we could expect nothing but regret and shame for having fled, and so on.

363

46. Why the soul cannot wholly control its passions.

There is a special reason that prevents the soul from being able at once to alter or arrest its passions, which led me to say, in defining them, that they are not only caused, but also maintained and strengthened, by some particular movement of the spirits. This reason is that they are nearly all accompanied by some excitation that takes place in the heart, and in consequence also in the whole of the blood and the spirits, so that until this disturbance has subsided, they remain present to our thought in the same way that sensible objects are present there while they are acting on our sense organs. And as the soul, in rendering itself very attentive to some other thing, may prevent itself from hearing a slight noise or feeling a slight pain, but cannot prevent itself in the same way from hearing thunder or feeling fire burning the hand, in the same way it may easily get the better of the lesser passions, but not of the most violent and strongest, except after the disturbance of the blood and spirits has been appeased. The most that the will can do while this disturbance is in full force is not to yield to its effects, and to restrain many of the movements to which it inclines the body. For example, if anger causes us to lift our hand to strike, the will can usually hold it back; if fear incites our legs to flee, the will can arrest them, and so on in other cases.

364

47. In what consists the conflict we imagine to exist between the lower and higher part of the soul.

And all the conflict we are in the habit of conceiving to exist between the lower part of the soul, which we call the sensitive, and the higher, which is rational, or, as we may say, between the natural appetites and the will, consists only in the opposition between the movements that the body, through the spirits, and the soul, through its will, tend to excite in the gland at the same time. For there is within us but one soul, and this soul has not in itself any diversity of parts; the same part that is sensitive is rational, and all the soul's appetites are volitions. The error that has been committed in making the soul play the part of various personages, usually in opposition to one another, proceeds only from the *365* fact that we have not properly distinguished its functions from those of the body, to which alone we must attribute everything observable in us that is opposed to our reason. Thus there is here no conflict, except that the small gland that exists in the middle of the brain, being capable of being thrust to one side by the soul, and to the other by the animal spirits—which, as I said earlier, are mere bodies— it often happens that these two impulses are contrary, and that the stronger one obstructs the effect of the other. However, we may distinguish two sorts of movement excited in the gland by the spirits. One sort represents to the soul the objects that move the senses, or the impressions met with in the brain, and makes no attempt to affect its will. The others do make an effort to do so—that is, those which cause the passions or the movements of the body accompanying the passions. And as to the first, although they often hinder the actions of the soul, or else are hindered by them, yet, because they are not directly contrary to them, we do not notice any conflict between them. We notice only the conflict between the latter and the acts of will that conflict with them: for example, between the effort by which the spirits push the gland in order to cause a desire for something in the soul, and that with which the soul repels it by the will it has to avoid the very same thing. And what chiefly causes this conflict to appear is that the will, not having the power to excite the passions directly, as has already been said, is con- *366* strained to use its industry, and to apply itself to consider successively several things as to which, although it happens that one has the power to change for a moment the course taken by the spirits, it may turn out that what follows does not have this power, and that the spirits may immediately afterwards revert to that same course because the previous arrangement in the nerves, heart, and blood has not changed, and thus it comes about that the soul feels itself almost at the same time impelled to desire and not to desire the same thing. It is this that has occasioned our imagining in the soul two powers in conflict with one another. At the same time, we may still conceive a sort of conflict, inasmuch as often the same cause that excites some passion in the soul also excites certain movements in the body to which the soul does not contribute, and which it stops, or tries to stop, directly it perceives them—as we see when what excites fear also causes the spirits to enter into the muscles that serve to move the legs with the object of flight, and the will we have to be brave stops them from doing so.

48. How we recognize the strength or weakness of souls, and what is lacking in the weakest souls.

Now it is from the success of these conflicts that each individual can discover the strength or weakness of his soul. For those in whom by nature the will can most easily conquer the passions and arrest the movements of the body that accompany them without doubt possess the strongest souls. But there are those *367* who cannot bring their strength to the test, because they never cause their will to do battle with its proper arms, but only those with which certain passions furnish it, so that it can resist certain others. What I call the will's proper arms are firm and determinate judgments concerning the knowledge of good and evil, according to which it has resolved to conduct the actions of its life. And the weakest souls of all are those whose will does not thus determine itself to follow certain judgments, but allows itself continually to be carried away by its present passions, which, being frequently contrary to one another, draw the will first to one side, then to the other, and, by employing it in conflict with itself, place the soul in the most deplorable condition. Thus when fear represents death as an extreme evil, and one that can be avoided only by flight, ambition on the other hand presents the infamy of this flight as an evil worse than death. These two passions agitate the will in different ways, and in first obeying one and then the other, it is in continual opposition to itself, and thus renders the soul unhappy and enslaved.

49. The strength of the soul is not sufficient without the knowledge of the truth.

It is true that there are very few men so weak and irresolute that they wish nothing except what their passion dictates to them. Most participate in determinate judgments, following which they regulate a part of their actions. And although their judgments are often false or even founded on certain passions by which the will formerly allowed itself to be overcome or led astray, nevertheless, since it continues to follow them when the passion that has caused them is absent, they may be considered its proper arms, and we may reflect that souls are stronger or weaker by reason of the fact that they are able to follow these judgments more or less closely, and resist the present passions that are contrary to them. Yet there is a great difference between the resolutions that proceed from a false opinion, and those that are founded only on the knowledge of the truth— inasmuch as if we follow the latter we are assured that we will never regret or repent it, whereas we always do so when we have followed the former, and hence discovered our error in doing so.

50. There is no soul so feeble that it cannot, if well directed, acquire an absolute power over its passions.

And it is useful here to know that, as has already been said above, although from the beginning of our life each movement of the gland seems to have been joined by nature to each one of our thoughts, we may at the same time join them to others by habit. Experience demonstrates this to us in the case of words: these excite movements in the gland, which, so far as the institution of nature is concerned, do not represent to the soul more than their sound when they are uttered by the voice, or the shape of their letters when they are written, and which, nevertheless, through the habit acquired in thinking of what they signify when their sound was heard or their letters seen, usually make us grasp the meaning rather than the shape of the letters or the sound of the syllables. It is also useful to know that although the movements both of the gland and of the spirits of the brain, which represent certain objects to the soul, are naturally joined to those that excite in it certain passions, they can at the same time be separated from these by habit and joined to others that are very different—and also that this habit can be acquired through a single action, and does not require long usage. Thus, when we unexpectedly meet with something very bad in food that we are eating with relish, the surprise that this event gives us may so change the disposition of our brain, that we can no longer see any such food without horror, although we formerly ate it with pleasure. And the same thing is to be observed in brutes. For although they have no reason, not perhaps any thought, all the movements of the spirits and of the gland that excite the passions in us, are nonetheless present in them, and in them serve to maintain and strengthen, not, as in our case, passions, but the movements of the nerves and muscles that usually accompany them. So when a dog sees a partridge he is naturally disposed to run toward it, and when he hears a gun fired, this sound naturally incites him to flight. But nevertheless, setters are usually so trained that the sight of a partridge causes them to stop, and the sound they afterwards hear when a shot is fired over their heads, causes them to run up to us. And these things are useful in inciting each one of us to have the courage to try to control our passions. For since we can with a little industry change the movements of the brain in animals deprived of reason, it is evident that we can do so yet more in the case of men, and that even those who have the feeblest souls can acquire a very absolute dominion over all their passions if sufficient industry is applied in training and guiding them.[18]

The Search After Truth by the Light of Nature (1641?–1649?)[19]

This light alone, without the assistance of religion or philosophy, determines the opinions a gentleman should have about all matters that may occupy his thoughts and penetrate into the secrets of the most curious sciences   X, 495

A gentleman does not need to have read every book, nor to have carefully learned everything taught in the Schools; it would even be a kind of defect in his

---

18. *The Passions of the Soul* continues with two more parts, containing another 162 articles.

19. This incomplete French manuscript was listed in the inventory of Descartes's papers made at Stockholm after his death. The manuscript survives only in a copy G. W. Leibniz made of approximately half of it, and in a published Latin translation (*Opuscula posthuma*, 1701). It is not clear when Descartes wrote it. Some speculate that it was one of Descartes's early works, others that it was written for Queen Christina at the end of his life. What is evident is that it was intended to be a large work ("two books"); thus the project was either abandoned by Descartes or cut short by his death. The setting of the work seems to be a courtly one—perhaps meant to be familiar to Christina—though it evokes the castle in which Descartes lived during 1641, at Engedeest in the Netherlands, when he was preoccupied by the objections of his Scholastic opponents.

education if he had devoted too much of his time to the study of letters. There are many other things to do in life, and he has to direct that life in such a manner as to reserve the greater part of it for the performance of good actions, which his 496 own reason ought to teach him, if he learned everything from it alone. But he comes into the world in ignorance, and, as the knowledge of his earliest years rests only on the weakness of the senses and the authority of masters, he can scarcely avoid his imagination being filled with an infinity of false ideas, before his reason has the power of taking his conduct into its own hands. In consequence he needs to have good natural endowments or else instruction from a wise man, both in order to rid himself of the false doctrines with which his mind is filled, and to build the first foundations of a solid knowledge and discover all the ways by which he may carry his knowledge to the highest degree it can possibly attain.

In this work I propose to explain what these things are and to put into evidence the true riches of our souls, by opening to each one the means by which he can find in himself, and without borrowing from anyone else, the whole knowledge which is essential to him in the direction of his life, and then by his study succeed in acquiring the most curious knowledge that human reason is capable of possessing.

But so that the greatness of my scheme may not begin to fill your minds with an astonishment so great that confidence in my words can no longer find a place there, I warn you that what I undertake is not as difficult as might be imagined. Those items of knowledge which do not extend beyond the capacities of the 497 human mind are, as a matter of fact, linked by a bond so marvelous, and are capable of being deduced from one another by sequences so necessary, that it is not essential to possess much art or address in order to discover them, provided that we begin with the simplest and know how to rise gradually to the most sublime. That is what I shall try to show you here by a system of reasoning so clear, and yet so common to all, that everyone will be able to judge for himself that if he has not observed the same things, it is solely because he has not cast his eyes in the right direction, nor fixed his thoughts on the same considerations as I have, and that no more glory is due to me for having discovered them than is due to a casual passerby for having accidentally discovered under his feet a rich treasure that had successfully eluded the searches of many for a long time.

And certainly I am surprised that among so many distinguished minds much better equipped than I to succeed in this, none has had the patience to find his way out of his difficulties; instead, nearly all have followed in the footsteps of those travelers who, abandoning the main route to take a crossroad, find themselves lost among briars and precipices.

But I do not desire to examine what others have known or have been ignorant of. It will suffice for me to note that even if all the knowledge we can desire is 498 to be found in books, what good they contain is mingled with so many useless things, and confusedly dispersed in such a mass of large volumes, that, in order to read them, more time would be needed than human life can supply us with, and more talent in discovering the useful would be required than in discovering it for ourselves.

That is what makes me hope that the reader will be happy to find here an easier path, and that the truths I shall advance will not fail to be well received, even though I do not borrow them from Aristotle or Plato, but show that they have currency in the world, just as money has no less value when it proceeds from the purse of a peasant than when it comes from the treasury. I have also taken pains to make them equally useful to all men. I have not been able to discover a style better adapted to this end than that of genuine conversation, in which each one familiarly explains to his friends the best of his thoughts. And under the names Eudoxus, Polyander, and Epistemon, I assume that a man endowed with ordinary mental gifts, but whose judgment is not spoiled by any false ideas, and who is in possession of his whole reason in all the purity of its nature, receives as his guests in the country house he inhabits, two of the most distinguished and inter-   *499* esting minds of their time, one of whom has studied not at all, while the other is well acquainted with all that can be learned in the Schools. And there (in the midst of other discourse that everyone can imagine for himself, as well as the local conditions and particular surroundings from which I shall frequently cause them to take examples in order to make their conceptions clearer), they thus introduce the subject that will occupy them until the end of these two books.

Polyander, Epistemon, Eudoxus.

Polyander. I consider you so fortunate in having discovered all these wonderful things in Greek and Latin books that it seems to me that if I had studied as much as you, I should be as different from what I now am as angels are from you. And I cannot excuse the folly of my parents who, being persuaded that the study of letters would enfeeble the spirit, sent me to the court and army at so early an age that I should all my life have had to regret my ignorance, had I not learned something from my association with you.

Epistemon. The best thing you could be taught on this subject is that the desire for knowledge, which is common to all men, is an illness that cannot be cured, for curiosity increases with learning; and as the deficiencies that are present in our soul only trouble us insofar as we recognize them, you have a certain advantage over us in that, unlike us, you do not see that many things are lacking to you.   *500*

Eudoxus. Can it be, Epistemon, that you with all your learning can believe that there is in nature any illness so universal that there is no remedy to be applied to it? As for me, I consider that just as there are in each country sufficient fruits and rivers to appease the hunger and thirst of everyone, so there are in every matter truths that can be known sufficient to satisfy fully the curiosity of orderly souls; and I think that the body of a dropsical patient is not further removed from its normal condition than the minds of those who are perpetually worked upon by an insatiable curiosity.

Epistemon. I once heard, it is true, that our desire could not extend naturally to things that seemed impossible to us, and that it ought not to extend to those that are vicious or useless; but so many things can be known that appear possible to us and are not only good and agreeable, but also very necessary in the conduct of our actions, that I cannot believe anyone ever knew enough of them not to have legitimate reasons always to desire to know more.

501   *Eudoxus.* What, then, will you say of me, if I tell you that I no longer feel any desire to learn anything at all, and that I am as happy with my small knowledge as Diogenes was with his tub, and all this without my having any need of his philosophy? For the knowledge of my neighbors is not the limit of my own, as are their fields that surround here the small piece of ground I possess; and my mind at its own will disposing of all the truths it encounters does not dream that there are others to discover. For it enjoys the same tranquillity that the king of an isolated country would have, if he were so separated from all others as to imagine that beyond his frontiers there was nothing but infertile deserts and uninhabitable mountains.

Epistemon. If anyone but you spoke to me this way, I should regard him as someone whose mind was either very vain or else too little given to curiosity; but the retreat you have chosen in this solitude, and the small amount of pains you take to become known, removes from you the charge of vanity; and the time you formerly devoted to traveling, visiting learned men, and examining everything that is most difficult in each science, suffices to assure us that you are not lacking in curiosity. So all I can say is that I consider you very happy and I am convinced that you must be in the possession of a much more perfect knowledge than that of others.

Eudoxus. I thank you for the good opinion you have of me, but I do not desire
502   to abuse your courtesy to the point of desiring that you should believe what I have just said solely on my word. We must not advance opinions so far removed from common opinion without at the same time being able to demonstrate certain effects from so doing; that is why I beg you both to be good enough to spend this delightful season here, so that I may have the opportunity of openly showing you some part of what I know. For I venture to flatter myself that not only will you recognize that I have some reason for being content in this knowledge, but, in addition, that you yourselves will be fully satisfied with the things that you will have learned.

Epistemon. I would not wish to refuse a favor that I already so ardently desired of you.

Polyander. And I shall have great pleasure in being present at this discussion, not that I believe myself capable of deriving any profit from it.

Eudoxus. On the contrary, Polyander, it will be you who will derive advantage from it, because you are quite unprejudiced, and it will be easier for me to set a neutral person on the right track than to guide Epistemon, whom we will often find taking the opposite side. But in order to make you conceive more distinctly the sort of knowledge I am going to treat, I beg you to observe the difference between the sciences and those simple items of knowledge that can be acquired without the aid of reasoning, such as languages, history, geography, and generally everything that depends on experience alone. I readily grant that the life of a man would not suffice to acquire the experience of everything in the world; but
503   I am also persuaded that it would be folly to desire that it should be so, and that it is no more the duty of a gentleman to know Greek and Latin than it is to know

the languages of Switzerland or Brittany; or that he should know the history of the Empire any more than that of the smallest state in Europe. Such a person should devote his leisure to good and useful things alone and occupy his memory only with those that are most necessary. As to those sciences which are nothing but the judgments that we base on some previously acquired knowledge, some are deduced from common objects of which everyone is cognizant and others from rare and well-thought-out experiments. And I confess likewise that it would be impossible for us to treat in detail each one of these; for we should first of all have to examine all the herbs and stones brought to us from the Indies; we should have to have beheld the Phoenix, and in a word to be ignorant of none of the marvels of nature. But I shall believe myself to have sufficiently fulfilled my promise if, in explaining to you the truths that can be deduced from common things known to each one of us, I make you capable of discovering all the others when you care to take the trouble to seek them.

Polyander. For my part I believe that this is likewise all that it is possible to desire, and I would have been satisfied if you had merely taught me a certain number of propositions so celebrated that no one can be ignorant of them, such *504* as those that concern the Deity, the rational soul, the virtues, their reward, etc., propositions which I compare with those ancient families that everyone recognizes as the most illustrious, although the titles of their nobility are concealed under the ruins of antiquity. For I do not really doubt that those who first induced the human race to believe in all these things had excellent reasons for proving them; but their arguments have been so rarely repeated that no one knows them any longer: and yet they are truths so important that the dictates of prudence tell us we should believe them blindly at the risk of being deceived, rather than that we should await a future life in order to be further instructed in them.

Epistemon. As far as I am concerned, I am a little more curious, and I should like you to explain to me certain particular difficulties that suggest themselves to me in each branch of knowledge, and principally in what concerns the secrets of the human arts, apparitions, illusions, and in a word all the wonderful effects attributed to magic. For I believe it to be useful to know all that, not in order to make use of the knowledge, but in order that one should not allow one's judgment to be beguiled by wonder at an unknown thing.

Eudoxus. I shall try to satisfy you in regard to both; and, in order to adopt an order which we may make use of to the end, I wish first of all, Polyander, to talk with you of all things that the world contains, considering them in themselves, on the understanding that Epistemon will interrupt our talk as little as possible, because his objections would often force us to leave our subject. We shall finally *505* consider all these things anew, though under another aspect, insofar as they relate to us, and as they may be termed true or false, good or evil; and it is here that Epistemon will find occasion to set forth all the difficulties that will remain to him from the preceding discourses.

Polyander. Tell us, then, the order that you will follow in your explanations.

Eudoxus. We must begin with the human soul, because all our knowledge depends on it; and after having considered its nature and effects, we shall reach its author; and when we come to know who he is and how he has created all the

things in the world, we shall observe what is most certain regarding other creatures; and we shall ask how our senses perceive things, and how our reflections
become false or true. Then I shall place before your eyes the works of man upon
corporeal objects, and after having struck wonder into you by the sight of
machines as powerful as possible, automata rarer than any others, visions
entirely specious, and tricks as subtle as artifice can invent, I shall reveal to you
secrets so simple that you will henceforth wonder at nothing in the works of our
hands. After that I shall reach the works of nature and, after having shown you
the cause of all its changes, the diversity of its qualities, and the reason why the
506   soul of plants and animals differs from ours, I shall place under your consideration the whole building up of sensible things. First I shall report what is observed
in the heavens, and what we can judge with certainty about them, and pass on to
the most reasonable conjectures regarding what we cannot determine positively,
in order to try to give an account of the relation that sensible things bear to those
that are intellectual, and of both to the Creator, the immortality of creatures, and
the state of their being at the end of time. Then we shall come to the second part
of this discourse in which we treat of all the sciences in detail, select what is most
solid in each one, and propose a method by which they may be carried on much
further, and so find by ourselves, with a mind of ordinary ability, everything that
the subtlest minds can discover. After having thus prepared our minds for judging perfectly of the truth, we must also apply ourselves to the direction of our
wills with respect to distinguishing good from evil, and observing the true difference between virtue and vice. That being done, I trust that your desire for
knowledge will not be so violent, and that everything I will have said to you will
seem so well established that you will come to believe that a man with a healthy
mind, had he been brought up in a desert and never received more than the light
of nature to illuminate him, could not, if he carefully weighed all the same arguments, adopt an opinion different from ours. In order to begin this discourse we
must ask what is the first knowledge that man comes to, in what part of the soul
507   it is to be found, and why it is so imperfect to begin with.

Epistemon. All that seems to me to explain itself very clearly if we compare
the imagination of children to a *tabula rasa*, on which our ideas, which resemble
portraits of each object taken from nature, should be placed. Our senses, our
inclination, our masters, and our intellect are the various painters who have the
power of executing this work; and among them, those who are least adapted to
succeed in it, that is, the imperfect senses, blind instinct, and foolish nurses are
the first to busy themselves with it. The best comes last, that is, the intellect; and
yet it requires an apprenticeship of several years, and it has to follow for a long
time the example of its masters, before it dares to rectify a single one of their
errors. In my opinion, this is one of the principal causes of the difficulty we experience in attaining true knowledge. For our senses really perceive only what is
most coarse and common, our natural inclination is entirely corrupted, and as to
our masters, although there may no doubt be very perfect ones found among
them, still they cannot force our minds to accept their reasoning before our intellect has examined it, for the accomplishment of this end pertains to it alone. But
the intellect is like an excellent painter who had been called upon to put the last

touches on a bad picture sketched out by apprentice hands, and who would   *508*
employ in vain all the rules of his art, correcting little by little first a trait here,
then a trait there, and would finally have to add to it from his own hand all that
was lacking, and could nevertheless not prevent great faults from remaining in it,
because from the beginning the picture had been badly conceived, the figures
badly placed, and the proportions badly observed.

Eudoxus. Your comparison places perfectly under our eyes the first obstacle
that stands in our way; but you do not show the means of which we must avail
ourselves if we wish to avoid it. And according to me it is this: that just as your
artist would have done much better to start the painting all over again, by spong-
ing out all its features, rather than losing his time in correcting it, so each one
who has reached a certain term of years known as the age of knowledge, should
set himself once for all to remove from his imagination all the inexact ideas that
have hitherto succeeded in engraving themselves upon it, and seriously begin to
form new ones, applying to this all the strength of his intelligence with such zeal
that if he does not bring them to perfection, the fault will not at least be laid on
the weakness of the senses, or on the errors of nature.

Epistemon. That would be an excellent remedy if we could easily employ it;   *509*
but you are not ignorant that the opinions first received by our imagination
remain so deeply imprinted there, that our will alone, if it did not employ the aid
of certain strong arguments, could not arrive at effacing them.

Eudoxus. It is certain of these arguments that I hope to teach you; and if you
wish to derive some fruit from our discourse, you must give me your whole
attention, and allow me to converse a little with Polyander in order that I may
begin by upsetting all the knowledge he has hitherto acquired. And as it is not
sufficient to satisfy him, and cannot but be bad, I may compare it to a badly constructed edifice whose foundations are not solid. I know no better remedy than
absolutely to raze it to the ground, in order to raise a new one in its stead. For I
do not wish to be placed among the number of these insignificant artisans who
apply themselves only to the restoration of old works, because they feel themselves incapable of achieving new ones. We can, however, Polyander, while we
are busy destroying this edifice, at the same time form the foundations which
may serve our purpose, and prepare the best and most solid materials that are
necessary in order to succeed in our task—provided you are in any degree willing to examine with me which of all the truths men can know are those that are   *510*
most certain and easy of knowledge.

Polyander. Is there anyone who can doubt that sensible things (I mean by this
those that can be seen and touched) are much more certain than the others? As
for me I should be very much astonished if you would show me as clearly some
of those things that are said of God and our soul.

Eudoxus. That, however, is what I hope to do, and it seems to me surprising that
men are credulous enough to base their knowledge on the certainty of the senses,
when there is no one who is unaware that they frequently deceive us, and that we
have good reason for always mistrusting those who have once betrayed us.

Polyander. I am well aware that the senses sometimes deceive us when they
are ill affected, just as a sick person thinks that all food is bitter; when they are

too far from the object this is also so, just as when we look at the stars they never appear to us as large as they really are; and in general when they do not act freely according to the constitution of their nature. But all their errors are easily known, and do not prevent my being now perfectly persuaded that I see you, that we are walking in this garden, that the sun gives us light, and, in a word, that everything that usually appears to my senses is truthful.

511   *Eudoxus.* So to make you fear being deceived by the senses on occasions when you cannot recognize this, it is not enough for me to tell you that they sometimes deceive you. I must go further and ask if you have ever seen one of those melancholics who believe themselves to be pitchers, or who think some part of their body is of enormous size; they would swear that what they see and touch is just as they imagine it to be. And it is true that any gentleman would be indignant if someone told him he could have no more reason than they of his opinion, since it rests equally with theirs on what the senses and his imagination represent to him. But you cannot be annoyed if I ask you whether you are not, like other men, subject to sleep, and if you cannot think when you sleep that you see me, that you are walking in this garden, that the sun gives us light, in a word, all these other things that you imagine yourself now to be certain of. Have you never heard in comedies this expression of astonishment, "Am I awake or asleep?" How can you be certain that your life is not a perpetual dream and that all that you imagine you learn by means of your senses is not as false now as it is when you are

512   asleep? More particularly, [how can you be certain of this] when as you have learned that you have been created by a superior Being who, being omnipotent, it would not have been more difficult to make us such as I have described, than such as you believe yourself to be?

Polyander. Certainly, these are reasons sufficient to upset all the knowledge of Epistemon if he is reflective enough to give his attention to it; as for me, I should fear becoming a bit too much of a dreamer for a man who has never studied or been accustomed to turn his mind in this fashion away from the things of the senses, if I were to enter into meditations a bit too abstract for me.

Epistemon. I too think it very dangerous to go too far in this mode of reasoning. General doubts of this kind lead us straight to the ignorance of Socrates or the uncertainty of the Pyrrhonists. This is deep water where it seems we could not find our footing.

Eudoxus. I admit there would be danger for those who do not know the ford to cross it without a guide, and many have lost their lives by doing so; but you have no reason to fear if you cross it after me. Indeed, such timidity has pre-

513   vented most scholars from acquiring a doctrine that was solid and certain enough to deserve the name of science; when, imagining that there was nothing on which they could rest their faith more firm and solid than sensible things, they built on this foundation of sand rather than by digging down further to find rock or clay. But we must not stop here. Even if you did not want to examine further the arguments I have just stated, still in their principal effect they would already have done what I wanted, as long as they had so affected your imagination as to make you fear them. For that is an indication that your science is not so infallible that you may not fear to see its foundations shattered by making you doubt every-

thing. Consequently, you are already in doubt about it. And this proves that I have accomplished my end, which was to undermine the whole of your doctrine by showing you that it was not well founded. From fear, however, that you may lack more courage and refuse to follow me further, I declare to you that those doubts which alarmed you to begin with, are like those phantoms and vain images which appear in the night by the uncertain glimmer of a feeble light. If you flee, fear pursues you, but if you approach and touch them, you will find nothing but wind and shadow, and you will ever after be better able to face a similar encounter.

Polyander. Convinced by your reasoning, I desire to set all those difficulties *514* before myself in the strongest possible manner, and to apply myself to doubt whether I have not been dreaming all my life, and whether even all those ideas that I thought could only enter into my mind by the door of the senses, might not have been formed of themselves, just as similar ideas are formed when I am sleeping, or when I am certain that my eyes are shut, my ears closed, and, in a word, that none of my senses are in operation. In this way I shall be uncertain not only as to whether you are in the world, if a world exists, if there is a sun, but also whether I have eyes, ears, a body, even whether I am talking with you, or if you are addressing me; in short I shall doubt all things.[20]

---

20. The French manuscript breaks off here. The 1701 Latin translation of it continues with a discussion of some of the themes of Meditation Two.

INDEX